Routledge Revivals

The Phenomenology of Modern Legal Discourse

Originally published in 1998, *The Phenomenology of Modern Legal Discourse* recovers the suffering which is concealed as lawyers, judges and other legal officials resignify a harm through the special vocabulary and grammar which constitutes legal language. At the moment of re-signification, an untranslatable gap erupts between the knowers' special language and the embodied meanings of the non-knower. *The Phenomenology* claims that the gap can be unconcealed if the knowers of the special language reconsider their assumptions about legal meaning, the body and desire.

With a broad grasp of diverse problematics from the legal procedures, legal discourses and legal theory of three jurisdictions to exemplify his claims, the author interweaves arguments which draw from Edmund Husserl's and Maurice Merleau Ponty's insights about meaning. The author's effort demonstrates how one may unconceal lived laws through a re-reading of the role of the experiential body in legal signification. The author's effort to retrieve the embodiment of legal meaning de-stabilizes deep assumptions of contemporary lawyers and legal theorists.

The Phenomenology of Modern Legal Discourse

The Juridical Production and the Disclosure of Suffering

William E. Conklin

Routledge
Taylor & Francis Group

First published in 1998
by Ashgate

This edition first published in 2024 by Routledge
4 Park Square, Milton Park, Abingdon, Oxon, OX14 4RN

and by Routledge
605 Third Avenue, New York, NY 10017

Routledge is an imprint of the Taylor & Francis Group, an informa business

Publisher's Note
The publisher has gone to great lengths to ensure the quality of this reprint but points out that some imperfections in the original copies may be apparent.

Disclaimer
The publisher has made every effort to trace copyright holders and welcomes correspondence from those they have been unable to contact.

A Library of Congress record exists under ISBN: 1840140712

ISBN: 978-1-138-36079-2 (hbk)
ISBN: 978-1-003-47475-3 (ebk)
ISBN: 978-1-138-36081-5 (pbk)

Book DOI 10.4324/9781003474753

THE PHENOMENOLOGY OF MODERN LEGAL DISCOURSE

To Annalijn

THE PHENOMENOLOGY OF MODERN LEGAL DISCOURSE

THE JURIDICAL PRODUCTION AND THE DISCLOSURE OF SUFFERING

WILLIAM E. CONKLIN

Ashgate

DARTMOUTH

Aldershot • Brookfield USA • Singapore • Sydney

Published by
Dartmouth Publishing Company
Ashgate Publishing Limited
Gower House
Croft Road
Aldershot
Hants GU11 3HR
England

Ashgate Publishing Company
Old Post Road
Brookfield
Vermont 05036
USA

British Library Cataloguing in Publication Data
Conklin, William E.
The phenomenology of modern legal discourse : the juridical production and the disclosure of suffering. – (Applied legal philosophy)
1.Semiotics (Law)
I.Title
340.1'1

Library of Congress Cataloging-in-Publication Data
Conklin, William E.
The pheonomenology of modern legal discourse/William E. Conklin.
p. cm. — (Applied legal philosophy)
Includes index.
ISBN 1-84014-071-2 (hardcover)
1. Law—Language. 2. Discourse analysis. 3. Semiotics (Law)
4. Semantics (Law) I. Title. II. Series.
K213.C657 1998
340'.01'4—dc21 97–40987
CIP

ISBN 1 84014 071 2

Typeset by Manton Typesetters, 5–7 Eastfield Road, Louth, Lincolnshire, UK.

Printed in Great Britain by Galliard (Printers) Ltd, Great Yarmouth

Contents

Series Preface

The objective of the Dartmouth Series in Applied Legal Philosophy is to publish work which adopts a theoretical approach to the study of particular areas or aspects of law or deals with general theories of law in a way which focuses on issues of practical moral and political concern in specific legal contexts.

In recent years there has been an encouraging tendency for legal philosophers to utilize detailed knowledge of the substance and practicalities of law and a noteworthy development in the theoretical sophistication of much legal research. The series seeks to encourage these trends and to make available studies in law which are both genuinely philosophical in approach and at the same time based on appropriate legal knowledge and directed towards issues in the criticism and reform of actual laws and legal systems.

The series will include studies of all the main areas of law, presented in a manner which relates to the concerns of specialist legal academics and practitioners. Each book makes an original contribution to an area of legal study while being comprehensible to those engaged in a wide variety of disciplines. Their legal content is principally Anglo-American, but a wide-ranging comparative approach is encouraged and authors are drawn from a variety of jurisdictions.

TOM D. CAMPBELL
Series Editor
The Faculty of Law
The Australian National University

Preface

Modern legal discourse conceals human suffering. The suffering about which one ordinarily reads in a newspaper or sees in a television bite focuses upon the physical body of the child or adult who has been the victim of war or poverty or a crime against the person. There is another type of suffering, though. This suffering also involves the physical body, though indirectly. Here, I have in mind someone's experiential pain which goes with the failure of an authoritative professional knower to recognize and to respond to the addressee through his/her verbal, gestural or written expression. This suffering emanates from a deep untranslatable gulf between the authoritative discourse of the professional knower and the everyday discourses of the addressee. One experiences the world and brings prejudgments and expectations from prior experiences into the world. But the failure of the person in authority – whether parent, judge, policeperson, social worker, legislator or what you will – to recognize and to respond to the experience of the addressee in his/her language impacts upon the addressee's physical body. Indeed, the gulf between modern legal discourse and the everyday discourses of the non-expert may have a great deal to do with more open manifestations of physical suffering.

The aims of this little book are, first, to identify why and how modern legal discourse so effectively conceals just such a suffering inside the play of special signs and gestures which carry such serious consequences for the non-expert; and second, to explain why an unconcealment or disclosure of the suffering remains possible. With respect to the latter, I wish to raise questions as to what sort of discourse would entertain the possibility of such unconcealment.

It is not easy to write about the knower's production of such suffering when one is just such a professional knower. It is even more difficult to unconceal such suffering when one is also immersed in a popular and academic culture, including a university culture, which appears to exist by and for the professional knower. The knower I have in mind is not the student of an Enlightenment discourse, whether of philosophy or literature or classics or law, which may presuppose that a transcendent Truth dwells beyond the knower. Nor is it the knower who critically pierces the veil of social appearances which just such a discourse may well construct. Nor is it the scientific knower who observes, measures and interprets physicochemical matter. Rather, I have in mind the knower of the special signs which represent the rules, procedures and unspoken assumptions of a bureaucracy or organizational pyramid of like-minded officials who are authorized to interpret and to enforce their own rules in a modern organization. Struggling to survive in such an environment, I have found a quiet, increasingly appreciated, haven at the Northrop Frye Centre of Victoria College, University of Toronto, where I have rewritten this book over several years. Without the tranquillity and civility of this College, my writing could not have been completed in a publishable state or, if it were, my effort would have been for the worse. The stimulating environment of the Centre for Law and Society at Edinburgh University helped me to bring my final draft together.

This book mirrors my own environing world as much as it does my effort to expose the juridical production and unconcealment of human suffering. With that in mind, I often write in the first person singular. I describe how, as a professional legal knower, I bring my bodily experiences into a text or reported social event. I describe how, as a non-knower drawing from my own experiences as a non-knower, I attempt to understand the modern legal discourse. And I endeavour to displace my own analytic legal training with a phenomenological description which exposes the problematic of that discourse.

My environing world particularly suggests to me that a legal discourse and the study of that discourse can be other than the production and concealment of human suffering. In this regard, I must give credit to the many conference panelists and referees, too numerous to mention, who have listened intently and criticized my arguments over the past few years. I am also grateful to Millie Bakan for having demonstrated to me that one may grow older and wiser without losing one's passion for the suffering of others.

William E. Conklin,
University of Windsor Law Faculty

Introduction: The Problematic of Modern Legal Discourse

The environing world of K in Franz Kafka's *The Trial* is stark, confused and pained. Self-confident as he rises from his sleep to observe the arresting officers at the doorway of his bedroom, K responds as an author of his own acts. Within seconds, though, his environing world begins to become distanced from the utterances of claimants to legal knowledge. K's environing world had hitherto been signified through his everyday expressions as a tenant, a lover, a nephew, a banker and a citizen. He does not understand who these men are nor why they stand at his doorway. He does not understand their gestures, their utterances, their assumptions or their questions. K is a law-abiding citizen in a liberal state. He possesses a respectable job in an esteemed and powerful profession. He is a good tenant in a boarding house. He attaches meanings to the police officers' actions from the viewpoint of such a citizen, employee and tenant. One such meaning, for example, is drawn from the privacy which K takes for granted as a citizen in a liberal state. As K is shuffled through one procedure after another, from one office to another, he strives to understand what external objects are constraining him. Self-described expert knowers of legal discourse posit those external objects. The knowers fail to respond to K's utterances in a manner which K can understand. His meant objects fail to link with the objects which the expert knowers take for granted. The harm to the invasion of his privacy is then overtaken by a deeper pain – the pain which he experiences when his utterances remain unrecognized – and his environing world collapses. As K repeatedly fails to understand and to be understood, his experiencing body slowly deteriorates until only the remnant of a biological body remains. But that remnant reminds all expert knowers that something alien to legal discourse remains concealed within the discourse. The body, the last material evidence of an alien language, must finally be expunged. K's execution constitutes the final remainder of the assimilationist project of the modern legal discourse.

The violence of a modern legal discourse, which Kafka so explosively exposes, poses two sets of important questions for the study of the legal discourse of a modern state.

First, how and why does the legal discourse of a modern state conceal the experienced meanings of a non-knower such as K? If one has been harmed, does the legal discourse recognize the harm? Does the harm sometimes slip through the juridical categorizations? If recognized, is the harm re-presented through a vocabulary, grammar and gestural style which are familiar to the expert knowers but not to the person harmed? Can the legal discourse of a modern state even signify an indigenously experienced event in the idiom of the person harmed? If not, why not? How does the legal discourse disperse other languages? Why does it do so? Is the modern legal discourse immersed in a particular sense of authority which carries the expert knower in a linear direction away from the embodied meanings of someone harmed? At what moment does legal discourse make no sense to the litigant? Can one write of the harmed as an aggrieved to the official discourse itself? Does the wound lie dormant, though alive, ready to erupt? Must the juridical agents of a modern legal discourse ultimately coerce the other who cannot, or will not, recognize the dominion of the categories of the legal discourse?

A second set of issues concerns the unconcealing of the addressive experiences of someone harmed. The term 'addressive experience', which I take from Mildred Bakan, connotes the experience of responding dialogically with another person in a concrete, socially contingent circumstance. What happens to the dispersed everyday discourses which a litigant has experienced before he or she represents his or her case to a lawyer? Are his or her dispersed embodied meanings concealed forever from the legal discourse of a modern state? Or is it possible to retrieve the meant objects of someone harmed? Is it possible to retrieve a discourse where one addresses the experiences of the other in the language of the other? What would characterize such a discourse? Would the discourse still possess the sense of authority which characterizes a modern legal discourse? Would the lawyers and judges continue to desire to reach some final source or foundation as they do today? Would the partners to such a different discourse even desire this? Would desire be embodied with experiences? Would such a sense of desire contrast with the cognitive search for an absent foundation as characterizes the modern legal discourse? Would there always remain an intertextual space between discursive partners? Could we even call such a discourse "law"?

These issues go to the production of human suffering inside the legal discourse of a modern state. Here, I am not writing of the suffering derived from a circumstance where one individual or group harms the person of another. I am writing of a suffering which transpires as the legal discourse subtly and slowly transforms one's story into a narrative which fails to address an individual's meanings as he or she has experienced them. Indeed, is it possible that a legal discourse, at the moment of the dispersal of someone's meant objects, really induces a double suffering? Does the person harmed suffer twice over? First, does one only suffer at the moment of assault, libel, abuse, torture or denial of the fulfilment of a promise (that is, as a mere indigenous experience)? Or, second, does one also suffer when the knower of an official discourse recognizes such an indigenously experienced harm? If so, what is it about such a moment of recognition which excludes the individual's embodied meanings from the official discourse? Does the official discourse exclude the language of the other by resituating it through the knower's special vocabulary and grammar? Can the non-knower who comes to the lawyer for advice present his or her indigenously experienced harm through her or his own idiom? Must the harm be re-presented and must it be re-presented retrospectively? Must it be re-presented as the expert knowers recognize the harm through signs with which the expert knower is already familiar? Indeed, must the harmed individual re-present his or her indigenously experienced harm through a re-presenter of the official discourse through the re-presenter's language? Is such a double suffering an inevitable phenomenon of the legal discourse of any modern state? Would the retrieval of the embodied meanings of an aggrieved individual undermine the authority of the state's official discourse?

Kafka's *The Trial* points to the manifestation of concealed meanings by a non-knower inside an official discourse. K *means* his words and thoughts as he experiences his world. He *embodies* his words with his experiences. K's language, though, lacks the authority of the language of the claimants of legal knowledge. Both the painter and the lawyer recontextualize K. They treat him as a sign. That sign gains its signification from the other signs which the two expert knowers take for granted as constitutive of legal reality. The knowers attest to the wrongfulness of K's act or omission by situating K and their knowledge of his act in the official discourse: as a sign, K is resituated in a grand invisible spectre of the Law all the while that they leave K's context-specific meanings untouched.

The painter, the lawyer, the judge and all the other claimants to legal knowledge aspire to *know* the labyrinth of procedures and doctrines of the legal discourse. They talk about the legal world as if K were the centre of that world – as if the case were K's case. Their discourse begins as if it were secondary to K's environing world. After all, this is a liberal democratic regime and the juridical agents wish to ensure that due process is followed. But as the expert knowers "respond" to K's queries, the experiential connection with K's environing world is distanced, then forgotten and lost. Although the knowers refer to it as K's case, they resituate him in a discourse which seems to lead somewhere else. Even K himself loses sight of his initial search of what legal harm did he commit, becoming lost in the never-ending search for a centre beyond his own experiences – a centre of the Law. As he does so, the objects of his utterances remain unfulfilled. As neither K nor the expert knowers can fulfil the intent which K puts *into* his utterances, K also fails to fulfil the objects which the expert knowers intend. The knowers try to situate K under their categories as they search for the categories which the judges will ultimately accept. K's indigenous sense of the harm to his privacy is forgotten as his meanings become continually unfulfilled in the official discourse. The expert knowers just cannot understand K's utterances because they cannot address the meanings which K's experiencing body implants into both his own utterances and his interpretations of their actions. K's pain is sanitized inside the official discourse. Even his eventual execution is taken as a matter of course, as a "natural" outcome of the official discourse.

The secondary signs of the official discourse disperse K's meant objects. The secondary discourse becomes primary and, indeed, self-referential and self-binding. The problem for the arresting officers, the tribunal, the lawyer, K's uncle, Fraulein Burstner's friend, Leni, the manufacturer, the painter, Block, and the gatekeeper is how to signify K's words, actions and inactions. As they try to signify K in a legal context, K's own embodiment of meaning loses any experiential linkage with the objects intended by the professional knowers, causing K to become an aggrieved to the official discourse itself.

K struggles to understand the official discourse. His body experiences pain, first, when the expert knowers do not respond – or rather respond unsatisfactorily in a manner which fails to fulfil K's intent in asking his questions. Second, when he himself fails to make sense of the gestures and words of the expert knowers. The body to which I refer is a phenomenal body, not a physiological body as a physical/chemical mass. K's experiences begin with the movement of his phenomenal body. When the arresting officers, the investigating judge, the lawyer, Block or any of the others posit a "fact" as a "given" during their discursive encounters, they analyse those, not K's felt experiences. They analyse by identifying categories which the other knowers will accept as legitimate; they then ask whether K's conduct falls *under* the category. Thus, their categories enclose K's (in)action inside metaphysical boundaries. Such an analytic project emanates from the signs which the knowers take to represent such categories. The closest access which the knowers can gain to K's pain is an *image* of K – an image which begins and ends with the knowers. The effort to signify K becomes the legal event which itself is continually reinvented as the knowers recirculate K through procedures and questions and utterances. The tactics and procedures circulate K. K's circulation through tactics and procedures is never-ending, and with a ravaging appetite, the knowers consume K's case as if it were a commodity. The expert knowers play with this consumptive circulatory game:

> 'Well, but how do you come to know about me and my case?' asked K. 'Oh, that's it,' said the lawyer, smiling. 'I'm a lawyer, you see, I move in legal circles where the various cases are discussed ....'[1]

Indeed, the game takes on a self-binding character. The event, as signified, becomes the true/real for all expert knowers. The knowers' desire to situate K's case inside the authoritative discourse painfully divorces that discourse from K's embodied meanings.

Neither K nor the representers of the authoritative discourse can respond to the other since the monologic character of their respective discourses distances and, indeed, immunizes the knowers from the violence of their acts. Likewise, K's monologue distances himself from recognizing the violence of his discursive acts towards the women in his life. As K slowly comes to recognize the naked violence of the legal monologue against his own embodied meanings, the boundaries of K's environing world slowly collapse. With the *dis*-embodiment of his meanings, K's body becomes a mere sign which may be consumed, excluded or, ultimately, executed.

The Problematics of Modern Legal Discourse

K is not alone, though. We too experience the juridical discourse of a modern state in a similar way. K's effort to understand and to be understood inside a scientized language remains the problematic of the modern legal discourse. Consequently, a deep wound lies hidden inside any legal discourse, however formalistic and universal its pretensions. For without the knowledge of categories which the special signs represent, we remain outsiders to the modern legal discourse at the very moment that the discourse includes us within its grasp. We lack the means to describe and argue about our indigenously experienced pains in our own language. The web of interrelated authoritative signs is so complex that even if we have mastered the vocabulary, we lack knowledge of the signifying effects. Our everyday languages are not even possible because, in order to be possible, our languages must be signifiable in the official discourse. The modern legal discourse cannot recognize our everyday languages because to do so would contradict the monologic hold which the legal discourse, to be authoritative, must maintain. Our meant objects, like K's, are distorted and inserted into a different signifying context. My aim in this book is to show how that dispersal of meanings occurs in a modern legal discourse and to ask whether or not it is possible to retrieve the concealed meanings inside the modern legal discourse.

The problematic of a concealed suffering inside the modern legal discourse raises three sets of issues.

First, is the legal discourse accessible to a non-knower? To what extent can a non-knower, such as K, gain access to the legal discourse without losing his or her embodiment of the secondary signs? In other words, can one know the magic nomenclature without becoming an expert in the authoritative signifying relations? Does the inaccessibility of the legal discourse produce a further suffering? As the discourse of the expert knowers re-presents the pain through the investigative, prosecutorial and adjudicative process, are the embodied meanings of the non-knower transformed into a discourse which experts can recognize as "valid" or "authoritative"? Is the non-knower's own language excluded as invalid or unauthoritative? Is the non-knower transformed into a juridical entity bearing little resemblance to a human being with an experiential body and a biography? Does this juridical entity represent a related category which the expert knower superimposes upon a human being? Are the authoritative magic terms, which represent such cognitive objects as typifications or fact categories, substituted as a referent for the non-knower's pain?

Second, when the legal discourse does recognize harm, is the harm idealized through the legal discourse? If a non-knower can only gain access to the legal discourse through authorized representers of the discourse and through nomenclature and gestures which make no sense to him or her, does even a scholar's study of the legal discourse *idealize* events? Does the lawyer's analytic method ignore the addressive experiences which citizen and expert alike bring *into* a discourse? In other words, is meaning constituted from the interpreter's forestructures and expectations of meaning (or what Georg Gadamer calls *prejudice*)? Although the expert may also embody the secondary signs of the official discourse, does the secondary signification intellectualize about the signs representing the aggrieved's harm? Do the non-knower and the expert embody a sign with prejudgments and expectations which they take for granted because their experiences seem so real and universalizable? Can they only communicate meaningfully with each other if they share similar *prejudice*? Does the traditional study of legal language, influenced by Algirdas Greimas and Charles Peirce, ignore such *prejudice*? Does the legal discourse of a modern state erase the *prejudice* of the non-knower or is the *prejudice* merely concealed? Does the secondary signification of a non-knower's indigenously experienced harm become an event itself? Does the risk of failing to recognize the primacy of the secondary discourse lead to an underlying coercion in the legal discourse?

A third set of issues concern the unconcealment of the wound of the modern legal discourse. Can the embodied meanings concealed inside the secondary legal discourse be retrieved? If so, how? Would such a retrieval undermine the need for force? Indeed, would such retrieved meanings be considered authoritative if, instead of searching for some absent object such as the "facts", a text or the intent of the Founding Fathers, the professional knowers responded to the non-knower through addressive experiences as dialogic partners? In such circumstances, would the experts remain professional knowers and would the dialogue remain authoritative, at least as one has come to understand authority in a modern state? If an expert knower listened and responded to the other's embodied meanings, a dialogue would characterize their social relations. They would not respond face-to-face: a multiplicity of possible configurations of signs would remain in the intertext between them. Because the dialogic partners would respond to each other through this intertext both the knower and non-knower would be addressees to the other. Their experiences would be addressive experiences. The legal discourse would no longer need to be enforced against the story of the non-knower because their dialogic relations would take on a *meant* sense. Yet, whether one could describe such a dialogue as authoritative would remain open to question.

Argument: the Juridical Production of the Concealment of Suffering

In order to address the language of the other, one must come to terms with two aspects of the phenomenology of modern legal discourse. The first set of issues concerns the production of the concealment of suffering inside the legal discourse. Here, drawing from the work of Jean-François Lyotard, I explore the nature of a suffering which arises from the non-knower's inability to address juridical agents in the non-knower's own idiom. I demonstrate, with reference to examples from the United States, the UK and Canada, how the legal discourse of a modern state produces such a suffering through the phenomenon of the displacement of signification. I argue in particular – again with examples – that the language of displacement is monological vis-à-vis the person harmed in that the harmed cannot *respond* to juridical claims through his or her own idiom. Again, using examples from the UK and the USA, I argue that the monologue is the consequence of the juridical agent's linear search for a foundation, or grounding, of all legal objects. That foundation is believed to dwell in the *knowledge* of an externally situated inaccessible Object. I connect the legal knower's search for an inaccessible foundation to a particular conception of juridical desire which posits a passive subject to given externally posited cognitive objects. Such a desire is part and parcel of the legal monologue.

In Chapter 1, for example, I show how an official discourse typified a woman of colour who had repeatedly applied for a job without being granted an interview. I link this example to the general claim that contemporary legal theory – especially certain strains of critical legal studies and feminist legal theory – presupposes a paradigm of consciousness in which the interpreter aspires to gain a presence, or face-to-face social relationship, with the non-knower by bringing the non-knower *into* the consciousness of the knower. Such a paradigm assumes that the author expresses his/her consciousness through words, terms, gestures or, to use the technical term, through signs as if the signs were transparent conduits of the author's intent. Against such transparency, the only constraint to a liberatory legal order, it is believed, is the class, race or gender of the authors of legal categories. By shattering the categories of glassy signs, we would reach each other in face-to-face social relations. Legal critique has sometimes aimed to retrieve such face-to-face relations to the exclusion of considering the opaqueness of the legal sign.

In Chapters 2 and 3, I isolate the moments through which the juridical agent transforms the embodied meanings of a non-knower. Even if one's indigenously experienced harm is recognized in the secondary discourse, a juridical agent recounts the harm in such a manner that the harm is reconfigured into a 'sentence', situated in the secondary signifying relations of the juridical agent. The 'sentence' then takes on the signification of an 'utterance' for the expert knower; the physical marks on a page are transformed into an embodied meaning. Slowly, almost imperceptibly, legal signification *produces the event as signified;* that is, the web of signs becomes the event itself. Through the moments of the juridical agent's meaning-conferring act, the embodied meanings of the non-knower become concealed *inside* the legal discourse. What is concealed are the prejudgments and forestructures of meaning which the non-knower may have brought *into* the indigenous event of the first form of harm. The legal discourse becomes so distant from the meanings which the non-knower has experienced that the latter are first frustrated and then concealed inside the secondary signifying relations of the legal discourse.

More specifically, the thrust of my argument in Chapter 2 is that modern legal discourse possesses a *secondary genre-like* character. The discourse re-presents an indigenously experienced harm as a referent and, in the act of re-presentation, conceals the meanings which the non-knower experiences as he/she is addressed through primary genres. In a primary genre, he or she participates in immediate spoken and written social relationships with others. People embody their stories with *meant*, not externally posited, objects. The *embodiment* of their meant objects with their past experiences and future expectations brings life into their language. The interpreter *means* the object of a text. Because the interpreter *means* the object through the medium of an utterance, legal discourse displaces the non-knower's embodied meanings, although the displaced meanings remain *alive*, but concealed in that they are embodied with the prior experiences and expectations of the interpreter. Professional knowers of the legal discourse guard the discourse and, ultimately, enforce its signifying relations on the primary genres of a non-knower. The enforcement of the secondary signifying relations is considered legitimate or authoritative because the professional knowers of the signs claim to know how to trace the signs to some external source or grounds. This ensures that the enforcement is authoritative. A *differend* or gulf dwells between the displaced embodied meanings of the victim and the authoritative signifying relations of the legal discourse. This *differend* rests *inside* the legal discourse.

Critique, then, must emanate from inside legal discourse rather than from a transcendent, third-party vantage-point. The displacement, transformation and concealment of a non-expert's embodied meanings offer such an inside engine of social critique. In a conscious effort to describe the knower's experiential act of interpretation, rather than to analyse the judicial interpretation of a text or "fact", I describe in Chapter 1 how juridical agents interpreted the social event of an individual's denial of a job interview. In Chapter 2 I draw from the assimilation of the student into a professional legal education as well as the assimilation of the witness's utterances into the narratives recounted at trial. And in Chapter 3, I describe the experiential moments which I, as juridical agent and professional knower, slowly interpret and analyse a legal problem. I take three such interpretive events in Chapter 3: the resignification of 120 000 American citizens and immigrants into the typification, 'persons of Japanese ancestry,' during the Second World War; the exclusion of an Inuit community from all social and legal protections in a modern industrial state; and a financial institution's call of a demand loan during the Depression of 1980–83 in Canada. I explain how legal doctrines, signified in the secondary discourse, function ideologically and conclude that the concealment of embodied meanings inside the modern legal discourse foments a crisis of modern legal authority.

Argument: the Retrieval of the Concealed Meanings

Chapter 4 aims to begin the project of retrieving the non-knower's concealed meanings. An important element of this project, elaborated in Chapter 5, is the retrieval of the embodied meanings of the expert knower as he or she encloses the non-knower's experiences with the secondary signs and their associated objects.

The key to the embodiment of meaning is the environing world or *Umwelt* which spreads about the phenomenal body of each organism. I connect the *Umwelt* of a human being to the communication between speaker and listener in a dialogue. In Chapter 4 I argue that modern legal discourse naively posits that the cognitive or physical object is external to, and constrains, the juridical agent. The agent searches for the external object and also for its grounding in a final, absent Object which is believed to end the trace for legal authority. The consequence of such a chase after absent objects, however, is that the embodied meanings of the non-knower are forgotten, lost, excluded and concealed.

In Chapter 5, as mentioned earlier, I take the concept of the *Umwelt* to the interpretive acts of two of the great jurists of this century – Viscount Haldane and Justice Holmes. I show how they constructed important constitutional doctrines as if the doctrines were absent standards, situated beyond their control. The two jurists read the world through very different lenses: the one as a formalist and the other as a realist. Yet, their very different environing worlds, drawn from their childhoods, adolescences and political, wartime and professional experiences, led them to conceal their own constitution of meaning as they constructed important constitutional doctrines. Haldane's and Holmes' legal analyses demonstrate how an authoritative discourse ignores or, at best, idealizes the judge's environing world. Legal analysis idealizes the environing world of a jurist by beginning with a posited external object as constitutive of the real. Even a non-knower's indigenous experience of pain is configured as an external object beyond the control of the professional knower of the secondary signifying relations. The knower *reacts* to the posited external object. The knower reacts passively with the consequence that the non-knower's meant object dissipates in this transformatory enterprise. I exemplify the transformative project of legal idealism by a reading of the infamous American desegregation case of *Brown* v. *Board of Education*.

In Chapter 6, in order to clarify my argument, I defend my claim that the monologic legal discourse of a modern state produces a concealment of suffering against a possible Derridean or Stanley Fish criticism. The possible Derridean criticism might suggest that I have implanted a nature–culture dichotomy in my argument: namely, that

I have posited a non-knower whose meanings are primary (and natural) and, furthermore, that I have posited an expert knower whose legal discourse acts as a supplementary social construction. The phenomenon of the displacement of meaning reveals, it might be argued, the language of metaphysics.

In Chapter 6 I respond to such a criticism by elaborating my own theory of meaning in more detail. I argue in particular that both a non-knower and a professional knower construct meant objects from their prior experiences and expectations. The key here is a very different sense of desire than that which motivates the search for an absent object. Returning to Spinoza, the environing world of an interpreter, even in a state of flux, *acts in* the world. This contrasts with the presupposition in modern legal discourse that the interpreter is "acted on" by external objects. The possible criticism of my argument, then, shares a trace of idealism for it idealizes the embodiment of meaning by concentrating upon the interrelationships of signs as constitutive of meaning.

I elaborate a general critique of the paradigm of legal consciousness in Chapter 7 while Chapters 8 and the Conclusion take up the challenge of the critique by setting out a theory of the dialogic relations concealed by modern legal discourse.

The concealed practices of social relations within the monologic discourse of the modern state are dialogic. There is no need to retrace the indicated signs of a parliament or court to an invisible foundation in a dialogue. A paradigm of knowledge presupposes that desire is a lack of an external object and, furthermore, that that lack of an external object draws one to assimilate the languages of others. A dialogic relation, in contrast, involves *action*. The phenomenal body, with its multiplicity of experiences, acts. The body acts towards meant objects through an environing world. In a dialogic relation, one *responds* to the aggrieved as an *addressee*. The response is an addressive experience.

Dialogic partners are *inter*preters. Their addressive experiences bring meaning *into* sign(ifier)–form relationships. Force becomes problematic in the retrieved dialogic relations – but so does the modern sense of authority.

Problematics of the Study of the Legal Sign

The study of law as a language is not something new. While H.L.A. Hart rejuvenated legal positivism during the 1960s and Ronald Dworkin popularized analytic jurisprudence during the 1970s, legal semiotics took hold in Europe. At this time, Georges Kalinowski and André-Jean Arnaud were suggesting that before a juridical agent tries facts or appeals to legal doctrines, one must become conscious that *signs* represent all facts and concepts.[2] They argued that signs ideologically mask the social values of interpreters of legal texts to the point that a neutral, impartial bourgeois peace encloaks social struggle. The peace exists because a rationally self-referential world hides the violence of social struggle. How do signs function ideologically? What constitutes a sign? How does a sign relate to social relations? Are there external objects beyond the signifying relation?

Linguistics

Do either linguistics or semiotics address these issues? Of course they do, in a way. Linguistics studies the structure of a language empirically. It identifies the physical properties of a language through a scientific metalanguage with technical terms denoting analytical concepts. Linguistics takes speech activity, as opposed to writing, as the source of its empirical studies. During the 1930s linguistics formulated the *phoneme* – the smallest abstract unit functioning within the network of structural relationships in a language – with some precision. The Prague School of Linguistics argued that the *phoneme* functioned as a sound which opposes another sound. The sound 'pit', for example, opposes the sound *'mit'*. Other linguists classified different physical sounds through such specialized terms as 'allophones', 'laterality of articulation', 'alveolarity' and the like. In all traditions, linguistics concentrated upon the spoken word, the written word being considered supplementary. By the 1950s acoustic data became an important source of empirical claims about language.

The linguist asks questions which miss much of the re-signification of embodied meanings. Some such questions are as follows: How does one pronounce a word? Why did the word take on that pronunciation rather than some other as may have occurred in a related language? What rules of grammar does a discourse follow? What tenses are commonly used? What tenses have dissipated over time? Does a language use verbs more than nouns to express an intent? How efficient are its utterances with words? Is translation possible? Is it possible to develop a common world language? Does language change through the speaker or through the altered functions of its words? What rules govern the manner in which different parts of an utterance are put together? These questions fail to address a great deal of the phenomenon of legal discourse.

Commentators on legal discourse have drawn primarily from legal semiotics rather than linguistics, partly because linguistics is preoccupied with verbal utterances and legal language is, to a large extent, a written language and, in its spoken form, gestures play as important a role as words. The preliminary pleadings in a common law action, for example, take a written form. The reasons for a judgment are written. A trial or a judgment may turn on the interpretation of one written word. For example, what did the legislature mean by a certain word? What did the earlier judge mean by a particular paragraph? Even verbal communications between lawyers, long before any lawsuit is in mind, are confirmed in writing. Although witnesses do verbally restate an event, their utterances are transcribed, and this transcription, rather than the indigenously experienced act of pain, slowly becomes the centre of later arguments. Moreover, it is the witnesses' non-verbal language – their clothes, facial expressions, demeanour, smiles, personalities, questions, silences – which are crucial in assessing their credibility or truthfulness.

Semiotics

In contrast to linguistics, semiotics focuses upon the written and gestural signs of a language. Semiotics is the science of signs. Gestures are signs in that they signify or represent an event or object even though they may not be spoken. They are especially important in primary genres where two partners identify immediately with their gestures to represent something.

One of the early students of legal semiotics, Algirdas Greimas, argued, for example, that a belief structure, magic terms, and hidden "unwritten" codes lie behind the physical texts called statutes and precedents. Similarly, legal theorists, influenced by the semiotics of Charles Peirce (1839–1914), focused on the relation of the sign to the physical/social object situated in the world of "fact" beyond the sign. This external object was called a referent. And still other scholars, influenced by Lacan, have exposed how a symbolic structure is very important in legal discourse. A symbol does not represent some external object. Though self-binding, the symbolic structure constructs an imaginary divine or phallic foundation of the authority of juridical language. Lawyers merely imagine the symbol and build a structure of signs in the belief that they can reach the absent symbol with which they immediately identify. Important approaches to legal discourse – such as those of Greimas, Peirce, Lacan or Derrida – draw from a semiotics of the sign rather than from the linguistics of verbal utterances.

Problematics of Studies of the Semiotics of the Legal Sign

Peirce and his Followers

Accordingly, it makes sense that legal discourse should be studied through a nomenclature which draws from legal semiotics. However, even here there is a diversity of specialized terms which are used in very different projects with different objects in mind. One project, led by Roberta Kevelson, relies heavily upon Charles Peirce, for example. While Peirce's nomenclature is a specialized language in itself, certain of Peirce's themes bear upon the primary genres concealed within a legal discourse. Peirce theorized about the dynamic and indeterminate possibilities of configuring signs, explaining in a letter to Lady Victoria Welby, for example, that 'all our thought and knowledge is by signs'.[3] A sign relates an object to an *interpretant* (a sign as interpreted). A sign stands to someone (an interpreter) for something (an object) as an *interpretant* sign in respect to a small part of an external object. One interpretant replaces another interpretant. Meaning is situated in the relationship between *interpretants* rather than from the intentions of the author of the sign or the equivalent representation of a sign to its object. According to Peirce, a fact is Firstness, an 'interpretant' is Secondness and the never-ending combinations of *'interpretants'* constitute language, known as Thirdness. Combinations of *'interpretants'*, or Thirdness, are indeterminate or unlimited in their reproduction of signification. The sign, then, does not represent a fixed conception or fact. Any one sign is interpreted. A sign, once uttered, never remains the same as the interpreted sign. Rather, an *interpreter* enriches each sign with a new signification. 'Meaning' is situated in the interrelation of one *interpreted sign* to another. The moment of reaching some fixed originary source of a sign is forever postponed because an 'unlimited semiosis' envelopes all meanings.

Roberta Kevelson and one strain of the Critical Legal Studies movement took up the Peircean point that an indeterminate flux of significations characterizes language. A legislature or judge, in the act of writing a text, may intend a certain object. But the relation of two opposing signs overtakes the object, Kevelson has argued. The text is resituated from an authorial to a signifying context. When joined in different configurations, a discourse constructs new objects, and the author's meant object dissipates.[4] This means that any one judicial decision signifies other representations. The interpretation of a referent or external object changes as each interpreter interprets a referent differently through different configurations of signs.

An important point in Peirce's semiotics needs to be isolated here. Although all experience is represented, according to Kevelson, there remains "out there" a referent which pre-exists the signifying relation. The referent is external or absent from two opposing *significants*. The referent is a given. The interpreter reacts to the referent. The legal discourse, embedded in the indeterminate configurations of opposed significants, inevitably idealizes social practice or natural facts as referents. The lawyer even represents a client's unanalysable feelings through the authoritative *interpretants* of legal language.[5] Even the ultimate foundation of laws is situated in Thirdness or the ever-changing combinations of *interpretants*.

Roberta Kevelson's Peircean analysis of legal semiotics has no place for such *prejudices* independent of signifying relations. Meaning, for her, rests in the *significant*, not in the constitution of meant objects. The structuralist studies of Julien Greimas and Bernard Jackson do acknowledge that the social-cultural *prejudices* constitute a deep semiotic code. However, for them, the deep code is self-referential and therefore misses the indeterminate character, which Revelson recognizes, of signifying relations. Both strains of thought concentrate upon the mind – the images of the sounds and marks – to the exclusion of the experiential body. As a consequence, the engine of social critique for traditional efforts in legal semiotics remains with the mind. The suffering of the experiential body is forgotten or, indeed, concealed within the very analysis of concepts because the most which one can do is to imagine or picture an external object within the mind itself.

Saussure

Legal semiotics changed tack on the Continent during the 1970s when a series of lawyers argued that legal discourse does not need an external referent. Bernard Jackson and André-Jean Arnaud suggested, in particular, that signification is so 'total' that even the "facts of a case" are signified. Furthermore, they argued, legal discourse even produces signs which themselves construct the external object of legality (or what Arnaud called 'juridicity'). One combination of magic terms represents other combinations of magic terms and so on in the direction of some final, absent source or *arche*-point. Legal discourse is self-referential. The relation of a sign to a signified object, as Saussure argued, is arbitrary. Saussure seems to have first coined the nomenclature which I shall take for granted.[6] He argued that a 'signifier' *fuses* with a 'signified' so as to produce a 'sign'. A signifier or 'language sign'[7] is more than just a physical word on a page or a sound in the air; it is a sound image or mark image of the pattern of sounds or marks. Because of the insecurity which the reader may experience with such a term as 'signifier', I use the term 'sign' as synonymous with the signifier in the balance of this book.

Kafka's *The Trial* exemplifies what is meant by a signifier (which I shall abbreviate as a 'sign') and signified. The story begins with K being awakened by commotion at his doorway by uninvited intruders. One of the officers utters sounds to the effect 'Y-o-u-a-r-e-a-r-r-e-s-t-e-d'. These sounds possess a material or physical character which physical scientists can perceive and examine. However, language constitutes much more than physical–chemical matter. For example, even if K hears physical sounds, uttered at his bedroom doorway, K himself embodies the sounds with a *meant*, not an external, object. The noise may indicate that the men in his doorway are looking for someone else, that they have reached the wrong apartment, that they are new tenants, and more. These may or may not be be meant objects constituted by K. K's experiences may also have led him to possess *prejudices* which he brings into the sounds and influence his picture of the external objects beyond his environing world. These objects may be physical or categorical. Saussure called such objects *signifieds*. Thus, when K hears the arresting officers at the doorway of his bedroom, he pictures the officers as meant objects. He imagines what their utterances and grunts represent; they signify objects for him. The sound images are what Saussure calls a 'signifier', and the images themselves are drawn from a web of opposing *significants*, to use Peirce's term.

However, whereas Saussurian analysis is confined to the signifier and signified, K *embodies* the utterances of the officers with his particular felt experiences. This is the crucial element which contemporary theories of the legal sign miss, whether the theories are derived from Peirce, as with the American version of Critical Legal Studies, or from Saussure, as with the European students of the legal sign. K brings his body *into* the utterances, independent of the meant objects of the officers. He constitutes the meant objects from his experiences. Science can only take us so far in understanding the constitution of such meaning. K's meaning is directed toward the sound 'a-r-r-e-s-t-e-d'. If K identifies sounds such as 'a' 'r' 'r' 'e' 's' 't' 'e' 'd', he already puts meaning *into* the sounds, as for that matter, do the arresting officers. K and the arresting officers bring different meanings into the same sounds so as to produce different sound images or signifiers. Their meanings are something other than matter. As a consequence, K on the one hand and, on the other, all the expert knowers – the lawyer, Leni, the painter, the examining magistrate and the others –mean the same utterances differently. Whereas the expert knowers assimilate K into their conceptions, K em*bodies* their gestures, utterances, silences, actions and inactions with his own meanings.

Where does such a conception as a *signified* enter into an analysis of legal discourse? The officials in *The Trial* take each sign as signifying or re-presenting something. That 'something else' is believed to be an external object – the signified. The painter, the lawyer, Leni and the gatekeeper search for that 'something else'. They claim to know the rule, principle or doctrine for which a sign stands. Because the object is external to the historically contingent signs, its externality drives a claimant to knowledge in a colonizing enterprise. The claimant to knowledge desires what he or she lacks – a cognitive object or signified – and so situates utterances into the interrelations of signs which the knower can recognize. After all, the knower knows signs. In so transfiguring an utterance, the knower re-presents the external object. Configurations of signs now represent the object and the context-specific meant objects of the non-knower are enclosed in secondary transfiguring signifying relations. Thus, the Peircean focus upon the never-ending reconfiguration of *significants* lops off the constitution of a meant object. A social event, such as K's embodied meanings as he awoke one fine day, slowly merges into significations of the event. The signified event is recontextualized amongst differentiating signs which represent objects meant by the expert knowers, not for K.

For example, the gestures and inquiries of the two police officers at the doorway of K's bedroom trigger images inside K's mind concerning the right to privacy which he believes to constitute reality in his own country, a liberal–democratic state. In addition, the absence of certain action (namely, his morning coffee and biscuit) raises images in K's mind of his landlady's role and K's need to rebuke her on their next chance meeting. K's image of his landlady also concerns her role of scrutinizing all visitors to the house. K's questions to the police officers, in turn, raise associations in their minds of K as a delinquent to authority. His incredulous attitude frustrates, indeed challenges, the images which the police take for granted as actors in a rigid hierarchy of officials. The officers do not care what role the landlady plays or whether she has served K's coffee. The officers do not need to know what text K has contravened or how flagrantly K has contravened it. They need only know that a more senior official has ordered them to arrest K. The officers presuppose that others know the right cognitive objects and the right procedures under which K will be tried. Expert knowers will fill in the gaps to the officers' knowledge. Whereas the utterances of the police officers are only physical–chemical sounds to K, the same utterances signify important conceptions to the officers and to all the experts who eventually "hear" K's case. K and the officers work through different idioms. These configurations, in turn, represent radically different conceptions about the role of the state, the person, authority and what matters at 7 am on a particular morning. No matter how hard he tries, K cannot respond to the police officers through their own discourse. Nor can the experts respond to K's utterances in a manner which makes sense to him. The nomenclature and the represented conceptions continue to be of no significance to K.

Greimas

The signifier–signified relationship becomes the subject of Algirdas J. Greimas' (1917–92) contribution to the discourse of legal semiotics. Notably in his essay 'The Semiotic Analysis of Legal Discourse' (1990), Greimas first departs from the Peircean line by dropping the externality of the referent from the semiotics of legal discourse. Signs alone (the juncture of a signifier and a signified) constitute existence for Greimas. The lawyer's first job is to represent an object and to predict how the representation will combine with other representations. Juridical officials treat the representation, not some external object, as the Real according to Greimas. Legal discourse represents its own signifiers through its own nomenclature and grammar. There is no outside to the legal discourse – no facts, no social practices, no objective "rule of law", no Constitution. Thus, there is no transcendent external standard of justice with which to evaluate any particular configuration of signs. Since there is no pre-existing social practice, the lawyer must remain content with extending old nomenclature to hitherto unsignified events. An event does not exist until it is recognized as an event through legal nomenclature and grammar. Signifying relations constitute the true/real, order the true/real, and authorize further action. Accordingly, one must abandon induction as a method of understanding law, whether one is a lawyer within the system or a scholar situated without. One must also abandon the idea that law is reified, because there is no given external social reality from which legal norms may have become estranged.

Second, Greimas distinguishes between a deep and surface grammar of a text. Binary relations signify the surface grammar. The deep structure sets out the minimum conditions for a script to bear signification. This deep structure has no outside: it is self-referring. Signs even endow a legal institution with personality.[8] Put another way, a lawyer is an *acteur* at the surface level and an *actant* at the deep level. The *actant* plays a role in a grander narrative synatactic unit which autonomously exists vis-à-vis all other signifying systems. In a sense, the deep structure of a semiotic system possesses a "life" of its own where small units combine into a system which is greater than the sum of its parts. This is so even though it is said that a legislature in a democratic state promulgates a statute. Such a claim suggests that a legislature transforms a posited social/natural reality into recognizable signs. And yet the deep structure of the signifying relations mediates the script of the legislature. Indeed, the legislature "promulgates" phrases which lawyers already recognize as authoritative signs in the structure of signifying relations. Within 'the law', there are many *groupes semiotiques* who communicate messages with each other through signs which possess meanings only for the experts. In this manner, the signifying systems of law function secondarily to natural or everyday languages, although not secondarily to a prior external object as the Peircean tradition of legal semiotics presupposes. This is not to say that the legal semiotic structures are isolated from the social–cultural realm, according to Greimas. The structures possess signifying effects upon other signifying systems.

Bernard Jackson

To analyse cognitive objects or to induce conclusions from social "facts" – as if the facts were beyond the interpreter's control as legal positivists claim – and to do so without recognizing the nomenclature and grammar of legal discourse, reinforces the concept of an *Alice in Wonderland* world divorced from the 'reality' of signifying relations, according to Greimas and Bernard Jackson. Legal conceptions simply do not exist, let alone possess efficacy, unless and until signs represent cognitive objects through a familiar nomenclature and grammar. Jackson further maintains that lawyers and judges apply the nomenclature and grammar through little stories which share narrative structures with other legal stories, thereby reinforcing the importance of the specialized nomenclature and grammar of lawyers. In one of his important essays along these lines, Bert van Roermund argues that the coherence of a legal narrative ensures that the little stories will be taken as real and true.[9]

The most important factor in a coherent narrative, of course, is the lawyer's belief that some transcendent source grounds any one configuration of signs. The ultimate source ends the trace for authority because it is external or beyond historically contingent signs. Without such an external Object to found the trace, the indeterminate circulation of signs would encourage disorder and uncertainty. Any one configuration would be a fragment. How could any particular configuration of signs be considered authoritative? Indeed, Jean-Paul Arnaud argues in one of his earlier studies that the cult of *juridicity* itself, or what Lon Fuller calls *legality*, requires that the foundation be projected 'out there' in an objective, politically neutral, external situs.[10] Such a situs is absent from a historically contingent configuration of signs. The import of Greimas' and Jackson's works is that the nomenclature and grammar of lawyers create the external foundation in order to maintain the authority to enforce lawyers' own configurations. Since it is absent from their signifying relations, lawyers and judges can only picture or imagine such an absent foundation.[11]

Problematics of the Social Critique of the Legal Sign

The Saussurian approach to the legal sign leaves one with this critical question: what is the engine of a social critique of legal signs if the ever-changing signifying relations of interpreter and sign represent all factual and metaphysical objects? Indeed, this same question applies to the works of Duncan Kennedy and other American followers of Peirce's approach. The key to this question is, I believe, that both the Peircean and the Saussurian strains of legal semiotics have been preoccupied with the *cognitive* aspects of signification or representation. The relation of the sign to the external object (or referent), for Peirce, is a cognitive relation. Communication, for Saussure as well, involves the transfer of thoughts from one human mind to another through signs. Cognitive objects are considered the prime movers in the speech circuit for Saussure.[12] A speaker's cognitive objects are translated into sound images which, in turn, are translated back again into conceptions of the hearer. The hearer pictures or represents an object or signified in Saussure's case, or a posited referent in Peirce's.

The discourse of semiotics thereby displaces a very important element in the concealed dialogic relations of a non-knower. The meanings of a non-knower are not drawn entirely from the relation of the sign to the *interpretant*, as Kevelson suggests, or the equation of one signifier to a signified, as Saussure argues, or the ever-changing relation of one signifier to another, as Derrida claims. Rather, one's meanings in a primary genre are embodied with what Gadamer calls *prejudice*,[13] in that one's experiences are brought into any configuration of signs. *Prejudice* draws from the forestructures of meaning and the expectations which one brings into one's reading of a sign. An object is thus embodied. The embodiment of one's experiences into a sign makes meaning alive. But the authoritative signifier–signified relations in juridical language displace the embodied meanings which a non-knower brings into shared signs.

Moreover, a focus upon the given, externally posited referent, as with Peirce, or the signifier-signified relation, as with Saussure, misses how a professional knower embodies signifying relations with the knower's past experiences and forestructures of meaning. I shall show in Chapter 3, for example, that the legal discourse of a modern state tends to project authoritative signifiers as the referent of a prior signifier: the signifier–signified relations tend to become self-referential and self-binding. As the signifier–signified relations of the knower displace the signifer-signified relations of the non-knower, the embodiment of both sets of relations with one's experiences is lost – though not forever. The embodied meanings of the non-knower, in particular, remain alive but concealed inside the signifier–

signified relations of the modern legal discourse. The legal discourse only appears to be self-referential because its own signifying relations, so crucial to the privileging of legal discourse as secondary to the lived meanings of the non-knower, deny the role of the embodiment of meaning by the knower. The possibility that the *prejudice* of the body enter into the interpretive act contradicts the objectivism and impartiality so dear to the expert knowers' sense of legality. Why objectivism is held so dear lies in the presupposed externality of the object to the signifier, whether the object be "the facts of the case" or a legal rule or policy. As a consequence of such a belief, legal discourse takes on a homogeneity. Take any lawyer from any country in the world, locate her or him in some unfamiliar building with other lawyers, and he or she will soon be speaking through the magic vocabulary which lawyers universally share.

The Phenomenology of Legal Language

I aim to raise the above issues by describing how juridical agents displace, transform and then conceal the embodied meanings of someone who has harmed another or someone who has been harmed. My arguments describe the experiences of juridical agents in diverse and familiar social contexts during this century. In contradistinction with the traditional analytic project of a common law lawyer, I describe the experiential moments of the juridical agent's *meaning* towards the given "facts", statutes, precedents and other projected objective standards of the common law lawyer. Here, I am less concerned with the analytic lawyer's traditional analysis of rules and principles but instead aim to bring into the open the importance of what the analytic lawyer leaves unsaid, or what H.L.A. Hart calls the 'pre-legal'. I aim to describe the intuitive moments before the lawyer or legal theorist begins to articulate and justify a rule or principle. My project, then, is very different from that of H.L.A. Hart or Ronald Dworkin and all the many others who have attempted to give explanatory power to the juridical official's enterprise. I show how the juridical agent becomes immersed in a web of secondary signs to the point of excluding some persons from consideration (such as a forgotten Inuit community). By playing in the web, the juridical agents sometimes avoid recognizing the indigenous experiences of a group who have been harmed (as in a racial discrimination case or the forgotten Inuit community). On still other occasions, the agents abstract from the particulars of the experiential being so as to construct a typified person. In still other contexts, the juridical official expels a particular subject as an other to the legal discourse, as did the US Supreme Court Justices in the internment of 'persons of Japanese ancestry'.

Legal discourse excludes the particular experiences of the non-knower by offering signs to represent the non-knower as a cognitive object.

In addition, the juridical officials read social events by ushering forth very special terms, such as "free speech" or "emergency" or "reasonable time", which reorganize the social world according to the cognitive objects which such terms represent. When one considers how a juridical agent reads social events, it is remarkable how the agent constructs the "facts", as did Viscount Haldane in elaborating the doctrine of an "emergency" for Commonwealth legal discourses or as did Justice Holmes when he elaborated the famous 'clear and present danger' doctrine through his own experienced and very special world. The juridical agent reads statutes and precedents and "facts" in search for an absent foundation of legal authority. The foundation is believed to ground the signs which represent or signify the non-knower's experiences. Such a search leads the agent away from the embodied meanings of the non-knower directly towards the foundation. With the production of more and more signifying effects, the modern legal discourse continues like a disembodied ghost whose shape continually shifts as its signifying context takes shape.

I depart from the different approaches of linguistics and semiotics which I have briefly outlined above. I do so in order to overcome the problematics which both the Peircean and Saussurian traditions represent. Influenced by Edmund Husserl's theory of *embodied* meaning in the *Logical Investigations* and drawing from the phenomenological theories of meaning elaborated by von Euxkull, Merleau Ponty and Vygotsky, I argue that one brings one's body *into* a sign by reading the sign through one's prior experiences of which one's forestructures of meaning and expectations constitute important elements. One's meaning is *lived* because of the bodily experiences with which one reads a sentence. Such an embodiment of meaning characterizes the act of interpretation, whether of the legal knower or the non-knower. I shall show with reference to the judgments of Viscount Haldane and Justice Holmes, however, that a jurist's environing world may well deny the role of an embodied interpretation. The jurist, immersed in a secondary discourse for a long professional career, may *mean* the world as externally posited. Thus, whether or not the interpreter experiences the constraining gaze of an external author, one *means* such a spectre. One embodies legal discourse with the spectre of such a transcendent author. I aim to recover nothing less than the interpreter's embodiment of meaning, however deeply concealed inside the modern legal discourse.

It is important to bear in mind, then, that when I read judicial decisions, statutes, doctrines and the like, I read them with a view to understand the moments through which the author/interpreter experiences the world. I do so, for example, by focusing upon the social, educational, personal and cultural *prejudices* of Haldane and Holmes. I glean their environing worlds from a rich library of their diaries, speeches, academic essays, books and judgments. I show how each judge reads the juridical world through his or her own experienced environing world even though that environing world encourages each judge to begin and end all legal analysis with an externally posited object, whether it be a social fact, a legal doctrine or a statute. When I write about judicial decisions, I refer to the experiential moments which a juridical agent incurs when he or she reads a statute, a social event or an earlier precedent. As a juridical agent and professional knower for almost 25 years myself, I read judicial decisions, statutes and other common law texts in a manner which aims to respect the author's and the interpreter's own embodiment of signs through his or her own environing world or *Umwelt*. Rather than abstracting cognitive rules and doctrines, playing with them, "applying" them and reconfiguring them, I experience the texts of the other in order to reach the language of the other from the intertext between us.

The possibility of an unconcealment of the embodied meanings of a non-knower offers the engine to a social critique of the legal discourse of a modern state. Legal discourse displaces embodied meanings at the very moment that expert knowers of the authoritative signs recognize the non-knower's signified event. Legal recognition occurs as the knower posits a sign to represent the other. The knower situates the sign into a trace of authority to some final source. Because of the loss of the non-knower's (and the knower's) embodied meanings in this transformatory project of juridical language, expert knowers must ultimately rely on an enforcement of their discourse upon the language of the other. Legal discourse is a master discourse.

The traditional critique of a modern legal order, as I said, is sited from afar – beyond the legal discourse. Thus, a series of discourses have arisen which presuppose that laws were separate from the situs of critique: law and society, law and psychiatry, law and literature, feminism and the law and so on. Such traditional critiques often long for a moment of immediacy between juridical agent and non-knower. As I shall discuss in the next chapter, feminist critics, for example, have often described such an immediacy as offering the potential for an emancipatory legal order. And, again, as I shall explain in the next chapter, an early moment of Critical Legal Studies attempted to ground a social critique of law in the moment of immediacy, sometimes described as 'intersubjective zap', between the lawyer and the client. The presence of the non-knower dwells inside, rather than outside, the official discourse of the knower, as I intend to argue and demonstrate by examples in the next two chapters. The nostalgia for face-to-face social relations, though, ignores the opaqueness of the legal sign in the official discourse. Moreover, once one takes account of the embodiment of the legal sign with *prejudice*, one can better appreciate that the modern legal discourse, to be authoritative, cannot address the other in the language of the other.

Where does justice lie, then? Is justice accessible through human laws? Is justice accessible at all? Justice lies in the unconcealment of the languages of the other. The challenge presented to the social theorist is to retrieve embodied meanings and to ask what a legal order would look like if such meanings were unconcealed. Would it be ordered? Would it be law? I argue that a clue can be found to such a challenge in Spinoza's ethical writings. There, I retrieve a very different sense of desire than the cognitive search for an absent foundation and describe such an alternative view of legal desire. I further argue that justice can be situated in the intertext of a dialogic relation and that such an intertext seems quite alien to the monologue of the modern juridical empire. I conclude that if such dialogic relations were unconcealed, the search for an external Object would collapse and, with that, so would legal discourse as we know it today.

Notes

1 Franz Kafka, *The Trial* (New York: Schocken Books, 1937, 1956): 103.

2 Arnaud, André-Jean, *Essai d'analyse structurale du Code Civil francais: la règle du jue dans la paix bourgeois* (Michel Villey Pref; Georges Mounin Postface; Bibliotheque de Philosophie du Droit, vol. 16; Paris: Librarie Générale de Droit et de Jurisprudence, 1973).

3 Charles Hardwick ed., *Semiotic and Significs: The Correspondence Between Charles S. Peirce and Lady Victoria Welby* (Bloomington and London: Indiana University Press, 1977): 31–2.

4 This contrasts with Husserl's sense of indeterminacy in *Logical Investigations*, vol. 2, nos 5, 6 (Evanston: Northwestern University Press, 1970).

5 Roberta Kevelson, *Semiotics and the Human Sciences: Peirce and the Law*, vol. 1 (New York: Peter Lang, 1991).

6 Ferdinand de Saussure, *Course in General Linguistics* (Charles Bally and Albert Sechehaye with Albert Riedlinger eds.; Wade Baskin trans.; New York: McGraw-Hill, 1955, 1966).

7 The term is Mieke Bal's in *Narratology: Introduction to the Theory of Narrative* (Christine van Boheeman trans.; Toronto: University of Toronto Press, 1985): 5.

8 Algirdas Julien Greimas, 'The Semiotic Analysis of Legal Discourse: Commercial Laws that Govern Companies and Groups of Companies' in *The Social Sciences: A Semiotic View*, Paul Perron and Frank H. Collins trans. (Minneapolis: University of Minnesota Press, 1990): 102–38.

9 Bert van Roermund, 'Narrative Coherence and the Guises of Legalism' in Patrick Nerhot ed., *Law, Interpretation and Reality: Essays in Epistemology, Hermeneutics and Jurisprudence* (Dordrecht/Boston/London: Kluwer Academic Publishers, 1990): 310–54.

10 André-Jean Arnaud, 'Fact as Law' in D. Carzo and Bernard S. Jackson eds., *Semiotics, Law and Social Science* (Rome/Gangemi: Liverpool Law Review, 1973): 129–44. Lon L. Fuller, *The Morality of Law* (New Haven, Conn.: Yale University Press, 1964).

11 The judiciary's elaboration of different images of a constitution in one modern state is exemplified in William E. Conklin, *Images of a Constitution* (Toronto: University of Toronto Press, 1989).

12 See especially Roy Harris, *Reading Saussure: A Critical Commentary on the 'Cours de linguistique génerale'* (London: Duckworth, 1987): 205–18. However a very different interpretation, which privileges the phenomenal body in Saussure, is Paul Thibault, *Re-Reading Saussure* (London: Routledge, 1996).

13 Hans-Georg Gadamer, *Truth and Method* (New York: Crossroad, 1985): 225–341.

1 The Paradigms of Legal Consciousness and Legal Language

An individual's concrete experience is recognized in the legal discourse of a modern state at the cost of the concealment of the experience itself. The legal discourse belongs to the knower of a very special vocabulary and grammar, and juridical agents isolate special terms from that vocabulary. In this way, the indigenously experienced harm of a non-knower is re-presented by signs which only the knower can claim to know. It helps that the knower belongs to a profession which carefully controls who can claim to know the legal signs. Juridical officials differentiate one legal doctrine from another, one pertinent "fact" from another, by situating the appropriate sign in a network of familiar signs. The juridical agents privilege some signs, ignore others and exclude others as just not relevant to the practice of law. The sign which represents the winning doctrine or "fact" becomes "magical" in such a network, although the sign may have little signification for the non-knower since the web of special signs is usually configured in a manner which denies the knower's active role in constructing a cognitive object. A legal rule, a doctrine, a principle or a policy exemplifies such a cognitive object.

This is the tragedy of both old and newly independent modern states: the authoritative discourse of the state produces a suffering at the very moment that the discourse claims a universalist character to the typifications which the legal signs represent. For the universalist doctrines fail to fulfil the *meant* objects of someone harmed. An individual's meant objects draw from his or her own indigenously experienced context. The gap between the meant objects of someone harmed and the cognitive objects of the professional knower of the legal discourse creates a silent bloodless wound *inside* the legal discourse. The person harmed does not know the special legal doctrines. The non-knower cannot present his or her experience of harm again, even as a witness in the courtroom. The best that he or she can do is to re-present the harm and, then, only through a professional knower who re-presents his or her representation as a cohesive narrative. The lawyer and judge recognize the harm, but the recognition is achieved through signs which only secondarily derive from the person who has been harmed. Even when political leaders claim to instil a revolutionary new ideology, a new discourse simply displaces an old one, and there remain non-knowers who are "other" to the new official discourse. The official discourse recognizes the non-knower as signified in the official discourse, not as meant by the non-knower. As such, the bodily experiences, which the non-knower brings into his or her meant objects, are concealed inside the secondary signifying relations of the knowers. Once the official discourse conceals the significations meant by such bodily experiences in primary genres, it is a short step for the official discourse to ignore, indeed to exclude, the non-knower's physical body through which he or she experiences meanings. This, I shall show in Chapter 3 with respect to the internment of 'persons of the Japanese ancestry' in the United States, the silence of the community of Davis Inlet and the confiscation of assets during a receivership. The juridical assimilation of the non-knower's experienced meanings, in turn, impacts upon the readiness of the juridical agents of the official discourse to imprison, torture or terminate the physical body of the non-knower. After all, the physical body reminds the knower that something always remains beyond the knower's grasp: namely, the experiential meanings of the non-knower. The physical body of the non-knower remains after the knower has intellectualized about the pain and suffering of the non-knower. Not surprisingly, then, when one official discourse tried to displace another official discourse between 1900 and 1989, over 18 059 000 persons were killed.[1] This bears repeating: the struggle of discourses to recognize and to be recognized as authoritative has caused the deaths of over 18 million human beings within less than 90 years – that is, 5 million human beings per year. The struggle to have an official discourse recognized has worked to maim and torture many more millions. Ethnic cleansing, openly manifested as in Bosnia or subtly exemplified with the internment of American and Canadian citizens during the Second World War, always remains a possibility for an official discourse. For the legal discourse of a modern state claims to represent all. Yet, that act of representation cannot recognize the other through the language of the other.

What is the connection between an official legal discourse and – to take an extreme case of suffering – ethnic cleansing? The key nexus is the body – the experiential body. The non-knower cannot bring his or her body into the complex web of the signs of the official discourse. However vigorously juridical agents claim a universalism for their doctrines and rules, the experiential body of someone harmed remains unassimilated in the official discourse. Yet his or her meant objects remain alive and become concealed inside the official discourse. Thus the non-knower's physical body reminds the juridical agents that the assimilationist project of the official discourse always remains incomplete.

How are everyday embodied meanings concealed? First, someone who feels harmed cannot re-present his or her harm as he or she had *meant* it in an indigenously experienced context. The best that he or she can do is to retain a professional knower to represent the harm in the official discourse. Second, the professional knower of the official signs will recognize a harm by re-situating the complainant into a secondary configuration of signs representing doctrines which intellectualize *about* the knower's cognitive world, not the complainant's felt experiences. The knower signifies a *signified* pain, not the indigenously experienced pain itself. The secondary signs take on a magical power for the knower. The knower claims to know what cognitive objects to associate with that signified pain. What makes the knowers' signs authoritative? Why are the knowers' signs used rather than those of the complainant? Why may the knowers' signs be enforced against those of the complainant?

Slowly, the knower traces one sign to another in an effort to reach some ultimate foundation which can finalize the knower's project. There are no opportunities for the non-knower to respond in his or her own idiom. Or, more correctly, there may be opportunities, but the non-knower's response is resituated into the secondary signifying relations which the knower will recognize. The non-knower cannot respond to the knower except through the secondary "magic" terms nor can the knower respond to the non-knower's stories in a way which makes sense to the latter's felt experiences. Mikhail Bakhtin (1895–1975) describes such a failed interchange of responses as a monologue. The key to the monologic path of the modern legal discourse is the belief in an external object, beyond the knower and the knower's own discourse. Such an external object is believed to ground legal reasoning. The trace of authority immunizes the knower from any charge of bias, but also prevents the knower from even recognizing the violence of his or her own interpretive acts. The trace of signs continues indefinitely and affords no opportunity for a non-knower to respond.

In contrast, in a dialogue, a discursive partner finalizes his or her utterance so that the other may respond. One response invites another response and the dialogue may depart from the original intent of the first utterer. In the authoritative discourse, the trace of secondary signs idealizes the story of the non-knower. The biological body of the non-knower reminds the knower of the secondary genre that there remains something other to the modern legal discourse. This bodily remainder threatens the cohesiveness, the inevitability and the civility of the knowers' discourse and can be erased only with the imprisonment, torture, maiming and the execution of the non-knower's physical body. Without a physical body, the non-knower cannot experience. The concealment of a non-knower's meanings disembodies those meanings. There is method in the madness of the authorized killing of 18 million human beings within 90 years.

As Jacques Derrida suggests, the condition of all possible justice is the language of the other.[2] Because modern legal discourse cannot address the other in the language of the other, laws, however legitimately posited, are not and cannot be just. Derrida does not clearly define this "other".[3] I shall argue in later chapters that a multiplicity of concealed embodied meanings of the non-knower constitute the "other" to the modern legal discourse. Legal discourse, at the moment of recognizing a non-knower's story, resituates the story into chains of magic terms which take on a special signification for the knower. The knower's signification is secondary to the story as retold by the person harmed. The secondary chains of signs configure the non-knower's story. Such a secondariness contrasts with the non-knower who has experienced an event as a primary felt experience.

I shall shortly argue that traditional efforts to retrieve a justice presented in face-to-face social relations have failed to appreciate how a legal discourse resignifies the story of a non-knower. I shall document how strains of contemporary social–legal theory have underplayed the opaqueness of the legal sign which has been considered transparent. The concepts of the mind have been privileged. Such an approach to justice works within a paradigm of legal consciousness.

The legal knower's consciousness fails to account for the non-knower's embodied meanings. Legal consciousness of the non-knower's concrete experience privileges the cognitive over the discursive. Laws become a matter of the meeting of the minds of professional knowers. Such a meeting occurs as if the legal signs were transparent. The legal doctrine, hitherto presumed to enclose the person harmed, is invisible in the sense of being inaccessible. Can the knower categorize someone without a sign to represent the category? Can the knower reflect about the legal doctrine without a sign to signify the private thought? As soon as a knower refers to a cognitive object through voice or written text, another knower imagines the sound or mark.

The legal sign, though, does not stand alone because it is embodied with prior experiences and future expectations. One brings one's experiential body *into* a sign as one thinks about the object which the sign is supposed to represent. The sign is *meant*. One means an object as signified by a sign. The embodiment of a sign raises the possibility that one's meant object remains unfulfilled by a listener or reader. The converse also occurs. A knower may embody a sign as if his or her meant object were posited beyond the knower's control. The privilege of the posited object constructs a condition where the interpreter remains passive. For the posited object is a given. But because the knower actually *means* such a posited external object, the belief in the givenness of the external object idealizes the knower's own embodiment of his or her meaning. This belief in the givenness of the external object creates a condition where the person harmed is accepted as a passive supplement to the given object, and the embodiment of both the knower's and the non-knower's meanings become a side issue. This means that the legal discourse of a modern state exudes a violence against the phenomenal body. In order to appreciate the devastating impact of that violence for the 19 million victims of an official discourse, we must turn to its discursive character.

Laws as Legal Consciousness

Kafka's K in *The Trial* manifests the devastating consequence of someone who attempts to understand others entirely in terms of one's consciousness of the other. K tries desperately hard to conceptualize what is happening to him. He tries to meet the minds of the professional knowers, but fails to appreciate that he is embodying the world with his prior experiences and expectations as a bank clerk, lover and citizen in a liberal state. He endeavours to enclose the knowers under invisible categories of which he is conscious. As a result, K believes that the legal world is posited external to himself. From the viewpoint of K as well as the lawyer, the painter and all the other expert knowers, the apparently uncontrolled and uncontrollable facts dwell "out there" beyond the actors. In addition, the legal procedures are taken for granted, as givens, beyond the control of the claimants to legal knowledge. The only thing that the knowers claim to do is to conceptualize about the externally posited facts and procedures and then situate K into that conceptualization. The knowers strive to reach a coherent picture of social "reality".

Such an intellectualized picture remains untainted by opaque signs. This is the problematic of the professional knowers and of K. Everyone fails to realize that the other imagines the legal world through signs which each embodies with meant objects. Both the knowers and K aspire to reach the other's mind without considering the embodied meanings of the other. Everyone fails to appreciate that, as a consequence of such an embodiment of meaning, an untranslatable discursive gap lies between the knowers and K. Such a gap lies hidden *inside* the legal discourse. However successfully the professional knowers enclose K inside their intellectualized world, K's physical body reminds the knowers that their effort to intellectually colonize K will remain forever incomplete until K's body is exterminated.

K and the professional knowers are not alone in this regard. Even contemporary legal theorists accept that laws concern a consciousness of cognitive objects through transparent legal signs.

Let me now concentrate upon theories of law which have attempted to overcome the experiential distance between knower and non-knower. Each theory, I now wish to emphasize, has attempted to transcend such a gap by advocating a radical change in legal consciousness.

The Phenomenology of the Human Sciences

The two most important legal theorists who attacked the problem of reification early in this century were Georg Lukacs and Alfred Schutz. Not surprisingly, they understood laws in terms of interconnected conceptions in legal consciousness. According to their view, a rule or principle became reified vis-à-vis the citizenry in a liberal–democratic state when the legal knower did not represent the interests of the populace. Georg Lukacs claimed in his important essays, 'Reification and the Consciousness of the Proletariat' and 'Legality and Illegality,' that legal consciousness was highly reified vis-à-vis what he called 'concrete experience'.[4] If juridical agents could transform their legal consciousness, laws would reach the concrete experiences of the oppressed. Such a transformed legal consciousness would be legitimate if legal doctrines were authored consensually. Instrumental rationality characterized the dominant legal consciousness of a bourgeois society, according to Max Horkheimer and Theodor Adorno.[5] The legislated means constituted the ends of society. But if juridical agents could continually critique the means, legal consciousness would transform instrumental rationality into an emancipatory reason.

Alfred Schutz looked closer at the character of a legal doctrine. He argued that the important thing to appreciate in the reification of laws is that a doctrine typifies about all persons. The typification, one should note for our context, is a cognitive object. A person must fall either inside or outside the boundaries of a typification which was a general ideal-type of person or event – for example, "any person who intentionally commits violence against another person is guilty of assault". The ideal-type transcends the particular traits of any isolated individual or concrete circumstance. In the example above, the particular person charged may be a well-meaning highly intelligent being, but the criterion which distinguishes the ideal-type is neither motive nor intelligence but the act of violence of one person against another. How the violence is committed, with what instrument it is committed, whether others help in the commission of the violence: these factors are involved in the application of the typification. Schutz's term, 'typification', seems to represent what Saussure meant by a 'signified' except Saussure added that a signified could represent a physical–chemical mass as well as a categorical object. A typification is a cognitive object and encloses many particular persons. The enclosure is an intellectualized enclosure, although the consequences may well involve someone's physical detainment once a judge has applied the typification. The typification transforms the face-to-face relations of everyday life into abstractions.[6] The relations between typifications are conceptual relations – for example, the typification of those who commit assault is conceptually related to the typification of "possession of a dangerous weapon". Consistency and logic are important factors in producing these relations. By privileging the typification in his analysis, Schutz's whole project assumed that laws were a matter of legal consciousness.

Early Critical Legal Studies

In a series of essays published during the 1980s, Peter Gabel and Duncan Kennedy continued to examine legal reification as an issue of legal consciousness. According to Gabel, legal theory should aim 'to realize the unalienated relatedness that is immanent within our alienated situation'.[7] The bourgeois legal order had structured an alienated social condition. Like Horkheimer's critical theory and Husserl's phenomenology, Gabel and Kennedy failed to account for the non-knower's embodiment of meaning *into* the legal sign. They only disagreed as to whether one could disrupt the invisible boundaries of legal consciousness and, if so, how. Scant attention was paid to the opaqueness of the legal sign which represented such boundaries. As a consequence, in their dialogue, 'Roll Over Beethoven',[8] Kennedy and Gabel ignored how both juristic agent and non-knower are distanced because each lives through a different language.

The problematic of the Gabel–Kennedy dialogue was that they defined emancipatory law in terms of the face-to-face/legal consciousness opposition.[9] Their enemy was legal consciousness. Emancipation from a reified legal world would entail an emancipation from legal consciousness. Their dialogue presupposed an "either/or" situation: either the categories of legal consciousness dominated or one could live a face-to-face or unreified social existence. Reification lay in a lawyer's *knowledge* of a categorical object. For Kennedy, laws were a form of consciousness – a 'belief-cluster'.[10] For Gabel, metaphysics projected 'a false form of unity that is imaginary in nature'.[11] Because they set up law in the manner in which they did, the key to retrieving an unalienated existence was to break through the metaphysical structures which lawyers had always posited on to face-to-face social relations. The alternative was for intuitions to rule the day. Only the particular individual, not a lawyer, could represent one's own intuition.[12] Intuitions would ensure 'authentic' face-to-face social relations or 'intersubjective zap'. Duncan Kennedy continued such a line of thought by privileging poetry,[13] jokes,[14] paradox[15] and dialogue as the tools to destabilize and disrupt the boundaries of legal consciousness. Jokes, for example, better justified 'the integrity of our communication, the reality of our community' than did the 'classic, very abstract phrasings of the dilemma of the human condition'.[16] Poetry, jokes and paradox avoided the permament abstractness of a legal category. All that was needed was a radical change in legal consciousness: this, they believed, would overcome the gap between I and thou, between lawyer and client, between reader and text.

What did Gabel mean by his term, 'intersubjective zap'? And why were the categories of the mind the source of all human alienation? According to Gabel, social alienation arose from cognitive representations which *re*-presented past particular experiences.[17] Once one re-presented an experience, he suggested, the re-presentation froze an experience in abstraction. Social relations displaced 'the immediacy of connection'.[18] Gabel and Kennedy longed to return to the unreified social relations which, they believed, constituted the real. Instead of jokes and paradox, according to Gabel, one should theorize about such experiences. We need to make 'as explicit as possible a general theory of life', he added. One should describe the 'existential reality at the level of reflection'.[19] By failing to take account of how the experiential body is brought into one's meanings, the problematic for Gabel was 'to *understand* in words with each other; in other words, to *theorize* or *imagine* with each other the meaning of what it was that just happened'.[20] We could share expression 'in *knowledge* of what we already intuitively comprehended'. Even the phenomenon of intersubjective zap required a theory of knowledge.

Feminist Legal Thought

One more moment in the effort to overcome legal reification understood law in terms of legal consciousness. This was the early moment of feminist legal theory. Legal consciousness was believed to enclose the particular context-specific experiences of the particular other. Only here, the other was of a particular gender – female.[21] Because the male gender had invariably authored statutes and judicial decisions, a male voice had been institutionalized to the exclusion of the female voice. Women's experiences would therefore remain unrecognized so long as the authored doctrines remained unchanged.[22] In an important essay in the mid-1980s, for example, Martha Minow took for granted that the traditional feminist analysis of difference should focus upon the authors of legal categories.[23] Robin West carried the author concept further in that, because men had authored the dominant philosophies of law, their theories had silenced women's particular experiences.[24] The very preoccupation of lawyers with rights and duties, according to Janet Rifkin, reflected the voice of the male author.[25] In contrast, women were said to relate with each other experientially. Man: abstract concepts; woman: face to face relations. Man: the mind, formality, and universality; woman: the body, informality, particularity. Legal consciousness, authored by men, had divested all juridical persons of 'real individual life'.[26] Male authored categories had transformed the physical body of the woman into an invisible categorical object. Once again, as with the earlier efforts to overcome legal alienation, legal consciousness was opposed to face-to-face social relations: either/or, general/particular, form/substance.[27] Feminist legal theory could not escape from the paradigm of consciousness.

Indeed, women of colour were quick to point out that even the dichotomy of male categories/female experiences was itself an abstract category which typified all men and all women.[28] The context specific experiences of women of colour were thereby enclosed under typifications about all women even though the authors of the 'male categories/female experiences' binary were usually white, middle class women whose experiences radically differed from the experiences of women of colour. Men of colour took up this point and stated that even the liberatory project of Critical Legal Studies generalized about the experiences of all people, including the radically different experiences of male scholars of colour.[29] Once again, the author of the categories of legal consciousness was projected as the enemy. An emanicipation from such a metaphysics was believed to dwell in a world of pure, unreified, immediate experiences.

The Problematic of Legal Consciousness

In sum, recent moments of legal theory have longed to retrieve direct, immediate and face-to-face social relations which legal consciousness has overlaid. The effect of this analysis has been to project the particular other within the consciousness of the knower of cognitive objects. The aim of a critical analysis of laws has been to transform the invisible boundaries of legal consciousness so as to carry the knower's mind to the other's mind. Such a connection is an intellectual nexus. The lawyer knows the other through the knower's mind.

A problem colours each effort of legal theory to break from the strictures of legal consciousness. If the problem of reification and its solution are understood in terms of a consciousness of the mind, the knower may self-consciously stretch his or her mind in order to reach the other as a categorial object. The knower's mind meets with the other's by widening its boundaries.[30] However, such an intellectualized project continues the problematic of *alienation* because the non-knower is enclosed inside the invisible boundaries of the knower's mind. The mind of the knower pre-exists the biography of the non-knower. Yes, the knower and non-knower may face each other without an intermediary concept. But such a face-to-face relation dwells *inside* the knower's typifications. The knower possesses a *knowledge* of the other. The knower's knowledge reflects the *knower*'s, not the other's, concrete experiences. However well intentioned, the particular other is assimilated into the knower's consciousness.

As a consequence, the retrieval of "love" or "community" takes on a *oneness* where the particular other *fuses* into the consciousness of the knower. An abyss no longer separates the non-knower from the metaphysics of the juridical realm. In the fusion, the knower posits the non-knower as existing prior to metaphysics. Sartre described such a non-knower as a 'pre-reflective cogito'.[31] But the knower's consciousness of the other presupposes a "we" which authors the community's knowledge of the other. Who is this "we"? Judges and lawyers, as expert knowers of signs, construct the "we". The knower constitutes the community within the boundaries of the knower's knowledge, however the knower verbalizes the other's experiences as from an unreified or pre-reflective cogito. As a result, the consciousness of juridical agents posits the presence of the particular other's experiences *inside* the knower's consciousness. The knower's intuitive presence with the other's intuitive experiences is *known*. The other to the laws no longer exists independently of the knower's mind.

Thus, so long as legal theory remains within a paradigm of consciousness, the legal critic necessarily fails to escape from the very consciousness within which the critic posits the source of alienated existence. If a juridical agent works from within the paradigm of legal consciousness, he or she can recognize the other's particular experiences only at the cost of assimilating them into the horizons of his or her own consciousness. The knower can overcome the gap between his or her own experiences and those of the outsider only if the knower gains a presence with the other. The knower gains such an immediacy by sharing an imagined common context and by *imag-*

ining with the other the shared meaning of what happened during a moment when the other was harmed.[32] The knower situates the other's experience inside his or her own cognitive picture of the juridical world. All this takes place in the knower's, not the other's, mind.

The consciousness of the lawyer and judge thereby conceals the experiences of the particular other. Here, I wish to elaborate three points which help to reinforce such a concealment.

First, the social critic who puts forward the possibility of a face-to-face social relation between lawyer and the person harmed presupposes that unreified social connectedness begins with a shared experience. If two people do not possess a shared experience, then they embody their meanings differently. However, the belief that everyone may share a face-to-face experience in a particular social context idealizes or typifies the multiple context-specific experiences which any one person, let alone several, may incur in one situation. Each context-specific experience is unique. Each individual brings a different experiential past and different anticipatory expectations into an experience. The more diverse the experiences and expectations, the greater a range of the possibilities that an external object – whether categorical or physical or experiential – will fulfil one's meant objects. Each moment of time is embedded in fragments of consciousness from one's own experiences. Such fragments emanate from a particular individual with a biography. A knower *exports* a conception *over* a non-knower's experience as the knower reads a text or hears a story. If asked 'what was the time when the non-knower experienced the pain?' the expert can hardly appeal to the time on a clock because the standard of a clock simply quantifies what is unquantifiable: the moment of the experience itself. The quantified time encloses the non-knower's experience, reconstructs it and conceals it. Because a knower's signification may or may not recognize a non-knower's embodied meanings, the non-knower's moment of experience remains indeterminate. The greater the diversity of shared experiences between knower and non-knower, the greater the chance that the expert's interpretations of the non-knower's conduct will diverge from what the non-knower had intended in an utterance.

If diverse *prejudices* and forestructures of meaning affect the interpretive acts of a knower or a non-knower and, even if their intentions were indeterminate in that they remain unfulfilled in the expert's signification, how is it possible for the knower and non-knower to share an experience at one experiential moment? Even if experiences were shared amongst all women, for example, the shared experiences would only be possible for those women with similar *prejudice* – to use Gadamer's term – and anticipatory expectations. That is, the shared experiences would only be experiences of like-minded people.

The paradigm of consciousness raises a second problem. The effort to close the gap between legal consciousness and the embodied meanings of a non-knower assumes that the knower and the non-knower alike actually wish to close the gap or to zap intersubjectively. They must possess "a sense" of face-to-face social relations just as John Rawls began his *Theory of Justice* with the assumption that participants in an original position must possess a 'sense of justice'.[33] In like vein, Immanuel Kant explicitly claimed that one must have an 'interest' or desire to be moral before one can even address the grounding of the metaphysics of morals.[34] But do the knower and the non-knower possess such "a sense" of face-to-face relations? Is it not possible that lawyers and judges, for example, are so entangled in the metaphysics of legal consciousness that they just do not wish to break free from it?

Third, the face-to-face relation is not a moment of otherness. As Peter Gabel acknowledges, '[b]ut the zap is in the moment of common recognition of something that was being denied. It's in the sudden experience of connectedness, not "otherness".'[35] The face-to-face relation is a *fusion* of the knower with the non-knower as a particular other.[36] The face-to-face relation occurs at a moment when there is no self and other. Indeed, because knowers and non-knowers may experience an absence of a reciprocity and because they may also fear the very possibility of social reciprocity, they may imagine that universal rights and duties represent a unity. Both knower and non-knower intellectualize a fused social interest through the knower's consciousness.

The Problematic of a Transparent Language

The key to legal consciousness is the mind. One strives to understand the non-knower's concrete experience as a cognitive object. The sign which represents the cognitive object, let alone the concrete experience itself, is not recognized as problematic. The legal sign is utilized as if the sign could not possibly interrupt the passageway between knower and non-knower. Although Martha Minow and Patricia Cain caution legal feminists against imposing their own metaphysics upon others,[37] too many self-described feminist legal studies suggest that laws are synonymous with male authored categories. To Ann Scales, for example, 'law, like the language which is its medium, is a system of classification'.[38] When Robin West advocates a 'reconstructive jurisprudence', she believes that it is possible to institutionalize a 'direct language that is true to our experience and our own subjective lives'.[39] Janet Rifkin likewise claims that men extend their cognitive objects through the glassy conduit of language.[40] The alternative to a male metaphysics is the concrete and personal experience of a woman.[41] As with Peter Gabel, the only alternative to a cognitive male consciousness is a face-to-face relation. Even Alfred Schutz and his students failed to study how language complicates the retrieval of face-to-face social relations.[42]

By failing to address how knower and non-knower *embody* the legal sign with their respective *prejudice,* this question is begged: 'how can a woman's particular experience humanize and transform patriarchy if legal consciousness is signified through obfuscating signs?' Further, if one embodies a sign with one's *prejudice,* is it not possible that, by focusing solely upon the categories of legal consciousness, the legal critic conceals the *prejudice* of both the knower and the non-knower? Is not the critic's effort to overcome legal reification misdirected to the extent that the critic gazes towards a moment of presence 'beyond' contemporary laws as Mari Matsudu believes[43] or 'after the law' as Martha Minow offers.[44] Is it possible that such a focus conceals the particular experiences of men as well as women, of knowers as well as non-knowers? If such were so, then does not the posit of an external, transcendent vantage point – the particular experience of the class-conscious theorist, the woman, the man of colour – reinforce the very consciousness which avoids the complexity of the embodiment of the legal sign? Might the engine of social critique dwell *inside* legal discourse, in the concealing phenomenon of the legal discourse itself?

In order to illustrate the point, we return to Kafka's *The Trial.* K tried so hard to understand the professional knowers – the painter, the lawyer, the court official and the other agents – by conceptualizing them inside his familar cognitive world. The same might be said of the knowers. As a tenant or a bank clerk, K spoke directly with others as the day-to-day events unfolded. But the knowers spoke *about* his case as if it were an event of the past, as if it were now uncontrollable and uncontrolled. Each knower claimed to know the procedures and the doctrines of the legal world as if these too had been posited beyond their control. Each knower tried to piece K's actions and questions into the knower's story *about* the case. The knowers took the boundaries of their legal consciousness for granted. K tried desperately to understand the knowers' knowledge cognitively and tried to enclose the others' actions and utterances *inside* his own consciousness.

And yet, both the knowers and K himself failed to understand the other. The knowers and K failed to appreciate that the other was uttering a different language albeit with similar vocabulary and grammar. They failed to realize that, in order to understand the other, one must take account of one's own embodiment of prejudgments and expectations in the constitution of meaning. Neither the knowers nor

K addressed the embodied meanings of the other. The knowers just could not hear or understand K's meant objects. Indeed, the expert knowers, for their part, spoke with each other as if K's experiences and life-world did not even exist. When they represented their meant objects as synonymous with K's utterances and gestures, the expert knowers did so through the indirect voice. The knowers spoke about K's case, not to K at K's "level". K entered into the official language as a sign *after* K had spoken or acted. The expert knowers spoke *about* K's actions in a manner which *assumed* that the expert knowers shared hidden legal significations about K's past actions. The discourse of the knowers began as a supplement to K's actions. But as the official discourse became increasingly centred about K's case, the more did the discourse refer to its own special significations as constitutive of the harm which K had allegedly committed. Indeed, it was not even necessary for one to know the harm that K had allegedly committed. The official discourse became primary and K's meanings became forgotten.

Georges Kalinowski argued at an early moment in the study of legal language that before juridical agents could attempt to typify the social, the agent had to familiarize her/himself with the *significata* – or special language and vocabulary – of legal language.[45] The *significata* designated objects which could be intentionally meant or externally posited. The expert knower did not respond to the non-knower and the non-knower could not respond to the knower. Why not? Because each possessed special *significata* with special objects unknown to the other. The same utterance or gesture could represent a different significance to the knower and the non-knower. Each lived through respectively different idioms.

But because the legal discourse – the discourse of authority – may be enforced against all other discourses, it produces violent effects. Such effects are sometimes hidden when the *significata* of the juridical agents seem sanitizing to the non-knower. Human rights legislation makes claims and offers remedies, for example, against individuals and groups who discriminate on grounds of race, national origin, gender, sexual preference and the like. The authors of a bill of rights may aspire to reach the best of humanitarian and progressive-minded ends. Well intentioned judges may also interpret legislation as if the legal discourse remedies social injustice. Inculcated with the belief that the rule of law is objective, politically neutral and distanced from the "wear and tear" of politics, progressive-minded non-knowers not infrequently look to legal texts as offering the one possibility to hear the voice of the non-knower. Human rights legislation offers the prime example. Written constitutions, legislation and judicial personnel frequently do attempt to address racism and sexism directly. Yet, notwithstanding the goals of these texts, the legal discourse *assimilates* the story of the particular non-knower at the very moment that the discourse recognizes the non-knower's story.

Legal Recognition as Concealment: a Human Rights Case

How is this transformation possible, one might ask, when so many contemporary statutes address the discriminatory exclusion of subjects from social institutions? Let me exemplify just such a transformation of a non-knower's story with reference to a human rights code. The human rights code under question – which could have been the human rights statute of any modern state – stated that all persons were guaranteed the freedom to work without discrimination on grounds of race, ethnic origin, sexual preference and the like. All persons were deserving of being recognized of a mutual respect. If any statute is intended to retrieve face-to-face social relations, then surely a human rights code can be said to be one such text. The case I choose is well known in Commonwealth legal discourses because of the legal principle for which it is said to stand: that if a remedy is available through an administrative law procedure, one is precluded from suing for damages in a civil court. I wish to address how the different judges read the complainant's particular experiences through a very special language to which the complainant was a non knower. I shall show how that legal language concealed her experiences at the very moment that her experiences were recognized in the *significata* of the legal language. The recognition of the *significata* became the event itself, and the complainant's particular experiences were forgotten.

From June 1974 to May 1978, Ms Pushpa Bhadauria had been denied an interview for ten separate applications to become a member of the teaching staff at a large college in Canada.[46] A court reported that Ms Bhadauria was 'a highly educated East Indian woman' holding a Bachelor of Arts, Master of Arts, and Doctorate of Philosophy in Mathematics. She was qualified to teach in the province of the college and she had seven years' prior teaching experience. The positions for which she had applied had been publicly advertised. The sense of emptiness and worthlessness experienced when one receives a rejection letter for employment can readily be appreciated. Indeed such an experience is difficult to represent in writing. After an initial feeling of self-doubt, the applicant might become angry with him or herself or deny the experience by rejecting the employer as unworthy of professional respect. Nevertheless, this particular applicant overcame these initial feelings of pain and applied ten times for ten different advertised openings with the same employer. Finally, the applicant decided to consult a lawyer who launched a civil action, alleging that the employer had discriminated against his client on the grounds of her ethnic origin.

The trial judge agreed that a reasonable cause of action had been disclosed but dismissed the action with a brief endorsement that Ms Bhadauria fell under a doctrine posited in an earlier case. This doctrine had excluded civil suits, such as Ms Bhadauria's, when a remedy by means of an administrative law procedure, such as that set out in the Human Rights Code was available. The doctrine typified all persons who fell under it. The legal effect of the typification was to place a limit on the amount of recoverable damages in any case before the human rights tribunal: a civil court would have awarded a far higher amount. In addition, Ms Bhadauria's lawyer would have lost control over her case had the Human Rights Tribunal possessed sole jurisdiction.

The Court of Appeal reversed the trial judge's decision. Ms Bhadauria's case was categorized as a 'civil proceeding', not an 'adminstrative law proceeding'. Subsequently, the Supreme Court re-endorsed the trial judge's categorization: namely, that Ms Bhadauria fell under the Human Rights Code procedures rather than the civil law proceeding. In so deciding, the appellate courts did not respond to Ms Bhadauria but, rather, to the factum and verbal representations of Ms Bhadauria's lawyer. Ms Bhadauria was a "case" whose social situation was beyond their control. The discursive partners were the professional knowers *inter se*, not the knowers with the non-knower.

The knowers carried on a written dialogue with each other without giving the complainant, Ms Bhadauria, an opportunity to intercede through her own language. The knowers' dialogue denied her the opening to shout or scream or politely interject with 'But what about my humiliation?' In other words, the judges' dialogue was monologic vis-à-vis Ms Bhadauria's language. Although secondarily dependent upon her for the initiation of the legal discourse, Ms Bhadauria's own idiom became unnecessary to the discourse itself. Her pain was forgotten, lost, dissipated and concealed in the recirculation of what the judges considered authoritative magic *significata* whose associated doctrines only the judges claimed to know. The legal discourse displaced the complainant's language at the very moment that the judges recognized that 'this Court must assume that the facts alleged by the plaintiff can be established'. The discrimination was taken as a fact, out there, a given, beyond the control of the juridical officials. The judges passively integrated the "fact" of racial discrimination into the web of signs which the knowers would recognize. The "facts" were resignified. But because the "facts" were believed to exist externally to the narrators, the resignification was considered objective, impartial and authoritative. The knowers endeavoured to situate Ms Bhadauria's lawyer's complaint inside the familiar language of the knowers. Nor could it have been otherwise, it seems.

Each judge responded to the earlier judge, and the trial judge to Ms Bhadauria's representative. In their cognitive enterprise the only issue was: 'How should they enclose Ms Bhadauria's experiences?' It was vitally important for the judges to settle what institution possessed the jurisdiction to lay down the *significata* of the legal discourse. My point is that such an inquiry into the appropriate typification – in this case, either administrative law or civil proceeding – misses the role of the legal sign. Once the sign is taken into account, one can better appreciate that the harm of denying Ms Bhadauria a job interview only worsened once she was immersed into the legal discourse. She had to retain an expert knower to represent her as a "case" through a language which only the knowers claimed the privilege of knowing and enforcing. Indeed, Ms Bhadauria was just that – a case. The judges recirculated her case into different configurations, but employing the same verbiage: Ontario Human Rights Code, *Macdonald* v. *283076 Ont. Inc.* (1979), *Christie* v. *York* (1940), *Rogers* v. *Clarence Hotel* (1940), *Constantine* v. *Imperial Hotels Ltd.* (1944), *Ashby* v. *White* (1703), *Re Wren* (1945), *Walkerville Brewing Co.* v. *Mayrand* (1929), Halsbury (2nd edition, 1944), *Re McDougall and Waddell* (1945), *Prosser*, section 4 of the Code, and Wilson JA. To make the knowers' language more obfuscating, the names were abbreviated into 'the Code' or *Christie*, for example. Sometimes, the names were even renamed. And yet the lawyers and judges treated each sign as "legal" or authoritative. One chain of signs combined to represent the category "administrative law"; another combined to represent "civil proceeding". Together, each configuration of names signified a special typification and consequence for Ms Bhadauria. The names took on the aura of *significata*. Judges and lawyers – even her own[47] – wrote to each other using, of course, *their* special language. Without knowing the cognitive objects which the *significata* or signs signified, a non-knower, such as Ms Bhadauria, could hardly understand why one combination of names would lead to one typification and another combination would lead to another. Nor is it likely that the non-knower would appreciate that she had become a "case". A new type of suffering displaced Ms Bhadauria's experience of receiving her rejection letters.

During the assimilation of Ms Bhadauria's felt experience of pain into the secondary authoritative discourse, Ms Bhadauria was transformed into a juridical person – a plaintiff. The judges did not write about her initial felt experiences of humiliation, indignity, loss of self, bitterness or anger when she had received the ten letters of rejection without an opportunity to be interviewed. Nor did the judges write about her disillusionment when she failed to hear from the college after the college had sent her a notice of the vacancy with the promise that she would be contacted for an interview. Such pain was not presented to the judges. The judges did not write about the workings of the hiring process at institutions of higher learning – something which Ms Bhadauria would have experienced on the basis of her seven years of teaching and her advanced graduate degrees. Nor did they write about the context in which her own interpretation of her rejection would have made sense: the networking; the perceived hierarchy of graduate schools within Canada and the United States; the hierarchy between the First World universities and those of the Third World; the prior networking of recruitment committee members with the referees of some applicants; the loyalties which faculty members retain with graduates of their own *alma mater*; their unconscious projection of their own self-images or idealized self-images in the recruitment process; the desire of some committee members to hire applicants in their own fields; their wish to perceive a faculty weakness in their own fields; or their fears/and/or speculations which they may project into their picture of an applicant whose name looks so different from their own. The judges found an examination of such factors unnecessary. Why? Because the legal discourse mattered, not her lived context-specific meanings. Although a secondary legal discourse parasitically "lived" from the event of signification, not from the non-knower's felt experience, it took on a life of its own like an overbearing machine, as it 'recognized' Ms Bhadauria's pain as a signified event.

Exclusion by Inclusion

The phenomenon of the displacement of a non-knower's everyday language with that of the knowers brings into question the paradigm of consciousness which has infiltrated this century's efforts to overcome legal reification, since the attribution of law to a legal consciousness ignores the discursive gap between the official discourse of the knowers and the language of the non-knower. Even if the critic succeeds in ensuring that juridical agents are conscious of the other's painful experience, the latter's harm will not be eradicated. The key to the indigenously felt harm is the sign, not the cognitive object which the sign represents. And the knower attempts to gain signification of the sign by situating it into a web of other signs which are familiar to him or herself. Even for the knower to contemplate the harm requires that he or she recognize signs to signify the harm in his or her solipsistic act of contemplation. Without considering the discursive context, the path of legal critic is, at best, naive. At worst, the critic's path produces a further suffering. Only the expert knowers claim to know what cognitive object to associate with each configuration of signs. And they alone can shift any one sign into different combinations, privilege some and omit others, in their game of signification. Expert knowers – or, at least, persons authoritatively certified to be expert knowers – write to each other *about* their game, calling their writing an "opinion" or a "judgment". The non-knower is merely a typified "case". Even the name of the aggrieved/non-knower signifies a cognitive object or typification which, once uttered, becomes another sign in the house of language with its never-ending maze of corridors and rooms. The non-knower's indigenously felt pain may well stimulate him or her to seek legal recognition. But the secondary discourse signifies the pain as a sign in a foreign language. The non-knower is reinscribed into an atemporal and aspatial signifying context. Slowly, imperceptibly, the non-knower's pain is transformed into a discourse for and by a privileged group of knowers of the signs of that discourse.

In failing to consider the discursive element of phenomena, juridical officials retreat to cognitive objects – doctrines, rules, principles, policies and other allegedly objective standards. Ignoring the sign which represents such doctrines as cognitive objects, the experiential body of the non-knower is lopped off. The non-knower is recontextualized from the social into the discursive. The expert knower recognizes harm independently of the knower's context-specific meanings.

Drawing from Levinas,[48] the knowers' discourse 'neutralizes' suffering. The knowers' representation of suffering sanitizes the pain and redirects it as a meant object of professional knowers. The resituated non-knower becomes a theoretical external object. The non-knower is purged of a biography. The expert knowers are not conscious of the non-knower as a concrete, meaning-constituting being. A conscious knower constitutes the non-knower as a sign, all the while that the knower tries to intellectualize *about* the harmed as if all signs were transparent. Thus, interestingly, the expert knowers typify the social world. They even *constitute* themselves. But, as Merleau Ponty argues, one simply cannot posit an other as a subject if one does so in one's consciousness.[49] One's own consciousness works to construct the identity of the knower and the non-knower, all in the name of the non-knower as a typified case. The horizons of the *knower's* consciousness emigrate *into* the non-knower. The non-knower, as a typified person, mirrors the mind of the knower's intellectualized world. When the knower recognizes the non-knower as a signified other to the legal discourse, the non-knower has been effectively assimilated into a cohesive picture, and the non-knower's meant world is disembodied of meaning. The face-to-face relations of embodied beings become fused, but the fusion takes place within the knower's consciousness, the consciousness of the "we" of the juridical agents, the "we" who recognize the pain of the non-knower by assimilating the non-knower into our signifying relations. The non-knower "exists" *for* the consciousness of the "we".

Once again Kafka's *The Trial* illustrates how the non-knower's embodied meanings are displaced in favour of the signifying relations of the official discourse. K's experiences were radically different from those of the knowers of the official discourse. One is led to surmise that the knowers would have been able to recognize K's anxieties only if K had learned their gestures, their style of speaking, their texts and their assumptions about place and time. But this would mean K learning a whole new language and becoming a knower himself. If K had adopted the knower's language, he would have lost his own discourse and thereby the means to express his felt experiences – the language which he had used in his interchanges with his landlady, Lena, his banking colleagues and his uncle. Either a non-knower must accept the emancipatory discourse of the humanist, also a professional knower or, alternatively, he or she must remain an outsider, an other, an outlaw. The suffering of the non-knower vis-à-vis a legal discourse collapses into a unity of oneness, of sameness, of identity with the expert knowers at the very moment that the expert knowers claim to speak on behalf of the non-knower. The expert knowers do not experience K's experiences. They possess an *outer*, rather than an inner, perception of K's experiences. Nothing really passes between the expert knowers and the non-knower. A *differend* dwells between their languages. Any possibility of an intersubjective experience between knower and non-knower is illusionary.

The pain, the anxiety, the violent struggle: these experiences dissipate in favour of what André-Jean Arnaud has called a bourgeois peace where all juridical persons equally share juridically defined rights and duties.[50] The circulation of signs masks the social values of the knowers. The most important value in this discourse of knowers is the cult of legality, sometimes called *juridicity*, which the knowers perpetuate through their self-imposed neutral, impartial, objectivist claims about their own interpretive acts. Juridicity allows the knower to insist that he or she is situated outside the "wear and tear" of social struggle. From such an extrinsic situs, the expert knower recognizes his or her own discourse as the true/real. The discourse of the knowers excludes all other signifying relations as illegitimate. The knowers exclude them as "policy", as the "wisdom" of the sign, as "oughts" and, being unreal, therefore as "invalid".

Of course, certain feminist legal theorists have attempted to break out of this vicious circle. Martha Minow and Elizabeth Schneider, for example, suggested that rights offer a situs for conversation.[51] And Lucinda Finley recognized the problematic of a gendered language although, understanding laws as a matter of legal consciousness, she urged that 'we lawyers' widen the patriarchical legal language to incorporate more women's perspectives, experiences and voices *into* that language.[52] One is left to speculate as to how such a transformed legal discourse would be possible once one appreciates how and why the knower speaks a different language from the non-knower. Further, if the *sign* is important in an analysis of suffering, then is it not possible that an emancipatory legal discourse exists for feminist lawyers alone in that they are certified as expert knowers of that discourse, just as are the male lawyers? Would not such a discourse simultaneously *conceal* the context-specific experiences of particular women who cannot present their experiences through such an alien discourse as that of the feminist lawyers?

Indeed, how is it possible for any knower to become present with the non-knower when the knower must recognize others through a secondary discourse, as feminists of colour believed? Can legal discourse be considered a conversation between the knowers and the non-knowers, as legal feminists have sometimes considered possible? Is it possible for face-to-face relations to erupt through an authoritative discourse as Gabel and Kennedy have believed? Is it possible for a knower to understand a felt experience of a non-knower in the same manner as the non-knower did? If not, why not? How can one even address the issue of the reification of laws without taking into account the *prejudice* of knower and non-knower alike. Even to typify someone as a woman or as a person of colour or an administrative law case or as K's case homogenizes the particular experiences and thereby conceals the heterology of everyday languages through which each classified individual lives.[53]

The particularity of an individual's experiences is camouflaged, if not denied, by the knowers' play inside the legal discourse of a modern state. Indeed, if one adds the factor of embodied meanings to the old analysis of legal consciousness, how can expert knowers who know the secondary chains of signs, reach or even address a heterology of voices which non-knowers experience? Are those voices more than mere pictures in the professional knower's mind, pictures which the professional knower continually reinforces as he or she comes to recognize more and more of the non-knower's world? Or are the voices lived through the body of a victim? If the latter, is the victim's body a mere physical–chemical mass or is it an experiencing body whose identity is postponed, without source or end? As Trinh Minh-ha counsels:

> ...trying to find the other by defining otherness or by explaining the other through laws and generalities is, as Zen says, like beating the moon with a pole or scratching an itching foot from the outside of a shoe.[54]

Notes

1 Compared with 69 229 000 persons from international wars. World Bank Report as quoted in *Toronto Globe and Mail*, Monday, 14 August (1995): A10.

2 Jacques Derrida, 'The Force of Law: The "Mystical Foundation of Authority"' in *Cardozo Law Review*, vol. 11 (1990): 919–1045, 949.

3 This ambiguity is elaborated in more detail in William E. Conklin, 'The Expressivity of the Invisible Author in the Modern Legal Genre' in Wilhelm Wurzer ed., *The Expressivity of the Author* (Evanston: Northwestern University Press, forthcoming).

4 See Georg Lukacs, 'Reification and the Consciousness of the Proletariat' and 'Legality and Illegality' in *History and Class Consciousness* (Cambridge, Mass: MIT Press, 1971); also see generally *Soul and Form* (Anna Bostock trans; London: Merlin Press, 1974).

5 Their theory of legal consciousness is explicated in W.E. Conklin, 'The Legal Theory of Horkheimer and Adorno' in *Windsor Yearbook of Access to Justice*, vol. 5 (1985): 230–57. Also see Leonard V. Kaplan, 'Can Rational Instrumentalism Do All That? A Reply to Professor Conklin' in ibid., 381–404.

6 See, for example, H. Taylor Buckner, 'Transformations of Reality in the Legal Process' in *Social Research*, vol. 37 (1970): 88–101; Michael Salter, 'Towards a Phenomenology of Legal Thinking' in *Journal of the British Society for Phenomenology*, vol. 23, no. 2 (1992): 167–82.

7 For Peter Gabel's effort to retrieve face-to-face relations, see Peter Gabel, 'The Phenomenology of Rights-Consciousness and the Pact of the Withdrawn Selves' in *Texas Law Review*, vol. 62 (1984): 1563–99; 'Reification in Legal Reasoning' in *Research in Law and Sociology*, vol. 3 (1980): 25–51; 'Intention and Structure in Contractual Conditions: Outline of a Method for Critical Legal Theory' in *Minnesota Law Review*, vol. 61 (1977): 601–43.

8 Duncan Kennedy and Peter Gabel, 'Roll Over Beethoven' in *Stanford Law Review*, vol. 34 (1984): 1–55.

9 Kennedy begins by suggesting, for example, that 'an essential, metaphysical/spiritual paradox in our real situation' is that we should apply 'the limits of knowledge, the limits of *conceptual* understanding' to the Critical Legal Studies viewpoint: ibid., 1.

10 Ibid., 31.

11 Ibid., 29.

12 Ibid., 50.

13 Kennedy describes 'nothingness is the worm at the heart of being,' as exemplifying poetry: ibid., 19. He says that poetry is to be preferred to such 'a reified abstraction' as 'alienation is ontological'.

14 Kennedy is drawing from Jean-Paul Sartre here. As Kennedy puts it, no concept is any more defensible than is 'making the kettle boil' or 'nothingness is the worm at the heart of being': ibid., 17. The actual text, as translated by Hazel Barnes, reads 'nothingness lies coiled in the heart of being – like a worm': *Being and Nothingness*, 7th (special abridged) edn (Hazel E. Barnes trans., New York: Citadel Press, 1971): 21. Sartre's metaphor, according to Kennedy, is 'an image, a metaphor, almost a joke' which should not be confused with philosophy: it is 'a joke on philosophy'. 'Roll over Beethoven', note 12 *supra*: 11. Such metaphors are 'a distanced, mocking ironization of the mode of discourse in which you have to abstract, analytically specified goal language, which is supposed to be the context and set the boundaries and be the reassuring structure for behavior', ibid., 11.

15 Kennedy believes that 'paradox and *unconsciousness* allow one experien-

tially, existentially, to exist outside of the contradiction-space of separateness and unity', ibid., 23.

16 Ibid., 11.

17 Ibid., 2.

18 Ibid., 6.

19 Ibid., 10. And again, 'I think we can be explicit about what it is that other human beings are trying to do. What the good things in life are in other words', ibid., 5.

20 Ibid., 8.

21 See, for example, Heather Ruth Wishik, 'To Question Everything: The Inquiries of Feminist Jurisprudence' in *Berkeley Women's Law Journal*, vol. 1, (Fall 1985): 64–77; Ann C. Scales, 'The Emergence of Feminist Jurisprudence: An Essay' in *Yale Law Journal*, vol. 95 (1986): 1373–403, at 1374–80, 1402–3.

22 Ibid. Also see the admittedly early writing on feminist legal theory in Ellen C. DuBois *et al.* 'Feminist Discourse, Moral Values, and the Law – A Conversation' in *Buffalo Law Review*, vol. 34, no. 11 (1985): 11–87; Catharine A. MacKinnon, 'Feminism, Marxism, Method, and the State: An Agenda for Theory' in *Signs*, vol. 7, no. 3 (1982): 515–44, and vol. 8, no. 4 (1983): 635–58.

23 Martha Minow has emphasized that this focus on the categorical underlies traditional feminist analysis of difference. See Martha Minow, 'The Supreme Court 1986 Term, Foreword: Justice Engendered' in *Harvard Law Review*, vol. 101 (1987): 7–95, at 35, 76–8. Also see, for example, Catharine MacKinnon, 'Difference and Dominance: On Sex Discrimination' in *Feminism Unmodified* (Cambridge, Mass.: Harvard University Press, 1987): 40–45.

24 Robin West, 'Jurisprudence and Gender' in *University of Chicago Law Review*, vol. 55 (1988): 1–72.

25 Janet Rifkin, 'Toward a Theory of Law and Patriarchy' in *Harvard Women's Law Journal*, vol. 3 (1980): 83–117.

26 Margot Stubbs, 'Feminism and Legal Positivism' in *Australian Journal of Law and Justice*, vol. 3, no. 63 (1986).

27 See Ann Scales, note 21 *supra*; and Robin West, note 39 *infra*. Katherine Bartlett states the need for 'consciousness-raising' in 'feminist knowing in law' so as to expand the scope of the categories authored by males: 'Feminist Legal Methods' in *Harvard Law Review*, vol. 103 (1990): 881–82, at 829. Also see Martha Minow, note 44 *infra*. Margot Stubbs claims that male authored categories should be continually linked with the concrete experiences of women through a new praxis. The male legal consciousness is believed to regulate the oppression of women. See Stubbs, 'Feminism and Legal Positivism' in *Australian Journal of Law and Society*, vol. 3 (1986): 63–91. Also see Mari Matsuda, note 43 *infra*.

28 See Patricia Cain, 'Feminist Jurisprudence: Grounding the Theories' in *Berkeley Women's Law Journal*, vol. 4 (1989): 191–214; and Marlee Kline, 'Race, Racism and Feminist Legal Theory' in *Harvard Women's Law Journal*, vol. 12 (1989): 115–50.

29 See, Richard Delgado especially 'The Imperial Scholar' in *University of Pennsylvania Law Review*, vol. 140 (1992): 1349–72. Also see Mari Matsuda, note 43 *infra*; and Alex M. Johnson, 'Racial Critiques of Legal Academia: A Reply in Favour of Context' in *Stanford Law Review*, vol. 43 (1990): 137–65.

30 Husserl certainly tries to argue otherwise in the *Cartesian Meditations*: Edmund Husserl, *Cartesian Meditations* (Donion Cairns trans.; Dordrecht: Martinus Nijhoff, 1960): s. 46, 101.

31 Jean-Paul Sartre, *Being and Nothingness* (New York: Citadel Press, 1985, 1965): Pt ll, ch. 1.

32 Ibid., 8.

33 John Rawls, *A Theory of Justice* (Cambridge: Harvard University Press, 1971): 567–77.

34 Immanuel Kant, *Grounding for a Metaphysics of Morals* (James W. Ellington ed., Indianapolis: Hackett Publications, 1981, 2nd edn): 42–4. At 48 Kant states that '*whoever, then, holds morality to be something real*, and not a chimerical idea without any truth, must also admit the principle here put forward'.

35 Ibid., 14.

36 That explains why Gabel scolds Kennedy for identifying zapness with the 'false duality' of 'union and otherness', note 8 *supra*, 21.

37 Martha Minow, 'Feminist Reason: Getting It and Losing It' in *Journal of Education*, vol. 38 (1988): 43–60. Also see Cain, note 28 *supra*.

38 Ann Scales, 'The Emergence of Feminist Jurisprudence: An Essay' in *Yale Law Journal*, vol. 96 (5), (1986): 1373–1403.

39 Robin West, 'Jurisprudence and Gender' in *University of Chicago Law Review*, vol. 55 (1988): 1–32, 70–72.

40 See especially Rifkin, 'Toward a Theory of Law and Patriarchy' in *Harvard Women's Law Journal*, vol. 3 (1980): 83–139.

41 See especially Mari J. Matsuda, 'Liberal Jurisprudence and Abstracted Visions of Human Nature: A Feminist Critique of Rawls' Theory of Justice' in *New Mexico Law Review*, vol. 16 (1986): 613–30.

42 See, for example, Thomas Luckmann, 'The Constitution of Language in the World of Everyday Life' in Lester E. Embree ed., *Life-World and Consciousness: Essays for Aron Gurwitz* (Evanston: Northwestern University Press, 1972): 469–88.

43 Mari J. Matsuda, 'Public response to Racist Speech: Considering the Victim's Story' in *Michigan Law Review*, vol. 87 (1987): 2320–81; 'Looking to the Bottom: Critical Legal Studies and Reparations' *HarvCR-CLLRev* vol. 22 (1987): 323–99.

44 Martha Minow, 'The Supreme Court 1986 Term: Justice Engendered' in *Harvard Law Review*, vol. 101 (1987): 7–95, 10.

45 Georges Kalinowski, Introduction à la logique juridique: Elements de semiotique juridique, logique des normes et logique juridique (Paris: LGDJ, 1965).

46 Bhadauria v. Seneca College (1981), 37 NR 455 (SCC per Laskin, CJC) overruling (1979), 11 CCLT 121 (Ont. CA per Wilson JA) overruling Justice Callaghan.

47 See the article by the lawyer who represented Ms Bhadauria: Harry Kopyto, 'The Bhadauria Case: The Denial of the Right to Sue for Discrimination' in *Queen's Law Journal*, vol. 7 (1981): 144–63.

48 Emmanuel Levinas, *Totality and Infinity* (Alphonso Lingis transl., Philosophic Series no. 24; Pittsburgh: Duquesne University Press, 1969): 132, 124.

49 Maurice Merleau Ponty, *Phenomenology of Perception* (Colin Smith trans., London: Routledge & Kegan Paul, 1962): Pt 1, c.6.

50 Jean-Paul Arnaud, 'La Paix Bourgeois' in M. Troper ed., *Le droit trahi par la philosophie* (Rouen: Biblioteque du Centre d'Etudes des Systems Politiques et Juridiques de Rouen, 1977): 51–80.

51 Minow, note 44 *supra*; E.M. Schneider, 'The Dialectics of Rights and Politics: Perspectives from the Women's Movement' in *New York University Law Review*, vol. 61 (1986): 589–622, at 622–3.

52 Lucinda M. Finley, 'Breaking Women's Silence in Law: The Dilemma of the Gendered Nature of Legal Reasoning' in *The Notre Dame Law Review*, vol. 64 (1989): 886–910.

53 Randall Kennedy, 'Racial Critiques of Legal Academia', *Harvard Law Review*, vol. 102 (1989): 1745–1819, 1784.

54 Trinh T. Minh-ha, *Woman, Native, Other: Writing Postcoloniality and Feminism* (Bloomington & Indianapolis: Indiana University Press, 1989): 76.

2 The Transformation of Meaning into a Modern Legal Genre

Sometimes, one describes a particular legal event as a "travesty of justice". Such a statement suggests that justice precedes posited laws. Justice is often believed to transcend any historically contingent event. And when one turns to legal philosophers, justice is frequently associated with the founding authority of authored laws. Thomas Hobbes and Jean-Jacques Rousseau accepted such a juxtaposition between authority and authored laws when they distinguished historically contingent laws from their foundation in a prior state of nature. Jeremy Bentham and John Austin, too, elevated the evaluation of posited laws to what Bentham called a 'metaphysics' of 'the greatest happiness of the greatest number'. For Hans Kelsen, one *a priori* norm, the *Grundnorm*, lay at the foundation of all legal reasoning. H.L.A. Hart insisted that 'unspoken judicial practices' grounded the concept of law and that lawyers could only approximate such unspoken practices. Joseph Raz and Ronald Dworkin also understood authority in terms of a source (in Raz's case) or a grand narrative (in Dworkin's) to differentiate laws from the violent acts of an outlaw. The authority of civil laws was projected external to the laws. If one could only identify such an external transcendent source, suffering would be eradicated it might seem.

Stanley Fish, alone of contemporary legal theorists, has questioned whether the authority for laws ultimately dwells in an external transcendental realm.[1] Through a diversity of examples in his book, *Doing What Comes Naturally*, Fish exposes how lawyers and judges create, and then defer, to a belief in the externality of legal authority. No constitution, no legislature, no founding fathers found a particular legal order. Professional training assimilates the future lawyer into tacitly accepted norms, standards, evidentiary criteria and assumptions which the lawyer takes as natural and universal. Shared experiences reinforce what is a good legal argument, what evidence is compelling and who is a reasonable person. The creation of an external grounds is not the work of a conscious conspiracy. The lawyer interprets a text *from* the assumptions, needs and purposes of the genre within which a lawyer acts. 'At times courts seem to be themselves constituting the authority (the rule of recognition) they subsequently cite as legitimizing their actions' he notes.[2] All conclusions follow from the lawyer's self constitution of authority.[3] For example, lawyers take the "rule of law" as alien to force, but the search for authority in some external source or grounds masks the violence of the "rule of law". Legislators and judges commit 'daily acts of violence' as they enact laws and interpret texts. Such violent acts are 'more sinister' than those of gunmen because the legal official wears 'the face of legitimate authority'.[4] One cannot escape from the violence of the interpretive act. As Hart puts it in one essay, 'authority rests with whoever seizes an opportunity to act and then makes the action stick' in the sense that, quoting approvingly from H.L.A. Hart's 'remarkable statement', 'all that succeeds is success'.[5] Instead of the gunman working outside the law, the legal officer is a gunman who colours his or her brute force with the neutral externality of the foundation of legal authority.

Fish's claims leave one with a simple problem: if the assumptions, ideals, and unwritten practices of lawyers and judges actually work to construct a belief in the externality of legal norms, does not the non-knower also live within his or her own discourses? If so, do not these discourses also work to project external objects as constraining the non-knower him or herself? Both the professional knowers and the non-knowers live through their own genres. The differences between their genres raise the prospect that when a witness verbally describes what he or she experienced in an indigenous event, the embodied meanings may be transformed into an objectivist and neutral discourse which takes on a life of its own. The modern legal discourse depends upon witnesses to provide verbal statements and gestures about the indigenously experienced pain. But the professional knowers link these utterances to secondary configurations of signs. This recirculation of the witness's utterance, I now intend to argue, transforms the embodied meanings of the witness into a recontextualizing narrative which takes its cue from the presupposed externally situated source of law. The trace of the legal narrative to such an external ground ensures the narrative's authority. Elements of the witness's story may be included in the narrative; other aspects may be excluded. The narrative may be enforced. And the witness, as a non-knower, may become an aggrieved to the legal discourse itself. The knower may not understand the witness through the idiom through which the witness meant her utterances. Nor may the non-knower be able to understand the idiom of the professional knowers.

I shall argue in this and the following chapter that the modern legal discourse produces a concealment of suffering. The suffering arises not just from the pain which may have been experienced in an indigenous event, but in the non-knower's effort to be understood through his or her own idiom. My argument will proceed through three stages. First, I shall claim that the legal discourse is secondary vis-à-vis the idioms through which one experiences day-to-day events. Second, I shall claim that juridical agents, whom I call professional knowers, assimilate the signifying relations of a non-knower into narratives which draw their coherency from a trace of signs to some presupposed externally situated grounds or foundation. I shall argue that legal narratives re-present the concrete context-specific meanings of a non-knower, that the non-knower's signification of his or her own meanings are resituated into the secondary legal discourse, that the secondary chains of signs represent doctrines which the professional knower claims to know and which function ideologically, and that the phenomenal body of the non-knower is concealed through the assimilative recirculation of secondary signifying relations. As a result, a complainant and defendant may both become aggrieved to the legal discourse itself. The secondary signifying relations produce a suffering different from the harm which may have been experienced in a particular social context, and the modern legal discourse takes on the character of a monologue. The key to the character of the monologue is that the non-knower cannot respond to the knowers except through the knowers' secondary genre. Only a professionally trained cadre of expert knowers may gain access to the secondary genre, even though the knowers may claim to act on behalf of the non-knower.

Third, as a consequence of the transformation of a witness's meanings, the non-knower suffers. For one thing, the non-knower's initial pain, experienced before the legal discourse began its enclosure, is left unrecognized in the idiom of the pained individual because the legal discourse, preoccupied with cognitive objects, assimilates the experiencing body of the pained being into the secondary signifying relations. A witness's utterance is re-presented in an indirect voice. The knowers narrate *about* the utterances of the witness. The utterance takes on signification inside a web of secondary signs which, though appearing as the true/real for the professional knowers, may well seem to be mere grunts and noises to the non-knower. Furthermore, once a non-knower gains access to the legal discourse through a professional knower, the non-knower can only re-present his or her pain through the knower's secondary representations of the event. The facts and circumstances of the case become a signified event even though the knowers may project the significations as uncontrollable and uncontrolled givens. Expert knowers, not the non-knowers, help the discourse along. The secondary signs represent special doctrines which typify the signified event. The knowers search for some absent foundation to their discourse. I shall describe in the next chapter how, in such a search for authority, the experiential moments of a juridical agent produce a concealment of suffering.

The Genre-like Character of Legal Discourse

It is important to appreciate at this point that the modern legal discourse possesses a genre-like character. What is a genre? And how is the legal genre secondary to other genres?

A genre, Mikhail Bakhtin suggests, is a particular way of perceiving the world.[6] It is a collective phenomenon which organizes utterances and texts. People learn to cast their speech in generic compositional nomenclature and grammatical structures. A specialized training teaches the law student how to identify and frame the issues using particular terms and grammar which other knowers will recognize. Other knowers speak and write in a similar manner; they associate similar doctrines and rules with special terms; and they may understand each other with a mere grunt which the genre members take as significative of important concepts. So, for example, if a Canadian lawyer voices the 'word' 'POGG' to another lawyer, the latter recognizes the 'word' to signify 'Peace, Order and Good Government' as set out in section 91 of the Canadian *Constitution Act, 1867–present*. But to a non-knower who overhears the two lawyers talking while waiting in line for a movie, the 'word' is just a grunt, a noise with no signification except that the lawyer might be mad. Notwithstanding the fact that the narrator/judge describes the "facts" of a case as unique, the reasons for decision in one narrative share common discursive properties with other legal narratives. One such shared characteristic is a distinguishing written or oral style.[7] A passive, impersonal and objectivist style characterizes legal narratives both at the trial and at the appellate levels. Certain discursive properties characterize different *fora* for narratives, whether the forum be a civil trial, a criminal trial, an appellate judgment, a statute or a regulation. As a group, these *fora* contrast with other genres such as the novel, play, poem or autobiography. A genre functions, as Tzvetan Todorov puts it, as a 'horizon of expectations' for a reader and as a 'model of writing' for an author.[8] The lawyer and judge read legal narratives with a view to integrating them into the genre.

The legal discourse is a secondary genre in that it parasitically lives off primary genres. What is a primary genre? A witness may recount an event through a primary genre.[9] When we share a primary genre with another individual we take much for granted. Events seem to naturally follow, and explanation may be unnecessary. For example, my daughter has pointed out that she knows what I mean when I say "Oh" by the tone and gestures which accompany it. She does not need to reflect about the meaning. I present it to her through my body. Taking a term from Hegel (who borrowed it from Plato's *The Laws*), the assumptions in a genre take on a 'second nature'. Habit and education socialize one to the point that one speaks "without thinking". H.L.A. Hart had the genre-like character of law in mind when he wrote that the foundation of the concept of law rests in 'unspoken judicial practices'. Juridical officials immediately experience the practices without having to reflect on them. In a primary genre, one embodies utterances with experiences.

Oral dialogue manifests such an embodiment of meaning. Physical gestures may speak as much as words. And words are intoned to represent felt experiences. It is possible for expert knowers within a secondary genre to share such an immediacy with their signs and gestures. Indeed, the bonding induced in professional law schools, I shall argue shortly, functions to inculcate just such a sense of immediacy. But a primary genre lacks the mediating role of reflection. An immediacy between body and utterance characterizes a primary genre as, for example, in a rejoinder in a dialogue, a letter, a diary, or a story, according to Bakhtin.[10] The bodily connection brings life into one's meanings as one speaks and writes. One speaks spontaneously. Moreover, one speaks rather than writes in a primary genre.

In contrast, a secondary genre loses this sense of immediacy between an author and his or her utterance or gesture. It may involve complex intellectual arguments and, furthermore, it is primarily written with highly organized grammatical structures. A secondary genre may not even possess specific addressees who can respond, as with a primary genre. The secondary genre searches for the original intent of the author of a text. The discussants write *about* the authorial intent as if the author and the author's text constrained the discussant. The discussion in a secondary genre is at least one step removed from the lived utterances in a primary genre which draw from the context-specific social circumstances of everyday life. The novel, play, scientific research and scholarly commentary exemplify highly organized cultural forms.[11] In some schools of narratology, the story, narrative and discourse represent three forms of a secondary genre.

A secondary genre re-presents another's experience. It resituates an utterance into chains of signs which other members in the secondary genre will recognize. It mediates context-specific meanings. Although expert knowers may share an unwritten sense of immediacy with their texts in the sense that they embody the texts with their own deeply felt experiences, they and they alone know how to combine the nomenclature of the texts in a manner which other experts can understand. That combination lifts the non-knower's utterances and texts from their specific social context in an indigenously experienced event into a supplementary signifying context. The resituated event signifies, or stands for, something to other expert knowers, but how the non-knower understands the resignified event is another matter. Although the expert knower's resignification may have an immediacy, as in a primary genre, the relationship between the knower's resignification and the non-knower's lived meanings is distant. This is so because the invisible boundaries of the knower's cognitive objects enclose the non-knower's utterances.

The distinction between a symbol and a sign helps to clarify the primary and secondary character of genres. One identifies immediately with a symbol, whether it be a flag, a national anthem, a school uniform or even a name. A symbol has a presence; a symbol moves the experiential body; it is felt. Intervening objects, such as legal doctrines, do not stimulate reflection about the symbol: a symbol is something which is lived *through* in a primary genre.

A sign (or, more adequately, a 'signifier'), however, represents an external object which may be a concept or a physical entity. The interpreter passively brings oneself *to* the object in order to be present or immediate with it. But the sign defers such a moment of presence in the external object because it actually represents, or stands for, the object. One sign is differentiated in terms of another sign. Without this interrelation of signs, a sign lacks signification. This is what I mean when I say that an indigenously experienced event is resignified. The event is represented by signs which gain their signification from other signs.

The Displacement of a Primary Genre

The genre-like characteristics of legal discourse are very special. Like medical discourse and the discourses of other professions, legal discourse is secondary to primary genres through which a non-knower has hitherto lived. The legal knower resituates the non-knower's utterances in the search for cognitive or factual grounds for a legal opinion or court judgment. The secondary discourse may recognize the non-knower's pain through terms and phrases which stand for special "facts", doctrines, rules, principles and other external standards. The non-knower's pain is thus experienced in the non-knower's own significations. The non-knower, in turn, recontextualizes the utterances into a network of secondary signifying relations so that the knower's picture of the indigenously experienced pain becomes twice removed from the event. The re-presentation of the non-knower's own re-presentation takes the non-knower's gestures and utterances from the indigenously experienced event to a signified event which is signified *for* the knower. Because the non-knower cannot respond through his or her own idiom without the expert knower recirculating the response into nomenclature and a grammar quite distanced from that idiom, the modern legal discourse takes on a monologic character with regard to the non-knower. It is the expert knower's knowledge of the signs in the secondary discourse that really matters. Indeed, the knower substitutes signs for physical–chemical matter. As already stated, the person harmed becomes a non-knower, an outsider to the legal discourse. The secondary legal discourse, as a result, strangely produces a suffering which comes after one has allegedly been harmed.

The legal opinion or judgment or argument of the professional knower, then, functions as the *site* for the displacement of embodied meanings. The lawyer's prejudgements involving class, gender and race ideologically saturate the secondary signifying relations which reconfigure the sentences of the aggrieved. Carolyn Strange shows, for example, that even though judicial decisions or jury verdicts may rule in favour of women and even though lawyers may restate "the law" in order to signal that women possess the right to be free from sexual assault, the male lawyer reaffirms his presupposed prerogative to defend women as weaker beings.[12] Douglas Hay also illustrates, with richly studied resources, how expert knowers reaffirm class prejudgements about non-knowers in an indigenously experienced social event.[13] The secondary discourse freezes the contingency of a non-knower's felt experiences.

Displacement takes place through the secondary signifying relations. As an example, take the word "freedom". A lawyer may interpret the word "freedom" to represent 'the equal treatment of all juridical persons under the same law'. For the politician, the same word may stand for the freedom to express political views. For the physician, "freedom" may involve the right to prescribe chemicals for patients without government interference. For the businessperson, "freedom" may signify the unlimited acquisition of private property. One conception of the sign "freedom", corresponding to that of the lawyer, the physician or the businessperson, may displace the conception intended by someone unfamilar with the languages of such professionals and businesspeople. This may occur even though the same word, freedom, is used. The lawyer's displacement ultimately matters most because the lawyer claims to be an expert in authoritative signs and because the lawyer's superior, the judge, may authorize the *enforcement* of the lawyer's displacing signification. The later displacement freezes the contingency and concreteness which the others associate with the same word.

Acculturation into a Professional Law School

The imperial project of the legal discourse begins – if there is a beginning – in the professional law school. The student, as a newcomer to the secondary discourse, slowly absorbs the gestural and verbal expressions expected of one who "thinks like a lawyer". More particularly, in the formal setting of the lecture hall, both teacher and student speak and write *about* the reports about subjects who claim to have experienced harm. Outside the classroom, the teacher and student absorb the unspoken and unwritten gestures expected of a professional knower of the secondary discourse. The genre-like character of legal discourse is overpowering. So, for example, from the first weeks as a law student, the student quickly learns to order the "facts of a case" with a start, a middle and an ending. The facts are considered "givens" external to the viewpoint of student and teacher alike. Judges' reported decisions are read as if given, externally imposed facts constrained the knowers: the facts cannot be changed except to make analytic points of argument. The facts are externally posited to be "out there", beyond the knowers. The rules and principles are also unconcealed as if they had always existed and as if the legal official were constrained by them. A series of facts and doctrines may be collated into a cohesive narrative. One narrative is joined with another within clearly demarcated boundaries of style, grammatical usage, etiquette and even content.

The acculturation process has been the subject of many penetrative studies. My point is that the acculturation of an individual into the legal profession plays an important role in constructing the genre-like character to a modern legal discourse. Gestures become as important as verbal and written vocabulary, and the grammar in the legal language. The educational project encourages the student to perceive, and to conceive of, the world as if the signs in the legal discourse constituted the true/real. The world which environs the future lawyer places objects as "givens" beyond the professional's intellectual grasp. The budding knower identifies with such an environing world. As partners in knowledge-seeking, teacher and student explore the reported facts, produce arguments and interpret facts and texts as if the "facts of the case", now absent and hypothetical, had been originally experienced as they are now signified. As partners, they use a great deal of energy in preventing an audience (that is, themselves) from forgetting the "facts".[14] But what are the "facts of the case"? They are represented as signs which the knowers will recognize as coming under authoritative typifications. The students of legal knowledge learn how to analyse authoritative signs, not the non-knower's indigenously experienced meant objects. The non-knower is resignified as John Doe or the plaintiff. The non-knower's last name becomes a new sign to be configured in the web of authoritative signs which the student must "learn". What is sought, in the end, is what Roland Barthes calls a 'work' which may be 'consumed' as a commodity.[15] The well trained student/lawyer consumes the signs as if they were commodities. And, in effect, the secondary genre into which he or she has become acculturated becomes primary.

Social bonding is pivotal in the enveloping legal genre. The exhausting social calendar during the first weeks of the first term, the annual interlaw school Law Games, Law Day, Person's Day, the Dean's dinner dance, the Formal, the moot courts, the intramural athletics, the Friday afternoon sojourn with students to the pub, the law school "talk" at the parties (which even spouses do not understand), the myths about various professors and all the other social practices peculiar to a professional law school: these experiences help to assimilate the law student's former everyday language into a secondary genre. Without such a shared environing world, legal reasoning might not appear so compelling. In this way, the law student becomes a knower. But, as a knower, he or she shares *prejudice* with other knowers.[16] Working inside the genre, the knowers might seriously disagree as to what counts as the external "facts", doctrines, rules, principles and other objects as signified by familar signs. They might also disagree about what configurations of signs are authoritative. But their *prejudice* sets tacit boundaries to their pictures of the facts, texts and other objects. Without shared *prejudice*, students would enter the legal profession with clashing expectations as to what counts as relevant, weighty, authoritative, "solid", or even "professional". Conversely, the deeper the assimilation of the genre into the student's consciousness, the narrower the range of disagreement amongst the professional knowers. The tacit inculcation of *prejudice* is critical to the social function of the professional law school.

The Phenomenon of Resignification of a Witness's Utterance

For the professional knower, this early training into a secondary genre works to create an environing world, or *Umwelt*, through which the knower reads, hears and communicates. The environing world makes one's intuitions seem natural. When confronted with a witness's story about a social circumstance, for example, I undergo a series of experiences as a professional knower. I "recognize" the story as similar to other stories which I have learned to classify under doctrines, rules, principles and other typifications. I typify the story even when the story sets out the "facts" of the case. I take certain assumptions for granted. Having lived through other genres, whether they be the language of tennis, track and field, afternoon television shows or of a rural school, I exclude some interpretations as unrealistic and include others as plausible.[17] In my role as a lawyer, I may not immediately identify with the utterances of witnesses. I do not enter into a 'concrete' relationship with the witness.[18] A witness embodies his or her utterance with a *meant* object which is *concrete* with him or her. As a knower, however, I take the utterance and resituate it as a sentence into a secondary configuration of signs. I integrate the sentence with other sentences so as to produce a new configuration of signs.

This act of elevating the sentence is what Husserl calls 'an objectifying act of reflection'.[19] I pass judgement upon the witness's story. I identify the story by a sentence or two, abstract the sentences into a standardized generalization about the "facts", and then connect that generalization to configurations of signs which I trace to other signs and, from there, to some presupposed founding Object. I *intellectualize* about the sentences even though I may claim to represent a pained witness who actually uttered the sentence in recounting his or her pain. Furthermore, I intellectualize retrospectively. However, I may do so intuitively, without reflecting on my typification because my peers share my understandings and expectations. I even situate the witness amongst differentiating signs which I, as a lawyer, consider to be "the law". As I correspond the witness's testimony to my discourse's pre-existing configurations of signs in the trace of authority, I integrate the witness's utterance into my secondary discourse *about* the witness. I transform the *meant* character of the witness's story into an external object which I signify through familiar terms. I mean the posited external object because I read the signification through my environing world as a professional knower. Yes, I may empathize with the witness. I may nod my head with a sympathetic grimace as he or she recounts the story. I may offer Kleenex and direct my secretary to bring the witness tea and biscuits. But, loaded with my special terminology, my client's utterance becomes a sentence which I resituate into a cohesive chain of signs which makes sense to me as a professional knower. I compare the chain with other chains of signs. I choose that configuration which seems most authoritative. I go through a similar transposition when I read documents which the witness may have brought to my law office.

The witness thus becomes "a case": I write letters to other lawyers about his or her "case"; I treat the witness as a plaintiff or defendent or as representing a legal claim. In this process, the indigenously experienced pain becomes irrelevant. I measure the signification of the client's story about his or her indigenously experienced harm against signs which represent prior external doctrines or typified "facts". The typifications enclose the non-knower's story. Slowly, almost imperceptibly, as I delve deeper and deeper into the "facts" of the case, the witness becomes a juridical person whose identity is gleaned from the rights and duties configured in the secondary discourse, not from his or her biography. The witness reports what others may have said in a prior specific context. Although the witness may only utter fragments of his or her thoughts and feelings when recounting them to me, I abstract them into themes and integrate them into one single consciousness as if the witness had no biography. My discourse – the secondary discourse – has taken precedence over the pained individual.

Rights and duties define the identity of this juridical person. The legal issue is whether a non-knower fits within the boundaries of a similarly situated juridical person configured in the secondary discourse. The juridical person is considered "real" "in the eyes of the law", even though his or her embodied meanings have been transformed into the seemingly objective formal configurations of signs in my discourse. So, a corporation, the Crown or a tree may be recognized as a juridical person with rights and duties even though the person does not look like a biological human being. And yet biological metaphors may be attributed to the juridical person. The juridical person may be said to possess "an intent". The evidence about the person may be said to have "weight". And the configurations from which the person is constructed may attribute eyes to the legal discourse – "the eyes of the Law".

The Act of Assimilation

The Phenomenon of Reported Speech

Let us look closer as I transform the embodied meanings of the witness. When I speak or write, I speak and write *about* my client's actions. A reported speech is a speech within a speech.[20] When I initiate a threat of a lawsuit or draft my pleadings or question my adversary's chief witness on discovery, I may report what the witness has said or what others have said. The witness's speech is without '…'. Although the witness may consider his or her speech as independent, complete, and as a part of his or her being, as a lawyer, I regard the same utterance as belonging to an author "out there", beyond my control. As Samuel Weber points out, the participants in a secondary discourse appropriate and alienate an utterance.[21] I report what was said in hindsight and after having configured it in a web of signs which my addressees – other lawyers – will recognize. The witness, as an original author of his or her utterance, no longer owns it. The re-report becomes an event itself. It is an event *after* the recounting of another event. As a lawyer, I unify the reported utterance into one unified context which I draw from my familiar signs. The witness's utterance is recontextualized into a secondary signifying relation. As a result, the witness's embodied meanings dissipate into my integrative project. Lifted from the witness's meaning-specific context, the witness cannot respond directly to other witnesses. That could have happened only in the uncontrolled and uncontrollable social concrete context before I and other lawyers were brought into the scene. The witness can only respond to sentences which the lawyer puts to her and, then, only in the context of the creation of a cohesive narrative. The lawyer is an 'officer of the court' with overriding duties to the court. The lawyer represents the master discourse.

The phenomenon of the 'reported speech' is important because, as Volosinov points out, one cannot mechanically transpose an utterance from direct into indirect voice.[22] In an indirect discourse, one 'hears' a message differently than does a listener who communicates, as a respondent, in a direct voice. During negotiations as much as in formal proceedings, for example, the lawyer redirects a quoted utterance into an argument. What the witness meant by his or her utterance is displaced in favour of how the lawyer signifies it in the secondary discourse. The knower situates the quoted utterance in a different configuration from what the original utterer had intended. Sometimes, the secondary discourse recognizes just such a transfiguration when the lawyer appeals to the 'constructive intent' of an author. The lawyer may also cite the author in the impersonal third person and in the passive voice. The lawyer does not cross-examine a witness as if the lawyer-witness relationship were a unique face-to-face or I/thou relationship. Rather, the lawyer employs formal pronouns such as 'you said that', 'he said', 'she said' or 'it was said that'. This contrasts with the active personal voice in a dialogue. The formal passive voice in the legal proceeding acknowledges and reinforces a belief that outside objects – "facts" and doctrines – constrain the knower. This induces one to believe that the knower merely represents what has already happened beyond the knower's control.

An impersonal writing style helps to produce a signified event as if it were posited beyond the knower's control. The narrative seems to descend from above. The lawyer reinforces this style with immaculate clothing, thick leather briefcase, formalistic gestures, self-confidence, clarity, articulateness, attention to detail and an enviable memory. Further, the lawyer re-presents the client's story logically and in a linear direction, each sub-plot making articulated assumptions and each argument building upon the strength of the earlier. Pleadings are drafted in the third person and in the passive voice: 'it was submitted that ...', 'it was held out by the witness that ...', 'it was provided in section one that ...', 'the general principle in this line of cases has been that ...'. The words belong to no-one. The passion and evaluative context-specific meanings of a non-knower evaporate. The lawyer's passion may be verbalized; but the verbalization will take the form of 'it is the concern of the plaintiff [not the lawyer] that...'. The narration exists independently of the client, the non-knower. The addressee/client passively listens to the narrated events. A non-knower, as an addressee, cannot respond to the represented events through his or her own signifying relations without the lawyer resignifying the latter through the lawyer's idiom. What matters is the narrator's unfolding (retelling) of the narrative concepts in terms of the secondary genre's signs, not the client's interpretation of his or her own report. The non-knower takes on an implicit identity. From the standpoint of the non-knower whose destiny depends upon the outcome of the narrative struggle, the narration is a 'naked corpse of the world'[23] which gives little insight into a non-knower's own context-specific meanings. The non-knower becomes an outsider, detached from the narration, although the narrator strives to consider all stories within the narration.

The formalistic and argumentative style of a legal discourse also reinforces the assimilation of an utterance as a signified external object. The utterer cannot respond as can an active participant in a dialogue.[24] In a dialogic relationship, an utterer carries the dialogue one step further, perhaps in an unintended direction. Utterer and listener are addressees to each other, each seeking a shared understanding of objects which each *means*. Their objects are not situated external to their environing worlds. Such a responsive relation is absent in a legal proceeding. Even a discovery is *led* by questions from the lawyer, questions which, ultimately, will be integrated into a cohesive narrative. The lawyer leads questions which he or she implicitly situates within authoritative doctrines and rules which the judge will recognize. The implicit doctrines exclude the irrelevant and underplay the less weighty. Boundaries of the doctrines act to pre-censor the utterances as if the external world of doctrines, rules and other typifications constrain the utterer. Indeed, as a client responds to questions during a discovery or a trial, a lawyer may well raise further questions and objections, all in an effort to make the lawyer's narrative cohesive. The client's utterance is integrated into the secondary discourse.

Returning to my interpretive act as an analytic lawyer, let us look closely at the civil procedure of a common law jurisdiction in order to appreciate how the procedure works to assimilate the non-knower's utterances through reported speech. Pleadings aim to define the legal issues. They are made *for* the secondary discourse, not vice versa. Each stage of the civil procedure proceeds from the first pleading, not from the non-knower's indigenously experienced meanings. Lawyers draft the plea so as to integrate evidence into a cohesive story about the facts as signified in the pleadings. The evidentiary rules exclude certain documents and utterances, include others, and attribute differing weight to the evidence. The discovery and pretrial conferences continue the process of integrating witnesses' reported sentences into a cohesive re-presentation of the client's story. Opportunities exist for further assimilation in the opening address, the re-presentation of the evidence in a certain order, the witnesses called, witnesses not called, and the actual leading of evidence in examination-in-chief. The lawyer cross-examines in order to integrate further evidence into the lawyer's story and in order to weaken the opponent's. The coherence of the story is tested in cross-examination. Leading questions, diction, phraseology, facial gestures, movements of parts of the body, asides, repetition of questions and other gestural and verbal factors work to depreciate some utterances and to privilege others as consistent. On re-examination, the knower embarrasses the unexplained and incomplete evidence. The argument collates the evidence into an integrated story. Like a good narrative, the plot may not become clear until the end of the reproduction of evidence.

The Utterance and the Sentence

Through this intricately complex re-reporting of events, the witness's speech is transformed from a felt utterance into a grammatically functioning sentence.[25] When making an utterance, the utterer embodies a series of physical sounds or marks with meant objects. The utterance is authored. When the utterance is transfigured into a lawyer's narrative about the event, the utterer's speech becomes a sentence. The sentence, composed of physical–chemical marks, is an external object to be reintegrated into the *lawyer*'s, not the non-knower's, story. As the sentence is lifted into the secondary story, the non-knower's utterance is de-authored: the author no longer owns the utterance. Further questions and answers then integrate the sentence into the lawyer's signifying relations. At that moment, the sentence becomes an utterance again although, this time, one which belongs to the lawyer. The sentence acquires a legal signification only within the context of the lawyer's whole reporting of the signified event.[26] The signification of the sentence is made concrete in the second-level discourse. The lawyer shapes and develops the sentence into secondary signifying relations which signify something authoritative for the lawyer although, perhaps, nothing for the original utterer. In argument, the lawyer re-presents the evidence through a retelling of previously told stories. The lawyer *interprets* the witness's sentence in such a manner that the sentence is linked with the lawyer's overall narrative. An integrated and internally persuasive narrative is reached.

New boundaries of commonality between lawyer and witness accompany the shift from utterance to sentence to utterance. Both in negotiations and in formal proceedings, lawyers utilize the witness's sentence to refute, supplement or argue in response to the claims of other lawyers. The lawyer *means* the same sentence differently than does the non-knower. In a sense, the lawyer authors the witness's original utterance. The new object of the lawyer's utterance, also meant, gives ideological content to the former utterance of the witness. The witness's own words have been transformed into a signifying context with which he or she does not necessarily mean. This alien signifying context functions as 'verbal–ideological thought'.[27] Only other professional knowers, who work/play within the secondary discourse, can recognize the signifying context. The new 'author' thereby directs the witness's utterance to an object which other lawyers will recognize as falling under authoritative typifications. During the transformation of the utterance, the lawyer reaches out to *enclothe* the sentence, left naked of embodied meaning, 'like a garment'.[28]

And yet, at the very moment that the witness's utterance is transformed into the secondary legal discourse, the discourse itself induces the lawyer to believe that the lawyer is constrained by the externally situated "facts" beyond the lawyer's control. The witness's utterance is believed to be one such "fact" even though it has become a sentence to the lawyer. Indeed, the term "bias" constrains the professional knower from ever admitting personal ownership of a witness's utterance. Many evidentiary rules also reinforce such a proscription. To admit that the lawyer actually authors the utterance of a witness would challenge the objectivism which the lawyer's discourse projects. The knower would no longer be considered a professional or a reporter of evidence.

As a consequence of the phenomenon of assimilation, the secondary discourse *defaces* the witness as the master and author of his or her own utterances. The witness's utterance is disembodied.

The ultimate moment of the assimilative project of a modern legal genre transpires when configurations of the lawyer's utterances take on a narrative structure. When initially interrogated, a client or witness narrates a story about his or her experiences through his or her own familiar nomenclature and gestures. The client's utterances may be cognitively resituated into doctrines familiar to the lawyer. At the early interviewing stage of the legal process, even the witness's story abstracts from the prior context-specific meanings which he or she had experienced during an indigenously experienced event. In discovery, counsel slowly elicits responses which fill the gaps in the counsel's story and which will rebut opposing stories. A lawyer possesses a subtle opportunity to bring different moments of the plot of the story at diverse points of the legal proceeding: the summary of "facts" through correspondence with opposing counsel; the pleadings; objections during discovery regarding the felt experiences which the witness had brought into his or her utterances in the indigenously experienced event. And, as the knower re-reports an author's utterance through the secondary signifying relations, the knower reinforces the boundaries of the secondary discourse.[29]

The Narrative as the Displacing Medium

The ultimate moment of the assimilative project of a modern legal genre transpires when configurations of the lawyer's utterances take on a narrative structure. I have identified above how the various stages of a civil proceeding offer ample opportunity for the knower's to assimilate the non-knower's utterances through reported speech. Such an assimilative phenomenon even begins when the lawyer or police officer in a criminal proceeding first interviews the client. When interviewed, the client recounts a story about his or her indigenously experienced event through his or her familiar nomenclature and grammar. Even the client's story abstracts from the prior context-specific meanings which he or she had experienced during the indigenously experienced event. The lawyer or police officer may then resituate the story or a fragment of the story into code sections or doctrines familiar to the official. At each situs of shaping a coherent narrative, the lawyer converts stories recounted through primary genres into secondary language signs. By so doing, a lawyer's story integrates the witness's lived meanings into a continuous structure or whole. The lawyer transforms fragments into a coherent order of events which mean something special to the expert knower.

A story is drawn from a *fabula* or a series of logically and chronologically related events. During an initial interview, again, each witness gives his or her story. An immediacy joins the witness with his/her story. In contrast, a narrator, such as a lawyer or a judge, acts as an impartial agent for others who tell their stories.[30] The lawyer arranges the witness's utterances temporally. In a sense, the lawyer as narrator brings the witness's stories *into* a shared secondary discourse which parasitically feeds from stories initially uttered within primary genres. By so doing, the narrator eventually authors the witness's story. Like narrators in general,[31] the lawyer narrates about what others have impliedly authored. The lawyer is an actor *within* a secondary discourse. The secondary metacode of concepts gives *form* to the witness's utterances. The true event, for the expert knower, is not the witness's indigenous experience of pain; rather, juridical truth lies in the authoritative *re-presentation* of the witness's story. And that story is *about* the witness's indigenous experience. The expert's signs become the referent for the expert knower[32] – that is, the secondary discourse becomes self-referential. And the witness's embodied meanings are displaced into a resignified narrative.

The trial court judge, in turn, narrates a story about the witnesses' combinations of signs by synthesizing the stories of all the lawyers or by privileging one lawyer's story over another's. The judge differentiates one concrete human experience from another by situating its memory and situs in a grand narrative *about* the witnesses' stories and *about* other judges' stories (about which signifying chains are authoritative). An expert knower questions the authenticity of a witness's story at the moment when the knower resituates the story in a grand narrative.[33] At that point, the witness's story is neither final nor complete. So long as the trial judge impartially recounts the witness's story continuously and coherently vis-à-vis other reported stories, it is difficult for any lawyer or judge to break from the narrated order. The judge narrates the reported stories rather than dialogues with them. The narrative takes on an apparent objectivity within unquestioned boundaries of what count as authoritative configurations of signs.

Notes

1 Stanley Fish, *Doing What Comes Naturally: Change, Rhetoric and the Practice of Theory in Literary and Legal Studies* (Durham NC: Duke University Press, 1989).

2 Ibid., 504–5.

3 Ibid., 136.

4 Ibid., 503–24, 504–5.

5 Ibid., 518.

6 See, especially, M.M. Bakhtin, 'Discourse on the Novel' in *The Dialogic Imagination: Four Essays* (Caryl Emerson and Michael Holquist eds.; Austin: University of Texas Press, 1981); 'The Problem of Speech Genres' in *Speech Genres and Other Late Essays* (Vern W. McGee trans.; Caryl Emerson and Michael Holquist, eds.; Austin: University of Texas Press, 1986).

7 Tzvetan Todorov, *Genres in Discourse* (Catherine Porter trans.; NY: Cambridge University Press, 1990): 18.

8 Tzevetan Todorov, 'The Origin of Genres' in *New Literary History*, vol. 8 (1976–71): 159–70, 163.

9 M.M. Bakhtin, 'The Problem of Speech Genres' in *Speech Genres and Other Late Essays*, note 6 *supra:* 61–2, 65–6, 98–9.

10 Ibid., 98.

11 Ibid., 62.

12 Carolyn Strange, 'Wounded Womanhood and Dead Men: Chivalry and the Trials of Clara Ford and Carrie Davies' in Francia Iacocelta and Marianna Valverde eds., *Gender Conflicts* (Toronto: University of Toronto Press, 1992): 149–88.

13 See, especially, Douglas Hay, 'Property, Authority and Criminal Law' in Douglas Hay *et al.*, *Albion's Fatal Tree: Crime and Society in Eighteenth Century England* (London: Allan Lane, 1975): 17–63.

14 Lyotard discusses this in another context in Francois Lyotard, 'A Memorial of Marxism: For Pierre Souyri' in *Peregrinations: Law, Form, Event* (New York: Columbia University Press, 1988): 46.

15 I use the term 'work' as Barthes uses it in juxtaposition with a text. See Roland Barthes, 'From Work to Text' in Josue U. Harari ed., *Text and Strategies: Perspectives in Post-Structuralist Criticism* (Ithaca: Cornell University Press, 1979); 'Theory of the Text' in Robert Young ed., *Untying the Text: A Post-Structuralist Reader*, (Boston: Routledge & Kegan Paul, 1981).

16 Hans-Georg Gadamer, *Truth and Method* (New York: Crossroad, 1985): 235–74.

17 Shlomith Rimmon-Kenan, *Narrative Fiction: Contemporary Poetics* (London and New York: Methuen, 1983): 125.

18 More generally, see Husserl's 'Appendix' to the 'Fifth Investigation' in *Logical Investigations*, vol. 2 (New York: Humanities Press, 1970).

19 Edmund Husserl, 'Fifth Investigation', ibid., 562.

20 V.N. Volosinov, *Marxism and the Philosophy of Language* (Ladislav Matejka and I.R. Titunik trans.; New York and London: Seminar Press, 1973): 115–24.

21 Samuel M. Weber, 'The Intersection: Marxism and the Philosophy of Language' in *Diacritics*, vol. 15, no. 4 (Winter 1985): 106–7.

22 Volosinov, note 20 *supra*, 129.

23 Mikkail M. Bakhtin describes the dead narration in this manner in 'The Discourse of the Novel' in *The Dialogic Imagination*, note 6 *supra*, 292.

24 This distinction is made by Volosinov, note 20 *supra*, 69.

25 Ibid., 80.

26 Bakhtin discusses this generally in 'The Problem of Speech Genres', note 6 *supra*, 82.

27 Bakhtin, *The Dialogic Imagination*, note 9 *supra*, 269.

28 The metaphor is Husserl's. Investigation VI, note 18 *supra*, 701.

29 Tzvetan Todorov, *The Poetics of Prose* (Richard Howard trans.; Ithaca, New York: Cornell University Press, 1977): 72.

30 Mieke Bal, *Narratology: Introduction to the Theory of Narrative* (Christine van Boheeman trans.; Toronto: University of Toronto Press, 1985): 5.

31 Ibid., 119–20.

32 Bernard Jackson comes to the same conclusion. See, especially, his *Law, Fact and Narrative Coherence* (Merseyside, UK: Deborah Charles Publications, 1988): 7–12.

33 Hayden White makes this point more generally in 'The Value of Narrativity in the Representation of Reality' in *Critical Inquiry*, vol. 7 (1980–81): 5–27, 23.

3 The Silence of Suffering

In early 1942, a strange – though perhaps not uncommon – political phenomenon transpired. The US government required a group of persons, mostly citizens, to report to a civil authority, imposed a curfew upon them, transported them to heavily guarded camps, confiscated their homes and businesses, and even deported some back to their ancestral country. Over 120 000 persons were treated to these special regulations. The Canadian government, for its part, shortly followed suit against 20 881 persons of the proscribed group. After the Second World War the Canadian government, unlike the American, continued the juridical project of exclusion. The detainees and internees were offered 'the option' of being relocated 'East of the Rockies' or, alternatively, of being 'repatriated' to the country from which their ancestors had emigrated several generations earlier.[1] The 'repatriation' programme was cancelled in 1947, $2\frac{1}{2}$ years after being implemented.[2] The evacuation and relocation programme was cancelled in 1949, four years after being implemented.

Who were the members of the proscribed group? In the United States, the official discourse called them 'persons of Japanese ancestry'; in Canada, 'persons of the Japanese race'.

The big question to this day is 'How was this mass movement of peoples into internment camps possible in such rights-conscious countries?' In both cases, the highest courts in the land validated the action. How was it possible that the legal culture would affirm such acts? For the most part, all we have is the expression of the judges in their judgments. Analytical lawyers are familiar with such texts as they seek out the grounds of the judges' holdings. I am concerned with the judges' texts, less for insights into their reasoning or justificatory acts, than for insight into the intuitive or prelegal *prejudice* which the judges brought *into* the "facts of the case". In other words, what was it about their environing world which encouraged them to read the legislative and executive acts as authoritative?

The obvious question is whether the judges read the "facts" through an environing world which took racism for granted. After all, both the United States and Canada had had a long history of legislated efforts to deny the franchise, to prevent the ownership of private property, to segregate schools, and even to deny citizenship on the grounds that one was typified a 'person of the Japanese ancestry'. For example, the general who had authorized the curfew against the proscribed group in the United States, General De Witt, had reported to the Minister of War in 1942 that the curfew was essential because 'the racial characteristics' of the proscribed group predisposed them to disloyalty against the American war effort. It is common knowledge that he also believed that biological complexion made it impossible for legal officials to differentiate one loyal member from a disloyal member. In 1982 Congress affirmed the role of racism in the internment of the 120 000 citizens and immigrants: 'race prejudice, war hysteria and a failure of political leadership shaped the decisions to exclude and to intern the proscribed group in camps.'[3] Despite General De Witt's racist disposition, the US Supreme Court judgments read as if the internment and deportation of the proscribed group were logically "natural", necessary and inevitable. Superficially, at least, the judgments seem cleansed of any indication of a racist environing world. Indeed, the US War Department had destroyed all drafts, records and copies of the military commander's original *Report* in which the commander had referred to members of the group in such biological terms. Racism may well have motivated the politicians, the media and the general public, but why did the highest judges in the respective countries (and, indeed, in the United Kingdom since the final court of appeal in Canada was the Privy Council), fail to recognize the racist flavour and effect of the regulations which were eventually challenged? Something more has to explain the Justices' texts in such a dark moment in the legal history of liberal democracies.

In particular, what was it about the Justices' environing world which made their validation of the internment camps seem so rationally natural? Can one explain the judgments on the grounds of military security? The official records document that military security was not the motivating factor for the military and political officials. The Congressional review of the evidence in 1982 concluded, for example, that 'not a single documented act of espionage, sabotage or fifth column activity was committed by an American citizen of Japanese ancestry or by a resident Japanese alien on the West Coast'.[4] Internment was imposed without regard for the security risk or disloyalty of individuals. Once the United States navy had gained control of the Pacific Ocean, no effort was made to disband the internment camps. How did the Justices read the "facts" in such a way as to support the authorization of internment practices?

In responding to the big question, I turn away from my analytic training as a common law lawyer and as a professional law teacher of constitutional law. Rather, I shall read the higher court judgments as if I, a juridical agent, were responding intuitively to the record. Put in other terms, what is it about my environing world, as a professional knower, which induces me to read the "facts and circumstances of the case" as did the US Supreme Court Justices? How do I embody the "facts" with my environing world into which I have been acculturated through long years of professional training, practice and academic teaching?

The Phenomenon of a *Differend*

The key to the judicial validation of the internment and deportation regulations in both countries is the non-knower's disembodiment of meaning. In terms of Saussure and Greimas, legal language might be understood as a subtext of relations between signs (signifiers) and signifieds. In terms of Charles Peirce, the indeterminate regress amongst legal signs might be the focus. Neither tradition grants an adequate role in legal discourse for the embodiment of the interpreter's sign and the disembodiment of the non-knower's. Using the tradition of Husserl and Gadamer, one can appreciate that an individual brings past forestructures of meaning and expectations *into* a sign as he or she reads, listens, speaks or writes. We lawyers *embody* our signifying relations with our shared experiences even if those experiences work to project the world as if it were posited external to us. The lawyer and non-lawyer may share the same signs, but our meant objects – the meant objects of professional knowers – differ as we address each other, if we do. The point I wish to make in the context of the American internment cases is that, as the official discourse addressed the lawyers for the internees, the signifying relations of the juridical agents displaced the embodied meanings of the internees in favour of a narrative which made sense to the Justices. The success of the displacing narrative, though, concealed a strident form of human misery. The latter arose from the untranslatable gap between the environing worlds of the everyday experiences of the internees, on the one hand, and the environing worlds of the Justices as professional knowers – indeed, the ultimate knowers – on the other.

The internees had lived context-specific experiences in fishing, business, farming, religion, and school before internment enclosed them. Once interned, they coped through humour, games, story-telling, and shared experiences. But the lawyers and judges interpreted the predicament of the internees as if the Justices were third parties, as if the internees' experiences were "out there" beyond the control of the Justices. After all, the legal genre had abstracted from the particular subjects who had previously and contemporaneously lived particular biographies and had typified them in the secondary genre as 'persons of Japanese ancestry'. That is, each and every internee had been signified by a sign which had represented something special to the juridical officials of the secondary genre. Such a sign, 'persons of Japanese ancestry', was immersed into pre-existing chains of other, more familiar, signs such as 'war power', 'emergency doctrine' and 'legal authority'. The knowledge of the professional knowers was a knowledge of such signs. The Justices on the US Supreme Court, then, wrote the judgments to other knowers, not to the internees. They wrote through a vocabulary, style and concerns which made little sense to the internees as they had lived as farmers and businesspeople, or as they had survived the day-to-day dread in the internment camps. In order to communicate the pain of their predicament, the internees had to retain a representer who could speak and write the language of the secondary genre. Such a language depended upon there being juridical persons who could be signified in the secondary discourse.

As such, the legal discourse supplemented the internees' experiences as a generalized other to the legal discourse. But, once signified in the legal discourse, the Justices wrote as if they had no choice, as if they were constrained by the configurations of signs which they had inherited from their language. Although supplementary to "facts and circumstances of the case", the constraints of the signifying relations in the legal discourse induced the latter to become a primary and secondary genre: a primary genre to the professional knowers who immediately identified with their secondary configurations of signs; and a secondary genre as the knowers proceeded to justify and reason about the signified event of internment. The internee became an other whose experiential and physical body must be controlled and regulated and, if necessary, exiled because, as juridically defined, the primary genres of the internees were unassimilatable into legal discourse. The internees' utterances and gestures could not be recognized as familiar and authoritative signs in the official discourse. Individual citizens, often citizens of second-or even third-generation immigrants, were resignified as signs which represented a universal typification. The discourse produced a *differend*, or fundamental rupture, between the authoritative signifying relations and the environing world of the internee. The internment camps of the world are the product of our discourse – the legal discourse of the modern state.

At this point one can appreciate that two types of harm had transpired in the US government's internment project. One form of harm is familiar. An internee experienced, in a sense, a familiar harm when he or she was detained and relocated without due process. The internee was harmed when he or she was isolated from his or her family and friends and then treated as a criminal – no, as worse than a criminal – because of the way juridical officials had typified the subject. A harm occurred when the internee's business was confiscated and sold without just compensation. The living conditions in the internment camps violated statutory and treaty standards of the day. And on it goes.

A second form of harm also transpired, however. This harm derived from the radical abyss between two genres, the one concealed inside the other. On the one hand, there was the dominant specialized genre of the juridical officials – the CIA, FBI, the military officials, the prison guards, and eventually the lawyers and judges. On the other hand, there were the primary genres which the internees lived each day. Borrowing Jean François Lyotard's term, I call this untranslatable abyss between two genres, a juridical *differend*.[5] In examining the inability of a holocaust survivor to put his or her experience into phrases, Lyotard has distinguished a *differend* from the activity of litigation. Without underplaying the terror of the context which Lyotard addressed, I am claiming, though, that there is a sense in which a *differend* even dwells inside litigation in a liberal legal order. The secondary legal genre slowly takes hold of the embodied meanings of the person who has experienced the first type of harm. The legal genre recognizes the harm by signifying it. This resignification becomes the event for the professional knower. At the moment of recognition, the litigant becomes an aggrieved to the official discourse itself, all the while that juridical agents claim to speak on behalf of the litigant.

In the resignification of the internment and regulatory control of citizens and immigrants in these liberal states, the second form of harm derived from the internees' inability to have their pain juridically recognized through their own everyday idioms They continued to live their everyday lives through their idiom. But the official discourse dispersed the internees' particular idioms. The indigenously experienced harm during the first stage of the dispersal of the internees went unrecognized in the official discourse. The archival histories of the road camps tell how officials, little acquainted with the cultural values, psychology and practices of the internees,[6] implemented rules and regulations without any sensitivity to their impact on the internees' environing world. The dispersal of the internees' everyday genres showed how the *differend* itself remained unrecognized inside the professional knowers' secondary genre.

The internees *meant* their objects, whether the objects were a game or a meal or the biting cold in uninsulated railway cars, as they embodied their meanings with concrete experiences from day-to-day. That embodiment of objects was lopped off, though, when the officials regulated and ordered the internees to remain in their houses during a curfew.[7] The bodily experiences of angst, the dread of the unknown and the pain of being treated irrationally were the means by which the internees *meant* their world. Their embodied meanings finally saw the light of day in the published diaries, letters, biographies and poems of recent years.[8]

The Search for an Authoritative Sign

Let us assume that the secondary legal genre did, indeed, displace the embodied meanings of the subjects who had been classified as 'persons of Japanese ancestry'. Let us assume that a serious gap persisted between the official discourse and the embodied meanings of primary genres of the non-knowers. This question now comes to the fore: what was it about the Justices' environing world which induced them to read the internment as if it were necessary or natural? I do not wish to analyse the "facts" as the analytic lawyer is trained to do. I do not wish to ask whether the Justices "correctly" abstracted principles of law from earlier institutional materials and then whether they had "correctly" applied the principles to the "facts and circumstances of the case". Nor do I even wish to ask whether the way the judges analysed the cases contradicted some deep political theory which judges in a liberal state might presuppose. Rather, I wish to describe the moments which professional knowers experience as they are presented with the legal problems before them. As I perceive through my environing world as a professional knower, I too disembody the possibility of an interpretive act of the internee. I do so through a series of experienced moments which cannot be measured in terms of some objective time or space standard. I live these moments because I bring my past structures of meaning and my future expectations, as a professional knower, *into* the signs with which I am familiar. I recognize others as a sign for something – a legal doctrine, a "fact" – which, in turn, is signified as another sign which my peers also will recognize as authoritative in the case.[9]

An American citizen, Mr Hirabayashi, was convicted of violating an Act of Congress because he had knowingly disregarded a military commander's order that 'all persons of Japanese ancestry' remain off the streets between 8:00 pm and 6:00 am. Mr Hirabayashi had also failed to report to a designated civil control station, this being the first stage of the evacuation of all 'persons of Japanese ancestry' to internment camps. Mr Hirabayashi also chose not to obey the curfew.

As I reread the judgments of the US Supreme Court, I immerse myself in the Justices' search for the *grounds* of authoritative signs by which they typified 'persons of Japanese ancestry'. The big question for the Justices was whether the military commander had exceeded his authority when he had proclaimed the round-up of the 120 000 residents and then their internment: 'in passing upon the authority of the military commander to make and execute the order, it becomes necessary to consider in some detail the official action which preceded or accompanied the order and from which it derives its purported authority', Justice Stone advised. The Justices situated the military commander's authority, in turn, into a chain of texts which stated that the Secretary of War was authorized to designate the 'Military Commander' with the authority to enact the orders. The Secretary of War, in turn, was situated in a chain of texts which the Justices traced to the president. Accordingly, the rights of all persons to enter, remain or leave the designated zones was subject to the military commander's determination. It did not matter whether the general had excluded some persons who might have committed acts of sabotage, nor was the extent of one's mobility relevant. The crucial factor was that some official had authority to so restrict the rights of persons juridically so defined.

By way of one further example, Justice Stone found it necessary to ground his own decision 'under the authority conferred upon us by that section' (s. 346 of 28 USCA, 8 FCA title 28). Stone traced that text, proclaimed by the military commander, to a presidential Executive Order no. 9066. Executive Order no. 9102, in turn, had created a new juridical person, 'the War Relocation Authority' which was authorized 'to formulate and effectuate a program for the removal, relocation, maintenance and supervision of persons designated under Executive Order No. 9066'. Executive Order no. 9066 created yet another juridical person, the Director of the 'Authority', who was posited authority 'to prescribe regulations'. Having traced the authority of the military commander up to the president, Justice Stone then traced the president's authority to Congress: 'the conclusion is inescapable that Congress, by the Act of March 21, 1942, ratified and confirmed Executive Order No. 9066.'

That did not end the tracing project. Since the Justices could trace the general's order to texts of Congress and the president, the Justices experienced a new moment: such texts were traced to the basic text called the American Constitution, and that required Justice Stone to resituate Articles 1 and 2 of the basic text into the prior and subsequent legal discourse. For example, the Justice circulated the magic phrase, 'the war power of the national government', into other statements, such as 'the power to wage war successfully' (recirculated from the jurist, Charles Evans Hughes). Dicta were recirculated to support the claim that the war power 'extends to every matter and activity so related to war as substantially to affect its conduct and progress'; or 'it embraces every phase of the national defense'. Justice

Stone immersed Articles 1 and 2 of Constitution, then, into configurations of signs. These signs privileged specially trained persons, lawyers and judges, to read them.

Ordinarily, Stone stated, the racial category of 'persons of Japanese ancestry' would control the constitutionality of the other texts 'were it not for the fact that the danger of espionage and sabotage, in time of war and of threatened invasion, calls upon the military authorities to scrutinize every relevant fact bearing on the loyalty of populations in the danger areas'. The "facts" related to loyalty collapsed into the overbearing signs of 'security', 'war power' and 'persons of Japanese ancestry', according to the Justices. The 'odious' typification of persons by race was outweighed by 'those facts and circumstances that are relevant to measures for our national defense'. Stone repeated again and again, for example, that the racial category was 'not wholly beyond the limits of the Constitution' because of 'the recognition of facts and circumstances'. It was not so much that the "facts" supported the orders, but that 'we cannot say that these facts and circumstances, considered in the particular war setting, could afford no ground for differentiating citizens of Japanese ancestry from other groups in the United States'. Furthermore, 'we cannot close our eyes to the fact, demonstrated by experience, that in time of war' ethnic affiliations 'may be a greater source of danger' than other affiliations. The trace of authority through familiar chains of signs coloured how the judges read the facts and circumstances. Indeed, Justice Stone admitted that the situs of a text in a series of other authoritative texts could warrant that the legal discourse ignore evidence of one's particular loyalty to the state.[10] In his *Final Report*: *Japanese Evacuation from the West Coast, 1942*, General De Witt quoted many texts which authorized the most minute details of the evacuation and internment of persons of Japanese ancestry. The signification of the 'persons of Japanese ancestry' became the event, with serious consequences in terms of the pain and suffering of the resignified subjects. Officials administered 6000 of the detainees' farms, aggregating over 260 000 acres which were valued at $73 000 000.[11]

The Resignification of Mr Hirabayashi

Having privileged the signifying context in which the Justices located Mr Hirabayashi, we professional knowers are taken into a new experiential moment as we begin to analyse the harm done to this individual. Here, we knowers focus upon the 'facts and circumstances of the case', as the Justices put it.

The Signified Facts

For one thing, the important facts were either judicially noticed or they were "recited" in the authoritative texts themselves. That is, an event was a fact if the event could be recognized as a prior authoritative sign. One judicially noticed fact was that, on 7 December 1941, the Japanese Air Force had attacked the US naval base at Pearl Harbor. Authoritative texts themselves also recited certain facts. For example, Executive Order no. 9066 recited the fact that 'the successful prosecution of the war requires every possible protection against espionage and against sabotage to national-defense material, national-defense premises, and national-defense utilities'. These facts, in turn, were defined by special terms in special sections of authoritative Acts of Congress. General De Witt had issued a Proclamation which recited another fact: namely, that the entire Pacific coast 'by its geographical location is particularly subject to attack, to the attempted invasion by the armed forces of nations with which the United States is now at war, and ... is subject to espionage and acts of sabotage'. These recited facts 'required the adoption of military measures necessary to establish safeguards against such enemy operations', according to the Court. Moreover, 'the present situation requires as a matter of military necessity' the establishment of a 'military zone'. General De Witt himself resignified physical landscape into a 'military zone' – landscape which may have been known for its beauty or expanse or urban sprawl prior to its reconfiguration in the legal discourse. The general issued another Proclamation which recited the fact that 'the present situation within these Military Areas and Zones requires as a matter of military necessity the establishment of certain regulations pertaining to all enemy aliens and all persons of Japanese ancestry, all alien Germans, all alien Italians, and all persons of Japanese ancestry within said Military Areas and Zones'. When pressed for his grounds for isolating 'persons of Japanese ancestry' as suspect of espionage and sabotage, after he had declared the curfew, the general recited the "fact" of the Japanese government's policy of dual citizenship. This "fact" was believed to ground the racial category.

Look closely at how the general's justification for the authority of his texts rested upon his self-referential circulation of nomenclature inside his own narrative. He locates the 'present situation' by associating it with other familiar signs – familiar, that is, to the knowers. One such sign was the sign 'person of Japanese ancestry'. Another was 'military zone'. Of course, the physical property to which the 'military zone' referred had once been a community of homes and businesses and farms. The sign 'dual citizenship' itself represented a whole series of other signs to professional knowers. Such a sign, though, apparently had little consequence for many of the persons who were expelled and interned. Although the juridical officials constituted the "facts" as meant objects, they signified the "facts" as if they had been posited beyond the knowers' control. The externality of the facts worked to objectify the knower's project of grounding a juridical action.

The Government Brief "recognized" another "fact": namely, the 'convention' that 'while many second and third generation Japanese born on United States soil, possessed of United States citizenship, have become "Americanized," the racial strains are diluted'.[12] The military commander incorporated other "facts" into the discourse: the dangers posed by vigilantes towards the ethnic Japanese; the concentration of ethnic Japanese near military sensitive zones (which the general, of course, had retrospectively recognized as 'military zones'); the number of Japanese ethnic organizations on the west coast; Japanese language schools; and the large percentage of 'aliens' in the ethnic populace. Of course, 'persons of Japanese ancestry' had been barred from citizenship and so were classified as 'aliens'.

And what role should a judge play in this context? This issue too hung upon the Justices locating their self-image in familiar configurations of signs. The Supreme Court Justices deferred to the judgment of the military officials about the external objects: the objects 'were then peculiarly within the knowledge of the military authorities';[13] and 'reasonably prudent men charged with the responsibility of our national defense had ample ground for concluding that they must face the danger of invasion, take measures against it, and in making the choice of measures consider our internal situation'.[14] The crucial issue was not that such an event had occurred but, rather, who could authoritatively signify the event and how was the event signified? The sign 'persons of Japanese ancestry', not the alleged events of espionage or disloyalty, became the referent. Knowers could recognize such a sign. Furthermore, although the signified referent was represented as external to the official discourse, the officials themselves constructed the referent as juridically recognizable.

The Exclusion of "Facts"

The legal narrative resignified other events by excluding them from the narrative. Thus, some American citizens were excluded from the sign, 'persons of Japanese ancestry': namely, 'families consisting of a Japanese wife, a non-Japanese husband ... and their mixed blood unemancipated children'; 'families consisting of a Caucasian mother, citizen of the US or a friendly nation, and her mixed-blood children by a Japanese father (either dead or from the family)'; 'mixed-blood (one-half Japanese or less) individuals ... whose backgrounds have been Caucasian'; 'Japanese unemancipated children who are being reared by Caucasian foster-parents'; and 'Japanese wives of non-Japanese spouses serving in the armed forces of the United States'.[15] The narrative also failed to recognize certain evidence about those included within the proscribed category. For example, 40 years after the Supreme Court had originally heard the *Hirabayashi* and *Korematsu* cases, it recognized that War Department officials had withheld certain of General De Witt's statements from the Justice Department lawyer who, in turn, could not represent them to the trial court. War Department officials had altered General De Witt's original *Report* to privilege the concern of espionage and to omit the general's biological stereotyping of 'all persons of Japanese ancestry'. The War Department had concealed records of the *Report*'s receipt; it had destroyed records of the *Report*'s preparation; it had created records that falsely identified the revised version as the only version; and it had withheld the original version from the Justice Department.[16] Indeed, the extent to which the War Department officials excluded evidence so as to make a cohesive narrative is impressive. Not least in this respect, officials suppressed evidence supporting the loyalty of 'persons of Japanese ancestry' as well as evidence countering their alleged commission of espionage. The lawyers for the government had alluded to the above exclusion of evidence and to the existence of evidence counter to the government's case in a footnote to their Brief to the Supreme Court in 1942. However, the War Department officials intervened and the Solicitor General, duly authorized, required a revision of the footnote.[17] Moreover, the trial and appellate judgments ignored the evidence of systemic discrimination against 'persons of Japanese ancestry' for the several decades leading up to the expulsion and internment.

Signified "Facts" Read Through a Trace of Authority

Once again, what the official discourse recognized as a "fact" was signified through an authoritative narrative. The key determinant in this moment of signification, again, was 'who had authority to recognize the the failure of Mr Hirabayashi to report to a civil authority?'. In this case, the authority of General De Witt and, ultimately the Solicitor General, determined what events could be signified as authoritative. As the Petition in the later Writ of Error in the *Korematsu* case stated,

> ... the "facts" upon which the Court relied, however, were not facts at all. Composed of half-truths and outright lies, the "facts" presented to the Court resulted from a deliberate and knowing attempt by the highest ranking military and civilian officials in the United States government to destroy, suppress and withold highly credible evidence ....[18]

Whether a fact "existed" hung upon the authority of a professional knower to recognize its existence. The knowers were 'reasonably prudent men', the Supreme Court had asserted in 1942. And the duty of the knowers was to trace texts to a 'possible or reasonable ground' or 'basis' or 'not unfounded' or 'a rational basis' 'in the light of all the facts and circumstances of the case'. The grounding, then, was believed to be situated in external posited facts. The facts were recognized, in turn, if and when they were situated in the trace for authority inside the discourse. So, for example, the 'relatively little social intercourse between them [persons of a Japanese ancestry] and the white population' was juridically recognized as an authoritatively posited 'reasonable grounds' for the curfew and Reporting Orders; and the Orders set out the category, 'persons of Japanese ancestry,' from which to differentiate all others. Once Orders were traced through the legal discourse to some external grounds, Justice Douglas agreed, 'our task is at an end'. For the judge was an umpire whose duty it was to uphold the boundaries of the typifications which the authoritative texts represented.[19]

In similar vein, the legal discourse also ignored events which concerned the historical context of the exclusion of 'persons of Japanese ancestry' from the official discourse. The 1982 Congressional Study found that the treatment of all persons described by this category contrasted with the 'more individualized and selective' treatment against enemy aliens of other ancestral origins.[20] In addition, the Study documented the success of the anti-Japanese groups in the United States during the first three decades of this century. Such groups wished governments to confirm that Asians should be forever barred from American citizenship.[21] Efforts had also been made to amend the Constitution to preclude children from becoming citizens if both parents were of an 'ineligible race'. Although the latter effort was unsuccessful, the Naturalization Act of 1790 had allowed for naturalization only of 'any alien being a free white person'. After the Civil War, this Act was amended (and upheld by the courts) to exclude any Chinese immigrant from citizenry.[22] The US Supreme Court extended this category to 'any Oriental' in 1922.[23] Furthermore, the financial recession of 1870 had been attributed to 'cheap Mongolian labor' to use the term of the day. According to the 1982 Congressional Study noted above, Japanese immigrants were effectively excluded from social and political life in the United States, and were also 'a convenient target for demagogues or agitators' in the 50 years preceding the Second World War.[24] In May 1905, 65 organizations combined to form the 'Japanese Exclusion League', resulting in the segregation of schoolchildren of Japanese ancestry. In 1913 the California Legislature enacted in the Webb–Henry Act that all aliens ineligible for citizenship were prohibited from future land purchases.

Subsequently, the anti-Japanese movement pressed for even more restrictive land laws and for the total prohibition of immigration from Japan.

The US Supreme Court's narrative about the "facts and circumstances of the case", then, ignored the above historical events as outside the trace of authority. Their inclusion would have disrupted the cohesiveness of the narrative, and the inferences to be drawn from the excluded events would have questioned the wisdom of the officials situated within the authoritative discourse. Mindful of the 'Speech of the Laws' in Plato's *The Crito*, such a scrutiny would have challenged the authority of the discourse to dominate all competing discourses. As the narrative about the authoritativeness of "the facts" took hold in the legal discourse, the historic systemic discrimination could be ignored. Reading the "facts" through the search for an originating grounds helped to re-present a cohesive narrative about the group in question. This narrative sanitized the violence as officials enclosed social phenomena within their sign, 'persons of Japanese ancestry'. It also privileged some statements and excluded others in order to convince the knowers of the threat which 'persons of Japanese ancestry' posed to military security.

The Silence of Mr Hirabayashi's Environing World

Having set out the key nomenclature and signifying context with which I, as a professional knower, interpret my signifying world, I search for a sign which will signify Mr Hayabayashi. As I do so, I increasingly distance my discourse from his environing world. My chain of signs represents *cognitive* objects: doctrines, rules, principles and institutions. What is critical to the phenomenological study of a modern legal discourse is that such cognitive objects possess *universal* components in that they encompass general categories. In our case, the professional knowers understood Mr Hirabayashi's experience as *indicating* or *representing* a *typical* experience. The typical experience remained undifferentiated vis-à-vis all the other internees within the boundaries of the cognitive object. Consequently, Mr Hirabayashi's experiential body was lopped off when that cognitive object took hold. The cognitive object enclosed his experiential body. Because the expert knower knew the sign cognitively, the *meaning* of Mr Hirabayashi's utterances and actions was swallowed into that cognitive typification. Needless to say, Mr Hirabayashi would be unlikely to share the same signification of the sign, 'persons of Japanese ancestry', with someone such as myself, trained as I am to recognize only certain signs as having legal signification. Mr Hirabayashi, in his everyday idiom, could hardly have interpreted his own particular experiences through such an impersonal category, for it was a term of the "we" – the knowers – not of Mr Hirabayashi.

We officials in the official discourse – not Mr Hirabayashi – posited the sign of 'persons of the Japanese ancestry'. We officials, not the internees, possessed and consumed the sign as if it were a commodity. Indeed, we juridical agents and our agents, in turn, gave signification to the sign as it related to other familar signs *inside* the official discourse. The paradox of modern legal discourse in a common law jurisdiction is that slowly, almost imperceptibly, we lawyers and judges in any one case begin to accept the authorized signs as constitutive of social reality. The critic is rejected as outside that reality, as impractical, as an idealist. As an expert knower of authoritative signs, one takes the judge's sign of a human subject or of an event as a "fact". In our US Supreme Court cases, the judges accepted the sign, 'persons of Japanese ancestry', as if the sign's cognitive object actually and accurately described particular human beings. We lawyers and judges built our legal analyses around the sign, as if it represented individual human beings who had lived particular biographies.

But by virtue of the universal character of the cognitive object of the sign, the givenness of the sign lost the uniqueness of Mr Hirabayashi's experiences. His particular biography was coloured over by the cognitive boundaries of a universal category. Indeed, to the judges, the legal sign seemed to carry a neutrality in that it could include anyone's particular experiences so long as one was characterized by the fact category or 'if' clause of the sign. Mr Hirabayashi was thereby treated equally before the cognitive object, whether one was included or excluded from its boundaries. The sign, 'persons of Japanese ancestry', then, idealized the particular internees by lopping off the internees' embodiment of their environing world. The Justices "knew" the cognitive object signified by the sign, but did not know Mr Hirabayashi's individual experiences. The judges and lawyers were privileged to belong to a profession which claimed an expert knowledge of a very special vocabulary and grammar. Moreover, their signifying relations protected that privileged position. They knew what categorical doctrines, rules, principles and "facts" to associate with each signifying relation. Using Gadamer's sense of the word, the judges and lawyers could not possibly "understand" the embodied meanings of the internees because the secondary signifying relations excluded those meanings. The sign, 'persons of Japanese ancestry', silenced the unique and individual experiences of each internee.

We narrators refused to question whether the typification, 'persons of Japanese ancestry', contravened a shared moral consensus or whether our signifying context was politically unwise. Indeed, Justice Stone asserted that 'it is not for any court to sit in review of the wisdom of their [the authorized officials and legislative institutions] or to substitute its judgment for theirs'. And, as Justice Douglas' judgment stated, 'the wisdom and expediency of the decision which was made is not for us to review'.[25] Nor did it matter that two-thirds of the internees were American citizens. Indeed, Justice Murphy, concurring, admitted that the impact of the authoritative Orders compared to 'a melancholy resemblance to the treatment accorded to members of the Jewish race in Germany and in other parts of Europe'.[26] For the narration about the authoritativeness of the proscribed category of persons took hold, and the narration treated all juridical officials as if they were *acted upon* by externally posited uncontrollable "facts". The judge's duty was to uphold the external "facts" since, unless we juridical agents did so, the world might come tumbling down. The 'inescapable duty' of the judical agent was to narrate events beyond our control, and we succeeded in doing so for over 40 years to the shame and pain of so many people.

Mr Hirabayashi and the 119 998 others became lost in our narration of an interconnecting web of juridically recognized signs. We even configured Mr Hirabayashi's name as an authoritative sign. Thus, when Mr Korematsu appealed against the government's decision to exclude Korematsu from his home, Justice Black recirculated the sign, Hirabayashi, because it now represented a special object "out there", beyond the judge's control – a given, posited. Mr Hirabayashi had become a signified event just like all the other signs. Justice Black wrote as if the sign, Hirabayashi, constrained Black in the later case of *Korematsu* v. *United States*. Hirabayashi had been transformed into an external object: this experiential body had been successfully concealed inside the legal discourse. The judges were elaborating a narrative, one which 'set up a figmentary and artificial situation', as Justice Roberts put it in dissent in *Korematsu*. To quote another dissenting Justice, Murphy, the signified person, *Hirabayashi*, lay 'like a loaded weapon ready for the hand of any authority that can bring forward a plausible claim of urgent need'. For 'every repetition imbeds that principle more deeply in our law and thinking and expands it to new purposes'.

The Non-recognition of the Particular Other: the Case of Davis Inlet

I have described the moments through which a iuridical agent may intuit a non-knower's experience. I have described how, in signifying the non-knower as a sign, the official discourse assimilates that sign *into* a secondary genre. But there is another signifying event which I should address. Sometimes, the secondary genre fails to recognize a non-knower and he or she slips through the cracks of signifying relations in that genre. I shall now work through such an event.

During the early 1950s the Federal Government of Canada had transported a nomadic community from the Arctic region to a locality on the Newfoundland coast called "Davis Inlet". The community had been a nomadic tribe for centuries. The government relocated the tribe with the promise that the location in Newfoundland would be temporary. "Davis Inlet" remained unrecognized in Canada's official discourse for over 30 years, until the winter of 1993 when eight children of Davis Inlet, ranging from the ages of two to twelve, attempted a group suicide, followed one week later by two more attempted child suicides. The national media described how almost all the village's adults were, or had been, alcoholics, very few were employed, and no police or social workers lived in the village. The inhabitants resided in homes without running water or a publicly supported sewage system. In addition, the provincial government had prohibited their one source of livelihood, fishing, by forbidding the use of the public dock because it was unsafe.[27]

Why had the community remained invisible to "the eyes of the law" for so long? Why had the community been left unrecognized in a society where other municipalities were entitled to a public sewage system, publicly funded education, health facilities and social services?

An Unsignified Community

The dominant official discourse had left the community unrecognized. First, the federal government did not recognize any special duty towards the villagers because, when the elders "consented" to move from the Arctic in the 1950s, the village elders had refused to recognize the protection of the national government pursuant to the Indian Act. Why? Because, the elders believed, such a recognition would undermine their legal claim that they remained an independent nation whose treaties with a former British government had recognized their special land and cultural rights as a nomadic tribe in the North. That is, the indigenous community realized that, to be recognized, they would have to acknowledge the mastery of the secondary discourse. Although two local brothers had trained and passed the exams needed to qualify as federally authorized police, they had not fulfilled the required high school completion for certification as police officers. As a result, they were unauthorized to act except as ordinary citizens. Neither did the provincial government recognize the villagers as a visible community in "the eyes of the law" because the village did not qualify as a 'municipality' under the provincially enacted Municipal Act. The villagers just slipped through the cracks of the secondary metaphysical order. The villagers were caught in a *chiasmus*, to use Merleau Ponty's term, without an authoritative language to represent their grievances: though living beings with painful experiences, they were juridically unrecognized as a group. Being thus unrecognized, they were not entitled to the benefits which earlier representatives of the Canadian state had undertaken towards other juridical persons in the legal discourse. Their non-recognition as juridical persons had the effect of undermining their social cohesion and pride as an Inuit tribe of an earlier day.

The Production of Suffering

Against the traditions of centuries of nomadic life and against the day-to-day upheaval of their settlement in Davis Inlet, the residents had shared a multiplicity of context-specific experiences. But in order to receive the social and legal benefits of the modern state, the lawyers, social workers, police and judges had to classify the behaviour of the indigents in a manner which made sense to others in the secondary genre.

On the other hand, the residents constituted *meant* objects as they tried to survive. Whether through alcoholism or suicide, the residents *meant* to escape from the monotony and distance of the artificially imposed Western bourgeois context. This context had been superimposed on to their collective memory – however unconscious after three generations – of a nomadic Arctic past. Their meanings constituted an environing world and were drawn from face-to-face encounters through *direct* speech and gestures between themselves. Their meanings linked their present experiences with their past and expected experiences. An immediacy joined their bodies with their everyday gestures and utterances.

When confronted with a report about the misery of the residents of Davis Inlet, however, I am confronted with a retelling of the pain through nomenclature and gestures which I, as a lawyer, will recognize. In order to make sense of the reported events, I resituate the reports into chains of signs which make sense to me. This resignification transforms the context-specific and embodied meanings of the villagers into recognized signifiers *about* them. The transformation of meaning occurs through a series of moments which the professional knower experiences.

The signification of the event First, as a lawyer, I search for authoritative words which will *signify* or *represent* what has happened, legally speaking. I isolate one part of the residents' experience and thereby reduce the residents' whole experiences into one category represented by one sign or configuration of signs. Of course, one cannot offer a complete picture of an experience, whether or not one is a lawyer. I *re*-present the residents' experience, as signified, during their relocation over a 40–year period. I assign this one sign with other representations which I recognize. I envisage the children's attempted suicide. I picture boundaries which include and exclude social factors as relevant. I typify the experiences into a standardized sign. So, for example, I may typify the villagers' experiences under such categories as 'young offender' or 'family' or 'welfare' or 'municipality' or 'Indian' or 'treaty' or 'assault'. I call the latter 'juridical facts' – 'matters.' As I reduce the experiences to one dominating "fact", that "fact" awakens different chains of signifying relations within my lawyer's consciousness. Each chain possesses a radically different legal consequence.

My authoritative signs, such as 'Indians and lands reserved for Indians' or 'municipal law', represent invisible typifications which silence the unique and individual experiences of each child who has attempted suicide. My typifications, as a knower, ignore the biographies of each villager except to the extent that my typifications (the typifications are really not mine because they pre-exist my own training as a lawyer) privilege an element of the child's biography as relevant to legal analysis. Indeed, my juridical typifications neutralize or sanitize the experiences in that I could include anyone's experiences within a typification, not just the individual residents of Davis Inlet. In our own example, I understand the experience of the residents as *indicating* or *signifying* a *typical* experience within which the residents remain undifferentiated vis-à-vis all the experiences of all others within the typification. Needless to say, my typification of the reported facts will not probably be shared with the villager/child who, in his or her everyday language of direct speech, would hardly interpret through my anonymous lawyerly categories. As a "competent" lawyer, I am presumed to "know" the various combinations of typifications – past and even future – which could possibly represent typifications concerning the plight of the Davis Inlet. My peers would consider me a "brilliant" lawyer if I could create a new combination of signs so as to offer a coherent, complete picture of all the past and possible signified events known to my discourse. What is extremely critical in this analysis "of the facts" is that I take my signified typification as constitutive of the "facts", even though the typification actually idealizes the events as experienced by the children who had attempted suicide.

The movement of the signified event Once I confidently identify the dominant characteristic with which to typify the experiences of the villagers as "fact" – a project which may well be debatable and therefore the subject of a trial if the residents have the strength and funds for such – I continue my exciting project of "legal analysis". At this second moment, I take my typification of the facts as given. More correctly, I take the configuration of signs as constitutive of the facts. I place the typified 'young offender' or 'family' or 'municipality' or 'assault' under one legal doctrine rather than under another. For example, the attempted group suicide might well be investigated under a provincially enacted Children's Aid Act, leading to a judicial order which would place the children in foster homes. However, if I had represented the event as involving 'young offenders' under the federally enacted Young Offenders Act or if I had classified the children as 'Indians' under the Federal Indian Act, the subsequent proceedings and outcome might be very different.

The trace of authority Having typified the reported story of the Davis Inlet children, I trace the resignified children through authoritative signs represented in statute books and law reports to texts believed to be authored by authoritatively recognized institutions. My aim is to associate the relevant typification with a grounds or source. Usually, I am satisfied if some text is cited as the grounds. Sometimes, I insist that the principle or policy of the typification be the grounds. In this tracing process, I insist that I am only applying the law. I function as a professional. I render an objective answer to my client, for I refer my utterances to external objects, whether they be "facts" or texts. I treat my choice of the dominant social trait as a "given" – as a "fact". My job is to analyse that fact in order to determine whether any government has contravened a previously posited duty towards the residents. I insist that a doctrine is *external* to my environing world because I believe my role, in a liberal–democratic state, is not to impose *my* will into the legal analysis of the reported suffering. Rather, majoritarianism suggests that, being an unelected official in a democracy, I should objectify the experiences of Davis Inlet residents and integrate them into the stream of other external objects such as statutes, precedents and the like. I must not make a personal judgment about any government or, for that matter, any action by a resident since that would take me beyond the legal discourse – outside the signs which I and my peers consider as the authoritative discourse of the modern state. I have been so successfully trained to believe that my role is to consider the event as an external object and to integrate the signification of the object into my stream of legal consciousness that I believe that the external objects constitute the whole of social reality. I respond to the retelling of the attempted group suicide as if my typifications are "second nature".

If I have immersed myself into a particular area of law for some years or decades, my peers will consider me as experienced. My opinion, however brief and coded, will command a substantial fee. But my experience is my experience *as an expert knower* who pictures or imagines indigenous experiences *after* they have occurred. I *post facto* assign a dominant sign to represent or indicate the signified event. Other experts may engage in dialogue, argue, speculate, predict or enforce my signs. Thus, I reproduce signs, not the event itself. My reproduction idealizes the indigenous event. Indeed, the event is dispersed, and my production of signs becomes the event. I need only cite a name such as *Guerin* or the Young Offenders Act and my fellow experts will just "know" a phalanx of "arguments" and doctrines associated with these names even before they hear about the indigenous experience about which I narrate a story. I uncover this nomenclature by searching for the grounds of *Guerin* or the source of authority of the Young Offenders Act. I join the grounds with other signs which represent a typification within which I fall as a barrister or solicitor. The latter in turn is said to authorize me to render a legal opinion or to represent a client before a court. If my peers in my office or opposing me in a courtroom challenge my interpretation of the dominant trait of the "facts", or if they challenge whether I am authorized to represent my client, I press on through the institutional signs which my fellow lawyers generally accept as authoritative. *Auctoritas, non veritas facit legem.* I search for the authority of my typification from historical sources higher in the court structure. Their signs may have been scripted at an earlier point in the discourse. My discourse may name the latter signs 'quasi-constitutional' or 'constitutional'. The more often that I find that other lawyers have deferred to the latter signs, the more assured am I that I have reached the closest expression of the spirit of the law.

The basic written text in the jurisdiction of Canada – the Constitution Act, 1867–present – for example, offers signs which awaken my legal consciousness. Any one phrase of the text has been the subject of debate amongst many earlier judges and lawyers. Section 91 of the Act, for example, provides that 'the exclusive Legislative Authority of the Parliament of Canada extends to all Matters coming within the Classes of Subjects next hereinafter enumerated; that is to say, – (24) Indians, and lands reserved for Indians… (28) The Criminal Law …'. But since their expulsion from the Arctic, juridical officials have failed to classify the residents of Davis Inlet as "Indians" because the residents had never consented to the supreme authority of the federal government and had insisted on their treaty rights as an independent nation. Similarly, s. 92 of the Constitution Act posits 'exclusive authority' to the provincial legislatures to make laws 'coming within the Classes of Subject' such as 'municipal institutions in the province' (8), 'property and civil rights in the province' (13), and 'generally all matters of a local and private nature' (16). But Davis Inlet is not a 'municipality' as categorized by the Municipal Act of Newfoundland, which Act had been enacted under the authority of s. 92(8) of the Constitution Act. Davis Inlet has not been juridically typified as a juridical person called a 'municipality'. Accordingly, the villagers are not legally entitled to the provincial support for public sewerage, public water, schools and all the other amenities of groups of residents who could be typified as a 'municipality' under the Act.

The reformulation of pain This "should" leave me unperturbed, as a lawyer, though. The concerns of Amnesty International or Aristotle or Eli Weisel are irrelevant in the transformation of the children's attempted suicide into legal language. We lawyers claim only to interpret *authoritative* texts, and the authority of one text must always be *author*ized. Such sources as the texts of Amnesty International or the UN Declaration of Social and Economic Rights do not lie in the line of authority within which I, as a juridical official, feel compelled to consider. I aspire to trace the strains of authority backwards from one source to another, always trying to reach an ultimate source or *arche*. The absence of such an *arche*, of course, drives me, as a lawyer, to *form*ulate the experiential world. Again, *auctoritas, non veritas facit legem*. Rarely will I be pressed to continually trace my sources to some final or ultimate foundation. If pressed, we may risk a constitutional crisis. Better to leave the foundation of my trace of justificatory grounds unspoken and unwritten. Indeed, if I come to envisage other events within the boundaries of my typifications, I may come to take the typifications as so real as to be of "a second nature". In the search for the authority of my typification of a reported event, the indigenous suffering of the residents of Davis Inlet becomes forgotten, lost, concealed inside and between my typifications. The referent is no longer the felt experience of an Inuit child with a biography. It lies entangled in a chain of signs which represent *my* spectre of the child as a generalized other to the secondary genre. Indeed, that the non-knower is even a child is forgotten. The past experiences of violent abuse against women, widespread alcoholism and attempted suicides by young and old alike – these indigenously experienced events no longer represent unique moments which particular human beings with a biography have experienced. Rather, the referents, being signs, *indicate typical* experiences. What the resident had experienced as concrete and what the resident had meant in a specific context is abstracted as I, a lawyer, participate in transforming the event into an anonymous, general fact category which compares a multiplicity of experiences with the sameness of that category. What had appeared context-specific to the point of seeming an unrepeatable unique experience to the villager becomes categorized as only one of many past and possible "fact" situations which arise in legal discourse. The individuality of the indigenous experience is lost. My significatory act itself becomes the event.

As a lawyer, I also *mean* my interpretation of the world just as do the residents theirs. I may bring my own professional experiences into the transformatory project. But my meaning goes to a second level which mediates between my own professional environing world and the signifying relations which I have learnt as a professional knower. The crucial issue for me as a lawyer is to categorize the *indirect* speech to which witnesses refer. I take the signifying relations of lawyers, not the residents of Davis Inlet, as authoritative. As I engage in dialogue with other lawyers in our search for the authority of our interpretations, the individual Inuit child with a biography slips from my face-to-face relations with others. My typifications lose the moments of anxiety, pain, shame, anger and frustration which the individual child may have meant when he or she spoke through his or her act of attempted suicide.

I face other lawyers too. Meaning becomes concrete for me as a lawyer as I too gain individual experiences with other lawyers as I engage in dialogue with them. I draw contextual meanings from the signifying relations which I take as *author*itative, as a lawyer. A new context arises – a context which lawyers embody, a context which disembodies the experiences of the Inuit child. I idealize the latter's experience by taking the authoritative signs of my professional, scientized language as the true/real. Thus, the children of the naming game are *de-faced*. Their experiences are disembodied. My production of their suffering is concealed.

My rhetoric with other lawyers confirms the resignification of the residents' everyday experiences. What began, prior to the lawyers' naming game, as a face-to-face cry for help in the first person, shifts into the third person once the legal process begins. As a lawyer, I simply do not say "I believe" or "I feel" or even "I am arguing". Rather, enclothed with black gown, I deferentially state "it is respectfully submitted to the court". I participate in objectifying the felt experiences of the residents of Davis Inlet. During the moment of individuality of pain, each child in Davis Inlet lives as an embodied "subject" who lives an instance with a biographical past and expectations for the future. But when my juridical utterance refers to the residents in the third person (such as do the pleadings and arguments of a lawyer or judge), my utterance neutralizes and objectifies.[28] I take the utterances of the residents – as others to the legal discourse – as a product rather than as an activity. Even the children become abbreviated substitutes for my "analysis of the facts". The residents are of the third person. The third person *represents* the unmarked member of a juridically authorized category. The typified member is only one of many subjects *within* the generalized category of juridical persons. The category of juridical person displaces the living subject with lived experiences. Even I become defaced. After all, I am an officer of the court – a juridical person. Only juridical persons count as the centre of my authoritative genre.

The concealment of my production of suffering is complete. The typification of the children at Davis Inlet comes *after* the children have meant their gestures of attempted suicide. My legal analysis subordinates life to categories whose signs I claim to be authoritative.[29] This enclosure of life precludes any active response from an addressee, such as the children of Davis Inlet, in advance and in principle. The experience of a particular child, before the legal discourse began its conquest, cannot correct or expand my own expectations, as a juridical official, unless the child as an excluded being recognizes the dominance of the sources or grounds external to the meaning-forming acts of us expert interpreters. The child is an excluded other to our juridical discourse. The excluded other is recognized *only* if I represent him or her through the chains of signs of the master discourse.

By defining one as a s. 91 or s. 92 federalism problem, a knower claims to know what juridical persons dwell inside and outside a legal discourse. The metaphysical order of the s. 91–s. 92 rhetoric assimilates even those who refuse to join into its assimilative journey. Juridical personhood swallows up the meaning-conferring subject.[30] Officials representing the legal discourse must consider as a threat any subject who resists its colonizing authority. Signs represent external objects. For the juridical discourse, the external objects are cognitive doctrines, rules and principles which emanate from, and which are directed towards, the mind. The body of the aggrieved is a remainder concealed within the concepts of the expert knower. The best that the expert knower's concepts can do is to classify, regulate and discipline the body of the aggrieved. This makes sense: because the body is a remainder, the juridical experts must ultimately force the body to recognize the authority of the secondary metaphysical order. The expert knowers may even redefine the outlaw's body as non-existent – that is, as a non-person without rights. This helps to explain why Patricia Williams compares legal discourse to a sausage-making machine.[31] The juridical officials in the sausage machine re-present a diversity of experiences which, in the end product, become uniform and the same with particular contents being undifferentiated. The meant objects of *individual* experiences of the particular beings remain unrecognized except through the legal categories which presuppose a sameness. We lawyers make the felt experiences of the Davis Inlets of our national and international societies into sausages through an analysis of cognitive objects. Because our peers think like us, we take the typifications as constitutive of the true/real. Suffering is produced cleanly. And our production of suffering is concealed inside that sanitized reality.

The Sanitized Pain during a Recession

Now, the reader may well reject my examples of the transformation of embodied meaning on the grounds that they are "public law" subjects – as if the public law were not really "law". The analytic lawyer, in particular, may view my examples as exceptions to the day-to-day practice of the secondary discourse. In order to address this objection I wish to turn to the resignification of harm to farmers and small businesspeople during the recession of 1980–83 in Canada and show how the non-knower's language remained alive, though concealed, inside the legal discourse.[32]

During the Canadian recession of the early 1980s, when the loans of many small businesspersons and farmers were 'called', the non-knower continued to express his or her harm through gestures and utterances in the privacy of his or her home. Such gestures included self-doubt, violence towards self and others, depression, racism, sexism and more. Through utterances and gestures, the non-knower might retell an experience: 'He beat me'; 'How can the Farm Loan program take my farm without any notice and after encouraging me to buy an air-conditioned tractor?'; 'I've been fucked!' But, as a lawyer, I hear such utterances as a lawyer, not as a non-knower. Yes, in the privacy of my office, I may gesture empathy and understanding towards the non-knower's plight, but I hear the utterance differently from him or her. I resituate his or her utterances into the chains of signs which I shall recognize: 'assault' in a Criminal Code, the 'reasonable time' doctrine of debtor/creditor law and the 'notice' provisions of a labour statute.

As soon as the non-knower begins to report events to me as a lawyer, I resituate the report into my signifying relations. The common law lawyer's magic situs for such a report, for example, is the longstanding doctrine of 'reasonable time'. During the nineteenth century, the term 'reasonable time' represented the legal principle that the banker had a legal duty to grant the debtor sufficient time to walk across his office and pull from a desk drawer the cash necessary to repay his loan when a banker demanded payment. By the late 1970s, expert knowers, especially in Canadian legal discourse, associated the term 'reasonable time' with another sign, *Lister*. *Lister* was more than the name of a litigant, however, for we knowers had situated *Lister* into another configuration of signs – specifically a six-point test setting out the circumstances when the call of a loan would be considered 'reasonable'. This six-point doctrine was represented by another sign, *Mr Boudloom* which typified "facts" that came within what the courts considered 'reasonable time'. By the late 1980s, the configurations surrrounding the term 'reasonable time' typified circumstances where a financial institution afforded a debtor several weeks' notice. On each occasion, the configuration of signs widened or narrowed the category of persons included under the typification. One's assets could be confiscated if they fell inside the boundaries of the doctrine. So, for example, whereas someone might be considered unprotected if, during 1980, he or she could not repay the loan within 20 minutes under the fact categories in *Mr Broadloom*, that very person might have been protected if he or she fell under the typification represented by the same term, 'reasonable time' as signified by *Whonnock Industries*.

However the term 'reasonable time' was interpreted by lawyers or judges, it signified one thing to the lawyer and quite another to the non-knower of legal terminology and grammar, whether a farmer or a social critic. To the lawyer, the phrase 'reasonable time' signified a special legal doctrine which authorized the lawyer or judge to justify a 'receivership'. But to the businessperson and the farmer as non-knowers, the same term, if expressed to them *meant* infra-family violence, unemployment, physical ailments and the general loss of self-respect. And to the observing social critic – also a non-knower of the legal discourse – the same term, 'reasonable time', meant the disruption of the family, the demise of rural communities, a negative rippling economic effect, the extraordinary rise in interest rates (of up to 28 per cent per annum for business loans), and many other social consequences. Moreover, even the doctrines represented by the sign 'reasonable time', presupposed that one possessed the financial means needed to enforce protection under the doctrines.

All these social, economic and financial factors impacted upon the felt experiences of the non-knower. The legal discourse, through its exclusions and inclusions, produced pain. Pain redoubled on to pain. The indigenous event, the call of one's loan pursuant to a demand contract, was retrospectively retold so as to resituate the pain as a signified event in a secondary narrative. The experiential body of the non-knower was forgotten inside the web. Yet, the non-knower's embodied experiences remained alive, though concealed, inside the enclosing boundaries represented by 'reasonable time'.

How, more precisely, did the legal discourse conceal its own production of suffering so well? The typified fact categories represented by the term, 'reasonable time', excluded two elements of the non-knower's experiential body. First, the non-knower's and the expert knower's experiences of time were concealed. The knower was preoccupied with a chronology of events and communications between the financial institution and debtor from the first signs of their partnership until the eventual repossession of an asset. Generally, the professional knower would organize the evidence, question the debtor on discovery and represent the evidence during a trial with a rigid adherence to such a chronology of events, moment by moment, day by day. Time would be measured by the clock. From the non-knower's experimental viewpoint, though, some isolated utterance by the creditor or some brief phone call might stand out amongst all the other moments of his or her recent experiences. Such an experienced time could not be measured. Indeed, the experienced moment might be so embedded in the debtor's consciousness that the debtor would link all other events, before and after the banker's phone call, to that single privileged moment. Reported judicial decisions do not describe the non-knower's long moments of intense anxiety, short moments of sharp psychic pain, and the exhausted silences which the non-knower and his or her family members experienced on the creditor's call of the loan.

The legal discourse concealed its own production of suffering in another way. The non-knower's experiences of space were concealed. The expert knower, situated in a conference room of accountants, lawyers, and bankers, might have been oblivious to the physical space in the conference room. Not so the debtor who had been presented with the 'consent to a receivership' form. The debtor's senses might have been overwhelmed by the cleanliness of the officials, their perfumes, the lightly textured carpet which required nightly cleaning, the original paintings on the wall, the dark clouds beyond the window, the solid walnut doors, the hierarchical seating of the officials and all the other trappings which went with the physical space of the conference room. Indeed, the non-knower might have intuited that the meeting space was emptied of other human beings. The sounds uttered from the officials might have been "understood" as just that: fragments of sounds. The space of the room might even have seemed as if the world were enclosing the non-knower's body.

In contrast with these experiences of time and space, the expert knower's cognate idea of 'reasonable time' measured time and space quantifiably and linearly. The doctrine of 'reasonable time' brought a metaphysical order to fragmentary experiences. First, the concepts associated with the transposing sign, such as 'reasonable time', enclose the non-knower's multiplicity of felt experiences. Second, a sign triggers hierarchies of evidence. Chains of signs allocated the admissibility, relevance, weight and credibility of the utterance accordingly. What the non-knower considered meaningful to his or her felt experiences, the judge or lawyer or legal scholar or police officer may well have excluded or given little weight, or consider self-serving, or rejected as a 'political' consideration or a 'policy' matter.

Secondary configurations of signs represented a metaphysical order which includes and excludes. Contrary to the early Barthes' view of a metalanguage, though, the metaphysical codes of the expert knowers were not self-creating; they needed the utterances of the non-knower in order to justify working on a chain gang – a gang on the chain of signs. The secondary discourse required the primary genres of the non-knower in order to "exist", however parasitically. Once the cognitive objects "existed" as signs, however, the expert knower could begin to consider the cognitive objects which the secondary signs represented as the true/real. The experiential body of the non-knower was assimilated into the concepts represented by the magic sign, 'reasonable time'. The felt experiences which the non-knower meant by his or her utterances dissipated.[33] Although the actors who lived through the primary and secondary genres might well have used similar vocabulary, the knower and non-knower configured such vocabulary within two very different intertextual combinations of signs with different associated objects.

More generally, if a judge chooses one lawyer's narrative over another's, the values and/or interests represented through the chains of signs in the first narrative "win" over the competing chain of signs. Similarly, a statute's signifiers "embody" a "winner". Both judgment and statute exclude as well as include.[34] Expert knowers struggle to dominate the signifying relations of other expert knowers. The expert knower privileges certain issues, signifies the issues in a certain context of secondary signifying relations (as a torts case rather than, say, a contracts case), recognizes the standing of a non-knower before the secondary genre, admits some reported speeches, excludes others, gives great weight to some and little weight to others, and hierarchizes the chains of signs according to their source (such as constitutional discourse over statutory, statutes over judicial precedents and judicial precedents over custom). The expert knower "uncovers" the signification of a secondary configuration by tracing it backwards historically in an effort to find the original intent of the first author who had written the text signifying the doctrine. The expert knower analyses the signified doctrines, clarifies their boundaries, and distinguishes the relevance of one configuration of signs vis-à-vis those of his or her antagonist. But because the expert knower frames his or her signifying relations as a neutral representation of the "facts", the empowering character of his or her signified concepts is immunized from serious critique. As Michael Shapiro remarks, a legal narrative prescripts a victim because its signifying relations produce silences and gaps before the victim is even signified.[35] The finality of a posited statute or judicial decision directs the expert knower to ignore these displaced silences and gaps. As an expert knower, I make the world. My imaginary reality precensors the meanings with which a non-knower has embodied his or her own utterances in a concrete social situation. I imagine the non-knower's pain and impersonate his or her suffering through the interrelated signs of my own secondary discourse. Indeed, I mirror my own genre's concepts as I signify in the name of the non-knower's pain. My impersonation therefore produces a disembodied event.

The Disembodiment of a Meant World

The social relations between knower and non-knower lack a dialogic character. The legal narrative, as I have described it, encloses the embodied meanings of the non-knower. Emile Benveniste hints as to why one should describe the internment cases, the Davis Inlet story or the events of the Canadian depression as a narrative rather than as a dialogue. Dialogic partners employ personal grammatical forms (such as the personal pronoun "I"), demonstrative pronouns and contemporaneous adverbs such as "here", "now", "yesterday", "to-day" and "tomorrow". In contrast, the judges in the internment cases described events authorizing the internment anonymously, in the third person. They centred the narrative about texts authored by others: the military commander, the president, and the Congress in the one case, the parliament and Newfoundland legislature in the second, and the judicially created doctrines in the third.[36] Furthermore, whereas a dialogue is characterized by the present, present perfect and the future verb tenses, the judges expressed themselves in the imperfect and the pluperfect tenses[37] which projected an objectivity and historicity absent from a dialogue. More generally, evidentiary rules, such as the rule against opinion evidence, reinforced the objectivity and "pastness" of the narrated events. In the appellate judgments which I have examined above, the Justices described the event in a distanced manner and as if the "facts" were uncontrollable. We lawyers and judges protect our authoritative discourse. Indeed, we are unable to understand how the non-knowers experience their indigenous pain as we reconfigure our signs for pain into a master discourse. The best which we can do is to picture the non-knower as an other to our discourse. As we picture the non-knower we envisage ourselves. We synthesize a complete coherent spectacle which includes all possible beings even when it excludes them. The spectacle lacks the personal pronouns and present tense which characterize the context-specific meanings which Messrs Hirabayashi and Korematsu, the Davis Inlet children and the depression families had indigenously experienced. Appellate judgments reinforce the past and objective character of the grand narrative about the experiences of non-knowers.

Although, from time to time Messrs Hirabayashi and Korematsu no doubt initiated utterances of their own in the privacy of law offices and although the debtors in the recession cases most certainly did, the judges write not only as if they are narrating a past event but also as if they do not, and cannot, control that past event even though their own chains of signifying relations become the event. More generally, in the *Hirabayashi* and *Korematsu* cases, the judges speculate as to what evidence the military must have had before them, as if this silent evidence autonomously spoke.[38] Other authoritative texts become the referent. The representer pictures the narrative as if it were objective, neutral and impartial. The objectivist and passive style of the judgments remind the reader that the judges – and, indeed, the lawyers – are not a party to the narrated events. And yet, as Hayden White explains, no one really speaks outside of a story.[39] It is not without reason that such phrases as "I believe that" or "I feel that" are absent from a lawyer's pleadings and oral argument. The judges just let the structure of the story continue as if an absent author enunciated the story.[40] Passive voice. Copula verbs. Such grammatical forms contrast with the action of context-specific meanings in primary genres. The pain and suffering of the 120 000 citizens and immigrants remained unexpressed as the antagonists inside the legal discourse searched for an authoritative enclosure of the pain. The non-knowers were already typified before they could even tell their stories to their lawyers. They were inevitably entangled in a language which the juridical narratives reaffirmed, defended and enforced.

Messrs Hirabayashi and Korematsu, the Davis Inlet children and the recession debtors were transformed into juridical persons with rights and duties which our narratives configured. The judges, lawyers, military commander, social workers, bankers, receivers and police officers were also juridical persons. Interestingly, the legal discourse displaced the juridical persons, Messrs Hirabayashi and Korematsu, with the military commander as the centre of the narrative. The juridical person's identity in the trace for authority is the situs for an 'agonistics' – or rhetorical struggle – between lawyers, just as Hayden White describes of the situs of the historical event in a historical narrative.[41] Lawyers succeed in the examination and cross-examination when witnesses reinforce the lawyer's narrative order of the signifying relations.[42] Indeed, the military commander had initially insisted that his racist comments should not be altered because, unaltered, they would support the government's legal case before the courts. The juridical person – not the individual subject with a biography – was the actor, author and authorizer of all action in the narrative. The non-knower, as a being with a biography, had to act as if he or she were a juridical person: ignorance of the discourse is no excuse, for example. Indeed, each non-knower was presumed to act reasonably at all times and with full knowledge of the secondary signifying relations. Even the military commander's original 1942 *Report* was displaced into a transformed and transforming secondary narrative of which the (substituted) *Report* was only a part. The lawyers' representations of events functioned to make for such a transformation. The *Report* was an object which lawyers re-formed and utilized in their trace for authority.

The narrator/lawyers and judges acted as the *agents of the narrative*. The narrative about Messrs Hirabayashi and Korematsu just happened; it was beyond their control. Once it began to unfold, it read like an overbearing, extremely complicated machine which was so overprogrammed that it could not stop without enormous effort from an agent outside the discourse. In general, once a lawsuit begins, a plaintiff may have only one or two openings to settle the dispute before the pretrial conference. Even then, the plaintiff may have to bypass the overprogrammed legal procedures in order to reach a settlement with the defendent. In the narrative about Mr Korematsu, the sign, Hirabayashi, signified importance because Hirabayashi now represented a juridically defined generalized other. Paradoxically, the reader loses touch with Messrs Hirabayashi and Korematsu as individuals with biographies, and with the debtors in the recession cases, as the institutions reproduced events. The narrative of the 120 000 interned residents became uncontrolled (because the narrators brought the narrative structure along) and yet controlled (because the narrative absorbed an imaginary character, the juridified person, which the narrators seemed to control).

Ironically, although the judges narrated as if the facts and circumstances of the case were posited external to the judges and beyond their control, their discourse, which configured also the judges as juridical persons, transformed the meant objects of the internees, children and debtors. I demonstrated in Chapter 2, as well, how even a professional legal training works to transform a law student into a juridical officer with special duties and privileged rights which the secondary genre recognizes. The continuing narrative, whether about internment or child abuse or a murder, offers no opening for the listener/client to intercede. One utterance is lifted into a secondary signifying context and, from there, to an utterance of the juridical agent. Each resignified utterance leads from the previous sentence in a continuous monologue, at least with regard to the non-knower. The juridical agent's utterance does not evoke a response from the *other* addressees: there are pauses in the civil and criminal legal processes. But the pause in the continuity of a legal narrative involves a linear time which can be measured on a clock; it lacks the experiential component of the indigenous event being narrated. The intensity of a pain knows no chronology of events: one moment may be privileged to the exclusion of earlier and later events. The pause which a judge allows in a witness's story is a grammatical, not an experiential, pause. An experiential pause would offer a moment for the witness to *respond* as an addressee. Without such an active response, we are left with an absent invisible author of our narratives. And 120 000 'persons of Japanese ancestry' in one country and 20 000 'persons of the Japanese race' in another may be validly interned. Some may even be authoritatively relocated or exiled. Another community may be uplifted and then forgotten for 30 years without any semblance of the social or economic conditions of a modern industrial state. And the experiential body of the debtor and his or her dependents may be expunged from the record.

Notes

1 Order-in-Council PC 7335 dated 15 December 1945.

2 On 24 January 1947.

3 Ibid., 237.

4 Peter Irons ed., *Justice Delayed: The Record of the Japanese American Internment Cases* (Middletown, Conn.: Wesleyan University Press, 1989): 105.

5 Jean-François Lyotard, *The Differend: Phrases in Dispute*, Theory and History of Literature, vol. 46 (Minneapolis: University of Minnesota Press, 1988): especially 12–13, 22, 24, 27. I do not intend to analogize the plight of the internees with the context (the Holocaust) with which Lyotard was concerned, although both situations manifest the loss of the body in the official discourses.

6 See, for example, the letter by Kinzie Tanaka to Inspector McGibbon, RCMP reprinted in Yon Shimizu, *The Exiles* (Wallaceburg: Shimizu Consulting and Publishing, 1993): 136.

7 Maryka Omatsu, *Bittersweet Passage: Redress and the Japanese Canadian Experience* (Toronto: Between the Lines, 1992): 33.

8 See, for example, Ken Adachi, *The Enemy That Never Was*, intro. Timothy Findley; updated Roger Daniels (Toronto: McClelland & Stewart, 1991); Yon Shimizu, *The Exiles: An Archival History of the World War II Japanese Road Camps in British Columbia and Ontario* (Wallaceburg: Shimizu Consulting and Publishing, 1993); Muriel Kitagawa and Roy Miki eds., *This is my Own: Letters to Wes and Other Writings on Japanese Canadians, 1941–1948* (Vancouver: Talonbooks, 1985); Yuko Shibata, Shoji Matsumoto, Rintaro Hayashi and Shotaro Iida, *The Forgotten History of the Japanese-Canadians: The Role of Japanese Canadians in the Early Fishing Industry in B.C. and An Annotated Bibliography*, vol. 1 (Vancouver: New Sun Books, 1977); Maryka Omatsu, note 7 *supra*; Takeo Ujo Nakano with Leatrice Nakano, *Within the Barbed Wire Fence: A Japanese Man's Account of His Internment in Canada* with Afterword by W. Peter Ward (Toronto: University of Toronto Press, 1980); Patricia E. Roy, J.L. Granatstein, Masako Lino and Hiroko Takamura, *Mutual Hostages: Canadians and Japanese during the Second World War* (Toronto: University of Toronto Press, 1990); Ann Gomer Sunahara, *The Politics of Racism: The Uprooting of Japanese Canadians during the Second World War* (Toronto: James Lorimer, 1981).

9 I describe the moments of the interpretive act in a Canadian context in 'The

Transformation of Meaning: Legal Discourse and the Canadian Internment Camps' in *International Journal for the Semiotics of Law*, vol. 9, no. 27 (1997): 227–56.

10 *Hirabayashi* v. *United States* 320 US 81, 106.

11 Ibid., 137–9.

12 Commission on Wartime Relocation and Internment of Civilians, *Personal Justice Denied* (Washington, DC: December 1982): 6–7 and reprinted in Irons, note 4 *supra*,108–9.

13 *Hirabayashi* v. *United States* 320 US 81, 94.

14 Ibid., 94.

15 Ibid., 145.

16 *Korematsu* v. *United States*. Petition for Writ of Error Coram Nobis, US District Court for the Northern District of California, 19 January 1983, as reprinted in Irons, note 4 *supra*, 128.

17 Irons, note 4 *supra*, 129.

18 Ibid., 137.

19 *Hirabayashi* v. *United States* 320 US 81, per Douglas, 109.

20 Commission on Wartime Relocation and Internment of Civilians, *Report: Personal Justice Denied* (Washington DC, 1982): 3.

21 Ibid., 35.

22 *In re Ah Yup*, 1 Fed. Cases 223 (Cir. Ct, D. Calif. 1878) per Circuit Judge Sawyer.

23 *Ozawa* v. *United States*, 260 US 178 (1922).

24 *Report*, note 20 *supra*, 31.

25 *Hirabayashi* v. *United States* 320 US 81, 106.

26 Ibid., 111

27 Dan A. Soberman, *Report to the Canadian Human Rights Commission on the Complaints of the Inuit People Relocated from Iniskjuak and Pond Inlet, to Grise Ford and Resolute Bay in 1953 and 1955* (Ottawa: Canadian Human Rights Commission, 1991); Government of Newfoundland, Labrador, *Background Notes on the Community of Davis Inlet* (St Johns: Government of Newfoundland, 24 February 1993); *Meeting Notes of Premier Wells' Meeting with Chief Prote Poker of Davis Inlet, 18 January 1991.*

28 This point is drawn from Benveniste's comments about the I/thou relationship during a dialogue. See Emile Benveniste, *Problems in General Linguistics* (Mary Elizabeth Meek trans.; Coral Gables, Florida: University of Miami Press, 1971; Miami Linguistics Series, No. 8): 218, 220, 221.

29 Emmanuel Levinas discusses this generally in *Totality and Infinity: An Essay on Exteriority* (Alphonso Lingis trans.; Pittsburgh: Duquesne University Press, 1969; Philosophical Series, vol. 24): 168.

30 Levinas makes this claim against Platonic philosophy generally. See Emmanuel Levinas, 'Time and the Other' in Sean Hand ed., *The Levinas Reader* (Oxford: Basil Blackwell, 1989): 53.

31 Patricia Williams, *The Alchemy of Race and Rights* (Cambridge, Mass.: Harvard University Press, 1991): ch. 6.

32 The research in this section is drawn from William E. Conklin and Jodi J. Morrison 'Public Issues in a Private Law World: The Appointment of a Receiver as a Case Study' in *Osgoode Hall Law Journal*, vol. 26, no. 1 (1988): 45–93.

33 That order is unstable so long as there remains the possibility that another metalanguage might represent the last one. This may help to explain why, through the doctrines of precedent and legislative supremacy, judges and legislators have found it important to ensure that a judicial decision is 'final'.

34 See generally, Michel Foucault, 'The Order of Discourse' in Michael Shapiro ed., *Language and Politics* (London: Basil Blackwell, 1984).

35 Michael Shapiro, *The Politics of Representation* (Madison: University of Wisconsin Press, 1988): 18–19.

36 Emile Benveniste, note 28 *supra*, 210–11. Also see Gerard Genette, 'Boundaries of Narrative' in *New Literary History*, vol. 8 (1976–77): 1–13, 8–9.
37 Benveniste adds the preterite tense as characteristic of a narrative.
38 See Gerard Genette, 'Boundaries of Narrative' in *New Literary History*, vol. 8, no. 1 (1976): 8 for an elaboration of this point more generally with respect to narratives.
39 Hayden White, *The Content of the Form: Narrative Discourse and Historical Representation* (Baltimore: Johns Hopkins University Press, 1987): x.
40 Julia Kristeva, *The Kristeva Reader* (Toril Moi ed., Oxford: Basil Blackwell, 1986): 46.
41 Hayden White, 'The Value of Narrativity in the Representation of Reality' in *Critical Inquiry*, vol. 7 (1980–81): 5–27, esp. at 6–10, 16–20. Also see Jean-François Lyotard, *Just Gaming* (trans. Wlad Godzich; Samuel Weber afterword; Minneapolis: University of Minnesota Press, 1985; Theory and History of Literature, vol. 20): 81, 102, 104–5.
42 Julia Kristeva makes this point generally about the subject in a narrative in 'The System and the Speaking Subject' in *The Kristeva Reader*, note 39 *supra*, 28.

4 Does the Knower Face External Constraints?

The monologic character of the secondary legal genre raises the question whether external objects really do constrain a juridical agent. For this issue, I wish to turn to the environing world of the professional knower. If the non-knower *embodies* his or her signs as he or she re-presents an indigenously experienced harm, does not the expert knower also embody the secondary genre's signs with prejudgments drawn from his or her own experiences and expectations as a professional knower? What role do the experiences of the professional knower actually play in passively responding to the given external objects? Is a statute or precedent binding beyond the control of the professional knower? Why does the knower frame his or her configurations of signs in terms of the authority of an absent object, a doctrine, rule, principle, political theory or the "facts and circumstances of the case"? Does the knower identify with the secondary genre so that there seems to be an 'immediacy' between knower and genre? Is the immediacy so apparent to the knower that any one statute or judgment or legal opinion or act of enforcement or "fact of a Case" *seems* to be posited in an objective world? Does that appearance of a posited statute or "fact" or the like seem necessary, natural and beyond the control of the knower? Does this appearance of a posited external world occur at the very moment that the knower embodies the posited statute, judgment or "fact" with his or her own previous experiences, his or her own prejudgments and expectations? Are the "facts of a case" givens? Are the secondary signifying relations autonomous vis-à-vis any knower or interpreter? Does the secondary legal genre really constitute a self-referential system of externally posited constraints?

Posited Constraints

The analytic positivism, which has informed the professional knower, assumes that an external Object, beyond the interpreter, stands alone as the source of all signification. The juridical agent's interpretive act gains its authority by being rationally linked to such an object. The absent object may be a cognitive typification in a statute or judicial precedent. The object may be a "fact of the case". The object functions as the grounds for the privileging of one sign over another and is believed to be measurable in time and space. The legal interpreter is preoccupied with the belief that the object exists "out there", separate from the interpreter. All legal analysis inside the secondary genre, it is believed, begins with such an external object which is believed to constrain one's interpretation of a text or event. As a consequence, the interpreter is passive with regard to the external source of knowledge.

The Agent's Movement Towards the External Object

The externality of the object draws the interpreter *to* it. The interpreter reacts to the object. Because the juridical agent lacks the object, he or she desires it. Such a desire drives the knower to reach out to gain access to the object. H.L.A. Hart claimed, for example, that a 'core meaning' or essence inheres in any word and that, without such a core meaning, lawyers would be unable to communicate with each other. Hans Kelsen defined a posited law as an act of will which a juridical organ directs towards an object. The agent's trace of signs towards some founding object, Kelsen and Hart claim, validates an utterance by a legal official as authoritative. Even Ronald Dworkin posits an external Object, an all-encompassing, cohesive purified theory of the laws, as the legitimizing source of all authored laws – "the law beyond law". The ultimate foundation of legal authority lacks a further object to which it may refer: it lacks a referent. The foundation of legal authority lacks a grounding. Even if the foundation is associated with social practices, as it is with Hart, the foundation possesses the character of an "in itself" because the foundation – immediate judicial practices – cannot be reached within the configurations of legal signs. Its situs as external to the secondary legal genre makes the foundation final. Put differently, the foundation is absent from texts which are posited as ordinary laws. It is believed to transcend the secondary legal genre even when its theorists claim that the laws are posited by human agents, that the grounding of authority pre-exists posited norms and rules, and that all laws are accessible from within the secondary genre.

The crux of legal signification in the secondary legal genre lies in the sign's *representation* of an externally posited object. It is assumed that a sign, or chain of signs, represents an externally posited object. Because the object is absent from the juridical agent and the agent's sign, the best that the juridical agent can do is to approximate the object by representing it with a sign. Even an invisible doctrine or principle, once conceived, is represented through a sign. Indeed, the doctrine cannot be conceived without a sign. So the sign also represents the posited "facts" by setting out cognitive boundaries which standardize or typify the facts. This explains why judges and lawyers refer to the *Oakes* facts or the principle of *Brown* v. *Board of Education* or why juristic agents incorporate a legal doctrine, such as 'the substantial interests test' or the 'reasonable time doctrine' or the 'duty of care' principle. Oakes and Brown are more than just well known names of persons who litigated in two different countries. Their names carry magic in the respective legal discourses because the mere citation of their names ushers forth an aura of authority and definitiveness about the cognitive object of their citation. The name signifies. The sign comes to represent a particular doctrine which the professional knower can trace through differentiating chains of other signs to some presupposed ultimate, yet absent, foundation. As the knower differentiates between signs, the knower imagines or represents the external object.

The Picture of the External Objects

All statutes, regulations, legal doctrines, "facts" and negotiation procedures are represented by signs which code a narrative about the "facts and circumstances of a case" or about the overall "intent" of a statute or constitutional text. The coded narrative makes sense to the expert knower. Because the representation mediates the object and the interpreter, the best that the representation can do is to typify what the object might look like by assigning a sign to represent it. The typification joins the sign to the agent's picture or image of the object. The interpreter is constrained by his or her image of that object. Even the non-knower's recounting of a story is pictured through the knower's familiar signs. Neither the representation nor the cohesive picture of the object can reach the witness's own recounting of his or her pain as the non-knower had experienced the pain. Nor can the non-knower's representation of his or her own story reach an immediacy with the non-knower's embodied meanings in a former indigenous event, since the latter dwells beyond the knower's gaze. The embodied meanings of the non-knower are either forgotten, being beyond the gaze, or are idealized within the typified boundaries of the knower's general picture of the non-knower's experience. The professional knower's picture thereby encloses the non-knower's embodied meanings. The signs of the representation ideologically encode the non-knower's story. Thus, the specific meaning context of the non-knower is transformed retrospectively into a signifying context through a representation which intellectualizes the non knower's stories. This intellectualization disembodies the non-knower as an experiential being, transforming him or her into a sign for a juridical person who represents some special object to the knower.

The Experience of the Body

The issue which we now face, then, is 'what role do the experiences of the professional knower play in the configuration of signs?' The problematic of legal interpretation is that if one believes that a posited object, such as a statute, dicta, regulation, other cognitive standard or "fact" constrains the juristic agent, that agent is subordinated to the object. The juridical agent reacts to the object and must be content to passively envision or picture the object through representations. The agent's forestructures and expectations of meaning may be ignored, if not denied, because what matters – indeed, what may even constitute "matter" or the physical–chemical mass of nature or a social event – becomes the juridical official's spectre of an inaccessible object. The agent even perceives a subject as a posited absent object to be observed and analysed in a science of psychology. Since even the agent's prior experiences and present expectations embody such an absent object, the knower's signification lops off such experiences. The knower's constitution of the absent object, as externally posited, excises the most important factor in the interpretive act – the interpreter's prior experiences which he or she reads *into* such a constitution of meaning. There is more to the juristic agent's understanding of what he or she takes to be "laws" than the sign, the object signified, and the circulation and reproduction of chains of signs. Lawyers em*body* the signs with narratives which their peers recognize as authoritative just as the non-knower embodies his or her story with signs which, because of his or her prior experiences, *mean* something to him or her.

The secondary legal genre has a very special absent object which all its agents share. Professional knowers in such a discourse search for one final object which can found or ground all others. In the quest for the *authority* of a configuration, the agent's embodiment is cancelled, forgotten, lost, put to the side. Although a sign possesses a bodily component in a physical sense, the trace of chains of signs to some transcendent *arche* works to conceal the phenomenal body.[1]

The phenomenal body of both the knower and non-knower cannot be situated in time or place. The litigation lawyer, one should recall, methodically and chronologically questions a witness from the early minutes of the witness's involvement with an alleged event to its end. Similarly, the lawyer may question a witness as to what was said and where it was said. The questioning presupposes a linear direction to the time and space of the witness's experience. The examination presupposes a start and finish to the event being re-counted. All this contrasts with the unquantifiable sense of time and place which the witness may have experienced during an indigenously experienced event.

Take a sexual assault, for example. To the sexual assault victim, there may be one moment, perhaps even a split second, around which the non-knower organizes her time – indeed, her life – thereafter. After that moment, her life has radically changed: distrust replaces trust, self-doubt displaces self-confidence, hate replaces love. So too, the victim may well organize all her thoughts and experiences about a flash of light from an automobile glimpsed as her attacker pinned her to the ground behind a hedge. She may well have experienced space as the attacker's particular cologne – a scent which now triggers nausea when she smells it on another man. Like the debtor during the repression of 1980–83, the non-knower experiences time and space in a manner which cannot be measured against the external standard of a clock. The professional knower's effort to situate the non-knower in terms of a measurable time and space takes for granted that time and space are external objects beyond them both. As the non-knower's experiences are reconfigured through legal analysis, she becomes an object of the interpreter and a non-knower to the legal discourse itself. The non-knower, as an externally posited object to the knower, is rationally connected with an authoritative discourse. And that discourse, in turn, is authoritative because, as with legal doctrines and the "facts of the case", the knower presupposes that he or she knows how to situate the non-knower within representations which, if pressed, can be traced to a foundation of the discourse. As the experiential meanings of the non-knower are concealed inside the secondary signifying relations, the latter lose the life which the non-knower's experiences brought into her story. To the non-knower, the transfiguration of her story seems to be a distant dead object, beyond her control. Yet, at the very moment of transformation, the immeasurability of the non-knower's time and space reinforces the legal discourse's projection of the object as a given. Moreover, the lawyers' discourse *about* the non-knower is dialogic vis-à-vis lawyers but monologic via-à-vis non-lawyers.

The Absent Foundation

If an absent foundation figures so importantly in legal discourse, why does it do so? To this issue, Martin Heidegger (1889–1976) offered an initial insight about Western metaphysics generally. In his classic essay, 'The End of Philosophy and the Task of Thinking',

Heidegger asks '[w]hat task is reserved for thinking at the end of philosophy?'[2] Philosophy has been unable to ask that question because it has hitherto been entrapped in metaphysics, he suggests. What distinguishes metaphysics? Heidegger argues that metaphysics, just like the trace of authority in legal discourse, searches for a grounding or *arche* in first principles which govern how one lives. A search for a final grounds characterizes the trace of precedents, statutes, doctrines, rules, principles and other standards in a modern legal discourse. The trace seeks a foundation which is believed to pre-exist the trace of configurations of signs. For Hans Kelsen, as noted above, the foundation dwells in an act of thought which, in contrast with an act of will which Kelsen calls a norm, is not directed towards any other referent. In like vein, H.L.A. Hart claims that the foundation of the concept of law dwells in "unspoken" judicial practices which later judges recognize through secondary rules. The Western tradition of metaphysics, Heidegger argues, has presupposed that beings originate in just such an unwritten transcendent foundation, before thought and language. Metaphysics aims to bring beings *to* the silent foundation. If one ever reached the presence of the foundation, such a presence would "end" philosophy in that philosophers would no longer need to represent conceptions.

Heidegger

The problem which metaphysics confronts, according to Heidegger, is that although philosophy, like legal discourse, attempts to reach the presence of such an unwritten foundation, philosophy can only do so through *representations* of the foundation. Philosophers represent conceptions with reasons. Such conceptions represent the originary moment, before concepts and before writing, when one's being was presented.[3] The task of thinking, then, is to unconceal the representations of the originary foundation of all thought. If philosophers could do so, they would reach a "clearing" without representations.

In his later works Heidegger believed that poetry could succeed in unconcealing such a metaphysics.[4] The thrust of his early works, though, suggests that one can retrieve the concealed beginnings of philosophy by tracing representational thought backwards through the history of philosophy to the moment when philosophers were not preoccupied with representations. According to Heidegger,[5] the early Greeks before Plato focused upon just such a presence of being. Plato changed such a project by searching for the Form of the Good through representations. If one could unconceal the deeply held representations of Western metaphysics, Heidegger argued, one could reach a clearing, and such a clearing would constitute a 'primal phenomenon'.[6] A representation excluded persons situated external to the represented concept but also included others inside such metaphysical boundaries. In order to exclude and include, philosophy needed an opening before representations began to exclude and include. In other words, to unconceal representations of a moment of silent presence, one must think outside the rational and outside the irrational. Such thinking would end philosophy's search for an end or *arche*.

Early Analytic Legal Positivism

The tradition of analytic positivism demonstrates Heidegger's insight that a foundation must be absent in order to finalize the trace of signs. With the Romans, lawyers began to search for the presence of just such a foundation. The foundation was believed to grant *auctoritas* to a juridical agent's action. A rational nexus to the *auctoritas* excluded statutes and official acts which were *ultra vires* and included those which were *intra vires*. The foundation finalized all posited enactments. Without the foundation, any one statute or official act would be a mere fragment – transient and unstable. Both Augustine and Aquinas continued the quest for a transcendent origin of all authority. With the early modern common law lawyers, such as Edward Coke, the "existence" of a legal rule is "confirmed" by the lawyer, learned from 'long Study, Observation and Experience', as Coke had held on more than one occasion.[7] When King James I claimed, in *Prohibitions del Roy*, that he himself could resolve legal disputes because 'the law was founded upon reason, and that he and others had reason, as well as Judges':

> ...true it was, that God had endowed his Majesty with excellent science, and great endowments of nature; but His Majesty was not learned in the laws of his realm of England, and causes which concern the life, or inheritance, or goods, or fortunes of his subjects, are not to be decided by natural reason but by the artificial reason and judgment of law, which law is an act which requires long study and experience, before that a man can attain to the cognizance of it.[8]

Any effort by the King to contradict the 'artificial reason' of the judges was held 'utterly void', Coke held more than once. In a note to one judgment Coke added that if the King so acted, he 'utterly' contravened 'reason' as well as law. For, as Coke and others held in the infamous *Dr Bonham's Case*, the artificial reasoning of the judges 'will controul Parliament, and sometimes judge them to be utterly void'.[9]

Even Coke's rival, Thomas Hobbes, sought to ground civil laws in some ultimate foundation which, for Hobbes, dwelled in a state of nature. Hobbes described the originary legislators in the state of nature as 'authors'. Once the authors agreed to covenants amongst themselves, the juridical agents of the state were 'actors'. The acts of actors were authoritative if an expert knower, living in the web of the common laws, could trace all juridical acts to the great Leviathan and, ultimately to the covenants of the authors in the state of nature. In one of his tracts, *A Dialogue Between a Philosopher and a Student of the Common Laws of England*,[10] Hobbes introduced the notion of 'the spirit' or 'life' of the laws. The 'spirit of the laws' went to the *authoritativeness* of rules which 'actors' 'pen' in civil society. Hobbes' Philosopher emphasized that '[i]t is not Wisdom, but Authority that makes a Law'.[11] Indeed, authoritative laws were *antecedent* to justice.[12]

Modern Analytic Legal Positivism

Early modern legal practice and legal thought manifested Heidegger's insight concerning the end of thinking in Western metaphysics. Of course, a juridical agent's reference to some social contract is rare today, though not unknown. Nevertheless, the search for some originary foundation to authorize legal reasoning continued into contemporary times. John Austin and Jeremy Bentham sought the authority of a juridical agent in the enactment of some sovereign author. In his early writings Bentham attributed the legislature as such an author. In his later writings, he described 'the People' in such terms. Yet, with respect to both final archemedian points, Bentham can be found acknowledging that one final concept, 'the greatest good of the greatest number', functions to authorize good from bad enactments by 'the People' or the legislature. That concept has no further justificatory object. The concept is an intrinsic good, valued in and for itself. Unlike an instrumental norm which an author wills, the foundation of all norms, according to Hans Kelsen, is a presupposed act 'of thought' which is not directed towards any object. Such an act of thought stands on its own without being dependent upon some higher object. Legislators and judges represent the act of thought through their own acts of will. H.L.A. Hart also gave an intrinsic character to the foundation of all primary and secondary rules: he described the foundation as 'unstated'. Juridical agents 'recognize' the foundation when they posit a 'rule of recognition' to justify the authoritativeness of all other primary and secondary rules. They can, at best, only approximate the foundation through a rule of recognition. Such a rule recognizes the foundation retrospectively.

Allow me to privilege one other legal theorist whose works exemplify Heidegger's insight about the search for an *arche* in Western thought. In his *Law's Empire*, Ronald Dworkin claims that legal authority dwells in the background political theory of a constitution. A mythic judge, Hercules, alone possesses the ability to gain a knowledge of the background theory and another mythic judge, Hermes, acts as a messenger from Hercules to the lesser lawyers. The best which lawyers can do is to shift back and forth between a text and the background theory in order to approximate the best application of the theory to the circumstances before the judge. Lawyers search for a cohesive, unified narrative about the Constitution in their resolution of a problem. That search, Dworkin posits, presupposes 'a law beyond the law'. Just such a search continues the project of metaphysics which, Heidegger argues, has permeated Western philosophy.

The external foundation of legal authority – the state of nature, the 'idea' of the 'greatest good of the greatest number', the *Grundnorm*, the 'unspoken' judicial practices, the 'law beyond the law' – functions as a radical other to the trace of posited laws. Such a foundation, the great theorists of legal positivism have insisted again and again, pre-exists the juristic agent's project. The identity of a legal system is believed to dwell in that external foundation. Kelsen went so far as to suggest that a change in the spectre of such a foundation constituted a 'revolution'. The juristic agent *desires* to be *present* with the foundation. Why else would lawyers work so hard to gain an encyclopaedic grasp of all efforts to reach the foundation of authority? The founding moment of a legal order brings the lawyer to a moment of presence and, at that moment, the lawyer need no longer represent the foundation: one's presence in the originary foundation of the trace of posited laws constitutes the other to posited laws. The legal positivist project manifests the very endeavour which Heidegger has attributed to the tradition of Western metaphysics.

Of course, Heidegger believed that there was a moment in Western culture when philosophers met an originary presence face-to-face without the aid of represented concepts. Although I do not wish to take on Heidegger's claim about the presencing philosophy of *moira* in early Greek philosophy here,[13] it is important to recognize that Heidegger's search for just such an originary presence, before the representations of thought, presupposes that all philosophy must be grounded in the presence of such a foundation.

The Spirit of the Laws

What, then, is the character of the originary presence towards which knowers direct their signified objects? If one believes that a rule is authored by a legislature or judge, the professional knower is drawn towards the external object which a text's phrase represents. The author's phrase *refers* to a distant object beyond text and author. A statute or regulation or 'reasons for a decision' refer to objects; these objects are usually typifications or categories. Likewise, a judgment, which summarizes the evidence in a trial refers to the event which the evidence, in turn, is believed to represent. The ordinary legal text represents an object as a referent. Hart argues that statements about primary rules refer to a rule of recognition as the source or ultimate criterion of validity of the rules. The object to which primary rules refer is *external* to the primary rules. In this case, according to Hart, the referent is an 'unstated judicial practice' which primary rules can only approximate.[14] Even a rule of recognition is *about* a further object – namely, the 'unstated judicial practices'.[15] Now, the foundation itself does *not* refer to some further object. If it did, the foundation would not be a foundation: it would not finalize, for there would still be some further object "out there" beyond the foundation. What had been taken as a foundation would be better described as an intermediate or second-order rule which judicial officials intend as a meant object. A founding criterion of validity, to be final, must lack a further object as a referent.[16]

The Problematic of an Absent Foundation

Unable to know the object to which the foundation refers (because the foundation lacks such a referent), the professional knowers of legal objects have a problem. For legal authority in a modern state, influenced by the juridical stoicism of the Romans, is associated with a foundation or ultimate source or *arche*. But that source, to be a final foundation, must be objectless: it must lack a referent. Notwithstanding his or her inability to experience the lost moment of immediacy with the foundation of authoritative rules, the expert knower claims to know which signs are authoritative and which are not – a claim which derives from the knower's ability to signify the former, silent, unspoken, presupposed presence before historically contingent authors began to represent the moment through signs. Because the genre-like character of legal discourse holds out a monopoly to such 'knowledge', it is a quick, yet subtle, shift for the 'knower' to consider a sign to be binding on him or herself and on all other persons to whom the author intends the text to apply. Or so Kelsen, Hart and others assume.

The need to find a finality to the seeming interminable trace of historically authored texts necessitates a moment of presence which no juridical agent can admit to knowing. That moment is a moment of purity, untainted by the ad hoc, social contingencies of a historical author. But the lack of knowledge of such an originating moment drives the professional knowers on and on in their imperial quest to represent the social and the *in itself* alike. The professional knower of the signs of a modern legal discourse is forever unhappy because he or she can never reach the originating foundation of a legal order, since, if he or she did admit to doing so, his or her authored laws and interpretation of such authored laws could no longer be considered finalized and therefore authoritative.

The Vision of the Foundation

The best that a professional knower can do in the search to 'know' the external, objectless foundation, is to *picture* or *envision* the foundation by representing the foundation through an interconnecting web of signs. This is the moment when the Roman notion of an 'author' enters into Kelsen's and Hart's legal analysis. For the professional knower fills the vacuum, left by an absent, objectless foundation, by drawing a vague figure as the ultimate creator or originator of the absent foundation. A picture delineates boundaries. Boundaries include and exclude, as I showed in Chapter 2. The boundaries *form* a shape. The shape is vague and transparent until the knowers fill in the details of the picture in constitutional law discourse. As they do so, the spectre of the foundation takes on an identity. The texts which are believed to be authored – statutes, judgments and the like – paint a picture of a vague, shapeless, silent, radically alterior other who stands beyond the texts as the first originator of a legal system. Such a radical other transcends historically contingent signs. Professional knowers, to use Hart's term, are 'haunted' by the constraints of this transcendent other.

Their representations give 'body' to the formless and unrepresentable foundation. The 'body', though, has no face behind which one might decipher a personality and is bodiless in that it possesses neither a physiological nor even an experiential character. The 'body' of the absent foundation cannot be perceived; it floats through physical structures and through our networks of concepts. Judges recognize the contours of such a bodiless body as they represent or, to use Hart's term, "approximate" the absent foundation through their signs. The more rigorously they analyse their picture of the vague foundation, the closer they apparently reach its identity. The picture of the professional knower is always a "second-best' – a picture of other pictures, a picture which represents a ghost-like *auctor* as the closest approximation of the foundation of authored laws.

The Gaze of a Spirit

Perhaps one could best describe this ultimate represented auctor as a spirit.[17] We professional knowers try to map out the identity of what cannot be identified: an absent, founding, formless, signless Object. Of course, the body of the final Object, as pictured, is not an organic or physiological body. Nor does it experience. One cannot picture the foundation with a particular dress or even with a face. The 'body' of the absent Object is transparent in that it seems to travel through all physical and social impediments. Like a ghost, the spectre of the foundation of legal authority just seems to be ever-present.

Why do I suggest that the vision of the foundation of legal authority possesses the shapeless form of a spirit? A spirit lacks a body with flesh. A spirit does not possess property – the personal and real property familiar to lawyers.[18] Furthermore, a spirit lacks a phenomenal body – one that experiences.[19] Yet, a spirit is the remnant of someone's body. That someone is, Derrida points out in *Specters of Marx*, a someone who is radically other than juridical persons. The radical other at the end of the trace of legal signs is ungraspable, irreducible and formless.[20]

Although lawyers cannot reach this spiritual other through our configurations of signs, we read, perceive, argue and write as if we can reach its identity by tracing one norm or rule to yet others. We treat our vision of the ultimate foundation of authority, this radical other to authored laws, as if there were one spirit, the Spirit of the Laws, which authored the grounding of all signs in the secondary legal genre. We act as if the Spirit gazed down upon us from a situs beyond any synchrony. Derrida describes the gaze in this manner:

> And even when it is there, that is, when it is there without being there, you feel the specter is looking, although through a helmet; it is watching, observing, staring at the spectators and the blind seers, but you do not see it seeing, it remains invulnerable beneath its visored armor.[21]

The Spirit gazes at us from afar. We picture the Spirit as a Creator or Author who may dress, dissimulate, create and protect juridical persons.

As officers of the court, we are guardians of the Spirit of the Laws. Of course, analytic positivism claims that the trace of our actions to the *arche* of authority is purified of morals and of history. Yet the mysticism of religion creeps into our tracing project when we must respond to the question, 'what is it that lawyers trace in their quest for authority?'. In addition to the Spirit of the absent foundation, we knowers are haunted by the possibility that at some point in time and space, some founding fathers had actually experienced the Spirit as a presence in their midst. We act and interpret as if the Spirit of the Laws gazed upon us from afar, as if the Spirit directed us to detain a non-knower, to confiscate his or her assets, to intern him or her, to deny her children of social amenities and the respect that comes with an identity with a community. The 'intent of the Spirit' assures that we may do all these things authoritatively, in the name of the Law, in the Spirit of the Laws. Our deference to the Spirit of the Laws induces us to believe that all signifying acts in the secondary genre represent the true/real. We feel constrained as if the Spirit actually willed our own juridical acts. We justify our judgments as if the Spirit warranted that we had no choice. The gaze of the Spirit of the Laws encourages us to imagine ourselves as *passive* representers and appliers of the Spirit's will. For those jurisdictions which escaped the influence of any realist tradition,[22] the necessary belief in some ultimate Creator or Author tempts the professional knower into believing that the knower does not bring his or her own meanings and own experiences into picturing the foundation.

The Spirit's Monologue

Professional knowers cannot possibly engage in dialogue with the spectre of the Spirit of legal authority because the Spirit is not, and has not been, an experiential being who is capable of responding verbally or even in writing. We do respond to each other through our special language. We usher forth new configurations of signs in order to represent a more rigorous picture of the Spirit's identity. The Spirit, situated "out there" beyond our configurations of signs, simply must be the final source for the authority of our acts. We must live our professional lives as if this mythical and mystical figure were represented by an historically contingent institutional source at some moment in a quantifiable time and space.

Indeed, the more rigorous our analysis, the closer our voyage seems to take us to the full vision of the rational beauty of the Spirit of legal authority. We knowers slowly and subtly construct an identity to our image of the Author/Creator, thinking that the image is the true/real even though it is only a vision. We envision the absent foundation in the image of a ghost who authors. We even give the image a proper name with capital letters. We call it the Rule of Law, or Justice, or the Law, or the Original Intent, or *Recht*. Montesquieu best represented the spectre of the foundation when he too acknowledged the foundation of posited laws as the 'Spirit of the Laws'. We professional knowers envision the ghost and render an identity to it as we play through our semiotic configurations. We struggle over whose spectre of the Spirit's identity should dominate all others. We compete by privileging some configurations of signs over others. We write editorials and demonstrate because claimants to other visions contravene the boundaries of our vision of the invisible founder. We even go to war in defence of the Spirit of the Laws. Precisely because we believe that the Spirit possesses a will whose gaze constrains us, the Spirit resembles a Roman *auctor*.

The moment of the Spirit's birth is unknown and has not been promulgated: if the Spirit had been promulgated, then the Spirit would not represent the final moment at the end of our vision of the foundation of legal authority. Nor may we say with certainty when the Spirit has died and some new identity has displaced the former Spirit of the Laws. The identity of the Spirit is not fixed nor quantified in time and space. Indeed, even after one picture of the foundation has replaced another through a revolution or a slow rereading of the texts authored in its spirit, its representers may remain haunted by its spectre. Such happens during a civil war. During a revolution or a civil war we may adhere to conflicting spectres of the identity of the Spirit. But at all times we are reconciled to the possibility that there must remain only one Spirit of authority at the end of our trace for legal authority. The will of the Spirit evolves as we make arguments or cite configurations of signs or make assumptions. As we continuously rediscover its will, we bring a rational unity to bear upon our own otherwise discontinuous fragments. We do so at the very moment that, in the name of the foundation, we claim that the Spirit's gaze constrains us.

Being unreachable from within represented forms and signs of the secondary legal genre, the possibility of reaching closer to the Spirit's will drives the juridical official to conquer all possible configurations of signs. No limit constrains the professional knower's quest to enclose all embodied meanings within the signifying relations of the secondary genre. Civil struggle is a struggle over the (self-)identity of the spectre of the foundation of the master discourse. One group of expert knowers dislodges the privileged signs of another group, all in the name of an archaic phantasm. The particular body of a non-knower reminds a professional knower that his or her spectre of the absent foundation of authoritative signs remains incomplete. Unless assimilated, the non-knower's physical body will pose as an unassimilated remainder outside the limits of the Spirit's gaze. Accordingly, the surrogates of the Spirit must be willing to imprison, subjugate, deny, starve, torture, rape, execute and exterminate the physical bodies whose meanings always pose as a threat to the unity and the coherence which the Spirit brings to otherwise fragmentary configurations of signs. The body of the outlaw raises the prospect that some primary genre may fail to recognize the mastery of the secondary legal genre of a modern state. Moreover, because the embodied meanings of primary genres are concealed *within* the secondary genre – in contrast with the Spirit which transcends the secondary genre – the body of the outlaw always threatens the authority of the secondary genre. The extermination of the body of the foreigner, though, is not a moment of happiness for the executioner because such an extermination can never complete the assimilative project of the secondary genre. For the secondary genre to be authoritative, there must always remain embodied meanings which the juristic agents may signify. The possibility that the "we" of the authoritative discourse may never institutionalize the foundation in "practice" leaves the professional knower in dread, for the prospect of unassimilated primary genres poses the possibility that a multiplicity of embodied meanings remain uncontrolled. The "best" that we expert knowers can do is to erase any opposing spirits from our monologue. Other languages, other music, other dress, other sexuality, other skin colours, other religious practices, other gods, the untouchables of civil society: all these particulars remind the expert knower of the possibility of another originary Justice preceding the commencement of our journey to find the identity of the Spirit of the Law. The possibility of Justice continually threatens the presupposed unity and rationally coherent will of the Spirit of authority.

Since the foundation of legal authority, and its spiritual surrogate, is so alien to what we juridical agents hold as authoritative signs, the Spirit of the Law incites a sense of concealment, of secrecy, amongst us. H.L.A. Hart, for example, quickly shifted from the anthropological 'unspoken' foundation of the prelegal order to the retrospectively inscribed primary and secondary rules of the modern legal system. The secrecy of the spiritual origins of the secondary legal genre is especially critical because, without its alien situs, authored laws would lack the finality necessary to be posited. What could be more foreign to primary and secondary laws – indeed, more ironic, contemptuous, even comic – than the possibility that their authority ultimately rested with a presupposed ghost-like spirit whose identity juridical agents could never reach within the posited signs of legal discourse. The non-knower's genres, lodged inside the secondary signifying relations, might be accessible if the belief that the source of laws lay in the Spirit of the Law were dissolved. However, the legal genre, to be authoritative, depends upon the inaccessibility of the Spirit of the Law for its very "existence".

The "Facts" as Givens

The Social Event as Externally Posited

The secondary legal genre takes on the character of a single, coherent and seemingly determinate monologue of some inaccessible Spirit. Rules, doctrines, principles and the like join together to constitute such a coherent structure. In addition, all evidence of a social event is taken as a 'given' – as fact. All evidence of this outside event is situated within a measurable space–time continuum. The legal interpreter applies categories to the "facts". The interpreter impartially draws the category from the core meaning of a statute. The interpreter acts as if he or she were a scientist. As a consequence, the experienced meaning of the interpreter is lost in the effort to reach the absent object as represented in a statute or judicial precedent. In its place, the legal interpreter constructs what Heidegger calls a 'wasteland' of objectification. The constitution of meant referents never comes to light, never receives a hearing. Nor do the non-knower's meant referents. The givenness of the object is presupposed to be superior to all experience in reaching the object. But why does the legal interpreter presuppose a primacy of the posited object in any circumstance? Heidegger puts the same question in this way:

> Whence do the sciences – which are necessarily always in the dark about the origin of their own nature – derive *auctoritas* to pronounce such verdicts? Whence do the sciences derive *the right* to decide what man's place is, and to offer themselves as the standard that justifies such decisions?[23]

An *optical illusion* characterizes the knower's act of interpretation. The knower claims to represent the absent "facts" by some configuration of signs, and yet the very representation of the given facts leaves the facts untouched, untouchable and forgotten.

In the American internment cases, for example, the US Supreme Court accepted the "fact" that all subjects signified as 'persons of Japanese ancestry', could subvert the American war effort. This "fact" was accepted by the military commander who had been 'authorized' to observe such "facts". Similarly, in the repression cases, the common law courts accepted that an individual had been given 'reasonable time' to find alternate financing if he or she fell under the typification represented by the sign, 'reasonable time', in the secondary genre. Likewise, the social circumstances of the Davis Inlet residents were not recognized as 'facts and circumstances' worthy of signification in the secondary genre for over a quarter of a century. In each specific context, the juridical officials read the "facts and circumstances" as if they existed externally to the environing world of the officials, as if they existed "out there" beyond their control. If the military commander, authorized to judge the "facts", determined that the ancestors of American citizens, twice removed, could be citizens of the enemy, then the juristic agent was authorized to begin the project of typifying the "facts" as if the agent played no role in so reading the social events. The "facts" could not be altered. The signs which represented the "facts" subsequently became the referent of the secondary legal discourse. They stood alone, divorced from the judges and commanders. They formed part of a single, coherent and determinate structure within a measurable space–time continuum.

This acceptance of the externality of social event is not peculiar to a modern legal discourse. Indeed, it runs through Western scientific thought, at least from the time of Galileo's positing of nature beyond the control of the scientist. It is difficult to appreciate the importance of the externality of the "facts and circumstances of a case" unless one gains a sense of early European science which, until recently, analytical positivism took for granted. Early modern science was preoccupied with causal facts of nature. Modern legal discourse has substituted social "facts" in place of natural "facts". But scientists of nature and scientists of the modern legal discourse have supposed the events to be external to the scientist's gaze.[24] Francis Bacon (1561–1626), for example, believed that the scientist did not, and could not, distort the natural movement of matter. For Galileo (1564–1642), Italian astronomer, mathematician and natural philosopher, space specified boundaries for the movement of matter. Such boundaries allowed the scientist to measure matter in space. The scientist could also measure time, much like the professional knower of legal discourse prepares and methodically situates the chronology of evidence in a contemporary lawsuit.[25] Isaac Newton (1642–1727), English scientist and mathematician, took positivism one step further in terms of the measureability of time and space.

Heidegger and the Quantification of Space and Time

Now, it is at this point that we can benefit from Heidegger's analysis of the externality of posited "facts". Heidegger asked, 'what task is reserved for thinking at the end of philosophy?'. That is, how would one think if one did not represent objects? This question is particularly important since the juridical agent thinks by representing an absent founding object. Heidegger traced the representative theory of meaning to Galileo's mathematical model of "experience". He pointed out the irony that Galileo's geometric laws of motion, presupposing a measurable space and time through Euclidian geometry, barred the scientist from the very scrutiny of experience which science claimed to study. First, according to Galileo, natural laws represented the essence of things when, as Hegel showed again and again,[26] natural laws abstracted propositions from nature. Second, the movement of objects dissipated from natural laws. Third, according to Galileo, external forces caused the movement of objects. Finally, Galileo's model itself prevented the scientist from considering the relationship of mathematics to experience. Galileo and Newton, for example, excluded the phenomenon of desire from nature. This contrasted with Plato and Aristotle who had attributed desire to nature. For Aristotle, matter was only a potentiality which desire fulfilled in a *telos* of the matter. The model prevented a primordial questioning of the meaning of the being of things.

As a consequence, Galileo and Newton had lost the being of experience just as the secondary legal genre loses the embodied meanings of a non-knower. As I documented with respect to the US internment and Canadian recession cases, juridical officials treated the "facts and circumstances of a case" as objects to be grasped, reduced and manipulated as useful commodities in the quest for the *arche* of authority. The professional knower of legal doctrines objectifies and never exposes a fact to the light; indeed, the knower does not even consider the social event except as signified through signs which are taken for granted in a secondary genre. The secondary genre claims a superiority over all other discourses, including the non-knower's, in its fulfilment of the will of the Spirit of the Laws.

Heidegger's question concerns the secondary legal genre just as it does scientific discourse: 'Whence do the [legal] sciences – which are necessarily always in the dark about the origin of their own nature – derive auctoritas to pronounce such verdicts?'[27] The juristic agent argues in a delusion because, notwithstanding the effort to ground the foundation of legal authority in 'judicial practices' (Hart) or in 'social facts' (Raz) or in experience (Hegel), the facts and circumstances of a case remain untouched, untouchable and forgotten. For the facts are enclosed by the universal forms of the "we" of juristic agents. The spirits of Bacon, Galileo and Newton are alive and well in the secondary legal genre.

The Concealment of *Phusis* in the External Object

Heidegger argued that the problematic of externally posited objects rests in the turn which Western metaphysics took with Plato. Plato drew a veil over phenomena by presupposing a world of invisible forms beyond the human being. A wise person searched for an immediacy with such cognate objects. Forms, external to appearance, informed matter (that is, earth, air, fire and water).[28] One could not perceive a "fact" except through a form of the fact. Forms were joined from one to the next until one intellectually stretched towards the Good beyond all other forms. The Good, since it was beyond being, could not be truly known. Plato thereby decisively concealed 'being' inside the forms. But what was the source or *arche* which originated the first being as a cognate object?[29]

Aristotle built a further layer of metaphysical concealment over phenomena by aiming to gain 'unimpeachable evidence of the senses as to each fact'.[30] Nature was believed to have posited facts. The philosopher and scientist simply could not alter nature. Every activity of nature had an end or *telos*, and the scientist aspired to identify the *telos* of any organism's activity. Aristotle showed in *The Constitution of Athens*, for example, how even civil laws naturally grow within a social organism towards a *telos*.[31] Aristotle's response to the question, 'what drives an organism to evolve from its genesis to its *telos*?' was that the absence of the completion of the *telos*, dwelling inside an organism, drives the organism onward to fulfil its *telos* or nature. Such a *telos* is the *arche* (beginning, principle or source) of the organism. In contrast with Plato's forms which dwell beyond the interpreter, Aristotle had the *arche* embedded inside the organism. The *arche* of an organism generates or originates the emergence of an object. *Phusis* or nature constitutes the originary mode of emergence.

Aristotle did not ask 'what does one *mean* by a being, unreified by conceptions?'. Rather, he limited himself to the representation of being insofar as it *is* as an objective entity. Only after analysing a particular being in nature did he turn towards Being or *ousia*. He believed that in order to apprehend a particular being as being, one had to strive beyond being to the final Being even though that final Being, as with the foundation of a positivist legal order, might be absent from all experience. Accordingly, even for Aristotle, the final *arche* of all beings is a reified, universal form without specificity. *Ousia*, as the foundation of the *telii* of matter, lies beyond all becoming and all passing away and, as the final form, is the metaphysical component of Aristotle's analysis.[32] Aristotle took the cosmos to be a hierarchy of beings where the potentiality of the higher becomes the *telos* of the lower. Motion permeates nature in this manner. But because the final form dwells beyond all particulars, the human being can never reach the universal Being. So, the search for an absent foundation in a legal order is not something new. Hobbes, Bentham, Kelsen, Hart, Dworkin and all the others carry forward a presupposition which has imbued Western metaphysics since Plato and Aristotle.

Now, Heidegger suggested that the focus upon the coming and passing away of objects concealed *phusis* or what Heidegger considered as an originary presence with nature. Heidegger did not rest content with the representation of external objects. He aimed to retrieve the presence or immediacy which metaphysics had enclosed with forms since Plato. For this retrieval of presence, Heidegger returned to the early Greeks.

In contrast with Aristotle and the long scientific tradition, which Bacon, Galileo and Newton represented and which began analysis with the givenness of external facts of nature, the early Greeks did not learn about *phusis* by observing the facts of nature.[33] To the early pre-Socratics, *phusis* included heaven and earth, stones and plants, animals and man. Most importantly, *phusis* included the gods who, in turn, were subordinated to fate or *moira*. Instead of observing the movement of beings as organisms of nature, the early Greeks understood *phusis* as the presence of being through gestural meanings of the body. *Phusis* means 'the emerging and arising, the spontaneous unfolding that lingers'[34] or, as Heidegger put it in 'The Origin of the Work of Art', *phusis* 'clears and illuminates the place which man calls his dwelling'.[35] This spontaneous unfolding of human experience, something which I shall elaborate with reference to a legal discourse in the following pages, contrasts with the givenness of externally posited objects in modern legal discourse. Beginning with Plato and Aristotle, *phusis* becomes concealed inside the trace of forms to some final absent foundation. As a consequence, in legal discourse, "the facts and circumstances of a case" can never be *presented* through thought and analysis. For example, the Romans substituted the word *natura* – meaning 'to be born' or 'birth' – for *phusis*. With Plato, Western thought took on a search for *the birth* of *thinking* in a rational grounds or foundation. The first principle or birth of thinking existed in a world above the sensations of physical–chemical objects. Hegel called this world a *supersensible* world. *Phusis* was restricted to the physical matter. Spirit, the living organism and the psychic were thereby displaced and *phusis* degenerated into a stale typification which concepts imitated.[36] Natural things existed "out there" in themselves, only to be observed for the asking. Facts were presented to the observer. Consequently, *phusis* became rootless or without a foundation. The 'highest exertion of thinking' separated it from the very phenomena which it originally moved.[37]

The Enlightenment completed the final moment of the concealment of phenomena.[38] Whereas Aristotle had concentrated upon the *telos* as constituting the "what" of knowledge, the moderns focused upon the mechanics. The ultimate *telos*, for Aristotle, was the Unmoved Mover. Newton, in contrast, excluded celestial bodies from his general theory of movement. All things, if left to themselves, would move uniformly in a straight line.[39] In addition, Newton rejected Aristotle's claim that a material thing possessed an inner nature or *telos*; rather, a thing rests only in relation to other things. If a thing changes its course, this change is due to forces *external* to the thing itself. Finally, Aristotle's ethics focused upon the ends embedded in nature, the highest natural end being the Good. Thus, all anti-natural activity was considered evil and violent. But, because Galileo and Newton erased the violent motion of the Aristotelian view (for Aristotle, external force moves things from their natural place), one no longer needed to distinguish the inward natural ends of a thing from the unnatural. There was no natural order of things. There was no *telos* inherent in a natural object. There was no transcendent invisible foundation to nature. Everything moved. God was dead.

The Non-knower as a Represented Object

Descartes introduced several themes which bear upon the posited facts by the legal process. First the legal proceeding is like a machine, much as Descartes describes of the body in 'Passions of the Soul'.[40] One should recall that Descartes considered the human body in the Galilean terms of a physical–chemical mass, rather than what I have considered as experiential. Any one movement of the physical–chemical mass causes other physiological movements in the body. Once the body machine is turned on, it cannot stop unless it breaks down physiologically. Descartes, at least in 'Passions of the Soul', considers the subject's mind as separate from the body machine.

It is not a coincidence that I liken a juridical proceding to a machine. The juridical agents of the legal proceeding, I shall argue in the next chapter, often consider the rules, doctrines, principles, statutes, judicial decisions and other legal materials as 'the true/real' or the *body* of the legal order. The body of rules, statutes and the like are considered "out there", posited, objective, practical, the 'is' of the legal order, beyond the control of the agent. This objective world is started through a legal proceeding. Such a proceeding, the institutionalization of the body of the modern legal order, is like a machine in that, once it is started with the first letters by a solicitor, the proceeding continues on and on with little opportunity for the parties, as non-knowers, to stop it. In some jurisdictions, even a plaintiff cannot discontinue the proceeding without being loaded with the defendant's legal costs.

Now, Descartes also used the word 'machine' to describe the human body I just noted . When the agent brings his or her own interpretation into the posited, objective world, the agent is considered as positing his or her subjective values, 'oughts' or policies onto the real world of objective rules. Such an imposition covers the objective body machine of a legal proceeding with the subjective 'oughts' of the juridical agent. Thus, this distinction between the uncontrollable objective world of rules and principles on the one hand and subjective values or 'oughts' on the other is traceable to Descartes' own distinction between the body (the real, the machine) and the soul (the 'ought' or subjective). Descartes even considered Spirit to have a material body. Nature was a perfect machine which possessed regularity, precision and inevitability in its behaviour. Predictability, a characteristic of the legal discourse, also characterized the interconnection of facts.

Descartes introduced a second element, though, which bears upon the externality of the "facts and circumstances of a case" in legal discourse. Descartes introduced the notion of the 'subject'. One might consider the word 'subject' to refer to a self-conscious, autonomous being who is considered and who considers him/herself separate from the family, the village, the city, the state, civil society or other particular subjects. This individual is believed to be self-conscious about him or herself vis-à-vis the community. Although Hegel believed that this idea of a self-conscious subject was absent amongst the Greeks, Socrates was arguably a self-conscious subject. Whether or not the idea of a self-conscious subject was shared amongst the Greeks, the modern epoch is usually considered modern because of this belief that a self-conscious, auto-nomous (or 'self-legislating') subject lies at the centre of the culture.

Now, Descartes believed that this subject could be represented, or re-presented, separate from the subject's physical–chemical body. Although Bacon's empiricism and Galileo's mathematical understanding of natural facts reinforced the extrinsic posited character of the object in European thought, Descartes connected the knowledge of such an object to the knowing subject. Descartes could not doubt his own presence because, to doubt at all, he just had to be present. Thus, he concluded, the "I", the subject, was beyond doubt. Heidegger suggests in his *Nietzsche Lectures* that Descartes succeeded in his argument that the ego was a certainty because he substituted *percipere* for *cogitare*.[41] By *percipere*, one takes possession of an object or seizes it by representing it in language. The object is re-presented to the subject. For Descartes, *cogitare* involves the representation of the representable *to* oneself. The subject calls the represented – the thing – to account or brings it to the subject. Descartes, of course, was focusing upon natural facts. I suggest that the externality of natural facts also bears upon the locus of social events. For both natural and social facts, the subject grasps towards the external object, whether the object be in nature or a social event.

In addition, both Descartes and the modern legal discourse consider the subject as a represented object, the juridical person. The represented and representing juridical person is believed to pre-exist the act of representation. Accordingly, because the subject is represented, consciousness of the external facts is a representation by a represented consciousness.[42] The represented juridical person is the ground or centre of the act of representation, just as Descartes claimed more generally. The juridical person, as centre, is believed to will or author the representation of the external object. Thus, Descartes' 'principle of all principles' – *ego cogito, ergo sum* – is 'primary and most certain *only* for *that* thinking which thinks in the direction of metaphysics'.[43] The paradigm of consciousness reigns supreme. Certainty lies in the *cogito ergo sum*. But, as Heidegger points out, the only certitude in Descartes' project is the *representation* from a *represented* centre – the subject. The only certitude is the interpreter as a represented object.

Until one reaches the advances of critical legal studies and certain moments of legal feminism, outlined in Chapter 1, legal interpretation imitates the scientific method in that the interpreter impartially observes the facts as if they were unchangeable, "out there", uncontrolled and uncontrollable. The interpreter categorizes the facts under doctrines and typifications which the interpreter claims to link to the absent object beyond both aggrieved and interpreter. But the scientific method involves more than observation, proof, exposition and summary. The Cartesian scientific method has the subject capture human experience as an object for the interpreter, as subject, to use.[44] Men and women become the measure of all things.[45] The object takes on a utility *for* the subject and the subject objectifies him or herself. The object is extracted, stored and manipulated. The subject's conceptions enclose all objects in order to reduce and then to decompose them – 'in order to depose and reduce it, and ultimately to decompose it'.

The Naivety in the Belief of an External Object: the Belief in an Emergency

Contemporary legal discourse, I demonstrated in Chapter 3, is permeated with the belief that juristic agents are constrained by posited facts and posited texts.[46] Here we look more closely how, much like the posit of a represented "fact", a famous judge accepted the external posit of a text as if the law emanated from the uncontrollable text itself. The judge I have in mind is Viscount Haldane (1856–1928) and the text is the British North America Act, 1867, which professional knowers have considered as the founding source of all laws in the state of Canada. Let me also illustrate how the judge, as an interpreter of the social world, attempted to extract, store and manipulate the *phusis* of human experience into a represented object. As a consequence of the represented act, the judge's interpretive experience as well as the experiences concealed in the represented object were lost and forgotten. Haldane reduced, abstracted and manipulated the experiences incurred in war, invasion or insurrection into a single sign, 'emergency'. In a series of judgments shortly after the First World War, Haldane read the 'peace, order and good government' clause of the basic text in a manner which 'implied' that the central government in the state could enact legislation during 'emergency' conditions. Without such a reading, in ordinary circumstances, the text signified that only the provincial legislatures could enact legislation, not the federal parliament. That is, Haldane reconfigured the phrase 'peace, order and good government' in 'circumstances' which one could label as an 'emergency'.

First, let us examine how Haldane believed that the 'peace, order and good government' clause possessed an essential core signification which *acted upon* the juridical official. In his first effort to define the clause, in In *re Board of Commerce Act, 1919 and the Combines and Fair Practices Act, 1919,*[47] Haldane writes that the POGG clause 'no doubt' authorized the national parliament to legislate for subjects 'which concern the Dominion generally'. Although he did not need to do so, Haldane adds as an aside, that 'in special circumstances, such as those of a great war', the national government possesses 'a great practical interest', and that '[s]uch an interest might conceivably become of such paramount and overriding importance as to amount to what lies outside the heads in s. 92, and is not covered by them'. Such a possibility was authorized, according to Haldane, 'in highly exceptional circumstances' when 'the interests of Canada as a whole' are at issue. Haldane makes it clear that it is the 'highly exceptional circumstances' which authorize the application of this doctrine.

Furthermore, Haldane insists that the doctrine is not a new one. He writes that a previous Privy Council judgment involving federal liquor legislation, *Russell* v. *The Queen*, 'appears to recognise this [emergency doctrine] as constitutionally possible'. Later in his judgment, Haldane writes more emphatically that *Russell* did indeed recognize the 'emergency doctrine'. Moreover, without offering examples, he writes that other such examples also exist. Haldane makes it seem as if he, the interpreter, has added no new insight into what he takes as the inherent objective meaning of 'peace, order and good government'.

During the following year, Haldane was given another opportunity to read the phrase, 'peace, order and good government' in the basic text of the Canadian constitution. In *Fort Frances Pulp and Paper Company* v. *Manitoba Free Press Company,*[48] Haldane reread his own earlier *Board of Commerce* judgment by claiming that the latter 'showed' the obvious need for the 'emergency doctrine' which he describes as 'implied *in* the constitution'. Two paragraphs later he writes that 'the character of the entire constitution' 'depends' upon the external constraint of the posited 'basic instrument'. Here, Haldane rereads that text as if the text itself – not Haldane's own theory of the Constitution – 'implied' the authority of the central government to declare an emergency. Haldane begins and ends his interpretation with the text. 'The language of s. 91', he writes a few lines later, 'protects' the state generally.

More than a signified doctrine was a "given". In the *Board of Commerce* case, Haldane also takes external posited facts as the trigger for the doctrine which he himself has constructed. He phrases this intriguing application of "the facts" as 'require[d]' by 'the national life'. That is, the social world, posited "out there" beyond Haldane and the authoritative texts, 'require' such a reading. The given and external situs of the text makes the court 'loath to enter' the issue whether the social circumstances dictate the application of the emergency doctrine. In sum, Haldane makes posited facts trigger the typification of 'emergency'; the pain experienced during wartime is reduced to the representation, 'emergency'; the representation intellectualizes the experienced events; and Haldane loses the possibility of either perceiving or understanding the actual "facts and circumstances of the case".

In short, Haldane represented Canada's social circumstances in a manner which configured them into a chain of authoritative signs which other professional knowers would consider authoritative of the will of the Spirit of the Laws. He reduced the context-specific experiences incurred during war, invasion and insurrection into the sign 'emergency doctrine' – a sign which signified something very special with important institutional effects. Haldane intellectualized *about* war, invasion and insurrection. He manipulated the word 'emergency', the single representation of the social events, in order to grasp the representation and to bring it to himself, just as Descartes argued. He enclosed the circumstances within the boundaries of his conceptions. As a consequence, Haldane lost the possibility of perceiving the actual social circumstances of war, insurrection and pestilence even though the "facts and circumstances" of an 'emergency' were supposed to trigger the application of the phrase, 'peace, order and good government'. Haldane admits as much in his *Board of Commerce* judgment: the factual circumstances 'requiring' the emergency doctrine are just 'conceivable' and a matter 'of the possible', to use Haldane's words. In *Fort Frances*, Haldane writes that a judge need not 'lay down a priori' 'an exact line of demarcation' as to when the "facts" trigger the application of the emergency doctrine, for, he insists, the national government itself will determine whether the social circumstances of an emergency actually exist: 'no authority other than the central Government is in a position to deal with a problem which is essentially one of statesmanship.' Here, Haldane admits that 'very clear evidence' that a crisis has ended would have to be admitted into court before a court would overrule the central government's determination that the emergency in fact existed. Haldane admits that it is not the war, invasion or insurrection which really triggers the emergency doctrine. Rather, it is the government's and court's representation of the circumstances, through configurations of signs deemed authoritative, that creates the existence of the emergency.

Haldane discloses the constitution of *his* meanings when he represents that drinking liquor 'at that time amounted in Canada to [an evil] so great and so general that at least for the period it was a menace to the national life of Canada so serious and pressing that the national Parliament was called on to intervene to protect the nation from disaster'. Haldane continues that 'an epidemic of pestilence might conceivably have been regarded as analogous'. Haldane constitutes meant objects when he rereads the *Russell* judgment as laying down the proposition that the 'evil of intemperance' was equivalent to an 'emergency' as signified in the constitutional discourse. Haldane insisted that the *Russell* court had grounded its judgment 'upon the facts, considered to have been established at this date rather than upon general law'.

However, in the text of *Russell*, Sir Montague Smith did not mention any emergency arising from the 'evil of intemperance' and, indeed, had represented the federal liquor legislation as related to the configuration, 'public order and safety' and 'public order, safety or morals' – 'that is the primary matter dealt with'. Smith then represented *that* representation of the statute, in turn, with the phrase 'criminal law' in s. 91 (27) of the British North America Act. Thus, what triggered the enclosure of "facts" with the configuration of signs, 'peace, order and good government', was the further representation, 'criminal and wrongful' acts, not the representation 'emergency'. Thus, Haldane abstracted from the actual text of *Russell* and reconfigured it in another chain of signs which he had configured as the 'emergency doctrine'. He *post facto* read *Russell* into an authoritative chain of signs and yet represented the *Russell* text as if it were posited just like the external constraints which Galileo and Newton had likened to nature. Intemperance, again, was 'a menace to the national life of Canada so serious and pressing' to 'require' the 'implied emergency' doctrine. The closest which Smith's text comes to Haldane's interpretation of the posited facts as an emergency is to write that 'the present legislation is clearly meant [once again, meaning is believed to inhere in the text itself] to apply a remedy to an evil which is assumed to exist throughout the Dominion'. It makes no mention of an emergency. Haldane goes even further in his next judgment, *Toronto Electric Commissioners* v. *Snider*,[49] when he writes that the text of *Russell* had rejected any authority in the central government to legislate 'for the general advantage of Canada, or is such that it will meet a mere want which is felt throughout the Dominion'. Again, he maintains that even this representation emanates from the text of *Russell* itself 'because it is not now open to them [later judges] to treat *Russell* v. *The Queen* as having established' that the federal government was so authorized to legislate the temperance legislation in *Russell*.

One is left to marvel at the facility with which Haldane abstracts typifications from the signified social circumstances, all the while insisting that he plays no active role in his own constitution of meant objects. Haldane articulates a representation into a phrase or clause; he situates the phrase in configurations of signs which may seem familiar to other professional knowers; he intellectualizes *about* the configuration; and then he manipulates the resituated representation in a manner which never reaches the *phusis* of the external constraints of "facts". Haldane constitutes meant objects which conceal and lose the actual social experiences of war, insurrection and pestilence.

And yet, Haldane pictures that externally posited emergency conditions require the invocation of the representation, 'emergency doctrine'. The latter, in turn, is believed to emanate from the text 'peace, order and good government'. He imagines that all legal analysis begins with externally posited facts and texts. He reads such an imagined world into chains of signs which he privileges over others. Such a configuration reinforces the boundaries of his picture. As a consequence, Haldane's representation of the text, the British North America Act, and his representation of the social events called emergencies, do not allow for the very possibility which Haldane himself *constitutes* from his own experiences.

Haldane's resulting picture is naive and idealizing. Furthermore, he does not allow his picture to return to his meaning-constituting acts. Indeed, his projection of the posited text and posited social world conceals the possibility that he himself is actually presenting his own experiences *into* the text 'peace, order and good government' and *into* the "facts and circumstances of the cases". Nor, indeed, does he allow that future judges may embody their interpretations with their own experiences.

The Knower's Embodiment of Represented Facts

The positivist tradition leaves the felt experiences of a non-knower untouched, untouchable and forgotten. If one wished to break from the naive assumption that "facts" and texts externally constrain the legal interpreter, then one must examine the representative act of the interpreter. There must be more to interpretation than configurations of signs which represent or stand for an absent object. Here, I wish to introduce the interpreter's *embodiment* of meaning. As Haldane exemplified, the interpreter brings *prior* intentional experiences *into* a configuration of signs. The representation of a fact or doctrine comes *after* such an embodiment of meaning.

When the professional knower *post facto* encloses a referent with a typification, the knower lacks a 'community of content', as Husserl put it, between his or her meaning of the represented typification on the one hand and a social–cultural referent on the other.[50] As just such an example, when Haldane accepted the text and the 'emergency' as external constraints, he lopped off his own addressive experience as he read the "facts and circumstances of the case". Haldane also excised his experience with the represented typification which he believed the text itself posited. When a judge *means* an apparent object, such as 'emergency', and the represented "facts and circumstances of the case", the *meant* object and the *represented* referent 'have nothing to do with each other', just as Husserl writes.[51] These words have come from Haldane as much as Husserl. The secondary legal discourse loses the sense of immediacy with the posited concrete objects even though the interpreter, influenced by the Cartesian project, aspires to bring the external object *into* the interpreter's metaphysical fold. The legal discourse of a modern state treats the phenomena of experience as objectified "givens" which the interpreter may analyse by configuring it within differentiating signs. The discourse transforms the event of the experience into the event of a secondary signification. The professional knower thereby takes his or her representation of a typification amongst configurations of secondary signs as the true/real.

Yet, this very configuration loses the experiences, in this case, of an emergency as well as the experiences of the interpreter as he or she reads a text or the (re-)production of evidence. The juridical official's reading of the text and of the "facts" loses the lived meanings of both the interpreter and the referent. When the interpretation concerns a non-knower's experiences, the distance of the non-knower from the legal discourse is magnified. The non-knower's meanings as to how he or she reads the "facts and circumstances of the case" remain unfulfilled. To be fulfilled, the discourse should address the jurisitic agent's *signative* intention as he or she points to his or her *experienced* object, as an experiencing being, before he or she encloses the object with a represented typification. This is what I mean by an 'addressive experience'.[52]

The objectivity of "the facts and circumstances of the case" breaks down because the professional knower constructs , during his or her interpretation, a metaphysical order which hides his or her own experiences. This metaphysical order, which also conceals the non-knower's meanings, cannot explain the interpretive act of the professional knower. As does the non-knower, the interpreter *intends* a meant object into the signified event. The interpreter signifies the event in a manner which denies the role of the interpreter's own meant object. What the knower takes as objective and independent of the knower's experience is really what Husserl calls an objective correlate of the knower's meaning conferring act: '[o]ur interest, our intention, our thought – mere synonyms if taken in sufficiently wide senses – point exclusively to the thing meant in the sense-giving act'.[53] I shall argue in Chapter 5 that the knower's sense conferring act lies in his or her experiential body, not in the secondary discourse's presupposed externally posited event.

Notes

1 Such a trace to a final absent foundation is the subject of my *The Divine Origins of Legal Positivism* (forthcoming).

2 Martin Heidegger, *Basic Writings* (David Farrell Krell ed.; New York: Harper & Row, 1977): 377–92.

3 Ibid., 374. Also see Martin Heidegger, *An Introduction to Metaphysics* (Ralph Manheim trans.; New Haven, Conn.: Yale University Press, 1959).

4 See, for example, Martin Heidegger, *Poetry, Language, Thought* (Albert Hofstadter trans.; New York: Harper and Row, 1971).

5 Martin Heidegger, *Early Greek Thinking: The Dawn of Western Philosophy* (David Farrell Krell and Frank A. Capuzzi, trans., Cambridge: Harper and Row, 1975, 1984).

6 Ibid., 385, quoting from Goethe.

7 Coke's theory of law is examined in William E. Conklin, *In Defence of Fundamental Rights* (Alphen aan den Rijn/Germantown: Sijthoff & Noordhoff, 1979): ch. 1.

8 (1606), 12 Co. Rep. 63 at 65, 77 ER 1342 at 1343 (KB). To this James was 'greatly offended' for if Coke were right, the King would be under the law and this would be treasonous to admit. One report records that the King became so physically angry, shaking his fists at Coke, that 'Coke fell flat on all fower' and begged James' pardon. See William E. Conklin, *In Defence of Fundamental Rights* (Alphen aan den Rijn/Netherlands, Germantown/USA: Sijtoff & Noordhof, 1979): fn 22.

9 *Dr Bonham's Case* (1610), 8 Co. Rep. 113b at 118, 77 ER 638 at 652 (KB). For Coke's appeal to some foundation in the common law, see generally the discussion in Conklin, ibid., 20–21.

10 Thomas Hobbes, *A Dialogue between a Philosopher and a Student of the Common Laws of England* (Joseph Cropsey ed. with intro. Chicago: University of Chicago Press, 1971).

11 Ibid., 55.

12 Ibid., 72–3.

13 See William E. Conklin, 'Hegel, the Author and Authority in Sophocles' *Antigone*' in Leslie G. Rubin ed., *Justice v. Law in Greek Political Thought* (New York: Rowman & Littlefield, 1997): 129–51.

14 H.L.A. Hart, *The Concept of Law*, 2nd edn (Oxford: Clarendon Press, 1994): 107.

15 Ibid., 94–5, 103.

16 The balance of this section is a revision of parts of an earlier essay, William E. Conklin, 'The Expressivity of the Invisible Author of Modern Legal Discourse' in Wilhelm Wurzer, *Invisibles* (Evanston: Northwestern University Press, 1997).

17 Jacques Derrida, *Specters of Marx: The State of the Debt, the Work of Mourning, and the New International* (Peggy Kamuf trans.; Bernd Magnus and Stephen Cullenberg intro.; New York/London: Routledge, 1994).

18 Ibid., 41–2.

19 Ibid., 131.

20 Ibid., 7.

21 Ibid., 100–1, 134.

22 William E. Conklin, *Images of a Constitution* (Toronto: University of Toronto Press, 1989).

23 Heidegger, 'What Calls for Thinking?' in *Basic Writings*, note 2 *supra*, 44 (emphasis added).

24 Francis Bacon took the positivist view of science in one direction. One could discover Truth by beginning with the determinate particulars of the senses, 'rising by a gradual and unbroken ascent, so that it arrives at the most general axioms last of all'. Francis Bacon, *Novum Organum*, Book I (Thomas Fowler ed.; Oxford: Oxford University Press, 1878): para. XIX. See also George G. Simpson, *The Meaning of Evolution* (New Haven: Yale University Press, 1967): 30.

25 Alexander Koyre, 'Plato and Galileo' in *Galileo Studies* (John Mepham ed.; Hassocks: Harvester Press, 1978): 404.

26 See, for example, Georg W.F. Hegel, *Phenomenology of Spirit* (A.V. Miller trans.; Oxford: Oxford University Press, 1977): paras 157–62, 197–99; also Hegel, *Natural Law* (T.M. Knox trans.; University of Pennysylvania Press, 1975).

27 Heidegger, note 23 *supra*, 44 (emphasis added).

28 See Martin Heidegger, 'The Thing' in *Poetry, Language and Thought*, note 4 *supra*, 163–82, 168.

29 Ibid., 185.

30 From *De Carlo*, III, 7, 306a 16–17 as quoted by Heidegger in 'Modern Science, Metaphysics and Mathematics' in *Basic Writings*, note 2 *supra*: 258. For an excellent study of how Aristotle concealed being see Werner Marx, *Heidegger and the Tradition* (T. Kisiel and M. Greene trans.; Evanston: Northwestern University Press, 1971): 17–37, 74ff.

31 Aristotle, *The Constitution of Athens and Related Texts*, (Kurt von Fritz and Ernst Kapp trans. with introduction and notes; New York: Hafner Press, 1950, 1974).

32 Marx, *Heidegger and the Tradition*, note 30 *supra*, 131–3.

33 Heidegger, *An Introduction to Metaphysics*, note 3 *supra*, 14.

34 Ibid., 61.

35 Martin Heidegger, 'The Origin of the Work of Art' in *Poetry, Language, Thought*, note 4 *supra*, 42. Phenomenon or *ta poioumena* are 'the things insofar as they are produced by the human hand and stand as such'. As defined by Heidegger in 'Modern Science, Metaphysics and Mathematics' in *Basic Writings*, note 2 *supra*, 250.

36 See Heidegger, *An Introduction to Metaphysics*, note 33 *supra*, 63.

37 Scc Martin Heidegger, 'Introduction' to *Being and Time* as reprinted in David Farrell Krell ed., *Basic Writings*, note 2 *supra*, 37–89, 41 ff. Also see David Farrell Krell, 'General Introduction: "The Question of Being"' in ibid., 1–36.

38 See, generally, William J. Richardson, 'Heidegger's Way Through Phenomenology to the Thinking of Being' in Thomas Sheehan ed., *Heidegger: the Man and the Thinker* (Chicago: Precedent Publications, 1981): 73–93, 80–82.

39 Heidegger, 'Modern Science, Metaphysics and Mathematics', in note 30 *supra*, 243–82, 262–3.

40 Réné Descartes, 'Passions of the Soul' in *The Philosophical Works of Descartes*, vol. I (Elizabeth S. Haldane and G.R.T. Ross trans.; Cambridge: Cambridge University Press, 1911): 331–427.

41 Martin Heidegger, *Nietzsche*, vol. 4 (Frank A. Capuzzi trans.; San Francisco: Harper & Row, 1982): 96–138, esp 106.

42 Ibid., 108.

43 Ibid., 100. See, generally, Joseph P. Fell, *Heidegger and Sartre: An Essay on Being and Place* (New York: Columbia University Press, 1979): 4–6; and Paul Ricoeur, 'The Critique of Subjectivity and *Cogito* in the Philosophy of Heidegger' in Manfred S. Frings ed., *Heidegger and the Quest for Truth* (Chicago: University Chicago Press, 1968): 62–75.

44 Heidegger, *Nietzsche*, note 41 *supra*, 120.

45 Martin Heidegger, 'The End of Philosophy and the Task of Thinking' in *Basic Writings*, note 2 *supra*, 369–92, 377.

46 This is elaborated in full in William E. Conklin, *Images of a Constitution*, (Toronto: University of Toronto Press, 1989, 1994).

47 [1922] 1 AC 191, 60 DLR 513 (PC), aff'g (1920), 60 SCR 456, 54 DLR 354.

48 [1923] AC 695, [1923] 3 DLR 629 (PC).

49 [1925] AC 396, [1925] 2 DLR 5 (PC), revising [1924] 2 DLR 761 (CA).

50 Edmund Husserl, *Logical Investigations*, vol. 2 (New York: Humanities Press, 1970); Investigation VI, s. 14, 711.

51 Ibid., Investigation VI, 712.

52 Ibid., Investigation VI, 727.

53 Ibid., Investigation I, s. 10, 283.

5 The Retrieval of the Knower's Environing World

As the professional knower proceeds to represent social events through configurations of signs which other knowers will consider authoritative, the knower constructs representations which fail to perceive the external events. Likewise, the knower's inability to reach a presence with the external objects drives him or her to try to reach the witness's story through configurations of signs. Even the "I" of the knower merges into the web of values, assumptions, style and gestures of privileged spectres of the absent foundation. The ability to rationally link one representation (such as 'emergency') to an accepted authoritative configuration (such as 'peace, order and good government') to another configuration (such as the British North America Act) to another (such as the Statute of Westerminster) to yet others fills in the boundaries of a picture of the final absent Object of the legal discourse.[1] Such a trace through configurations of signs assimilates the represented event into a picture of the whole. The trace disembodies the interpreter's signifying relations, just as the interpreter's signifying relations disembody the embodied meanings of the non-knower. The absence of the final Object from within the "known" secondary configurations drives the knower to assimilate all alien representations and to make them one of the professional knower's own.

This assimilative trace of authority, though, forecloses the possibility that the knower recognizes how he or she reads his or her own experiences *into* the privileged signs. The representation privileges the cognitive over the phenomenal body and the legal doctrine over the experienced meaning of the non-knower. Doctrines, which the secondary signs represent, codify through configurations of signs which abstract from the experience of the non-knower. The doctrines function to substitute a conception represented by one sign, such as the non-knower's, by the conception represented by the knower's sign. The secondary configuration of signs functions ideologically.

This raises a very important question. If the secondary discourse conceals the experiences of the non-knower, does it not also conceal the experiences of the knower as he or she interprets? Does not the knower embody meaning *into* the secondary configurations, all the while that the latter project the interpreter as subject to external constraints? If so, is the secondary legal discourse as self-referential as I initially suggested in Chapter 2? Are the knower's embodied meanings outside and prior to the knower's configuration of signs? Indeed, is it possible that professional knowers carry on a lived dialogic relation with other knowers at the very moment that their discourse monologically assimilates the non-knower's signified meanings?

The Embodiment of a Meant Object: the Case of Viscount Haldane

Haldane's belief that objective, externally authored texts and "facts" constrained him naively explains his own interpretive acts. After all, his interpretation of the texts and of the "facts" are acts. Interpretation is not an act which brings an externally posited text or social event *to* the knower so that the knower can reduce, abstract, intellectualize and manipulate the text or event as an object. Haldane writes, and others have interpreted him,[2] as if that were just what he did. Rather, Haldane himself read his own prejudgements and expectations *into* the posited text to the point that the text was no longer posited.

When Haldane read the words 'peace, order and good government' in s. 91 of the British North America Act, for example, he did not accept the words as a "given" and then bring the words to himself, although he wrote as if he did that. Rather, Haldane read his own prior experiences and anticipations *into* the words – he conferred meaning into the words. His constitution of meaning drew from his experiences as a child, as a failed lover, as a self-styled upholder of the British Empire, as a young lawyer who represented Canadian provinces before the Privy Council in at least ten cases, and as a student of the British Hegelians. Stephen Wexler has linked Haldane's tendency to hide his emotions behind abstract idealizations to the painful loss of his brother during their teens. In addition, two women refused an emotional relationship with him:[3] he withdrew from social relations for six months after the first and suffered a complete nervous breakdown after the second. As a young lawyer, he was deeply grateful for the fee he received for representing the Canadian provinces before British Courts.[4] Since his main litigation experience concerning the Canadian Constitution evolved from his representation of the provinces, he was sensitive to their plight to grow and diversify against centrifugal tendencies favouring the federal government. Of course, the studies of Haldane's political and social thought suggest that Haldane read additional experiences into his interpretation of 'peace, order and good government'. Haldane deeply believed in an Empire whose liberalism peacefully elevated its majesty and supremacy above regional and particular discord. Giving free rein to the local institutions would encourage the colonies to wish to remain within the Empire without the Imperial Court resorting to the use of force. As he put it to the Royal Colonial Institute in 1903:

> The constitution of the Empire resembles, not a machine, but a living and growing organism, and it is not possible to force the rate of growth of such an organism without danger of weakening the springs of life.[5]

Furthermore, like others of his generation, Haldane was heavily influenced by such British Hegelians as T.H. Green (1836–82), Francis Bradley (1846–1924), Edward (1835–1908) and John Caird (1820–98), and Bernard Bosanquet (1848–1923).[6] These influences encouraged him to read the British North America Act as if a general interest of the whole community dwelled behind the text and consequently induced him to imply the 'emergency doctrine' from the text. In his view, the judges and politicians had to allow institutions and doctrines to grow freely rather than suffer superimposed constraints from without. The provinces, he believed, were the natural *fora* for such an organic growth and, being closer to the populace and concrete social relations, best represented particular wills. However, all particular wills fused into a *Sittlichkeit* or collective moral life. The declaration of an unwritten doctrine, such as emergency, fused particular into general interests, which universally applied to the whole Dominion, and therefore reflected such a *Sittlichkeit*. Thus, Haldane found it "natural" to read the 'emergency doctrine' into the phrase 'peace, order and good government'. Such a reading thereby typified the social event of a war and configured the typification into the trace of authoritative representations. The state's central institutions could authoritatively override the local and private matters assigned to the provinces. The state was one and indivisible. When 'war, invasion or insurrection' challenged the very existence of the state, all particular and provincial interests became subordinate to the indivisible interests of the whole. At that very moment of unity, an immediacy between state and citizen discounted any evidence that an emergency did not exist. The represented fact was thereby transfigured into the legal discourse.

The Hegelian metaphor of the state as an 'organism' had two consequences for his interpretation of the 'peace, order and good government' clause. First, Haldane read a legal text as incidental, and even secondary, to the deeper unwritten organic practices with which the colony immediately identified. Whereas a text had a fixed meaning, practices changed with time. As he wrote,

> The Constitutions of our colonies are really in the main unwritten. The Acts which constitute them are but skeletons which the practice of the governors, ministers, parliament, and judges have to endow with flesh and blood before the dry bones can live.[7]

Second, the organism metaphor encouraged Haldane to "perceive" the provinces as the institutional source for social change and growth. A central government would place fetters upon the indigenous particular interests. Haldane interpreted the central parliament's specific areas of jurisdiction in s. 91 of the basic text as exceptions to the provincial authority to legislate. Only in the rare circumstance of war, invasion or insurrection would the invisible will of the whole prevail. Thus, Haldane's reading of the 'peace, order and good government' clause made the clause alive with his own experiences.

Haldane read one last experience into his interpretation of the 'peace, order and good government' clause. During the 1880s, he was very politically active in advocating Irish Home Rule. After being elected to parliament in 1885 under the leadership of Gladstone, Haldane's party became bitterly divided over the issue. A new government declared the Irish Nationalist Party illegal, and the British state sided with the Irish landlords. Haldane was so deeply disillusioned that he almost joined the underground movement as a revolutionary.[8] When faced with failure over Irish Home Rule, Haldane transferred his political frustrations to the context of Canadian federalism.

Haldane pictured the 'emergency doctrine' as springing from the textual object, 'peace, order and good government'. His experiences of the death of his brother, his failed love affairs, his Hegelian education, his political experience concerning the Irish Free State, and his liberal imperialism suggested to him that an idealized world of texts and doctrines denied any role to the judge in constructing doctrines. Habit and education had induced him to suggest that the founding fathers had assumed the 'emergency doctrine' when they had enacted the British North America Act. Haldane took the emergency doctrine for granted to such a point that he even reread the Privy Council's *Russell* judgment to support the claim that the 'evil of temperance' was 'so great and so general', 'so serious and pressing that the National Parliament was called on to intervene to protect the nation from disaster': he transformed the act of drinking liquor and beer into an 'emergency' and the state was justifiably reorganized accordingly! Haldane discounted any effort to mediate a legislative declaration of emergency with evidence or argument. And yet, he 'found it difficult to explain the decision ... as more than a decision of this order upon the facts'. Haldane's interpretation of the 'peace, order and good government' clause was alive, although his act of interpretation denied that life.

Haldane's lived meaning, though, was not a natural meaning in a biological sense. Rather, his interpretations were lived because he infused the text with experiences which he himself had previously lived. He embodied the text with his experiences. Accordingly, the other to the authoritative language of the state was not the 'nature' which Levi-Strauss and Jean-Jacques Rousseau had posited as the originary genesis of culture. In similar vein, Hans Kelsen had proposed that natural laws dwelt in a physical–chemical world; in contrast, human authors posited civil laws. Nature was a "given" around which even Kelsen elaborated a theory of law which he described as 'pure'. 'Nature never lies', Rousseau insisted. Now with Haldane, once again, a foundation, exterior to legal discourse, functioned as the *telos* of human action. Against such an exterior Object, Haldane writes as if the British North America Act were a text beyond his control, "out there", a given objectivity whose wisdom he could not question: 'a Court of law is loath to enter' the actual facts of a case.[9]

Contrary to the idealization which Haldane's experiences directed, however, a text is a meant object, just as Rousseau *meant* 'nature'. The interpreter *means* a text. Haldane directed his experiences and expectations, for example, into the textual phrase 'peace, order and good government'. He meant the text as if some founding father had determined its objective meaning. Haldane even constructed his judgments as if the text made his conclusions necessary, natural and uncontrolled. He wrote as if he, Haldane, only supplemented the text, although he did admit some role in teasing the emergency doctrine from the clause when he wrote that the doctrine was 'implied', rather than explicitly posited, from the text. We know now, though, that Haldane's conclusions were contingent upon his own experiences which he brought *into* the phrase 'peace, order and good government' as well as *into* the *Russell* judgment which he held as all-controlling. In sum, Haldane *embodied* the 'peace, order and good government' clause with *his* experiences. His experiences connected with *his* meanings. And yet, he represented his meanings as if they emanated from the text itself, as if someone else had authored the emergency doctrine.

The Haldane example raises an incongruity. On the one hand, the professional knower's whole life virtually takes place inside a prescientific, experiential world. The professional knower *means* this world.

On the other hand, the knower *represents* his or her meanings as if meaning were posited in his representations "out there". Moreover, the knower reads his or her meant significations as if the "facts and circumstances of the case" are also posited "out there" as external constraints upon the knower. The knower represents the given referents, such as a perceived war, invasion, insurrection or even the 'evil of intemperance', through authoritatively posited magic signs such as 'peace, order and good government'. The knower brings his or her experiential meanings *into* the referents and represents the meanings through a web of signs which other professional knowers will recognize as authoritative. The latter configurations include and exclude particular representations. For example, by categorizing "facts" as an emergency, the knower excludes other configurations, such as 'national dimensions' or 'new matters', from the authoritative disposition of the "facts". As a knower situates a term in a privileged configuration, the knower's own experiential meanings are forgotten or even denied a relevance because the signification, not the knower's experiences, becomes the centre of the secondary signifying relations.

Because the secondary discourse of the modern state can, at best, represent the experiential world, the resulting view that an absent object constitutes the true/real is naive. Haldane, for example, claimed to accept the "fact" of the emergency doctrine as well as the "fact" of an emergency condition as posited by some force beyond his control that the central government should rationally represent the whole territory in times of war, invasion or insurrection. He meant these "facts", though, on the basis of his own experiences. That is, the knower's meaning never penetrates the posited "facts" themselves. Further, the knower who immediately identifies with such a positivist world-view finds it very difficult to understand *how* this naivety even imbues the secondary discourse. The expert knower, as a knower of authoritative signs which represent the Spirit of the Laws, fails to return to his or her own meaning constitution of both the externally posited texts and "facts". The knower thereby both discovers and conceals. Even when the knower admits to the importance of the "I" in the interpretive act, his or her positivist world-view prevents him or her from realizing that a meaning-constituting project initially constructs the distinction of "non knower–Law", "I–thou", "interpreter–objective text". The givenness of the text or represented social event points in a direction which hides the accomplishment of creation – of life – within the interpreter's own constitution of meaning. The expert knower is blind to his or her own lived meanings in the construction of a juridical world of objective rules, principles and other standards which the knower and most others take as "law". The knower is open to the very charges which Husserl makes against Galileo, Descartes, Locke, Hume and Kant.[10]

The Concealed Interpretive Act

The problem is that, as my interpretation of Haldane's judgments exemplifies, the very meanings which the knower projects *into* chains of authoritative signs encourages the knower to deny that he or she brings his or her own experiencing meanings into what he or she takes as posited. To admit such betrays a legalism which privileges impartiality, formalism and instrumental rationality.[11] The constructed juridical discourse simply cannot allow for the possibility that the knower's meanings escape the closure of externally posited "facts" and texts. The knower's representation of this outside realm occurs *after* the knower has meant the representation. Nevertheless, the knower represents the posited objects "out there" as existing prior to the knower's own felt experiences. Consequently, the knower's representative project loses the knower's own lived experiences. His or her constitution of meaning remains untouched, yet it is an object of representation and manipulation.

Let us look more closely at the contrast between the representative character of the secondary discourse and the knower's concealed constitution of meaning as the knower intuits the signified world. The knower goes through several experiential moments in his or her representation of the externally constraining world. First, the professional knower, such as a judge or lawyer, takes a "fact", whatever its content, as a given. In the evidentiary project the knower's whole purpose is to "produce" the evidence to "establish" the "fact". Legal consciousness takes a magic sign to represent or stand for the "fact". Next, a knower then recognizes the "fact" by a certain sign, such as 'reasonable time', or 'persons of Japanese ancestry', or 'emergency' or 'national dimensions'. The sign represents a conception which abstracts from the particulars so as to produce a general and universal conception which enclothes or overlays the absent fact 'like a garment'. That is, the knower's consciousness 'reaches out beyond what it actually experiences' to the thing to which the non-knower refers.[12] The knower relates the "fact" to the sign just as Haldane connected intemperance to an 'emergency'. Next, the knower analyses whether that sign fits under one represented authoritative category rather than another. The knower "finds" such categories by tracing the grounds of one authored sign to another until, when pressed, he or she can claim that, together with all other authoritative signs, a cohesive picture of the absent foundation of the trace has been reached.

However, the knower's acceptance of a given fact results from his or her *constitution* of meant objects as he or she reads a text or social event. The representation of his or her meanings excludes some evidence, includes other evidence, gives varying weight and credibility to the included evidence, and reads the evidence through chains of magic signs which his or her peers take as authoritative. Such a sign and its represented legal doctrine do not attach to the non-knower's narration. Rather, the non-knower and knower undergo a series of meaning experiences which infiltrate into what the knower otherwise represents as an external neutral data. Of course, the data are not neutral because the knower parasitically overlays the represented "fact" with his or her own value-ridden experiences, including experiences which hold out the "facts" as externally posited. Further, the representation of his or her meanings of the "fact" by a signified category includes and excludes by joining with other configurations of signs which mark out the spectre of the absent foundation. In addition, when an earlier judge, such as Smith in *Russell*, has represented a social "fact" as a given (for example, that intemperance has a national dimension), the later judge (such as Haldane in *Re Board of Commerce*) may well accept the signifying relation (that the 'evil of intemperance' carries the signification of an 'emergency'), not the referent of intoxification, as the true/real. Thus, when the professional knower appeals to the "facts of a case", the representation that the "facts" are externally posited is already built into the knower's interpretive act. The knower plays with the earlier judge's statements through a game which distances him or herself from the objective realm. As he or she does so, he or she disembodies herself as well as the non-knower so as to produce a dead language vis-à-vis the non-knowers.

In sum, as Husserl so perceptively argues, a meaning-constituting experience does not begin with the two separate poles of interpreter and external fact or text. When a professional legal knower describes the "facts of a case", he or she carries on what Husserl describes as 'an objectifying act of reflection'. But, I have argued, the external constraints are not externally authored. One brings oneself into a signifying relation which represents how the knower means the represented facts. 'We attend to it [the fact] and pass judgment on it,' Husserl explains.[13] The interpreter's experience *constitutes* 'the full and sole presentation, judgment, etc., etc., of this object'.[14] When the knower situates a narrated event into familar and recognizable configurations of signs, for example, the knower *interprets* the narration. The knower does not interpret by adding new sensations to the narrated events or "facts of the case". Rather, interpretation is, in Husserl's words, 'an act character, a mode of consciousness, of "mindedness"'.[15] When a knower interprets narrated "facts" or a posited text, his or her ego experiences personal prior experiences not the narrated events which he or she may project as posited external to them. Each lawyer and each client, witness and judge, brings a different experiential past and different anticipatory expectations to bear into the stories of the other.

Thus, the representative project of the knower who feels constrained by externally posited "facts" and texts conceals what the knower is really doing. Moreover, the constitution of social events as externally posited conceals the non-knower's own meanings because he or she also cannot speak except through secondary configurations which deny the non-knower's own constitution of meaning. Whereas the representing knower cannot reach the posited fact and text, the representing world conceals that the object, as meant, is intuitively *presented* to the interpreter. The interpreter fuses into a unity with a meant object. The knower does not confront social data, such as statutes, doctrines and the "facts of the case", with mere empty represented doctrines. The knower *fuses* his or her experiences into his or her *meant* representations. This fusion makes the posited object determinate in a concrete context and also brings the knower's experiential body into the whole of the world. The knower, as interpreter, embodies the world first, by conferring meaning into it and, second, by living in the fulfilment of that meaning. When the knower represents the outside text or non-knower or "fact" as a "given" towards which the interpreter is drawn, the 'perceived' 'external constraint' is forever indeterminate. The interpreter can never reach the absent "fact"; he or she can, at best, only represent it.

The interpreter's placing of the represented "fact" under an invisible doctrine, rule, principle or other standard which is, in turn, represented by an authoritative sign, fails to explain how the knower constitutes this world which he or she takes as externally authored. Why? Because the corresponding relationship between the external "fact" and the invisible doctrine, which an authoritative sign represents, is constructed after, and external to, the interpretive act itself. No matter how deeply the knower believes in the practicality of his or her practice, he or she conceals his or her own constitution of the meaning of the "facts", the authoritative signs and the enclosure of the "facts" under the category which the signs represent. The authoritatively positioned interpreter even excludes his or her own experiencing body from his or her "analysis" of the case. The knower intellectualizes his or her meanings, and this intellectualization forgets about the particular experiential bodies in whose name the litigation was commenced. At best, the knower represents the bodies with magic names, like *Snider* or *Russell*, which the knower situates inside configurations of signs which delineate his or her picture of the absent Object. The secondary legal discourse thereby produces a world which becomes increasingly distant from the lived meanings of the non-knower. It also ignores that what the interpreter takes as "fact" is *meant* and that the meaning of the "fact" or text is constituted experientially *before* the interpreter represents it to his or her peers by a configuration of signs. As Husserl argues more generally in 'Investigation V', the interpreter does not enter into a real relationship with a posited fact or text about which he or she writes a story or narrative.[16] Regretably, this ignorance of a prior meant object is maintained in the name of the majestic sign, the "rule of law".

The Interpreter's Embodiment of Meaning: a Lesson from *Brown* v. *Board of Education*

The knower does not always constitute a representative world which denies the non-knower's own constitution of meaning. Sometimes, the higher courts of a state may recognize just such a dynamic act of meaning. Even that recognition, though, occurs through secondary configurations of signs which knowers, not the aggrieved, claim to "know". What do they claim to know? First, the secondary configurations of signs. Second, the invisible doctrines which the signs represent. At the very moment of the knower's recognition of the non-knower's constitution of his or her own meanings, the knower signifies the recognition through magic signs which he or she can trace through authoritative texts to a picture. The picture represents the final absent Object of the legal discourse.

Perhaps the best known judgment in modern legal discourse, *Brown* v. *Board of Education*, exemplifies how judges signify their own recognition of a non-knower's constitution of meant objects through secondary configurations of signs.[17] Oliver Brown and several other children in three other cases were the plaintiffs in the case which finally reached the US Supreme Court and was eventually known as *Brown*. The plaintiffs in *Brown* were Afro-American children who were denied access to state public schools attended by white children. What the court described as 'tangible' evidence of a good education (buildings, curricula, qualifications, teachers' salaries and the like) were equal between the two sets of schools: the publicly-funded schools attended by white children and those attended by Afro-American children. But such 'tangible' factors merely represented an outside world of education which lopped off the 'intangible', interpersonal and experiential factors which help constitute a child's meanings into the world. In the court's own words, an education 'is a principal instrument in the awakening of the child to cultural values'.[18] The experiential factors which an education brings into a child's world is 'incapable of objective measurement'. They are 'intangible considerations'. For example, to separate children on the grounds of race 'generates a feeling of inferiority as to their status in the community that may affect their hearts and minds in a way ever unlikely to be undone'.[19] Such a 'sense of inferiority affects the motivation of the child to learn'. This immeasureable, 'intangible' experiential character of learning connected with 'our democratic society', 'our most public responsibilities, even service in the armed forces', and 'the very foundation of good citizenship'.[20] These statements could be interpreted as supporting the very claim that one *means* an object and that such a claim is so important that legal discourse should recognize the meaning constituting act authoritatively.

Such a legal recognition, though, was represented through secondary configurations of signs which represented the particular experiences of each child. The critical representation was not drawn from any text. Rather, the court's narrative hung upon its interpretation of the word 'equal' in the phrase 'equal protection of the laws'. But why that phrase? And how did the court signify the experiential meanings of a child as opposed to an education which did not respect such phenomena?

Here, the court was preoccupied with tracing the authority of the signifying relations, and this trace led it to interconnected signs directed towards a presupposed external foundation of authority. For example, the court located the 'common legal question' in the four combined cases, known as just *Brown*, to the issue as to whether the children had been 'deprived' of 'equal protection of the laws'. That configuration was signified 'under' the Fourteenth Amendment which, in turn, had been properly amended shortly after the Civil War to the basic text called 'The Constitution of the United States of America'. The propriety of such an Amendment had a special signification, of course, because the United States had just gone through an extraordinarily violent civil war. The *Brown* court found that the authority of the Fourteenth Amendment derived from a prior authorized procedure which could be traced through other provisions posited in the basic text. The historical circumstances surrounding the Fourtheenth Amendment were 'inconclusive'. The crucial issue for the *Brown* court was 'what authoritative chain of signs best represented the word "equal" in the authoritative text, the Fourteenth Amendment'. Here, the *Brown* court excluded the configuration, 'separate but equal', as no longer representative of the authoritative configuration, 'equal protection'. The 'separate but equal' doctrine had been authorized in *Plessy* v. *Ferguson* (1896) according to the *Brown* court. And *Plessy* v. *Ferguson*, in turn, had held that the magic sign, 'separate but equal', typified 'not education, but transportation'. The US Supreme Courts had 'labored with the doctrine for over half a century'.[21]

How can one labour with a doctrine, such as the 'separate but equal doctrine', unless one believes that it actually represents the real? And how can a juridical agent believe in such a reality unless one transforms the *phusis* of phenomena into a represented world which is externally posited? Indeed, the *Brown* court described that previous judges had been 'involved' with the magic configuration, 'separate but equal' not with the particular experiences of the human beings who were separated from their racially different peers. Furthermore, even the court recognized the need to substitute a new configuration for the old one because a student constituted meaning by virtue of 'intangible' factors: even that recognition is 'amply supported by modern authority'[22] such as scholarly psychological studies of Afro-American children who learned in segregated schools. But the judges assimilated the academic studies into the legal discourse and, because of this, the studies had become 'authoritative'. The representation project was complete. The children, as non-knowers, were silenced at the very moment that their languages were recognized in the legal discourse. It was left to later US courts to devise a new sign to represent the reconfigured doctrine in the "facts and circumstances" of Oliver Brown. The new sign, of course, was just *Brown*. The particulars of Oliver Brown's experiences were forgotten; indeed, the particulars were substituted for authoritative statements about the 'intangibles' in learning. The *Brown* "facts" became authoritative. *Brown* v. *Board of Education* represented a doctrine. And an external object, a text called 'The Constitution,' 'prohibited' governments from maintaining the *Brown* facts. The legal discourse could recognize a non-knower's embodiment of meanings only by disembodying those meanings in deference to the trace of a spectre of some final absent Object of authority.

The Self-Image of the Interpreter: the Case of Mr Justice Holmes

If the legal discourse, as a secondary discourse, disembodies the non-knower's meanings and if the knower constructs the belief in an external foundation to legal signs, one is left to conclude that the professional knower him or herself embodies meant objects in his or her own self image as a professional knower. I now wish to illustrate my claim that professional knowers project their own institutional self-image into legal doctrines and that they do so even when they insist that it is improper for them to do so. Haldane exemplified such a situation. Let me take a second – equally famous but philosophically very different – judge, to show how a judge reads his or her own environing world into a secondary legal genre. Justice Holmes is reputed to be a great defender of the role of the democratic majority. He is also reputed to be a legal realist who insisted that a pragmatism replace any Kantian effort to shape laws according to moral "oughts". Even a very self-conscious judge, such as Holmes, acts as he or she interprets – embodying "facts" and texts with his or her own prior experiences. Let me show how Holmes embodied his key doctrine of judicial self-restraint.

One key to Holmes' doctrine of judicial self-restraint involved his insistence that law be separate from the judge's subjective moral convictions. 'I should be glad,' he wrote to the legal historian, Pollock, 'if we could get rid of the whole moral phraseology which I think has tended to distort the law.'[23] In his classic essay, 'The Path of the Law', Holmes wrote that 'every word of moral significance could be banished from the law altogether, and other words adopted which should convey legal ideas uncoloured by anything outside the law'.[24] The judge's institutional duty was to be concerned with the laws as they are, not as they ought to be.

Holmes' restrained institutional self-image was manifested in several ways. For one, in the early chapters of his important work, *The Common Law*, for example, he argued that all subjective moral culpability should be eradicated from the laws of crimes and torts.[25] 'Primitive' legal orders had required personal fault in civil liability whereas 'mature' legal systems had evolved to the point that one could be punished even when not morally blameworthy. A fixed standard, external to the defendant, should be the source of criminal and tortious liability. The defendant's personal motives were irrelevant. The defendant's personal biography was irrelevant. It was 'perfectly proper' for laws to consider an individual as a means, as a 'tool' for the general welfare.[26] Holmes feared that elements of subjectivity would bring the courts into a power conflict with interest groups and individuals.

Another manifestation of Holmes' institutional self-image drew from his freedom of speech cases. In *Schenck* v. *US*, Schenck had been charged with an attempt to obstruct recruitment into, and to cause insubordination in, the military.[27] The legal issue was whether s. 3 of the Espionage Act contravened the free speech provision of the First Amendment. Holmes held that Schenck's intent to change the government's policy was irrelevant. The key was the external standard of 'proximity and degree' of Schenck's pamphlet to a 'substantive evil'. Again, in other free speech cases, Holmes insisted that the judges appeal to an external standard, independent of judge and defendant. In *Debs* v. *US*, for example, Holmes looked to the 'natural and probable effect' of a speech upon what another institution – Congress – had considered a 'substantive evil'.[28] And in his *Abrams* dissent, he objectively assessed the immediacy of the alleged evil to a 'clear and present danger' and the 'appreciable tendency' of the defendant's conduct to magnify the evil.[29]

The judge's role was to remain as aloof as possible from social–political conflict. Why? Holmes offered that if a judge decided according to his or her personal predilection, he or she would be interfering with the natural evolution of the clash of political interests. Even to hold a trust or monopoly as 'invalid' or 'unjustifiable' or 'unconstitutional' ran counter to the natural flow of power. Judicial self-restraint vis-à-vis the legislature also permeated both his

Lochner and *Buck* v. *Bell* judgments. In *Lochner* a New York statute prohibited the employment of persons in bakeries for more than ten hours per day and 60 hours per week.[30] The majority of the US Supreme Court held the statute to be an unnecessary, unreasonable and arbitrary interference with Lochner's right of contract under the Fourteenth Amendment. Holmes dissented. Because the statute was attempting to ensure a human working condition? No. Because the majority of the Court had imposed an economic theory 'which a large part of the country does not entertain'. The judiciary should not intervene with the views of the majority which, he believed, supported such legislation: '...my agreement or disagreement with the economic theory has nothing to do with the right of a majority to embody their opinions in law.' The majority had imposed a personal, narrow economic 'social statics', which had been espoused by a long discarded theorist, Herbert Spencer. He concluded that 'the word "liberty" in the 14th Amendment is perverted when it is held to prevent the *natural* outcome of a *dominant* opinion'. There was one exception, he held: namely when the judge's view supported the longer-term fundamental principles of society which would situate the legislature's statute as an aberration of the overall evolutionary flow of events.

Then came *Buck* v. *Bell*.[31] A Virginia statute had authorized the superintendent of the State Colony of Epilectics and Feeble Minded to authorize residents' sterilization. Speaking on behalf of the majority of the *Buck* v. *Bell* court, Holmes held that the statute did not violate the due process clause of the Fourteenth Amendment. Why not? Because the legislature had spoken and the legislature represented the public interest. 'As a matter of law', the judiciary could not say 'the grounds [for sterilization] do not exist, and if they exist they justify the result'.[32] It so happened that the legislature's view towards such citizens corresponded with that of Holmes: if residents were discharged without being sterilized, he wrote, they would become 'a menace to society'.[33] He likened Carrie Buck's situation to that of wartime when the public good had 'call[ed] upon the best citizens for their lives'. The mentally disadvantaged were already 'sap[ping] the strength of the State'. Holmes concluded as follows:

> ...it is better for all the world, if instead of waiting to execute degenerate offspring for crime, or to let them starve for their imbecility, society can prevent those who are manifestly unfit from continuing their kind ... Three generations of imbeciles are enough.

The important point is that Holmes believed that he had no choice in these decisions which so seriously affected the constitutional rights of these citizens. He felt constrained by the external objects beyond his control. Holmes' letters to his friends Harold Laski and Pollock during the period when he was writing the *Schenck, Frohwerk* and *Debs* judgments, for example, affirm as much. He wrote to Laski on 16 March 1919, for example, that 'on the only questions before us I could not doubt the law'.[34] As to his *Debs* judgment, Holmes wrote to Laski as follows:

> I hated to write the *Debs* case and still more those of the other poor devils before us the same day and the week before. I could not see the wisdom of pressing the cases, especially when the fighting was over and I think it quite possible that if I had been on the jury I should have been for acquittal but I cannot doubt that there was evidence warranting a conviction on the disputed issues of fact.[35]

The sole consideration in the free speech cases was whether the external standard of 'clear and present danger' justified the legislature's restriction of a right in certain political exigencies. Thus, Holmes wrote in *Schenck,* 'in many places and in ordinary times' Schenck's conduct would have been constitutional. 'But the character of every act depends upon the circumstances in which it is done.' The intent had to be 'presumed' from the circumstances of wartime.

It is at this moment that the analytic lawyer asks 'how can one reconcile all these cases rationally and consistently?'. And the question comes to the fore when one reads the above cases against Holmes' own *Gitlow* dissent.[36] What I wish to argue is that one may best reconcile the cases, not in terms of Holmes' doctrines and reasoning process as analytic lawyers are prone to do, but in terms of the relation of his doctrines to his own environing world which he had lived over a lifetime.

Gitlow had published a newspaper, *the Revolutionary Age,* which advocated a communist revolution. He had urged 'revolutionary mass action'. He was charged with violating a New York statute which had made it an offence for one who 'advocates, advises or teaches the duty, necessity or propriety of overthrowing or overturning organized government by force or violence ... or by any unlawful means'. The state had not offered evidence of 'some definite or immediate act' of violence. The majority of the US Supreme Court had held that such evidence was unnecessary because the newspapers' statements were 'inimical to the general welfare' and 'entailed such danger of substantive evil' and 'danger to the public peace and to the security of the State'. Holmes held that such evidence was necessary because it was 'manifest' 'that there was no present danger of an attempt to overthrow the government by force on the part of the admittedly small minority who shared the defendent's views'. It was not in society's interests, he wrote, that the state repress political expression. But how could Holmes claim to act in society's interest when he had hitherto insisted that only the legislature could do so? Holmes had respected the legislature's demands in *Lochner*, *Buck* v. *Bell* and in the earlier free speech cases by insisting that the judiciary should not interpose its views upon the legislative will.

Holmes' appeal to external standards, as with Haldane, embodied his prior experiences before and after his professional life. These experiences related to his lived environing world. The *Gitlow* dissent can only be reconciled with Holmes' other judgments if it is realized that it is not his words and sentences which mattered, but his embodiment of his image of his environing world *into* the words and sentences. Holmes saw his own life as a constant struggle for survival. After all, he had been left to die on the battlefield in the American Civil War not once but three times, and he records that he believed himself close to death on at least one of those occasions. He had felt 'no pangs of conscience', he wrote later, of marching conscripts to the front lines of the battlefield with bayonets against their backs. He encouraged his troops to treat the enemy 'not even as a means but as an obstacle to be abolished'.[37] These wartime experiences led him to believe in Charles Darwin's theory of the survival of the fittest in the natural evolution of the species. Holmes was not alone in a belief in the self-interest of human action. His friend, John Dewey, shared a similar view.[38] As Holmes wrote in *The Common Law*, 'at bottom of all private relations, however tempered by sympathy and all the social feelings, is a justifiable self-preference'.[39] Holmes confided to Laski at one point that he understood all men and women as living and dying 'like flies – here swept away by a pestilence – there multiplying unduly and paying for it'.[40] The inevitable struggle in life eventually erupted into violence: violent conflict 'was the order of the world at which it is vain to repine'.[41] Talk about the exploitation of human beings 'always got my hair up'.[42] He continued, '[a]ll society rests on the death of men. If you don't kill 'em one way you kill 'em another.'

Another element of his environing world derived from the struggle for power which Holmes had had to face on the battlefield as much as in the courtroom. Holmes insisted that the ultimate outcome of the struggle for power brought happiness and joy: 'to use them [one's powers] to their height is one's joy and duty, so it is the one end that justifies itself.'[43] Holmes extended this struggle for power which he had experienced in his own personal life into his political and legal view of the state. Thus, in 'The Gas-Stokers' Strike', he wrote that '[i]n the last resort a man rightly prefers his own interest to that of his neighbors. And this is as true in legislation as in any other form of corporate action.'[44] Even when politicians were motivated by the greatest happiness of the greatest number, the political struggle for power took place in the legislative process, for any statute favoured one dominant economic or political group at the expense of others at any one point in time. Only in 'civilized communities' did the legislature function accordingly. When beliefs were deep in a group's consciousness, 'we try to kill the other man rather than to let him have his way'.[45] 'The '"ultimate ratio" not only "regnum", but of private persons', Holmes wrote then, 'is force'.[46]

How did Holmes bring his meant objects of struggle, conflict, violence and force into the configurations of signs such as judicial restraint, clear and present danger, rights, objective standards and the like? Judges could neither constrain nor redirect the power struggle: 'I see the inevitable everywhere,' he once wrote to Pollock.[47] Reason and argument were like 'argu[ing] a man into liking a glass of beer'.[48] Judges stood helpless by the wayside as power conflict inevitably erupted into violence. The best that a judge could do was to sit detached, to observe the conflict, and to predict which litigant represented the stronger political–social interests. In the public law realm, the legislature represented the forum for political struggle and the last thing a judge should do was to restrain that struggle by putting idealistic and rationally derived doctrines in its way. Holmes represented the legislative outcome of the power struggle with the term, 'public policy'. Public policy did not involve social "oughts", as one might associate with the term today. 'Public policy ... accurately measured social desires.'[49] In American society, according to Holmes, the legislative majority best represented the power struggle in the wider society. The legislature alone should create rights, condition the scope of the rights, and repeal one's rights. Correspondingly, a legal right represented the will of the dominant political groups in society. Whether an individual possessed a right depended entirely upon whether his or her conduct coincided with 'public policy'. Human rights or 'rights as trump', as Ronald Dworkin would later coin them, did not exist: 'I utterly disbelieve all postulates of human rights in general'; 'the rights of a given crowd are what they will fight for'.[50] On yet another occasion Holmes wrote that a legal right could vary from the protection of a religious belief to the right to a glass of beer.[51] A right functioned as an 'empty substratum' in the legal language.[52]

This takes us back to Holmes' doctrine of judicial restraint in *Buck* v. *Bell*, the 'clear and present danger' cases, and *Lockner*. When faced with these cases, Holmes projected his own environing world into the statutes and litigants' re-presented stories. His function was to predict what social desires the litigants represented and which desires would win out in the long term in the inevitable struggle for power. Not only was the legislature a better forum to entertain such a struggle, it was also a better indicator as to what social interests were winning. Thus, Holmes' role was to remain subservient to the will of the legislative majority. His life-world reconciled his free speech judgments with such a majoritarianism.

How, then, can one appreciate Holmes' *Gitlow* dissent in favour of free speech? Here, too, Holmes projected a meant object which he drew from his own experiences as a soldier, a student of philosophy and a lawyer/judge. Society was continually evolving as a result of the struggle for domination by differing social interests. What was a minority at one moment would become the majority at the next. Thus, in *Gitlow*, Holmes writes that Gitlow's Manifesto for Revolution 'offers itself for belief and if believed it is acted on unless some other belief outweighs it or some failure of energy stifles the movement at its birth'. There was no point in a judge or legislature obstructing political speech. Even the legislature could create obstacles to the inevitable struggle for power by artificially preventing the expression of political speech. According to Holmes, in the long term, history had demonstrated that the majority had often eventually adopted the minority viewpoint:

> If in the long run the beliefs expressed in the proletarian dictatorship are destined to be accepted by the *dominant* forces of the community, the only meaning of free speech is that they should be given their chance and have their way.[53]

Or, as Holmes wrote in his *Abrams*' dissent, 'time has upset many fighting faiths'.

If the expression had a political context then, as in *Schwimmer* for example, it must be protected in order to ensure the natural evolution of society.[54] Rosika Schwimmer had applied for American citizenship but, because she was an uncompromising pacifist, she had testified that she would not take up arms in defence of the state. Holmes, dissenting, held that Schwimmer did not pose a threat to the state because she was over 50 years of age and would not be allowed to bear arms even if she wanted to do so. Her opinions should be protected because they were as political as the more orthodox opinion that the president should have a seven-year term. Any legislative restriction on Mrs Schwimmer would obstruct the natural evolution of American politics. In contrast, a legislative requirement enforcing unilingualism did not create an artificial obstruction to the political process, according to Holmes.[55] Holmes' environing world restricted the judge's function to the ensuring of the free-flow of political expression. Holmes embodied the "facts" and the texts through an environing world which his prior experiences had constructed. Holmes' doctrines of judicial self-restraint and his focus upon predictability mirrored that world.

The Retrieval of the Interpreter's 'Environing World'

One thus begins to understand that an interpreter constitutes meant objects; the interpreter's prior experiences embody the objects; and the interpreter shares a community of content with the meant objects.[56] Such a community of content is lived because the content emanates from the interpreter's experiences. These lived meanings are generated before the interpreter ever represents or signifies the meanings through signs. Before Haldane ever represented the 'peace, order and good government' clause with the 'emergency' doctrine, for example, he presented his own *prejudice* into the clause. Whether citizens of a state have their assets confiscated, families interned and family members deported under emergency regulations during a war, the embodied meanings of the particular non-knower are left untouched, untouchable and forgotten if the knower presupposes that he or she is constrained by externally posited facts and doctrines. Even the living subject, the non-knower, is represented as a juridical person who is disembodied of experiences.

Once one takes account of the experiential *presentation* of meaning, the interpretive act discloses the non-knower's meanings as lived. Such meanings may well radically depart from the judge's representation of "facts" as externally authored. The juridical person, as an external object, remains indeterminate precisely because the juridically defined person is an "it" – a posited object towards which the interpreter is drawn. The positivist picture treats the non-knower as a homogenized typification which is represented in authoritative chains of signs. The picture takes such chains as the true/real. And that true/real rules out the possibility that a multiplicity of concrete meanings lie embodied in the displaced language of the non-knower. The addressive experiences of the non-knower are thereby lost. The representations which the juridical interpreter takes as the true/real are indeterminate and dead. The representations project pictures or spectres. The interpreter tries to make the spectres coherent and clear, rational and derivative through a narrative.

The modern legal discourse (re-)produces a suffering which its interpreters, whatever their good will, cannot erase because they live meanings which deny the possibility of lived meanings of a particular other. First, the juridical interpreter represents the pain of a non-knower through a language which conceals the meaning-constituting language of the non-knower. Although the non-knower and the representer may share the same signs to represent the non-knower's pain, the same sign may represent different conceptions for both of them. Second, when the juridical interpreter re-presents the stories of the non-knower, the interpreter's re-presentations enclose the non-knower within standardized forms which the interpreter represents through authoritative configurations of signs. The non-knower becomes disembodied as the juridical interpreter embodies the non-knower's stories. All this takes place in the name of the non-knower's pain and without touching the constitution of the knower's own embodied meanings, let alone the constitution of the meanings of the non-knower.

The representative character of the knower's signifying relation conceals the possibility of a multiplicity of meanings embodied in the non-knower. What is hidden is a non-knower who actually possesses a biography. What is forgotten is the social contextualization through which the non-knower meant his or her pain.

Let me begin to unconceal the forgotten interpretive act of the knower. In such a concealed interpretive act, the interpreter contextualizes by drawing from an experienced time and space. The interpreter's meanings point to meant objects which legal discourse encloses with representations of an absent object – a "fact", a doctrine, a grounding, a foundation. The concealed interpretive act points to a non-knower which the knower *means*. What the knower has taken as objective "fact" evaporates. For, the knower, as interpreter, no longer constitutes meanings which deny the interpretive enterprise by beginning and ending all legal analysis with externally situated facts and externally situated doctrines. The lawyer now *works*. The lawyer no longer passively observes the outside world as if he or she cannot control it, influence it, constitute it. The lawyer discloses his or her embodied meanings into the chains of signifiers which he or she has hitherto taken as the totality of the true/real. What lawyers have hitherto taken as objective and independent of experience are the meanings of the lawyers, not of the non-knower. Husserl puts it this way: '[o]ur interest, our intention, our thought – mere synonyms if taken in sufficiently wide senses – point exclusively to the thing meant in the sense-giving act.'[57] The knower *embodies* his or her spectre of the non-knower just as the knower *embodies* the text with meanings which the knower, not the non-knower, has experienced.

The narrative has played a role in the representative project. The legal narrative, I argued in Chapters 2 and 3, represents "the facts and circumstances of the case" within pictures which the knower recognizes as authorized. But now we have uncovered that such narratives *conceal* the very meaning-constituting acts which the narrator and interpreter alike bring into the narrative. The judge, as narrator, projects a world which begins with posited facts even though the narrator, through his or her own interpretive acts, leaves the posited facts forgotten.[58] The non-knower is one such referent which the narrator/interpreter proceeds to disembody. The loss of the possibility of the non-knower's meanings takes place just as the narrator denies his or her own meanings in the disembodiment project. The legal narrator *lives through* the non-knower, all the while denying that he or she does so. Accordingly, what a legal narrator takes as an actuality – the given "facts" of a case – is really only a possibility, and an unlikely one at that.

The expert knower of the authoritative language of the modern state thereby "suffers" from a double optical illusion. What the knower takes for the real is re-presented through secondary chains of authoritative signs at the same moment that, in fact, the posited facts are merely a possibility. The non-knower's pain, as meant by the non-knower, remains unfulfilled in the secondary configuration of signs. The knower hangs his or her analysis upon "the facts" but never reaches them. Second, because the knower constitutes meanings from his or her own prior experiences and expectations, what he or she takes as "actuality" conceals the knower's own role in the very constitution of the externality of the "facts". I have shown how Haldane's and Holmes' environing worlds manifested such a constitution of such externally posited "facts". The "true/real" is always changing as different interpreters bring different experiences into their meanings of a non-knower's story. Gadamer calls the past experiences *prejudice* or forestructures of meaning. The knower reads "actuality" in the light of his or her moving horizons, horizons which he or she has formed with the aid of a state-financed and state-regulated training. The knower gives form to the world even when the knower accepts the world as posited. The knower's form shifts from his or her *prejudice* into a continuous stream of consciousness which does not even take time and space as measurable, although it may project time and space in such a manner. An indeterminacy of result characterizes the adjudicative function.

The Environing World

I wish to prevent a misunderstanding. When I refer to the body of the interpreter or the body of the non-knower, I do not mean the biological body which one can perceive as a physical chemical mass; I mean the experiential body. The physical body may experience after the experiential body has begun to move.[59] Or the physical body may remain ostensibly unmoved and yet such a physiological body may experience. When one experiences, one reads an inner world (*Innerwelt*) against an environing world (*Umwelt*).

What is the character of the *Umwelt* of an experiencing being? The legal discourse may signify the non-knower as an objectified person, recognized with rights and duties. The juridical person is comparable and measureable in a vast whirl of presupposed causally related social events. But this signification, I have argued, conceals the non-knower's and the knower's constitution of meanings. If, as a professional knower, I gaze upon a posited text or a witness's statement, I may press my gaze towards represented objects further and further into the distance. Eventually, I shall reach an objectless region which dwells beyond my horizons of meaning. Merleau Ponty calls it a *chiasm*; Derrida calls it *differance*. Because the *chiasm* is without objects, the region cannot be measured nor can it be divided into determinate, discrete components. Each experiencing being will perceive a picture or spectre of the objectless region through particular horizons of visibility. Because each being reads different experiences into his or her picture, knowers and non-knowers are unable to share the same universal measurable objectivity. Thus, although modern legal discourse leads the interpreter to believe that the knower reaches nearer and nearer to the true/real as he or she reduces all particular "facts" into smaller and more rigorous analytic conceptions, such an exercise hides the fact that the interpreter will never reach the end of all analysis. The interpretive task is open-ended precisely because meanings vary how each living being perceives his or her surrounding environing world.[60] At the boundaries of my perception there is no objectivity; rather, there is an infinity of appearances. Thus, as von Euxkull says, 'the secret of the world is to be sought not behind objects, but behind subjects'.[61] The secret of legal authority lies not in the hidden, almost divine, foundation beyond the trace of posited norms, but in the concealed meanings which the interpreter retrieves as he or she interprets.

Let us examine the *Umwelt* or 'environing world' more closely. Sebeok uses such terms as 'experienced world', 'psychological or subjective or significant environment', 'behavioral life space', or 'mind set' interchangeably.[62] As the juridical official apperceives a text or a story or a narrative about an 'emergency', say, his or her interpretive act alters the spatial and temporal character of the story. I have demonstrated this effect of experiential space and time with respect to the nomadic residents of an "unrecognized" community, the farmer whose loan is called without notice during the recession of 1980–83, and Haldane's constitution of the emergency doctrine.[63] The appearance-world of each particular subject, knower and non-knower, carries a spell which surrounds the subject's story. It even conditions the conceptions and doctrines which the interpreter represents through configurations of signs which he or she means. As we have seen, if the representer of legal discourse pictures a visible world without objects there would be no space for, without objects, there would be nothing to measure quantitatively. Apperception brings spatial qualities into a common form. Apperception even incorporates qualities of time. The past and the future are lived through the present in a differentiated and concrete manner. The very act of apperception alters space and time by pushing the horizon of objectless space and time nearer or further from the experiential being. As Schrodinger notes, it is merely for convenience that the scientist projects the natural world as autonomous and objective.[64] The appearance-world mediates the scientist's observation of the most minute and fixed particles. The notion of the *Umwelt* or 'environing world' even anchors Kant's works.

How do signifying relations relate to the meaning-constituting 'environing world', then? Whereas von Uexkull seems concerned with the biological body which experiences meaning Sebeok, who interprets von Uexkull, claims that biology begins and ends in the signifying relations. That is, one's constitution of posited objects is itself represented through signs. Mark-signs which represent the 'internal' meanings of an interpreter connote the sensed world. 'External' mark-signs, which fulfil that meaning in the direction of the meant objects, connote action. And 'direction signs' direct meanings from the internal to external signs. A sign exists only if an utterance or gesture or mark has meaning for the interpreter's 'environing world'. Direction signs toward an object surge up from the unconscious or, quoting from Kant, from 'an art hidden in the depths of the human soul'.[65] Although protoplasm generates the physiological movement of the physical body, direction signs of an experiential body signify that movement. The signs of protoplasm script the future of living matter. The mark-signs even inform psychological sensations. Indeed, they signify the world. Thus, an experiential being may create new objects as mark-signs, and direction signs re-configure its 'environing world'. Mark-signs signify experience.

We are left to conclude, then, that mark-signs shape and reshape all matter until the matter functions as a useful *meaning-carrier* to the 'environing world' of an experiencing being. Each cell, one by one, undergoes the constitution of meaning until meaning informs a whole organ and then the whole organism. Even though material objects may stand beyond the interpreter, meant objects continuously fulfil the interpreter's own constituted meanings thereafter. The properties of the material object remain the same. A statute or report of a judicial decision lies in my hand as a neutral object, for example, until I enter into a meaning relationship with it. At that point, my meanings transform the statute from a material object into a meaning-carrier of my meant objects. That is, such texts remain a dead object until I begin to read them and bring my *prejudice* into the texts. I signify my meanings by representing them in signs which connote something for me.

Werner Karl Heisenberg (1901–76), the famous scientist, disclosed this meaning nexus between the interpreter and a neutral physical object when he demonstrated how the observer at one end of the microscope perceives the external object at the end of the interpreter's gaze. Initially, the scientist claims that the object is determinate. On close study, though, the interpreter brings meaning into his observations as he reads the signs of the observed object through the microscope. Drawing from Husserl's *The Crisis of European Sciences*,[66] the environing world of the lawyer or judge or other juridical official suggests horizons from which he or she understands what a text or "fact" states. The *knower*'s environing world cannot envelop the experiential meanings which another author, such as a legislature or a judge, intends. The more diverse the readers' experiences and expectations, the greater is the range of possibilities with which the readers may fulfil the author's meant object. This means that the characterization of professional knowers as manipulative may misdescribe their interpretive acts. The many experiential differences which exude from readers may undermine the very possibility of a single uniform configuration of meanings. It makes sense, in other words, that professional knowers will have constructed several configurations of signs (such as the 'reasonable relationship', the 'substantial relationship', the 'fundamental interests', the 'citizenship' doctrine and many other doctrines) to represent any one provision of a text (such as the 'equal protection of the laws' in the Fourteenth Amendment of the US Constitution). Husserl goes so far as to suggest that an 'environing world' implants a spiritual renewal in a text or posited fact.[67] It is crucial for the belief in the external constraints of "facts" and texts, then, that professional knowers bond together through common experiences and values. Otherwise, professional knowers, as listeners, risk interpreting the same narrated events differently from each other.

Embodied Meanings as Action

We saw above that experience begins with the movement of the experiencing body. Imbued with positivist science, psychologists often observe the biological body as the very external object which has characterized the modern legal discourse. Only recently, the discourse of psychology has returned to the phenomenological works of Lev Vygotsky, the Russian psychologist who, during the 1920s and 1930s, examined the meaning-constituting acts of children.[68] Vygotsky sought to uncover the origins of human consciousness in the emotional life, rather than in the behavioural acts, of biological beings. He attributed the genesis of consciousness in a child to his or her 'word meanings' of the 'internal aspect of speech'. Much like my sense of a 'meaning-constituting act' as elaborated above, Vygotsky suggests that a child means by bringing his or her social relations into a word: 'the primary function of speech, in both children and adults, is communication, social contact', he wrote.[69] A 'word meaning' unifies thought with communication. Vygotsky offered evidence that the child begins to form words *after* he or she gains meaning from the social context in which he or she utters words.[70] If he is right, speech originates in the pre-intellectual, sociocultural experience of the child. The body is a part, if not the most important part, of that experience. The child constitutes her meanings and fulfils his or her meant objects from his or her *Umwelt* or 'environing world'.

Interestingly, when an interpreter, such as Haldane, surrounds himself with posited objects which the interpreter idealizes, Vygotsky describes such an idealization as a 'pseudo-concept'[71] or 'primitive thought'.[72] Expert knowers who believe that posited texts and facts constrain the knower, then, tend to study the product rather than the concealed meanings of legal signification.

Indeed, the infamous tool of pedagogy in a professional law school, the 'crib', manifests a mechanism which considers laws as objects "out there" to be "learned" and utilized as things. The law student learns to translate words and sentences ready-made rather than to experience the words and sentences as her own, and as the author's, embodiment of meaning. The law student learns legal language as if it were addressed by and to an imaginary person, abstracted from any biography and signified as a 'keyword' in pre-existing signifying chains. A curriculum imposes a rigid timetable upon the student's ability to learn the intellectual tools and magic configurations of names. The timetable also treats the student as if he or she were without a biography – as if his or her experiences do not direct meant objects towards the tools and names. Without such lived meanings, the student cannot speak or write legal language fluently. The language is meaningless. Because the interpreter's 'environing world' draws from his or her experiential body, the professional knower *acts* when he or she reads, speaks and writes. Again, the student who is trained to translate a language is led to believe that both interpreter and text are passive dead objects over which the knower possesses no control. Such a belief involves the rule of "laws" rather than the rule of interpreters.

The importance of one's 'environing world' to the meaning-constituting act requires that one redirect one's focus from the trace of authority to some absent Object to the meaning-constituting acts of the knower and the non-knower.[73] When a knower begins legal analysis as if the "facts and circumstances of a case" are uncontrollable, the knower loses contact with perceptual experience. The knower projects the absent object, rather than a meant object, as real. The posit of the representation of the referent – a text, a "fact", a non-knower – and the corresponding concept of the representation *conceal* the whole of a knower's existence, let alone the client's, the witness's and other lawyers'. What has been taken as "legal analysis" of represented facts and represented doctrines constructs a reality which is painfully divorced from the experiential meanings of both legal interpreter and the non-knower. Accordingly, the statute, the precedent, the non-knower and the interpreter are treated as dead products.

The positivist's belief in a truth or reality of posited objects distorts more than the juridical official's meaning. Even configurations of signs, which supposedly represent the true/real, are distorted. How so? The official and the posited external text or fact are detached from each other. The three entities – the interpreter, posited object and sign(ifier) – become concepts or doctrines which the interpreter represent amongst differentiating signs. The posit of the text or fact severs the experiential links which otherwise unite an *embodied* interpreter with his or her meant facts and texts. The modern legal discourse, to the extent that it presupposes posited objects, maintains an arm's length between the interpreter and text or fact.

I can understand how a body lives only if I reject a posit of the body as physical–chemical matter. I must return to the body which I am experiencing at this moment: back aching, head throbbing, my mind/body wondering whether my rereading of my meant objects in this text will ever be joined in dialogue with others, my body searching for signs which I might mean and with which the addressee might also share. The experiential body is a work of art, Merleau Ponty points out, in that it links embodied meanings; it is not a work of science. As a work of science, the body would detach a posited object from a subject.[74] Instead, a subject gains access to a text or other object by reading meant objects into the text. So too can a novel, poem, painting, or musical work communicate as the addressee reads the sounds, colours and other percepts of the work. The addressee reads 'nascent movements' within the author's body as the addressee reads the author's texts.

Is there a juridical world, then, separate from the professional knower's meanings? As a professional knower, I live *through* the stories which witnesses represent to me. The stories take on a meaning for me as I integrate them into a narrative which means something to me, as a professional. Even when the witnesses and documentary evidence "establish" certain facts which a judge accepts as "facts", I perceive the facts. I do not perceive them by picturing them in an objectless world beyond me. Rather, I situate the facts within my horizons of meaning which I know because I have already experienced them. My horizons delimit whether the percept will mean something to me. My former experiences build up and strengthen the boundaries of my horizons. Thus, although my 'environing world' may induce me to picture the utterances of witnesses as representative of posited facts, I interpret when I perceive through sound and sight. I incorporate my horizons of meaning, drawn from concrete social–cultural contexts, into my interpretive act. My 'environing world', which I have constructed through my experiences, generates my interpretation of the world as externally posited, just as it did for Haldane. No external product – neither my biological body, nor the protoplasm of my biological body, nor a posited text, nor socially posited facts – generates meaning. In order to understand how my experiencing body means the social–cultural context, then, I must retrieve my experiences which lie *prior* to the constitution of such posited objects. When I do, I shall find that my experiential body actively *surges* towards them as I perceive them. My meanings interweave with the environment which I hitherto may have taken as also externally posited.

When I communicate with another professional knower or even with a non-knower, I project my meanings into the listener's 'environing world'.[75] It is possible, of course, that there is such a *differend* between my experiences and expectations on the one hand and those of the non-knower on the other. If there were, we do not share meanings. We may speak past one another even though we may utilize the same configurations of signs. We may carry on a monologue vis-à-vis each other. I communicate authentically with my peers and with a non-knower when my dialogic partner responds in a manner which challenges my horizons of meaning and thereby transforms me. I experience such a challenge, and that experience is built into my prejudgments and expectations, just as are other experiences. My listener will resume my gestures and carry them one step further. As Vygotsky demonstrates, sometimes a child responds to an adult in just this manner and, less frequently, the adult likewise responds to the child.[76] My gestures in a dialogic relation blend with the signifying relations of the other lawyer or the non-knower. With such blending, my gestures animate the gestures of the other. As a result, my gestures and utterances carry embodied meaning for the listener as well as for myself. The embodied character of my language is sustained.

A statute in a statute book says nothing; it makes marks on paper. The gestures of my body to and from the marks read the marks. My gestures embody the marks with my horizons of meaning which, in turn, have drawn from my experiences. Instead of the statute imprisoning my analysis, I reach out to the marks through the signs which I share with the statute's text. The shared signs mean something to me.

I reach out in order to *bring* meaning *into* the marks on the statute books. My gestures, not the given marks on the page, constitute meaning. The body gestures meaning. My embodied meanings bring life into the marks on the page. The marks come alive. This is what the Privy Council meant when it described a text, such as the British North Amercia Act, as 'a living tree capable of growth and expansion within its natural limits'.[77] Merleau Ponty similarly describes language as 'an organism'.[78] Even when I silently recall words or thoughts to myself, I gesture meaning towards the unspoken and unwritten words and thereby bring life into my thoughts through my gestures. Conversely, when a word loses meaning for me (such as the word 'fee tail' – an important word in any first year-property class in common law jurisdictions), it becomes empty – a dead, physical sound or particle on paper. As I read marks in a statute book, I bring what I already know and have experienced to bear into them. A unique existence takes hold, and the statute book becomes a text. The text, in turn, carries me beyond what I already know, almost as if I am its addressee. I *plunge* into the words on the page without even imagining or picturing a complete whole.

Of course, I may plunge into words in a manner which seems mysterious to another expert knower or even to a non-knower as the listener. I may, for example, analyse how some judge may have constituted his or her meanings rather than treat his or her doctrine as a posited magic object to be manipulated as a product – as a dead thing. My interpretive activity may yield strange sounds which seem strangely dissonant to the legal discourse. But soon, my words may draw the judge into modified horizons of meaning. He or she may gain access to the new horizons. And, in the judge's process of embodying my utterances and marks, he or she will bring his or her life into my signifying relations.

Here, we see the relevance of Husserl's and Heidegger's critique of the supposed determinacy of natural and social–cultural referents.[79] The horizons of meaning which surround my interpretation of a witness's stories are always open in that there is always something beyond my gaze. As soon as a story or a text ignites my meanings, I direct my prejudgments and anticipations into the otherwise strange sounds. This process is a 'never-ending synthesis' of my constitution of meaning with my meant objects. This synthesis is invariably incomplete. My gestured meaning changes the significance of any other dialogic partner's meant object. Gadamer cautions that all such meant objects, although they may exhibit a physical manifestation such as marks on a page, wait for my experiential body to direct meaning into them.[80] That meaning will always be indeterminate. As Merleau Ponty puts it, my perceptual experience is always 'of a world, that is ... an indefinite and open multiplicity in which relations are relations of reciprocal implication'.[81]

Against the background of the indeterminate fulfilment of meanings, my embodiment of words and sentences brings my appearance-world or *Umwelt into* them. I surround myself with a world which speaks to me of myself. This environing world situates me in a concrete context which contrasts with the network of posited abstract representations which professional knowers have hitherto taken as authoritative. A meaning of a statute or precedent or witness's story does not dwell behind the words "out there", a 'thing in itself'. A statute or other authoritative text is meant. At the end of my gaze, the text poses immanent possibilities for my further interpretations. A plurality of worlds imbues my interpretation of texts. My bodily gestures invest the texts with my humanity. To use Merleau Ponty's term, my horizons of meaning constitute an 'intentional arc' or 'field of experience' which contextualizes my meanings. The world is my life – my prelogical, premetaphysical, experiential life. So, when another lawyer or a non-knower speaks or writes, my life-world is already there. I read their signs through my life-world; others read my utterances through their life-worlds. As we engage in dialogue we move in many contexts of possible meanings, searching for shared meanings. Of course, although the years of training within a particular discourse influences the horizons of meaning which the professional knower learns to accept, through the constitution of meaning, the knower encounters what is other than him or herself. I do not know a non-knower through authoritatively posited doctrines, I experience that individual as I respond to his or her signs. My response brings my experiences to bear upon the non-knower's signs. I act with others through embodied meanings.

Interpretation through an Environing World

Given the indeterminacy or openness of fulfilment of meaning-constituting acts, listening and reading take on an inevitably interpretive character. Experience is interpretation. To understand a text, such as a statute or a precedent, one does not "get inside" the text: I do not fuse my experiences into the text so that I can play with its magic signifying relations. However, this is not to suggest that the text does not exist. Rather, because I encounter a multiplicity of meanings as my intentional arc meets with the marks in the text, a gap always remains between my 'environing world' and the text as a posited object. My horizons as a professional knower of the text intersect, rather than fuse, with the text as a meant object. In a sense, I engage in dialogue with myself as text, as I try to bring possible readings into my intentional arc. When I interpret dialogically, I understand the text.[82] The text always remains the same with the same title and the same provisions but, as I reread it, my interpretations of it continually rejuvenate meaning. I thereby come to understand the text and myself at deeper and deeper levels.

The critical point in the interpretation of "facts" and texts is the lawyer/interpreter's horizons of meanings in his or her 'environing world' or *Umwelt*. My 'environing world' makes the words in a statute or fact concrete. This contrasts with the traditional surface project which takes the statute as a posited object. Meaning is shared when the interpreters constitute the same meant object as they speak and read. As Gadamer points out in 'Man and Language', if one speaks a language that no one understands, then one does not really speak. This helps to explain why a professional law school expends such efforts to induce shared experiences and a shared formalist language amongst future lawyers. Lawyers must speak and write to other lawyers. If lawyers share a configuration of signs and if they attribute similar meant objects to the configuration because of their similar professional experiences, they may actually believe that their meant objects are "real" and "practical". Such a sharing may well be the social function of an oppressive pedagogy which presupposes that some absent holy ghost grounds authoritative doctrines. The student must learn to reproduce the doctrines as products – as things – when hired to give a legal opinion or to argue a case before a court. Lawyers share horizons of meaning. Gadamer argues that this sharing constitutes 'spirit'. This 'spirit', however, is not the external transcendent *a priori* foundation presupposed in modern legal discourse; it dwells in the intertext between interpreter and text, interpreter and particular other. The spirit permeates a dialogue in which an individual's utterance possesses a multiplicity of meanings until the respondent responds. Such a multiplicity of embodied meanings contrasts with the emptied transcendental foundation of legal authority.

In this manner a professional knower, as interpreter, connects the external world with his or her 'environing world' when he or she reads a word, hears an utterance or perceives an event. The interpreter brings the posited object into his or her 'environing world' so as to constitute a meant object. The text or the utterance are meant objects. In contrast, the modern legal discourse, as I argued in Chapter 2 and illustrated in Chapter 3, brings a passive interpreter *to* the posited text. Precisely because meaning precedes a represented thought, as Vygotsky noted, communication inevitably involves embodied interpretation. An interpreter charges the other's utterances with meaning. The sound images of the other reawaken meaning in the interpreter's life-world.

Professional knowers experience through language. Contrary to the classical episteme of knowledge, a sign does not represent a statute or precedent as if the object were a chemical–physical, measurable product. Contrary to the conventional reading of Saussure, a structure of signs does not autonomously differentiate representations.[83] An interpreter differentiates signs as he or she reads them through his or her 'environing world'. The interpreter experiences as he or she privileges one chain of signs over another and his or her prejudgments and anticipations therefore enter into that experience. In this interpretive act, a referent, such as a statutory provision or a judicial precedent, is contextualized in secondary signifying relations. The sign representing the referent is brought into the horizons of meaning of the interpreter's 'environing world'.[84] Thus, I do not "understand" the referent cognitively by reflection or representation. I understand the referent by embodying it with the *prejudice* of my 'environing world'. My 'environing world' humanizes the secondary chains of signs. As Gadamer suggests, the 'original humanity of language' imbues my being-in-the-world. My constitution of meaning is fulfilled in a meant object: both bring my humanity into language. Such a humanity, hitherto concealed within the modern legal discourse, is disclosed as I interpret a text or a story. The humanity of the interpreter is concealed because the modern legal discourse treats chains of signs as a product to be used and because the representer of the legal discourse naively and passively begins and ends his or her analysis with a posited object. Even the biography of the professional knower is abstracted.

Notes

1 This theme is examined in the context of the history of legal positivism in my *The Divine Origins of Legal Positivism* (forthcoming).

2 See, for example, Bora Laskin, 'Peace, Order and Good Government Re-Examined' in *Canadian Bar Review*, vol. 25 (1947): 1057–87; ibid., as reprinted in W.R. Lederman ed., *The Courts and the Canadian Constitution* (Toronto: McClelland & Stewart, 1964; Carleton Library No. 16): 66–104.

3 Stephen Wexler, 'The Urge to Idealize: Viscount Haldane and the Constitution' in *McGill Law Journal*, vol. 29 (1984): 608–47, 614.

4 Laskin lists the ten cases in which Haldane represented the provinces in 'Peace, Order and Good Government Re-examined' note 2 *supra*. Wexler documents how privately appreciative Haldane was for the opportunity to have some income from one Quebec case in Wexler, note 3 *supra*, 621–23.

5 Viscount Haldane, 'The Cabinet and The Empire' in *Proceedings of the Royal Colonial Institute*, vol. 34 (1902–3): 325, as quoted in Stephen Wexler, 'The Urge to Idealize: Viscount Haldane and the Constitution of Canada' in *McGill Law Journal*, vol. 29 (1984): 608–50, 628–29.

6 Jonathan Robinson, 'Lord Haldane and the British North America Act' in *University of Toronto Law Journal*, vol. 20 (1970): 55–69.

7 As quoted in Wexler, note 3 *supra*, 634–5.

8 See ibid., 636–7.

9 *Fort Francis Pulp and Paper Company* v. *Manitoba Free Press* [1925] AC 695, [1923] 3 DLR 629 (PC).

10 Concerning Husserl's views of Galileo's discovery and concealment behind ideal geometric constructions, see Edmund Husserl, *The Crisis of the European Sciences* (David Carr trans.; Evanston: Northwestern University Press, 1970): 50–52.

For Husserl's criticism of Descartes, see ibid., 82; re Hume, see ibid 88, 95 and *Logical Investigations*, Investigation V (New York: Humanities Press, 1970): 546–7; and re Kant, see *The Crisis*, ibid., 96.

11 The latter term is explained in William E. Conklin, 'The Legal Theory of Horkheimer and Adorno' in *Windsor Yearbook of Access to Justice*, vol. 5 (1985): 230–57.

12 Edmund Husserl, Investigation VI, note 10 *supra*, 701.

13 Husserl, Investigation V, ibid., 562.

14 Ibid., 560–62.

15 Ibid., 540.

16 Also see 'Appendix' to ibid.

17 347 US 483 (1953); 98 L Ed. 873. Citations are made to the latter Report.

18 Ibid., 493.

19 Ibid., 494.

20 Ibid., 493.

21 Ibid., 491.

22 Ibid., 495.

23 Mark de Wolfe ed., *Holmes–Pollock Letters*, vol. 2 (Cambridge: Harvard University Press, 1941): 200.

24 Oliver W. Holmes, 'The Path of the Law' (1920) *Collected Legal Papers* (New York: Peter Smith, 1952): 179.

25 Oliver W. Holmes, *The Common Law* (Cambridge: Harvard University Press, 1963): 38.

26 Ibid., 40.

27 *Schenck* v. *US*, 249 US47, 39 S.Ct247, 63 L. Ed.470 (1919).

28 *Debs* v. *US*, 249 US211, 39 S.Ct249, 63 L. Ed.566 (1919).

29 *Abrams* v. *US*, 250 US616 (1919).

30 *Lochner* v. *NY*, 198 US45, 25 S.Ct.539, 49 L. Ed.937 (1905).

31 *Buck* v. *Bell*, 274 US200, 47 S.Ct.584, 71 L. Ed.1042 (1927).

32 Ibid., 207.

33 Ibid., 206.

34 M.D. Howe ed., *Holmes–Laski Letters, 1916–1935* (Cambridge: Harvard University Press, 1953): 190.

35 Ibid., 203.

36 *Gitlow* v. *NY*, 268 US652, 45S.Ct.625, 69 L. Ed.1136 (1925).

37 Oliver W. Holmes, 'Natural Law' in *Collected Legal Papers*, note 24 *supra*. For his wartime experiences also see 'Deals and Doubts' in *Collected Legal Papers*, note 24 *supra*, 304. Reprinted in *Illinois Law Review* (1915): 109.

38 H.D. Aiken, 'Introduction' in W. Barrett and H.D. Aiken eds., *Philosophy in the Twentieth Century*, vol. 1 (New York: Harper & Row, 1962): 80.

39 Holmes, *The Common Law*, note 25 *supra*, 38.

40 Letter dated 23 July 1925, *Holmes–Laski Letters*, note 34 *supra*, 202–3.

41 Oliver Holmes, *Speeches* (1934) as quoted in F.E. Lucey, 'Holmes-Liberal-Humanitarian-Believer in Democracy?', *Georgia Law Journal*, vol. 39 (1951): 523, 538.

42 *Holmes–Laski Letters*, vol. 1, note 34 *supra*, 431.

43 Holmes, as cited in M. Lerner, *The Mind and Faith of Justice Holmes* (New York: Little, Brown, 1943): 42.

44 Oliver W. Holmes, 'The Gas-Stokers' Strike' in *Harvard Law Review*, vol. 44 (1931): 795–96, 795.

45 Holmes, 'Natural Law' in *Collected Legal Papers*, note 24 *supra*, 311.

46 Holmes, *The Common Law*, note 25 *supra*, 38.

47 *Holmes–Pollock Letters*, vol. 2, note 23 *supra*, 230.

48 Holmes, 'Natural Law' in *Collected Legal Papers*, note 24 *supra*, 311.

49 Holmes, 'Law in Science and Science in Law' (1899) in ibid., 225–6.

50 Letter dated 23 October, 1926 in *Holmes–Laski Letters*, note 34 *supra*, 888.
51 Letter dated 1 June 1927 in ibid., 948.
52 Letter dated 19 January 1928 in *Holmes–Pollock Letters*, vol. 2, note 23 *supra*, 212.
53 Emphasis added.
54 *US* v. *Schwimmer*, 279 US644 (1929), 49 S.Ct.448, 73 L. Ed.889.
55 *Meyer* v. *Nebraska*, 262 US390 (1923), 43 S.Ct.625, 67 L. Ed.1042; *Bartels* v. *State of Iowa*, 262 US400 (1923), 43 S.Ct.628.
56 Husserl uses this term in 'Investigation VI', s. 14 in *Logical Investigations*, vol. 2, note 10 *supra*, 711.
57 Husserl, Investigation I, s. 10, ibid., 283.
58 See Husserl, 'Investigation V', s. 7, ibid., 546.
59 Jacob von Uexkull offers a key to this question in *Theoretical Biology* (trans. D.L. Mackinnon; London: Kegan Paul, 1926) and in Jacob Von Uexkull, 'The Theory of Meaning' in *Semiotics*, vol. 92, no. 1 (1982): 25–82. Von Uexkull points to protoplasm as the driving force of the meaning-forming process. Protoplasm generates, repairs, moves and regulates the system without external help. Protoplasm initially generates organs from a physical mass. This genesis of organs is 'almost unlimited' in its formative possibilities. (*Theoretical Biology*, 355). Protoplasm drives an organism in a direction *internal* to the works themselves (ibid., 19).
60 Von Uexkull, *Theoretical Biology*, note 59 *supra*, 71.
61 Ibid., 29.
62 Thomas A. Sebeok, *The Sign and Its Masters* (Austin/London: University of Texas Press, 1979).
63 Ibid., 19.
64 Erwin Schrodinger, *What is Life? Mind and Matter* (Cambridge: Cambridge University Press, 1967): 99.
65 Sebeok, note 62 *supra*, 194.
66 Husserl, *The Crisis*, note 10 *supra*.
67 Ibid., 160. Also see Husserl, 'Denial of Scientific Philosophy' in ibid.: 389–95, 390; and 'The Vienna Lecture' in ibid.: 269–99, 275.
68 Vygotsky, *Thought and Language* was first published in Russian in 1934, reprinted in 1956 and 1982, and published in English in 1962 (Cambridge MA: MIT Press, 1962).
69 Ibid., 34.
70 See especially ibid., 80–95.
71 Ibid., 119.
72 Ibid., 126.
73 The *Umwelt* is not simply a response of the body. Even Whitehead argued that the environment is already sensory and that basic entities have sensory aspects.
74 Mildred Bakan, 'Mind as Life and Form' in R.W. Reiber ed., *Body and Mind: Past, Present and Future* (New York: Academic Press, 1980): 131–54, 150.
75 Maurice Merleau-Ponty, *Prose of the World* (John O'Neill trans.; Evanston: Northwestern University Press, 1973): 19.
76 See especially Vygotsky, *Thought and Language*, note 68 *supra*, 29–47.
77 *Edwards* v. *A.G. Canada* [1930] AC123, [1930] 1 DLR98 (PC).
78 Maurice Merleau-Ponty, *Phenomenology of Perception* (Colin Smith trans.; London: Routledge & Kegan Paul, 1962): 181.
79 For Werner Heisenberg's analysis, see his 'The Copenhagen Interpretation of Quantum Theory' in *Physics and Philosophy* (London: Allen & Unwin, 1958): 44–58.
80 Hans-Georg Gadamer, 'Man and Language' in *Philosophical Hermeneutics* (Berkeley: University of California Press, 1976): 59–68.

81 Hans George Gadamer, *Truth and Method* (New York: Crossroad, 1985): 345–47.
82 Ibid., 345–7; 'Man and Language', note 80 *supra*.
83 However, for a very different reading of Saussure – one which claims that the body did figure in Saussure's theory of language – see Paul Thibault, *Re-Reading Saussure* (London: Routledge, 1996).
84 Gadamer, *Truth and Method*, note 81 *supra*, 377.

6 The Idealism of a Modern Legal Discourse

An important problematic arises from my above argument. Are the embodied meanings of the non-knower, much like the Spirit of the Laws, unreachable within the play of authoritative signs? If so, do the non-knower's embodied meanings function as an invisible or inaccessible centre to the phenomenology of suffering in the modern legal discourse? Are the embodied meanings similar to a transcendent foundation at the end of legal reasoning? Do the primary genres serve as an "inside" and the secondary discourse the "outside"? Do the concealed genres represent an *arche* or foundation for the reformed professional knowers? Does the phenomenology of suffering follow the traditional effort to define difference in terms of identity, as Derrida maintains in his criticism of Hegel and Heidegger and the language of metaphysics generally? The secondary legal discourse supplements the meaning-constituting act. The legal discourse supplements the supplement. One metaphysics has been substituted for another, it might be claimed. The situs of Truth has merely been displaced. The new situs exiles the secondary discourse as a reification of embodied presentative meanings at the centre.

Another set of issues goes to the character of the retrieved meanings. Does the claim that an authoritative discourse conceals such embodied meanings simply perpetuate the age-old search for an origins of thought – this time in a particular other rather than in a transcendent other? Has the alien, silent foundation of legal authority been replaced with another which is equally alien, and silent? Would the retrieval of the embodied meanings share the monologic character of the secondary discourse? Would the authority of primary genres share the violence which is endemic with metaphysics? If not, why not?

In responding to these issues, I shall argue that a tinge of idealism permeates the modern legal discourse. Many hidden languages lie inside the legal discourse. The possibility remains that these concealed languages, through which one represents an indigenously experienced pain, remain alive.

Is the Foundation of Legal Discourse Accessible?

The exteriority of the *arche* of legal discourse is essential for rules to be considered posited. Why? If one posits an object, the object's situs must possess some finality. Without finality, the object fluctuates like a drop of water in a river, to use a metaphor from Heraclitus. One cannot identify the drop as "that" drop because it is immersed in an ever-changing stream. The ever-changing flux of the particulars of the stream makes it difficult to render an identity to the stream. A text manifests just such a transience when one cannot rationally link the text to an author who, in turn, can be linked to other authors. Without a finality, a text is a mere fragment. One would not know whether some other institutional source could authoritatively overrule any one enactment or decision. Without an exterior foundation, a rule would lack a posited character. With finality, a text can be joined with other texts to bring order and direction.

Now, the problem is that if the final grounds resembles all other texts, then it cannot be final. For how is one to know that one should stop one's trace to the "final" sign if the "final" sign resembles the character of a sign like all the others? No one text would be recognizable as posited because the trace of signs would continue *ad infinitum*. In order to be final, the ultimate foundation must be radically other than some configuration of signs. All of the leading positivists of modern legal thought realize that they must identify, or at least offer the possibility of, a foundation which radically differs from all other norms and rules. The foundation cannot be posited by expert knowers. The foundation must dwell beyond the configurations of signs in some transcendent situs. The presupposition that such a foundation actually exists opens the possibility that a sign can be posited. Without the inaccessible foundation, presupposed to dwell beyond the official discourse, any one rule would be temporary, ad hoc, unpredictable, and uncertain. Such a fragment could hardly be described as posited, because a posited sign, as understood in a modern positivist state, must possess some certainty, predictability, generality and universality to represent what can be considered a "law". The 'state of nature', the 'greatest good of the greatest number', the *Grundnorm*, the 'unspoken judicial practices', the coherent political theory of Hercules, 'second-level exclusionary reasons' of legal reasoning – these suggested foundations to a positivist legal order function to finalize the trace of texts, just as does the *arche*, *telos*, consciousness, God, man, Justice or *aletheia* in philosophic discourses.

The presupposed fixed origin or 'point of presence' orients, balances and organizes the coherence of a structure.[1] At the same moment that the state of nature, the *Grundnorm* or 'unstated judicial practices' governs the structure of rules and principles of a legal discourse, such signified foundations escape the structurality of signs of authored laws. The foundation must escape the structurality of signs represented in a legal discourse in order to be considered a foundation. Because Hobbes, Bentham, Kelsen, Hart and all the others situate the 'state of nature' or *Grundnorm* or other foundation beyond the structurality of authored texts, the foundation is a lack or absence. It is situated outside legal language in a prior unexamined or unexaminable centre.

The very lack of this centre motivates the juridical representer to try to reach it. The claim to know the signs which represent the centre brings cohesion to fragments. The inaccessible centre must necessarily be a Oneness; otherwise, the representers of the centre would have to continue their search for a foundation. In order to finalize all rules, this foreign Oneness must transcend all rules; it must be situated outside the contingent and the finite. All juridical officials "know" whether a text can be traced to such a transcendent foundation. The juridical official interprets in the name of this nameless and inaccessible foundation.

Of course, in the drive to reach such an inaccessible foundation, the embodied meanings of the non-knower become overlaid with layers and layers of secondary signifying relations. Juridical officials long to retrieve what is unretrievable. The closest to which the knower can reach the foundation of posited rules is a picture or spectre of the foundation. The picture delineates boundaries; it privileges figures and background considerations to the exclusion of others. The spectre articulates fantasies *about* the identity of the absent foundation. The more rigorous the analysis of the concepts associated with the spectre, the closer, it is presumed, is one to the absent foundation.

Being a self-contained Oneness beyond all cognition and all experience, this final, ultimate foundation to the posited laws is bodiless in the sense of a physiological and a phenomenal body. And yet, the representer – the knower – of the final source associates a semblance of authorship with the founding source: the Author of the Laws is believed to create and to constrain. In Chapter 4, I described the foundation of legal discourse as a 'spirit'.[2] A lonely figure gazing from afar, the Spirit of the Laws is believed to pre-exist the language of the knowers. However lawyers picture it, the Spirit remains transparent, bodiless, soulless, and inaccessible from within the networks of authored signs.

As the spectre of the foundation of the laws takes form through the configurations of signs, the foundation itself remains a secret.

Indeed, just as officials guard the massive doorways to the Castle of Law in Kafka's little story at the end of *The Trial*, we lawyers must guard against any threat to the secret that our trace of authority presupposes a grounding in a spirit. After all, what could be more offensive to our scientized language than the possibility that we can, at best, possess a spectre or picture of a foundation as we imprison over 1 million of our populace, many with the visible attributes of one race, in 12-foot-square dungeons, as we execute one such prisoner per week in Texas alone as I write, as we authorize the expulsion of tenants from the doorsteps of abandoned tenement houses, and as we have authorized the acts of other guardians who have shared in the "civil" killing of over 19 million human beings in the name of authority during this century? What could be more alien to the claims of formalism and objectivity of our spectre of the Spirit of the Laws than that our spectre rests upon a secret – the secret of a ghost who dwells at the end of our practical juridical reasoning of which we are so proud?

The secrecy surrounding the originary foundation of a secondary legal genre is important to my argument. For once one appreciates that a never-ending differentiation of signs displaces primary genres and once one understands that legal discourse is haunted by the ghostly spectre of a foundation, the phenomenon of displacement occurs in the name of the Spirit. The non-knower may well still mean his or her signifying relations. Indeed, his or her own languages may also presuppose the spectre of a Spirit at the end of his or her everyday genres. But his or her primary genres are concealed *inside* the dispersing authoritative chains of signs which the guardians of the Spirit take as authoritative. The haunted spectre of the foundation of the secondary legal genre violently displaces all other challengers as outlaws. Derrida exposes the very violence of a believed presence with such an originary foundation in his important essay, 'Force of Law'. The non-knower of legal discourse must either speak through the privileged signifying relations of modern legal discourse or retain a representer of the discourse to speak on his or her behalf.

Once it is realized that the professional knower envisions the foundation at the end of legal reasoning, all that is left of legal discourse is a potential multiplicity of differentiating signs or what Derrida calls 'grams' or finite, contingent units. Infinite substitutions of grams characterize the moment before juridical agents configure signs to represent an external object. In contrast, the foundation of legal authority dwells in the inexhaustible transcendent field beyond the finite and beyond the contingent. The play of grams continuously moves in supplementarity.[3] When a lawyer writes or speaks, he or she inevitably privileges some signs over others from an infinite possibility of substitutions without ever reaching the infinite of a transcendent foundation.[4] Similarly, legislators privilege configurations of signs in a statute or constitutional text. So too, do judges privilege special configurations when they elaborate a legal doctrine: they read a statute in terms of a web of configurations which they consider weighty and 'binding'. This substitution process recodes the configurations to give a sense of coherency and order to the play. This recoding situates the non-knower's story in terms of opposites: clear and present danger versus free speech; emergency versus national dimensions; reasonable time versus demand note; title versus possession. The trace of such opposites to some singular presupposed foundation beyond all grams adds a sense of coherency to the signification.

Without the spectre of a foundation to the trace of authority, gazing from beyond the discourse, the phenomenon of displacement becomes critical. The violence with which the secondary legal discourse displaces the inside non-knower's story, becomes naked violence. The configured spectre of the foundation sanitizes the violence of displacement into the objective aura of an impartial umpire.

Is the Non-knower an Invisible Author?

If an invisible author is believed to found the legal discourse of a modern state, do the concealed meanings of a non-knower share a similar inaccessibility? Is the non-knower an invisible author to the modern legal discourse? Is the non-knower also a ghost? Are there a multiplicity of such ghosts concealed inside the modern legal discourse? As with the Spirit of the Law, a moment of the presence of the non-knower's embodied meanings is lost in the play of grams. The best that the knower can do is to approximate the non-knower's meanings through representing signs.

Two invisible authors seem to characterize an authoritative discourse, then. On the one hand, there is believed to be a ghost-like author who, bodiless and voiceless, transcends the contingently configured signs of the legal discourse. This is the Spirit of the Law. Being exterior to the discourse, this transcendent origin is a radical other to the legal discourse.

On the other hand, there is a second radical other to the legal discourse. In order for professional knowers to recognize an indigenously experienced pain, the legal discourse assimilates the pain, as a signified event, into the secondary signifying relations of the legal discourse. Ironically, despite its assimilationist claim to represent the whole social order, the legal discourse depends upon the non-knower's primary genres in order to initiate the legal discourse. Without a particular other who pleads that his or her harm be recognized by juridical officials or, alternatively, without a particular other who must be excluded from an act of juridical recognition, the legal discourse would have no signified referent. Although dependent upon primary genres, the secondary legal discourse cannot reach the non-knower's story because the legal discourse, as a secondary discourse, possesses its own chains of signs which represent and resituate the non-knower's story, I argued in Chapter 2. The non-knower becomes invisible in that a particular non-knower, with a biography, is transformed into a juridical person whose rights and duties give him or her a legal identity. The secondary discourse cannot reach the primary genres except through the secondary signifying relations. The authoritative discourse cannot read the non-knower's stories through the non-knower's language.

In this respect, if justice is the language of the non-knower as a radical other to legal discourse, an authoritative discourse cannot be just.[5] The legal discourse is not, and cannot be, just because the discourse cannot recognize the grievances of subjects through their own primary genres. Legal discourse appropriates and assimilates the signs of a non-knower into the language of an 'implicit third' institutionalized by the objective, impartial and extrinsic situs of a judge.

Of course, the concealed signifying relations in primary genres do remain accessible to the non-knower, unless the juridical agents execute the non-knower's body or "succeed" in torturing the non-knower so that he or she loses her primary genres and can only utter meaningless sounds.[6] The embodied meanings of a knower, as well as the embodied objects of the non-knower, are lived – but not in a biological sense. Rather, a text becomes alive because the interpreter brings his or her past experiences and expectations towards an external object, I argued in the previous chapter. It would be a serious misunderstanding to believe that the immediate relation of environing world and text is natural in a biological or physical–chemical sense. Rather, taking a term from Hegel and from Plato in *The Laws*, the immediate relation between the interpreter's felt experiences and his or her meanings defines a 'second nature'. Habit and education induce the interpreter to speak "without thinking", so to speak. As H.L.A. Hart suggested, a judge applies 'unspoken' practices without recognizing them until after they have been applied. The relationship between interpreter to the text is context-specific, and the interpreter's environing world of past experiences and future expectations constitutes an important element of that context. Professional knowers may even share such an environing world to the point that an interpretation seems natural, inevitable and objective. Their picture of the Spirit of authority haunts their environing world. Indeed, one does not become a lawyer when one has passed the appropriate Bar exams. One becomes a lawyer when one begins to "think like a lawyer", when one's experiences, as a professional knower, begin to take a shape which other professional knowers will recognize as their own environing world.

The Idealism of the Secondary Play

If professional knowers embody their spectre of the Spirit of authority from a never-ending play of magic signs, then a particular configuration of signs is a "given" at any particular moment. The nomenclature and grammar of the configurations pre-exist the lawyer. The professional knower may hide, acting as counsel to another genre, such as journalism, the entertainment industry or a feminist research institute but, in order to address juristic agents, an expert knower will find him or herself drawing from the idiom of the knowers of the legal signs. As I argued in Chapter 2, the lawyer can represent pain and suffering only through familiar and recognizably authoritative chains of signs which are just "there". The modern legal genre encourages the juridical official to understand a configuration in terms of its ultimate absent foundation. But the project of justifying statutes and cases in terms of higher-order grounds is itself the effect of configurations which work to make one "think like a lawyer". The lawyer's ratiocination project possesses neither a genesis nor a *telos* as its foundation; the "facts of the case" are signified through familiar authoritative signs. Even the law reformer works within the chains of signs which are recognized as authoritative in the secondary legal genre. A legislature, judge or a scholar just cannot escape from legal language. As Derrida says more generally in 'The Ends of Man',[7] an interpreter cannot decide to escape from language, and by language, of course, he means the never-ending chains of signifying relations. Heidegger puts the point in this way: human beings 'must first learn to exist in the nameless'. Or, as Foucault claims, 'when he [an individual] tries to define himself as a living being, he can uncover his own beginning only against a background of a life which itself began long before him'.[8]

As a consequence of the "thereness" of the play of signs, the meaning-conferring acts of the non-knower remain frustrated. The non-knower is divested of the means to argue through his or her own idiom.[9] Even though the critic may phrase his or her project in terms of the harm to the non-knower, the latter's embodied meanings become forgotten, lost, unrecognized except in the alien configurations by and for the professional critic. Such lost meanings are what Mikhail Bakhtin calls the 'heteroglot … which insures the primacy of context over text'. He suggests that,

> At any given time, at any given place, there will be a set of conditions – social, historical, meteorological, physiological – that will insure that a word uttered in that place and at that time will have a meaning different than it would have under any other conditions; all utterances are heteroglot in that they are functions of a matrix of forces practically impossible to recoup, and therefore impossible to resolve … .[10]

Legal discourse fails to recoup the heteroglot of meant objects.

The Violence of the Modern Legal Discourse

Thus, a violence permeates the phenomenon of heteroglossia in modern legal discourse, first, in that as we lawyers interpret texts which are considered authoritative, we displace the non-knower's configurations of signs. Second, we lawyers displace competing languages in the name of their spectre of the Spirit which is believed to have originated, and therefore to have pre-existed, our trace of authority. This originary violence is neither legal nor illegal – it emanates from the first act of configuring authoritative signs. The violence is the imposition of the spectre of the final foundation without a gounding. No further norm or rule justifies the final norm. It just "is": it is a presupposed end. All non-knowers who believe in, and who live through, other languages must accept the originary violent act of legal language to avoid being categorized as an outlaw. They must accept the violence silently, deferentially and without question.

The secret absence of the *Grundnorm* or 'rule of recognition' or 'social facts' or other named *arche* point, familiar to the theorists of legal discourse, is not the only element which the juridical official forgets as he or she plays with the 'magically binding' signs. For meaning to be fulfilled, there must be a referent. However, I have shown that the referent for a juridical official in the modern legal discourse is another authoritative sign: the referent of Haldane's emergency doctrine was a sign, 'emergency', not the political circumstance of an emergency; the referent of Holmes' 'free speech' doctrine was a sign, 'clear and present danger', not the content of the speech. The referent, being another sign, could fulfil another sign, however absurd the social outcome at the time. But this fulfilment of a sign's representation in another sign misses the social context, even a signified context, where a non-knower embodies his or her signs with meanings. But precisely because the play of signs excludes an embodied subject as a referent – except in terms of authoritative signs which signify rights and duties defining a juridical person – the play remains forever unfulfilled and therefore indeterminate. An authoritative configuration only becomes fulfilled in another sign. The secondary discourse forever fails to reach the non-knower's pain as a social–cultural referent unless the secondary configurations themselves weave the significations of the non-knower's pain within authoritative chains of signs. Even then, though, the non-knower's embodied meanings become signified. The signified pain is thus recognized only if prior configurations of authoritative chains can give a place to the signified pain.

As exemplified in the case of the American and Canadian internment of 'persons of Japanese ancestry', the signified facts may be so transformed into the new secondary language that the facts may be unrecognizable to the non-knower. Even the non-knower's stories of angst, of curfews, of confiscated property, of the internment and deportation of citizens and 'aliens' became lost in the trace of authority. The sole issue became 'did the military commander possess the authority to signify the "facts" as conducive to sabotage and espionage?' The juridical recognition of the "facts" produced a concealed *differend*. The embodied meanings of the non-knower were displaced by, and for, the secondary juridical language of the modern state.

The juridical official is immersed in an idealizing production. The interpreter privileges a particular configuration which loses the particular social context of the non-knower's story. As a result, the interpreter becomes unable to address the non-knower in his or her own language. The sanitizing discourse conceals the ethnocentric interpreter's experiences, experiences which may well be induced through years of professional training in the genres of legal discourse. The particular non-knower's meanings are signified in a transformatory act which "makes sense" only to the expert knowers of the secondary legal genre. The non-knower cannot stop the enforcement of the transforming discourse even though the transformation occurs in his or her name. Ironically, without the non-knower's story, legal language could not become an enforceable secondary language since there would be no language of an other against which to enforce the legal discourse. In the trace of authoritative signs there must always be an other, but the other dwells hidden *inside* the displacing configurations of authoritative signs, rather than in some foreign transcendental *arche* or source which gazes from afar.

The Idealization of the Non-knower's Story

As the secondary discourse assimilates primary genres, the non-knower's embodied meanings are reconfigured and transformed into secondary signifying relations. The juristic agents of the Spirit of the Laws signify the non-knower's meant objects through signs which make sense to the 'environing world' of the professional knower.

Because the Spirit is an unexamined and unexaminable foundation, all professional knowers are driven to conquer competing stories and narratives. The linkage of a chain of signs to the Spirit of authority authorizes an official's speech. The juristic knower can never present the non-knower's story because the knower can only re-present the story through the configurations of signs which make sense to the profession of expert knowers, not necessarily to the non-knower. Professional knowers search in vain to enclose what the secondary legal discourse lacks – an inaccessible foundation. The legal discourse cannot complete the enclosure. The non-knower's biological body remains a reminder to all juristic agents that the enclosure remains incomplete.

In this imperial quest, the legal discourse loses the experiences of particular experiential beings. Secondary differentiating signs imperceptibly become the referents of the expert knowers who, at the same moment, claim to represent the non-knower. The secondary discourse begins as a supplement to primary genres through which witnesses tell their stories. But the supplement overwhelms (challenges) the primary genres by assimilating the non-knower's meanings into the authoritative signs. The secondary discourse refers to its own familiar configurations of signs in order to represent the non-knower's stories authoritatively.

Three elements of the secondary legal discourse work to idealize the suffering of a non-knower.

First, the referent for secondary signs is another sign. That is, although the professional knower claims to apply a doctrine to the "facts" of a case, the professional knower signifies the "facts" by a special term, such as 'emergency' or 'clear and present danger'. The knower draws out the signification from a network of signs which the lawyer takes as authoritative. The issue for Haldane, for example, was not whether an emergency existed as a political event but whether the sign, 'emergency', could be contextualized within the chains of signifying relations which had hitherto been associated with the founding text. Issues which are of interest to the social historian or the political scientist may be of little concern to the juristic agent because the professional knower reads the signifying configurations as constitutive of an emergency. The act of signification becomes an event. The professional knower takes such an event as practice.

In the leading contemporary Canadian judgment concerning an 'emergency', for example, the highest judge on the judicial hierarchy at the time (Chief Justice Laskin) admitted expert testimony as to whether an emergency existed. Yet, he wrote, such expert testimony did not go 'to the proof of the exceptional circumstances as a matter of fact'. 'The extrinsic material need go only so far as to persuade the

Court that there is a rational basis' to attribute the abstracted emergency to the dominant chain of signs, 'peace, order and good government'. The expert, after all, was a mere 'economist' who could not 'determine the answer' whether the central government may authoritatively legislate during an 'emergency' when the government could not do so ordinarily. The professional legal knower might recognize a referent, such as the social event of an emergency, only if he or she could situate it within recognizable configurations of semiotic differences. As a consequence, the knower reads the harm of the non-knower and the "facts" surrounding that harm as if the signs, not the experienced event, were 'tangible' and 'concrete'.[11]

Again, expert knowers have even described particular legal texts as a 'living tree'. The metaphor may connote that the recirculation of magic signs grows organically. Alternatively, perhaps, the recirculation may situate a text as if the text were an organism. In like vein, lawyers refer to the "body" of law, the "weight" of the evidence, the "heart" of the issue, the "scales" of Justice, the "intent" of the legislature, the "mind" of the legislature, and "the full weight of the law". Immersed for years in the play of authoritative signs, the expert knower may well believe that these chains of signs constitute the whole of social relationships. Ronald Dworkin quite rightly characterized the secondary legal genre as 'imperial' and the judges as 'princes'.

A second factor works to idealize the non-knower's embodied meanings into the secondary configurations of signs. Legal history becomes a history of the trace of signs which the professional knower considers authoritative. Although social classes and economic interests make for the enactment of a legislated text and although gender and race may constitute the 'environing world' of an interpreter, such factors are an aside to the issue of authoritative signs unless the signifying relations, such as those drawing from the American Civil Rights Act, recognize such factors as authoritative. What gives them the aura of authority is their situs in familiar chains which, professional knowers believe, can be grounded in still further chains and, ultimately, in a foundation of the whole trace to the Spirit of legal authority. Even Saussure admitted that the historical direction of particular configurations of signs might well contradict the direction of the social–cultural context surrounding the signs.[12] Since the professional knower is haunted by the Spirit of authority, the authorized sign may "exist", and that existence is what matters. As a consequence, the historical, the social and the moral take on special significations within the secondary legal genre. H.L.A. Hart emphasizes, for example, that once the juristic agent embarks upon the project of retrospectively recognizing the 'unspoken judicial practices' which lie at the foundation of laws, morality carries a 'justificatory' character distinguishable from the anthropological shared beliefs of the citizenry. The primary rules, posited by legislatures and judges, define what is social.

Indeed, particular configurations of signifying relations construct the juridical person itself. The non-knower does not possess a direct entry into the castle of signifying chains. The lawyer representing a non-knower must accept the signifying chains of the legal discourse, mimic them and collate them together into a network which other lawyers will recognize as a strong argument. Even women may not "exist" as juridical persons until judges recognize them within previously recognized authoritative signs. What matters is not the biological appearance of a woman nor the experiences of motherhood, but the situs of a person called 'woman' within chains of statutes and precedents which professional knowers will recognize as authoritative in the trace to the Spirit of authority. The juridical signification of 'woman' is an event itself. Configurations of authoritative signs give her an identity. The play amongst authoritative signs takes on "a life of its own". Signifying relations become events. "Facts" begin and end with such events. A juridical agent, as well as the juridical person who is the subject of the authoritative discourse, are immersed within secondary signifying relations. These signifying relations represent the non-knower's voice so that professional knowers will recognize it as significative. Creativity relates to the ability of one knower to play with the authoritative signs. Volosinov's perceptive commentary seems apt with respect to the secondary signifying relations: 'Language stands before the individual as an inviolable, incontestable norm which the individual, for his part, can only accept.'[13] Once one sign is privileged to the exclusion of another, such an event hierarchizes differences and chains are excluded. But this privileging emanates from signs which colour any lawyer's signifying action with neutrality and impartiality. The play is there, just as is a machine before an operator sits down to operate it. 'The play's the thing': As Foucault offers, 'meaning sleeps an almost invisible sleep in the words [one] momentarily activates by means of discourse'.[14]

Meaning as Social–Cultural Praxis

If the momentary configurations of signs are so effective in assimilating the embodied meanings of a non-knower, is there an engine of social critique of the secondary signifying relations? Traditionally, the critic has viewed legal relations from the vantage-point of the "transcendent" foundation of the legal order. When a juridical agent has become familiar with the knowledge of sociology or psychiatry or literature or Marxism, the agent has critiqued in the spirit of a project which studied laws from outside the vantage point of each discipline. Sometimes, the concept of the 'state of nature' has functioned to provide just such an external transcendent vantage point. For others, such as Kant, a 'perfectly good will' in a noumenal realm has functioned as a standard to judge acts in the phenomenal realm. For John Austin and Jeremy Bentham, in turn, the admittedly 'metaphysical' concept of the 'greatest happiness of the greatest number' served to evaluate the legal doctrines in a 'descriptivist jurisprudence'. Bentham called the discourse of critique, 'censorial jurisprudence'. For Hans Kelsen, the advocacy of a different *Grundnorm* radically transforms the authoritativeness of posited norms. H.L.A. Hart, for his part, elaborated a concept of law by differentiating the moment of inscription – of making 'statements' about primary and secondary rules – from an earlier inaccessible moment before writing, a moment of immediacy with judicial practices.[15] Hart and his commentators fell back upon the inscribed rules. The jurisprudential critic attacked the coherency of primary rules vis-à-vis the secondary rules which granted duties to juristic officials to posit primary rules. Thus, to share Aristotle's distinction,[16] the focus of legal discourse was directed towards a 'product' rather than an 'action'. The juristic agent uses the words in a statute or precedent in order to trace the picture of the externally situated Spirit of the Law. Once again, the play's the thing.

The professional knower cannot change the play, except through a radical shake-up from the outside – an outside which is inaccessible to the professional knower within the play. Thus, even the critic "loses sight" of the concrete and context-specific meanings of the non-knower's everyday genres. The Spirit gazes on to the juridical official from an origin which professional knowers can only represent. A radical shake-up challenges the nuances, shapes, colours and boundaries of the picture of the Spirit. The critic challenges the spectre of the foundation as if he or she had some insight into its situs. Bentham was such a critic. We know now that the critic chases after a singular spirit. Because the foundation possesses a ghost-like spirit, any one configuration of signs may be considered final if rationally linked to the picture of the Spirit. The professional knowers, not the Spirit, paint the picture. Their picture is self-binding. The non-knower's embodied meanings are unnecessary. What is necessary is that such embodiment be signified through a secondary network of signs which the professional knower will recognize as authoritative. The secondary play of signs is immunized from attack from within the discourse, for the non-knower's meant objects are distantly concealed. From the silent situs of the non-knower, the knower's discourse is someone else's discourse which the non-knower just cannot understand because his or her meanings remain unfulfilled and because his or her significations of those meanings are transformed into authoritative configurations of signs.

The Non-knower's Unfulfilled Meant Objects

The professional knower's failure to fulfil the non-knower's meant objects leaves the secondary discourse monologic vis-à-vis the non-knower. The fulfilment of a meaning is the second moment in the non-knower's experience of meaning, the first being the non-knower's conferring of a meant object into his or her story. A lawyer or judge may awaken meanings for the witness. The witness turns towards his or her own meant object and confers meaning on to the question asked. His or her response points in a certain direction. Conversely, the non-knower's response may arouse a range of possible interpretations in the professional knower. The knower, however, fulfils the utterances and writings of other expert knowers. The resignification of the non-knower's story becomes determinate at the moment of the fulfilment of the knower's retelling.

Yet, an indeterminacy characterizes the non-knower's response to the knower's questions.

An interpretation involves two acts. In one act, the interpreter brings an intentional direction towards an externally situated object. The closest to which he or she reaches the external object is to embody the object through a representation or sign. The object is embodied as meant. A witness responds to the lawyer's question, for example, by bringing his or her meaning *to* the question and also by bringing an intentional direction to other witnesses' stories, gestures and texts. The witness's conceptions do not autonomously stand alone, beyond the witness, as an objectivity which he or she represents. There is no *noumena* world: the witness lives *through* the *appearance* of the lawyer's questions and other witness's stories. The witness represents that appearance as a sign which the aggrieved *means*. A *noematic* nucleus characterizes the meant object, the *noema* being the intending sense.

The witness presents the witness's *own* significations as he or she confers meaning on to words and sentences which are uttered by him or herself or others. Only through his or her intentionality does the witness (or, for that matter, the professional knower) *experience* as meant. His or her meaning continues even *after* the narrated events have vanished.[17] Indeed, much of a lawyer's language takes place *after* the external referent has passed away. The witness thereby brings life *into* the lawyer's or judge's questions. But the lawyer's subsequent trace of secondary configurations of signs to the boundaries of a picture of the Spirit of authority covers up the above phenomenological creation of a meant object. At the moment of concealment, the witness becomes an aggrieved to the legal discourse itself.

The witness speaks or gestures. These sounds and actions, by themselves, do not seem to differ from a physical object. A mark or sound is 'intrinsically indifferent', as Husserl would say. Both the witness and the professional knower recognize a pattern to the witness's sounds and gestures. A sound/mark pattern is more than a word or a sentence. That is, nomenclature and grammar do not pattern sounds and marks. A pattern is recognized by its relation to another pattern. A witness's sound/mark pattern is unintelligible to the knower unless it awakens a sense-conferring awareness in the professional knower. That is the moment when the knower resituates the sound/mark pattern into a secondary configuration of signs. The cases of Haldane and Holmes show that the knower lives his or her own constitution of meanings in the reconfigured sound/mark pattern.

The movement towards such a resituated sound pattern makes the constitution of meaning an *act*. Meaning is an act because meaning always has an intentional direction towards an object.[18] The sound or mark pattern render the sound or mark into what I have called a 'sign'. When a pattern is conferred into a sound or mark, the resulting sign undergoes 'an essential phenomenal modification when its object begins to count as an *expression*'.[19] As Husserl explains in 'Investigation V', 'we live in the acts which give it [the object] sense: we are exclusively *turned* to the object that appears in such acts, we *aim* at it, we *mean* it in the special, *pregnant* sense'.[20] As I noted in Chapter 2, as one confers meaning on to an object through an utterance, the expert knower understands the utterance of the non-knower as a sentence to be resituated into the secondary genre. Because such an act draws from the knower's experiences and expectations, the knower can construct a pattern to the marks and sounds in order to make them meaningful. Thus, the conferring of meaning by both utterer and respondent becomes alive with each respondent's experience. In other words, life replaces the dead data of marks and sounds.

The problem is that, in the modern legal discourse, the professional knower situates marks and sounds within patterns which the knower believes to be separate from the meant objects of the non-knower.[21] Holmes succeeded in doing so with his doctrine of judicial restraint, as did Haldane with his doctrine of emergency. Holmes and Haldane insisted that they only observed, predicted and reacted to external objects, such as the event of an emergency in Haldane's case or the inevitable struggle for power in Holmes'. The sounds and marks of non-knowers stirred up, or awakened, definite intentional patterns. Taking language as posited external to themselves, Holmes and Haldane did not, and could not, possibly fulfil the meant objects of the non-knowers.

This conferring of meaning is the first moment in an interpretive act. However, the interpreter goes through a second moment. The witness's speech/mark pattern may be left unrecognized or the interpreter may fulfil it. The knower's questions function as a referent to the witness and the witness's response serves as a referent for the expert knower. Unless the expert knower recognizes the witness's conferring of meaning, the latter remains unfulfilled or unrealized.[22] Once again, the witness becomes an aggrieved to the legal discourse. The non-knower's meant object is not presented before the knower as a meant object *for the knower*. If unrealized, the witness's meaning-conferring act, which the witness represents as a sign in his or her own story, becomes a mere meaning intention unconnected to the significatory project of the legal discourse. The non-knower's utterances remain mere grammatical sentences because, being unfulfilled, they are unintelligible. The sentence is a series of marks and sounds or, more correctly, hylatic data which, for Aristotle, constituted the primary substratum of change, known by analogy rather than through direct observation. Of course, the referents for the professional knower are always mediated through the primary genres of witnesses and clients so that what is hylatic data to the knower is not so to the witness or client. Both non-knower and knower infuse meaning into what they take as data to confer meaning patterns drawn from the respective genres. But, as in K's case as well as the case of the residents of Davis Inlet and the interned 'persons of Japanese ancestry', the juristic agents may fail to "recognize" the meaning-conferring acts of the non-knower. Only when such a recognition takes place does the data become concrete with a specific context. In that context, the knower grasps the sentence as a referent which the knower, in turn, signifies in a pattern which is meaningful to the knower. Until the moment of reconfiguration is reached, the witness's meanings always remain open. However deeply concealed inside the knower's language, the non-knower's meanings retain the possibility of fulfilment. In contrast, the final Object of a legal discourse remains forever unfulfilled by virtue of its finality. That helps to explain why the professional knower becomes haunted by a ghost rather than by some contingent context-specific meanings of the non-knower.

The knower may fail to recognize the meaning-conferring acts of the non-knower in terms of the non-knower's meant objects. Why? In part because the modern legal discourse is so preoccupied with concepts and doctrines and "facts". A concept may inform the meant object of the professional knower.[23] The question which must be asked in the light of the example of Haldane and Holmes, then, is 'how can a knower's invisible conception, represented by such terms as "emergency" or "clear and present danger", fulfil the meaning-conferring intention of a witness if the professional knower's "environing world" lops off the bodily element of the meaning-conferring act of the juridical official as well as non-knower?'. Haldane and Holmes, like the residents of Davis Inlet, no doubt did bring sensory experiences into their typifications, as applied in the circumstances. They no doubt embodied their configurations of signs. Haldane's and Holmes' analyses of the basic texts, which had "created" Canada and the United States, exemplified this point. The knowers' lives were brought *into* the texts and "facts". The knowers' sound/mark patterns were *meant*. Their conceptions about judicial restraint did not stand alone as a represented objectivity. In contrast to a legal doctrine which offered only an *intellectual* foothold to a knower's sign, meaning *emanated from* the knower's act-experience which he or she brought into the signs representing doctrines. Only when the direction of the knower's act is met by the pain of the non-knower's body can the meaning-conferring acts of both knower and victim be *fulfilled* in a *determinate* context.

A non-knower's meaning-conferring act makes the pain perceptually apparent to the knower if the knower recognizes the non-knower's *statement* about the pain. For Husserl, a percept is a percept of a natural or physical–chemical object. However, by means of the examples of Haldane and Holmes, I have demonstrated that the knower perceives by enclothing the client's or witness's sentences with the *knower*'s 'environing world' or horizons of experience. What is missing from such an enclosure is the knower's understanding of the client's statement *as a percept*. In this respect, I am deviating from Husserl's use of the term 'percept' because I am using the term to refer to a statement rather than to a physical object.

The non-knower's meaning-conferring acts especially remain unfulfilled because the most that the well intentioned knower can do is to recognize the non-knower's meaning as signified in a secondary genre. The knower takes the signs as authoritative if he or she can trace them to a coherent picture of the Spirit of the Laws. The knower's meaning-conferring acts point to an external object, beyond the experiences of the non-knower and even beyond the experiences of the professional knowers. Without the non-knower's intentional act in the first moment of interpretation, unintelligible physical–chemical data are posited. Without the fulfilment of the non-knower's intentional conferring of meaning in the second moment of interpretation, the non-knower remains a linguistic monad whose meant objects are lost in a web of foreign signs.

Moreover, the non-knower's meant objects remain indeterminate as unfulfilled, though meaningful and therefore alive to the non-knower of the legal discourse. They remain indeterminate in the sense of being open and unspecified. To the knower, the non-knower's meant objects do not function as a referent to the professional knower. What is more important to the knower is that he or she can resignify the non-knower's statement into secondary configurations towards which the knower can confer meaning. The displacing signifying relations of the professional knowers cannot complete the non-knower's meant objects. The non-knower's meaning-conferring act fails to fuse with the knower's fulfilment of the non-knower's meant object. The discursive relation between non-knower and knower thereby lacks what Husserl describes as a 'unified stream of consciousness' – 'a real whole'. The non-knower's meant object faces an 'incompletely determined completion'.[24] Such indeterminacy characterizes the first moment of the will in Hegel's *Philosophy of Right*. The non-knower's universal object circumscribes a 'sphere' or boundary of meaning which remains open or unspecified until the knower grasps or encloses its representation as a sign.

Even the non-knower's sense of time and space remains indeterminate. I exemplified such an indeterminacy of time and space in the context of a financial institution's confiscation of one's assets under a 'demand note'. The professional knower often delineates the chronology of events leading up to the foreclosure of the assets. Such a chronology is measured in terms of "clock time". Rather than being an objective universal standard of measurement, though, each instant of time for the non-knower is embedded in a continuous stream of his or her own experience which does not possess an immanent standard which the professional knower may import into documents and physical exhibits. The knower's recounting of the time and place of events may well abstract partial experiences of the non-knower and thereby transfigure the non-knower's experience into what the non-knower perceives as merely fragmentary. Although other professional knowers will recognize the transfiguration, it leaves the non-knower's experience of time and space indeterminate. There remains an indeterminacy even as witnesses recount in the present. When a lawyer interprets a natural referent, a social circumstance, or a sound or mark of a witness, another lawyer or judge, he or she does so against the above time horizon. He or she also brings past experiences and future expectations into the meaning-conferring act just as a listening lawyer brings his or her past experiences and prospective expectations to bear into the speaking lawyer's signs.

When the knower's own sound/mark pattern points to a signified referent which the non-knower had meant, the thought of the knower is made determinate.[25] The meaning act of the non-knower is then realized in the 'this' of the knower's percept. The knower's actual perception *fulfils* the non-knower's conferring of meaning.

Such a prospect, though, seems difficult, if not impossible, so long as the knower chases after spectres of a Spirit. In such circumstances, the professional knower cannot respond to the non-knower through the non-knower's language. The language of the non-knower remains the language of an other to the authoritative language of the professional knowers. Perhaps, Kafka best characterizes the experience of someone who lives through the language of an other:

> All the more incomprehensible. ... At last he noticed that they were talking to him, but he could not make out what they were saying, he heard nothing but the din that filled the whole place, through which a shrill unchanging note like that of a siren seemed to ring.[26]

The Tragedy of Unfulfilled Meant Objects

The ultimate tragedy arises when, as in Kafka's *The Trial*, the non-knower and the professional knowers cannot fulfil each other's meanings, even though both respondents may be well-intentioned in their desire to understand the other. The non-knower's meaning-conferring acts remain unfulfilled in the expert knowers' responses. The authoritative discourse is violently imposed upon the primary genres of the other. In such a circumstance, the non-knower and the knowers speak and write through radically different languages. Neither can respond to the other because the acts intend different meanings to the same event or sentence. The crucible in such an abyss of meanings is that the professional knowers direct their meanings towards an absent foundation presupposed to be situated external to all accessible signs which the knowers mean. The professional knowers may identify relevant facts, typify them and analyse the enclosure of the facts by the universal typifications. The knower does all this in a search for the external Object/Spirit signified by the configured picture. The objects meant by the non-knower are lost or assimilated in this project. The search for authority colours the meant differences of the non-knower and, in their place, the meanings of professional knowers reconstitute a new world of juridical alternity. The trace for authority even transforms the 'environing world' of the juristic agent since he or she takes the displacing 'environing world' as the true/real. Consequently, the radically different meanings embodying the non-knower's pain and the knower's picture become events which neither respondent can understand. At that moment, a *differend* insinuates itself between the authoritative discourse and the language of the other.

K's unfulfilled meanings characterize K in Kafka's *The Trial*. The doors of the Castle remain forever open and yet, the Old Man from the Country can never gain access through the doors. When K is refused permission to even glance at the books of the Examining

Magistrate in an empty "courtroom", K responds with 'these books are probably law books, and it is an essential part of justice, dispensed here that you should be condemned not only in innocence but also in ignorance'. It is not just that the expert knowers fail to fulfil K's meanings. K also fails to fulfil the meanings conferred on his actions by women and by the expert knowers. Their meanings remain indeterminate with respect to each other.

When K enquires of his lawyer as to how he had known about K's case before K visited him, the lawyer replied 'I'm a lawyer, you see, I move in legal circles where the various cases are discussed ... .' When K fidgets before the lawyer and his uncle, the uncle likens K's questions to those 'of a child'. The lawyer rhetorically asks of K, 'whom shall I associate with if not with men of my own profession?'. The narrator describes the resulting frustration with which K meets the lawyer's actions:

> In such and similar harangues K.'s lawyer was inexhaustible. He reiterated them every time K. called on him. Progress had always been made, but the nature of the progress could never be divulged.
>
> The lawyer was always working away at the first plea, but it had never reached a conclusion, which at the next visit turned out to be an advantage, since the last days would have been very inauspicious for handing it in, a fact which no one could have foreseen.[27]

To the lawyer, the intricate and never-ending procedures are exhilarating and intellectually demanding; to K they are increasingly distant and alien to his initial understanding of a constitutional democracy. From the viewpoint of the painter, an expert knower of the legal knowledge and legal system, 'you don't seem to have any general idea of the Court yet ... . But since you're innocent you won't need it anyhow. I shall get you off all by myself.'[28] K does not even understand that statement: 'How can you do that?,' he asks. 'For you told me yourself a few minutes ago that the Court was quite impervious to proof.' Here, the painter understands the transformative character of the secondary genre: 'Impervious only to proof which one brings before the Court... . But it is quite a different matter with one's efforts behind the scenes; that is, in the consulting rooms, in the lobbies or, for example, in this very studio.' The professional knowers guard a secret behind the vast doorways of the Castle. In the chapter concerning the lawyer, the narrator describes the maze of legal proceedings:

> [T]he ranks of officials in this judiciary system mounted endlessly, so that not even the initiated could survey the hierarchy as a whole. And the proceedings of the Courts were generally kept secret from subordinate officials, consequently they could hardly ever quite follow in

> their further progress the cases on which they had worked; any particular case thus appeared in their circle of jurisdiction often without their knowing whence it came, and passed from it they knew not whither. Thus the knowledge ..., the final verdict and the reasons for that verdict lay beyond the reach of these officials.[29]

Each professional knower, the arresting officers included, could excuse his or her own inability to justify and even to understand his or her own actions by reference to the secret source of authority. Because knowers trace one configuration of signs to another in the hope of reaching closer to the final foundation of all authoritative laws, the foundation must remain absent from all expert knowledge. That is the secret of a modern legal discourse.

Now, the impact of the *differend* is devastating for the non-knower. First, the direction of his meant objects loses its certainty and clarity. As the narrator describes of K:

> ...he felt as if he were seasick. He felt he was on a ship rolling in heavy seas. It was as if the waters were dashing against the wooden walls, as if the roaring of breaking waves came from the end of the passage, as if the passage itself pitched and rolled and the waiting clients on either side rose and fell with it.[30]

Then, the body slowly becomes unwell, losing all ability to bounce back as one would expect of a vibrant being. The non-knower's self-esteem – indeed, his or her will to live – dissipates:

> It was humiliating even to the onlooker. So the lawyer's methods, to which K fortunately had not been long enough exposed, amounted to this: that the client finally forgot the whole world and lived only in the hope of toiling along this false path until the end of his case should come in sight. The client ceased to be a client and became the lawyer's dog. If the lawyer were to order this man to crawl under the bed as if into a kennel and back there, he would gladly obey the order.[31]

The non-knower's experiential body slowly dies and, with that death, comes suffering which the professional knower, as a professional knower, simply does not and cannot know. Indeed, this slow death occurs at the very moment that the expert knowers claim to 'know' the facts of a non-knower's case.

The Situs of Social Critique

The situs of the social critique of laws in a modern state, then, has been misdirected. Traditionally, the legal critic has examined authored laws from the vantage-point of a surrogate for the supreme author, the Spirit of authority. Gazing from afar, purged of all experiences which might taint an impartial inquiry, the critic attacks the coherency of particular configurations of signs vis-à-vis the accepted spectre of the grounding of legal authority. Alternatively, the critic claims that a different picture of the Spirit is better suited to the institutional materials of a state. Either critique takes one into the secondary signifying relations which transform the pain of a non-knower.

The traditional critique attacks the source or grounding of any configuration of signs in the legal discourse. But the critic him or herself presupposes that authority ultimately to rest in some final grounding. The external standpoint of the critique is projected into the gaze of the presupposed originating source. Even when the critic claims that juristic agents represent the wrong spectre of the Spirit, the critic remains within the traditional search for an absent foundation. He or she may challenge the inclusion or exclusion of certain agents, such as 'founding fathers'. He or she may insist on his or her vision of the Spirit to the point of advocating war or even participating in ethnic cleansing, torture, civil war and all the other ugly manifestations of the twentieth century. But he or she only differs with the 'enemy' as to the identity of the Spirit of authority in his or her state. The critic charges the reigning configurations of the spectre as "invalid" or "illegal" or "unauthoritative" or "unconstitutional". Both the critic and his or her constructed vantage-point of critique perpetuate a *violence* which subordinates the stories of the aggrieved to the critic's own secondary genre. The social critic's configurations of the signs are just: a crudely violent phenomenon in the constitution of the foundation and in the signification of embodied meaning.

The above predicament only remains so long as the social critic gazes from the "outside". I have argued, though, that the phenomenon of the displacement of meaning as well as the resulting *differend* between the languages of the knower and of the non-knower, are concealed *inside* the secondary signifying relations. The displacement produces suffering because even the social critic, as a professional knower, cannot fulfil the non-knower's meaning-conferring acts.

The question, then, is whether the non-knower's meanings may be retrieved. After all, we are now sufficiently aware that professional knowers have been chasing after a spectre.[32] If one is left with the possibility of a multiplicity of configured significations, is it possible for the non-knower and the knower to hear each other peaceably? Is it possible to retrieve a concealed social relation where both non-knower and knower possess the possibility of fulfilling each other's meaning-conferring acts? The *differend* concealed inside the modern legal discourse offers the situs for social critique.

The Collapse of the Lawyer's Play

Do the lived meanings of the non-knower reinstate Nature as the transcendent *arche* from which to understand and to critique any contingent configuration of authoritative signs? Concealed primary genres are invisible in the sense of being inaccessible from the secondary signifying project of the knower. The modern legal discourse is monologic at the expense of the concealment of embodied meanings of non-knowers. Such meanings, though displaced, are concealed *inside* the privileged configurations of signs. This distinguishes the concealed primary genres from the external transcendental grounding of authority. In addition, the concealed genres incorporate the phenomenal body, not a concept, into meant objects. That is, whereas an absent metaphysical Object – the *Grundnorm*, 'rule of recognition', or 'greatest happiness of the greatest number' – "grounds" the legal monologue, the monologue itself conceals culturally experienced phenomena. This constitutes the second manner in which the primary genres do not function as substituted ghosts of authority.

It is an error, then, to believe that the infinite differences of signs in legal discourse constitute social–cultural practice. Because any contingent configuration of signs produces a concealment of embodied meanings, the secondary signifying relations idealize the stories represented through primary genres. Indeed, the idealization takes the professional knower in a very different direction from the meant objects of a non-knower, for the knower searches for the boundaries of a picture of an absent foundation in order to authorize his or her own opinion.

Herein lies the problematic of any claim that the unconcealment of embodied meanings would continue the language of metaphysics. The play of possible combinations of signs takes place at two levels: at the level of the displacing or authoritative discourse and at the level of the displaced language of a non-knower. The legal discourse of a modern state can never recognize the displaced language without compromising its own claim to signify authority because the professional knower confers meaning into an Object which is necessarily absent – necessarily absent in order that laws be considered posited.

On the other hand, if it is realized that no absent "outside" foundation can transcend all configurations of signs, it becomes clear that the very phenomenon of displacement works to conceal other languages through which non-knowers (of the legal language) live. Non-knowers live their own languages because they confer their meanings on to an external object. Furthermore, they fulfil the meant objects of dialogic partners as they interpret the configurations of familiar signs. Additionally, if the end of legal reasoning only encountered the gaze of a Spirit, then what professional knowers have hitherto taken as posited, is transient, fragmentary and without rational coherence. Legal discourse lacks the absent foundation which can unify all significations of juridical officials.

The violence of knowers' interpretive acts stands naked. For, in delineating the spectres of the Spirit of legal authority, the displacing discourse assimilates the non-knower's languages into significations which are meaningful only to the professional knower who inquires whether the sign falls inside the familiar picture of the Spirit. The displacing language assimilates the language of the other in deference to spectres which the professional knowers construct, and in the name of a Spirit which the aggrieved may not share. The knower both interprets and constitutes the picture of the Spirit.

Indeed, both the signifying chains of the professional knower and the non-knower may be spoken and written by means of the same sounds and marks – the same words and sentences. Sounds and marks do not, of themselves, make a sign. The sound or mark must be *meant* for it to become a sign, and the sign signifies, or represents, that meaning. As a consequence of the dynamics of displacement, the professional knower and the non-knower *mean* the sounds and marks differently. Again, each points towards a different meant object. Each *patterns* the sounds and marks towards a different object. The knower, as a receiver, begins to understand the sentences of the non-knower when the receiver recognizes a pattern to the non-knower's marks and sounds. The problem is that the professional knower patterns the non-knower's sounds and marks through signs which the knower recognizes as authoritative.

Moreover, once uttered, the meaning-conferring acts of professional knower and non-knower remain indeterminate vis-à-vis each other in that they remain unfulfilled. The knower and non-knower write and speak past one another. Each configures signs differently in order to represent their unfulfilled meant objects. Different combinations of signs stand for, or signify, different meant objects. The same sound or mark may act to trigger different embodied meanings in the two respondents – knower and non-knower. Each *lives* their language, though, because each brings his or her own past experiences and future expectations *into* his or her configurations of signs. Haldane and Holmes were no different in this respect than the residents of Davis Inlet. The displaced signifying relations, however silenced, excluded, ignored, forgotten or reread through the displacing signifying relations, remains a language, short of the biological death or successful torture of the non-knower. Whereas Lyotard contrasts such a circumstance (which he names a *differend*) with 'litigation', a legal opinion or litigation itself may work to create a *differend* inside the displacing language. In such a circumstance the non-knower suffers.

Just such a *differend*, concealed *within* and between authoritative signifying relations, poses an opening from which to critique any one contingent configuration of signs. If the configuration displaces signs of another and if suffering arises from the inability of the displaced language to associate harm with the privileged signs of the knower, justice lies in the concealed languages of the authoritative signifying relations. Derrida admits as much when, in his essay 'The Force of Law', he suggests that law is not, and cannot be, just because justice is the language of the other.[33] Interestingly, though, the language of the other dwells *between* and *within* the very signifying relations which juridical officials posit as authoritative, not in the transcendental absent foundation, as the Enlightenment social critics believed, nor in the *differance* of a multiplicity of differentiating signs before any knower begins to play, as Derrida suggests. With respect to the Enlightenment view, the Spirit, believed to ground legal authority, haunts the expert knower of legal signs. The gaze of the Spirit of the Law (or what Derrida terms a Ghost) is believed to constrain the expert knower. In the quest to identify the picture of the Spirit, the significations of the non-expert are ignored, forgotten, lost or hidden. With respect to the second possibility, namely that justice dwells in a *differance* from which a language of metaphysics is configured, we know now that the other to legal language is concealed *within* the contingent configurations of signs. The other to an authoritative language is not the Spirit of authority, whom Derrida sometimes projects as the other to authoritative language, but the finite, contingently embodied meanings displaced and then concealed within the authoritative language. The significations of the non-expert are re-presented through the privileged chains of authoritative signs which signify something for the knower, though not necessarily for the non-knower. Any historically contingent, authoritative configuration of signs thereby idealizes the language of the particular other at the very moment that grammatology has its field day.

More generally, the modern legal discourse, which produces the concealment of a non-knower's embodied meanings, fails to account for the addressive experiences with which the professional knower *means* contingently configured signs. As I argued with respect to Haldane's and Holmes' interpretations of two basic texts, the 'environing world' of the professional knower may well induce readings which exclude just such expressive experiences. Thus, the situs for the social critique of legal discourse, as well as the situs for its understanding, are located inside the trace of differences amongst authoritative signs – not before or beyond it. The retracing of chains of authorized signs defines 'who harms', 'what constitutes harm' and 'when harm terminates'.

The modern legal discourse idealizes both the language of the interpreter and the language of the non-knower. 'Legal language as play' collapses. One is left with one penetrating set of questions. Is it possible for the nomos of the modern state to fulfil the meant objects of the non-knower when the knower's meant objects are believed to have been grounded externally, "out there", beyond the legal discourse? Is it possible for the professional knowers to reach the objects meant in the meaning-conferring acts of the non-knower when the knower signifies his or her own meanings in the name of a vision of a Spirit of authority?

Notes

1 This point is elaborated in Jacques Derrida, 'Structure Sign and Play in the Discourses of the Human Sciences' in *Writing and Difference* (Alan Bass trans., Chicago: University of Chicago Press, 1978): 278–93.

2 Derrida so describes the *arche* of legal discourse in 'Force of Law: The "Mystical Foundation of Authority"' in *Cardozo Law Review*, vol. 11 (1990): 919–1045; 'Before the Law' in Derek Attridge ed., *Acts of Literature* (London/New York: Routledge, 1992): 181–220; *Specters of Marx* (Peggy Kamuf trans., Magnus and Cullenberg intro.; London/New York: Routledge, 1994).

3 Derrida, 'Structure, Sign…', note 1 *supra*, 288.

4 Here, I am joining Derrida's earlier work with his 'Force of Law', note 2 *supra*.

5 Ibid., 949.

6 Elaine Scarry, *The Body in Pain: The Making and Unmaking of the World* (Oxford: Oxford University Press, 1985).

7 Jacques Derrida, 'The Ends of Man' in *Margins of Philosophy* (Alan Bass ed.; Chicago: University of Chicago Press, 1982): 131.

8 Michel Foucault, *The Order of Things: An Archeology of the Human Sciences* (New York: Vintage Books, 1970): 330.

9 Jean-François Lyotard, 'The Differend' (Georges van den Abbeele trans.; *Theory and History of Literature*, vol. 46; Minneapolis: University of Minnesota Press, 1988): paras 12-13, 22–27.

10 Mikhail M. Bakhtin, *The Dialogic Imagination: Four Essays* (Michael Holquest, ed.; Caryl Emerson and Michael Holquest trans.; Austin: University of Texas Press, 1981): 428.

11 Ferdinand de Saussure, *Course in General Linguistics* (Toronto: McGraw-Hill, 1959, 1966): 15.

12 Ibid., 54.

13 V.N. Volosinov, *Marxism and the Philosophy of Language* (Ladislov Matejka and I.R. Titunik trans.; New York and London: Seminar Press, 1973): 53.

14 Michel Foucault, *The Order of Things* (New York: Vintage, 1970): 323.

15 William E. Conklin, 'The Secret Foundation of Sovereignty in Legal Positivism' in *Rechtstheorie*, Beiheft, vol. 17, 75–84

16 *Ethics* 1139a–1139b.

17 Edmund Husserl, Investigation I in *Logical Investigations*, vol. 2 (New York: Humanities Press, 1970): 301.

18 Husserl, Investigation VI, ibid., 682–3.

19 Husserl, Investigation I, ibid., 283. Husserl's emphasis.

20 Husserl, Investigation V, ibid., 584.

21 Husserl, Investigation VI, ibid., 688.
22 Husserl, Investigation I, ibid., 280.
23 Husserl calls this a 'categorical' or 'non-independent form': Investigation I, fn. 1 ibid., 281.
24 Husserl, Investigation VI, ibid., 700.
25 Ibid., 683–4.
26 Ibid., 193–4.
27 Franz Kafka, *The Trial* (New York: Schocken, 1937, 1956, 1964): 124.
28 Ibid., 151.
29 Ibid., 119.
30 Ibid., 72.
31 Ibid., 193–4.
32 'The Invisible Author of Legal Authority' in *Law and Critique*, vol. 7, no. 2 (1996): 173–92.
33 Derrida, 'The Force of Law', note 2 *supra*, 919–1045.

7 Consciousness of the Absent Final Object

One question remains before I can retrieve the embodied meanings of professional knower and non-knower alike concealed inside a modern legal discourse. If I succeeded in retrieving such meanings, would the meanings also be associated with violence? If not, why not? Further, if the professional knower were able to retrieve the embodied meanings of both non-knower and knower, would legal discourse remain monologic? Indeed, would one be able to characterize the retrieved meanings as authoritative in the same sense that the authority of the modern state has been associated with an *arche* or foundation?

The question of the violence of legal discourse revolves about the absent object which the professional knower aims to represent. That absent object, posited "out there" beyond the social and signifying context of the knower, drives the knower to conquer all competing "facts" and doctrines through a secondary genre. The absent object may be what the knower takes as the "facts of the case", or a legal doctrine, rule or principle, or the Object, the final *arche* of the trace of signs. I argued in Chapter 4 that the ultimate foundation or grounding in a modern state, to be final, must remain absent from the secondary discourse. Hobbes and Rousseau, Bentham and Austin, Kelsen and Hart, Dworkin and Raz all acknowledged that legal discourse must possess some final source or author or 'law beyond the law' to be authoritative. The knower cannot reach a posited object. The absence of the object/Object requires that the knower *represent* it by a secondary sign. The closest which the knower can approximate the object is to share a spectre of it through configurations of signs which function to represent it. All legal signs are pictured authoritatively in the name of authority. The knower in his or her quest to fulfil the desire for the absent object, displaces all competing discourses monologically. The displaced configurations of signs are products to be consumed.

I now wish to turn to the task of retrieving a radically different sense of authority from the embodied meanings concealed in modern legal discourse. I shall do so in two stages. In this chapter, I shall contrast the desire for an absent object with one's recognition of a dialogic partner. The latter sense of desire has the knower produce, rather than consume, configurations of signs. In Chapter 8, I shall argue that a dialogue between knower and non-knower characterizes the retrieved social relations and that the idealizing narrative *about* the non-knower is no more. Legal discourse becomes a dialogue drawn from the intertext of the *differend* which separates the idiom of the knower from that of the non-knower. Force is unlikely in such a retrieved dialogue because each dialogic partner participates by bringing his or her meant objects *into* the intertext.

The Final Object

The secondary legal discourse is monologic in that the non-knower cannot respond to the professional knower except through secondary signifying relations. The knower strives to reach a final Archemedian point from which to gaze down at the contingently configured signs. Because the knower lacks such a final grounding, he or she represents it through chains of signs. As a professional knower of legal discourse myself, I trace the grounds of one configuration to another, backwards and upwards through the chains of surrogates who speak on behalf of the absent Object. The trace is my trace, not the trace of the founding source which I can only picture or imagine. I construct an identity of the foundation through my configurations of signs. I picture the foundation as a creative author or a basic rule from which all secondary signs may be derived. The origins or end-point of legal reasoning is the source, the centre, the founder of the trace of the authority of one sign to its authority in another. And when immersed in a legal problem, I act as if the event about which a non-knower testifies, exists "out there" beyond me, beyond my control – a "given" towards which my analysis is driven. I analyse the representations of such facts in terms of doctrines, rules and principles which, once again, I believe to be posited beyond me. I carry out a monologue vis-à-vis the non-knower through configurations which will never reach the external objects which I take as a "given". I do not, and cannot, address the embodied meanings of the non-knower so long as I attempt to bring myself *to* the posited objects, to the facts, the doctrines, the foundation, so long as my analysis begins with the posited, yet absent, object, so long as I take the posited object as the true/real. All I can do is to picture, or imagine, the posited object. My tools are signs which represent cognitive objects which enclose my own and the non-knower's particular meanings. The conceptions abstract and intellectualize through a cognate world of signified doctrines, policies, and facts. The professional knower aspires to *know* the other as a *consciousness*.

The effort to conceptualize the other in one's legal consciousness is not a new one. Since I cannot know the good life except in the sense of 'contemplation', Plato argued, I cannot do good except through rational reflection.[1] I strive to reach the unreachable eternal objects for they constitute reality and truth.[2] Existence lies in the eternal objects. That is, absent objects constitute true being.[3] Such absent objects transcendentally unify the multiplicity of particular differences which characterize bodily experiences.[4] Unless legal knowers (of course, Plato ridicules the professionalization of knowledge) desire the unattainable essence of the absent fact or absent doctrine, one non-knower will violently dominate another with no third source to mediate and to adjudicate.[5] Justice is believed to dwell in the final absent Object – the Good.

So long as the professional knower in legal discourse retains such a picture of transcendent Justice and the analysis of facts, such a discourse will be monologic, since the knower will 'understand' the "facts and circumstances of a case" and the legal doctrines in terms of absent objects which he or she can only represent. Such objects are posited external to the experiential body: an abyss lies between the body and the absent object of the mind. Because the knower can never reach the object of a sign, the knower's drive to conquer all difference, both inside and outside legal language, will never be satisfied. Such a drive to conquer what is absent from the knower, namely a multiplicity of differences, stems from a particular sense of desire which we have inherited from Plato. The juridical agent desires to enclose the differences, as objects, within the metaphysical boundaries of the knower's concepts, doctrines and the like. The desire is cognitive of the object. So, for example, the representers of the final Object – the foundation of the authority of a legal order – never succeed in completely appropriating the stories of the non-knower. Put in different terms, a Cartesianism permeates the knower's claim to be involved in "the practice of law". Because the mind is associated with desire as a lack and because the body is associated with production of matter and because there is an unbridgeable gap between the absent object and matter, for Descartes desire is a lack of a material object. Because the gap is permanent, desire is unlimited. Perhaps this may help explain why any bureaucracy, such as a university which claims to possess authority, seems to be continually recoding social practices into writing.

The absence of the posited Object requires that lawyers and judges – claimants to the knowledge of the Object – act as its surrogates. Since the Object is a Oneness (for otherwise, the trace of authoritative representing signs would continue, as Kelsen and Hart acknowledge), any institutional organization of surrogates must reach upwards with a single director, minister, or prime minister at the pinnacle of the hierarchy. Such a pyramidal hierarchy legislates, adjudicates and enforces conceptions against non-totalizable and non-totalized embodied meanings. The surrogates classify, standardize, normalize and unify a multiplicity of possible embodied meanings of professional knower and non-knower alike. A legal organization is built like the bricks of a castle. The castle represents a formless absent unity. Juridical officials act as if power emanates from deep inside the castle – so deep that one cannot experience its centre except through signs which approximate that centre. The surrogates signify or represent without signifying anything! The surrogates, then, invent such terms as the "rule of law" or "justice". The Panopticon, for example, represented how legal institutions could control, regulate, view and spy upon a prisoner's physical body, a constant reminder that a multiplicity of embodied meanings may remain unenclosed.[6] Even the architecture of courthouses, courtrooms, law school classrooms, student lounges (in the basements of law schools) and the invariable location of professional law schools on the fringes of university campuses reflect the search for the final Object of authority, as explained in Chapter 2.

What role does a judge play in this seeking of a knowledge of the absent foundation? When knowers engage in dialogue with each other about the absent Object or, perhaps more correctly, their ghost-like spectre of the Object, their debate or refutation assumes a consensus which goes to the identity of the founding source of legal authority in the particular legal order. As partners in knowledge-seeking, they explore the evidence, produce proofs and interpret texts as if the signified event, posited beyond them, existed as set out in their respective statements of claim. As partners in seeking to know what configurations of signs best represent the event, they energetically prevent an audience (and themselves) from forgetting the referent, the story of the non-knower, the story of the witness, the "facts and circumstances of the case" and the ghostly figure at the end of the objectless realm of doctrines, rules, principles and other standarized universals.[7] Rhetoric prevails. A third party – a judge – is needed in order to adjudicate the struggle over which configuration of signs best represents the externally posited referent. As Thrasymachus says:

> If then we oppose him in a set speech enumerating in turn the advantages of being just and he replies and we rejoin, we shall have to count up and measure the goods listed in the respective judges to decide between us.[8]

Throughout the judge's adjudication of the dispute between the professional knowers of the referent, the judge assumes an impartial and objective vision of all the other actors. This is not surprising in that the legal discourse may represent the "facts" and "the Law" as fixed in time, place and source. And yet, as Lyotard remarks, the moment when a judge or witness intervenes as a third party to a dispute, he or she becomes a partner to the dialogue.[9] At this point, all three take on the character of a surrogacy to the Spirit of authority.

The surrogates of the one, final Object, then, trace one sign to another linearly towards their vision of the final Object. The knower interprets as if he or she can reach the absent end of the reasoning. Any conclusion which seems to manifest such a linearity takes on a hue of inevitability: there is 'no choice' in the conclusion; it 'necessarily follows', 'my role is not to question the wisdom of the presupposed posited object, whether it be a statute or a doctrine or a fact'.

Both the professional knower and non-knower act passively. They passively depend upon the absent object for their own identities as knower and non-knower. Spinoza could have been describing the surrogate and non-knower in a legal discourse when he wrote that one is 'acted on': 'something happens in us, or something follows from our nature, of which we are only a partial cause.'[10] The posited objects and their representations constrain both the knower and the non-knower. The knower, then, may only consume, not produce, the representations in that he or she may not control them. As Deleuze pointed out,[11] because the non-knower and the knower are 'acted on', their lives thereby slip from their control. Others will impose values upon, and thereby reinforce, the externality of posited objects. In this respect, just as we observed with respect to K in *The Trial*, the legal discourse of a modern state privileges cognitive objects over life by judging life in terms of the concepts.[12] The legal discourse depreciates life in the Spirit of an invisible Object who dwells in a supersensible world. Life is reactive in such a discourse. And the professional knower does not yet think because thinking involves an *activity* of thought.[13] The typifications which the knower lacks *act on* the knower, and yet these typifications are unreachable because they are cognitive. What the professional knower takes for reality and "practice", then, is a fantasized reality. The knower of the legal discourse in a modern state produces a ghost-like fantasy which can, at best, be represented through configurations of signs which, in turn, deny their own function in the construction of the fantasy. The knower believes what is absent. The knower produces an imaginary object which functions as if there is a 'dreamed-of object behind every real object', to use Deleuze's phrase.[14]

The situs of absent objects beyond the knower prevents the knower from acknowledging his or her own role in the production of such a fantasy world. The juridical surrogate represents the outside forces of posited facts and posited doctrines. The non-knower's life is judged in terms of the representation of such external forces. The knower reacts to the outside. A time and space to laugh, to play or to dance are left unrecognized. Perhaps, more accurately, such a time and space are left as a remainder – a supplement to the project of tracing authority through representing configurations of signs. The legal discourse superimposes the cognitive over the lived meanings of knower and non-knower alike.[15]

Consciousness of the Particular Other Through the Mind

The absence of the object in a legal discourse influences how the professional knower recognizes a non-knower and his or her story. The professional knower privileges the theoretical life of a pure, disinterested contemplation of the absent object.[16] The knower cannot reach posited facts or doctrines except through conceptions which abstract from the multiplicity of particular meanings. The knower constitutes the non-knower's story *in the mind* of the knower. Such a cognitive contemplation lops off the experiential body of the other as a possibility of fulfilment of the knower's meanings. The knower's recognition of the non-knower is independent of the non-knower's context-specific meanings.

This point reinforces why I argued in the previous chapter that legal discourse idealizes the non-knower's stories. The knower neutralizes and sanitizes the pain of a non-knower who lives *in* the world.[17] Indeed, the knower's effort to bring him or herself *to* the posited object denies that the non-knower lives in the world. The concrete 'environing world' of the non-knower is lost, even expelled, from the linear reasoning towards a theoretical object which the knower takes as the originating source of legal analysis. The more rigorous such analysis, the further does the representer depart from the meanings of the non-knower.

The knower pursues a monologue vis-à-vis the non-knower. The knower clarifies his or her identity, as a professional, at the loss of his or her own social–cultural practice. An alien imagined "community" – "out of control" as it were – acts upon knower and non-knower alike. The knower intellectualizes *about* such an imagined community, communicates through one single language and recognizes the non-knower in the *knower's consciousness*. So, just as I showed from my several examples in earlier chapters, the non-knower is transformed into a replica of the knower. The non-knower mirrors the knower. The non-knower is signified through the knower's signifying relations, all the while that the knower "applies" and "justifies" a judgment as if the knower is acted upon by the "facts of the case". To describe the cognitive objects as "facts" continues the project of concealment. Those facts which qualify for juridical recognition enter the *knower*'s consciousness, not the non-knower's. All truth is the knower's and everything which is the knower's is true. Immersed in a private 'environing world', the knower fraternizes with his or her own constructed universe. Agreement becomes difficult between knower and non-knower to the extent that the non-knower also constructs a competing consciousness which denies his or her own 'environing world' at the very moment that the knower reaches for absent objects.

The cognitive object, whether signified as a "fact" or legal doctrine or policy, functions ideologically and is signified by a secondary sign which only an expert knower claims to know. "Ideology" here differs from its traditional sense. Georg Lukacs argued that an ideology severs the connection of a conception from its physical–experiential referent[18] be it, say, a social phenomenon or a natural object, such as a tree. Lukacs' sense of ideology presupposed that a transparent sign represented the conception. It is clear, however, that legal signs are not transparent. Indeed, precisely because a non-knower and an expert knower read the same sign differently and because the secondary discourse possesses authority over primary genres, a non-knower's conceptions are concealed within the secondary signifying relations. The secondary signs represent other signs and the prior "factual" world dissolves in favour of another very different "reality". The expert knower signifies a previous signifying relation. The non-knower signifies his or her embodied meanings and the expert knower recontextualizes the non-knower's sign into a secondary combination of signs. Contrary to Lukacs' tacit belief,[19] the expert knower can never reach an unreified concrete context.

Much as Louis Althusser argues in 'Ideology and Ideological State Apparatuses,' a sign represents a signified object which, being cognitive, is imagined or pictured. Thus, the signifying relation is an *imaginary* relationship between concept and the concrete context-specific meanings. The non-knower no longer exists as an embodied being in legal discourse but, instead is imagined.[20] The projected imaginary relationship of sign to non-knower performs an ideological function.[21] The expert knower inscribes concepts into his or her actions in the belief that he or she is uniting theory with practice. But the expert knower constructs this unity in terms of imaginary relations which the expert knower's concepts enclose. The expert knower inscribes his or her social practice with ideology at the very moment that the expert knower claims that his or her theory constitutes social reality.

There is a sense, then, that what Althusser calls 'a mirror structure' colours what the expert knower takes as a fact.[22] The expert knower's sign signifies a "fact" or event which merely mirrors a social event. The mirroring begins and ends with the expert knower's own signifying relations, not the non-knower's. The expert's conceptions do not, and cannot, actually reach the pain which the non-knower tries to signify through his or her own signifier–signified relations. The secondary signifying relations seem true. Professional knowers recognize the expert's signs as their own because their mutual training and education has been so effective in the production of a secondary genre: it just seems inconceivable that the non-knower's pain could be otherwise. Accordingly, a legal judgment is produced from signs which mirror the cognate objects of expert knowers. Such a self-authorizing mirroring produces serious political and social effects for the non-knower and others. The authorizing signs call for juridical officials, such as policemen, prosecutors, attorneys and social workers, to enforce the cognitive objects represented by an authoritative chain of secondary signs.

More generally, the phenomenon of mirroring produces an imagined history which mirrors the cognate objects which the professional knower associates with the secondary signs. In a sense, the imagined history becomes ahistorical and asocial in that the social referent dissipates in favour of secondary signs. A professional education, state-subsidized and rigorously regulated, begins the inculcation of such an imagined history. The secondary metaphysical order functions theologically in that it inculcates piety which, as Kenneth Burke once noted, attempts 'to round things out and to fit experience together into a unified whole'.[23] The modern professional law school, as I described in Chapter 2, aims to do just that. The expert knower *pro*fesses conceptions which secondary signs represent. The conceptions fix and then abstract from experience. Even though the expert knower claims to recognize "the facts of the case", the expert knower encloses and then masters the context-specific meanings of the other to the secondary genre. By privileging certain signs, the conceptions, which such signs represent, are empowered.

Let me return to the non-knower's experience of the banker's call of a loan, examined in Chapter 3. By the late 1970s the Canadian courts were confronted with two competing chains of signs. The one, called a 'demand note', authorized a financial institution to demand immediate payment if a contractee had failed to fulfil certain conditions. The 'demand note' was effectively a 'contract' which authorized the possession of an asset if the debtor could not pay a debt 'on demand'. A second chain of signs, called the 'reasonable time' doctrine, was read *into* the 'demand note' so that the financial institution had to give the debtor reasonable time to obtain alternative financing. With the Supreme Court of Canada decision of *Lister*, the courts sided with the latter chain of signs. Although the doctrine seemed to favour the debtor, the doctrine really mirrored the lawyers' values of due process, a fair hearing, reasonableness and all the rest.

In the mirroring projection of juridical values, the social and economic circumstances of the debtor were forgotten. Moreover, the privileged chain of signs ignored the fact that the economic circumstances were such that the financial institutions had effectively become a partner in the debtor's enterprise. The financial institution regularly monitored the debtor, advised the debtor, encouraged expansion when the bank officials considered such prudent and so on. In addition, the cognitive object signified by 'reasonable time' failed to take account, at least initially during the early 1980s, that the allowance of 20 minutes, or even a few days to obtain alternative financing contrasted with the practice of a ten-day wait for a minimal consumer loan. For the sign, 'reasonable time,' was situated in signifying configurations which were directed towards absent objects represented by other signs rather than towards the context-specific meanings of the non-knower – the debtor.

The Problematic of the Paradigm of Legal Consciousness

We have reached the fundamental problematic of contemporary legal thought. I documented in Chapter 1 how a certain school of thought in critical legal studies and feminist legal studies aimed to retrieve face-to-face social relations between professional knower and non-knower through one's mind. This school failed to give adequate attention to the language through which both non-knower and professional knower live. The basic problem is 'how can a professional knower's consciousness recognize the consciousness of a non-knower through concepts?'. A knower's consciousness might try to retrieve concrete social relations by reforming legal pedagogy. On occasion, legal scholars have argued that juristic agents could become vitally at one with the non-knower.[24] The knower has aimed to share a common 'environing world' with the non-knower. But that commonality emanates from the knower's 'environing world' as the knower stretches to reach the non-knower's utterance or text or action through consciousness alone. When a knower claims to "know" the facts of a non-knower, the knower intuitively takes the non-knower to be a living subject. But the knower does so by analogizing about the non-knower from experiences which the knower has had in the past. The non-knower is analogized *inside* the knower's constituting *consciousness*. If concepts house the being of a non-knower, the knower takes the non-knower's verbal expression to signify the *thoughts* of the non-knower as a speaker. The knower understands such utterances *intellectually* even though the non-knower's mental phenomena do not fall within the knower's grasp.[25] The knower does not experience the non-knower's recounted experiences; he or she possesses an outer, rather than an inner, percept of them. The knower perceives the non-knower's sentences as manifesting certain inner experiences. The speaker's words do awaken a meant object within the knower.

However, the knower signifies his or her meant objects through secondary signifying relations which the knower takes as transparent of the non-knower's will. Likewise, the knower's signs overlay the non-knower's meant objects so that the knower possesses a word and a percept at the same time, just as Husserl describes.[26] The knower posits the non-knower's experiences as an external object when the non-knower's experiences merely exist in the knower's consciousness.[27] The knower tries to transcend both the knower's and the non-knower's experiences through universalizing concepts. The knower is assured that the non-knower's experiences actually exist since the knower has constituted the non-knower as an *alter ego* within the *knower*'s consciousness.

And yet, a face-to-face relation with the non-knower, something which early critical legal studies and feminist legal theory aspired to reach, cannot be attained. The knower constitutes another monod in the *knower*'s consciousness. But the knower cannot be conscious of the non-knower because, to be conscious, the knower constitutes and the knower cannot constitute the non-knower as constituting. Merleau-Ponty acknowledges in *Consciousness and the Acquisition of Language* that 'it is repugnant to the other, by definition, to be only the consciousness that I have of him'. The non-knower is an other for him or herself just as the knower is for him or herself. One cannot experience an other. One cannot gain access to the other through consciousness. Even if the knower renounces his or her own *cogito* in order to posit the non-knower's *cogito*, the non-knower would still owe his or her meanings – indeed, his or her existence – to the knower.[28] The non-knower would remain the phenomenon of the knower.

Accordingly, the professional knower, however well intentioned, does not experience the non-knower's indigenously experienced pain if the knower works within a paradigm of consciousness. The best that the knower can do is to analogically perceive the non-knower as a replica of the knower. This suggests a second opportunity for the professional knower to understand the non-knower's embodied meanings as the non-knower's rather than as the knower's. In contrast with his success in *Logical Investigations* to demonstrate that every intentional act has a *meant* object and that the knower points to an experience in his or her own consciousness, Husserl attempts to elaborate a second effort for the knower to reach a non-knower in a face-to-face relation in the 'Fifth Meditation'. Here, Husserl claims that a knower and an aggrieved may possess intrinsically relational communication: the knower sees the non-knower looking at him or herself; but, as a subject, the knower transcends his or her own experiences by considering the non-knower analogically with the knower. The analogical apperception is an *intuition*. The knower experiences the 'other ego' not as a mere physical thing belonging to nature but as *in* the world. Here, the knower does not transcend the non-knower through conceptions. The non-knower is not absorbed into the knower's conceptions. The non-knower is believed to be beyond the knower's own experience when the non-knower addresses the knower. The knower relates to the non-knower through the non-knower's expressive body. The knower reads more than physical marks: the knower brings phonemes and graphemes into the sounds and marks of the non-knower in order to produce a sound/mark *pattern*. So too, when the knower sees the non-knower's body there in his or her law office or in the witness box, the knower does not perceive it as a physical body. The listening lawyer perceives the speaker as a subject who is expressing an utterance. The knower creates percepts of the non-knower's speech. To the extent that the knower perceives the witness as manifesting certain inner experiences, the listening lawyer also *perceives* those experiences without experiencing the experiences themselves.[29]

At first sight, the analogical intuition seems to explain a social relation between knower and a non-knower who has experienced harm in a context-specific situation. The knower's intentionality links with the utterances and testimony of the non-knower. This linkage encourages the knower to empathize *with* the other, not *to* him or her. The experience of the one informs the experience of the other. The knower thereby passively synthesizes the experience of the other through the *knower*'s meant objects. The knower does not experience the witness's experiences but, to the extent that the listening lawyer perceives the client or witness as manifesting certain inner experiences, the lawyer *perceives* the experiences or possesses an outer percept of them. The knower also brings his or her embodied meanings into the knower's perception.

If a client informs his or her lawyer of a harm which he or she has experienced, then, the knower does not perceive the story as if it were a given external event. The knower possesses an intuitive image of the circumstance. This involves a very different understanding of the non-knower's experience than when the knower associates the non-knower with the familiar signs in the secondary genre, as occurred in the contexts examined in Chapters 2 and 3. The lawyer's intuition is now what Husserl describes as an 'unmediated seeing'.[30] The knower places the non-knower's harm, as reported, into the knower's *own* intuitive idea of the circumstance. The knower gains an understanding of the client's statement, in Husserl's words, 'through the mere picture-work of fantasy'. The knower's understanding connects with the utterances of the client. The meant objects of the person harmed are fulfilled in the knower's meant objects as the knower intuits them.

But there remains this critical question: does the knower's intuition actually assimilate the non-knower's experience into the knower's conceptions in analogical apperception? According to Husserl's analysis, of course, the knower's intuition does not contribute to the actual meaning of a non-knower. However, the knower's intuition aids the witness in embodying a story with meaning. Without the lawyer's intuition of what the non-knower meant by his or her story about the indigenously experienced harm, the meaning of the non-knower's statement remains unfulfilled. As such, the non-knower's statement remains 'indeterminate in its abstraction'.[31] But the lawyer's intuition encloaks the client's otherwise indeterminate story with a *determinacy* which *fulfils* the witness's meaning-conferring act. The witness reaches a goal by telling the story. Without the lawyer's intuition as to what a witness means, the indicative character of the client's meaning would be 'empty' or 'impossible in the concrete', to use Husserl's words. Without a partner with whom to share the story, the client's story would be merely an indeterminate fragment.

The problematic of such an indeterminate fragment arises from the phenomenon that the partner only shares through, and in terms of, the knower's 'environing world'. Although the knower's environing world stretches out to the client's or witness's story in order to fulfil the latter's meanings, the knower fails to face the non-knower as an other who *embodies* his or her own meanings. The knower pairs the *alter ego as if the non-knower were independent of the knower's body*. Yet – and this is the important point – the alter ego really replicates the knower's body because the knower perceives the witness analogically as if the witness, as a non-knower, has had the knower's experiences. As with the effort of the knower to understand the pain of the non-knower intentionally, the knower fulfils the non-knower's meanings by fusing the non-knower's story into the knower's 'environing world'. The non-knower's embodied meanings live *in* the knower's 'environing world'. The knower constitutes the non-knower's world as the knower analogically apperceives. Such a constitution of the other occurs when the knower fuses with the other in a moment of 'intersubjective zap', to use Peter Gabel's term as elaborated in Chapter 1.

The consequence, then, is that the knower analogically 'projects' him or herself into what the knower takes to be an alien cultural community through a kind of empathy. Empathy takes effort and sensitivity. And, for that, the knower must try to put his or her own cultural expectations into abeyance. By virtue of the resulting 'single universal community', the knower erroneously believes that two 'environing worlds' coexist prior to metaphysics.

Yet, such a belief takes place through the transcendental conceptions of the knower and at the sacrifice of the bodily gestures of the non-knower. The knower may analogize that the non-knower, like the knower, constitutes meanings through his or her phenomenal body but such an analogical apperception leaves the non-knower exterior to the consciousness of the knower. Husserl especially succumbs to this problem in 'Investigation I'. Precisely because the knower's consciousness constitutes the non-knower as an other, he fails to deal with a situation where an intertext between the knower and non-knower possesses the possibility of multiple meanings. For example, the knower may be mistaken as to the identity of the non-knower as a meant object. The knower may be living in his or her own solipsistic world. To our error, we fail to account for the mediating configurations of signs which represent the utterance of a knower or a non-knower. We have worked within the same paradigm of consciousness which I recovered from critical legal studies and feminist legal studies. The knower analogically apperceives the non-knower *before* the knower represents the non-knower as the knower's meant object. The knower sees things which transcend the knower's monadic character before he or she directs his or her meanings, as meant objects, towards the non-knower. We must account for the language through which a non-knower lives in order to ensure that our analogical intuition remains respectful of the non-knower.

The knower's consciousness is able to uncover the non-knower's consciousness as an alter ego. But the knower's consciousness can never alter the radical otherness of the non-knower's embodied meanings because it fails to account for the non-knower's own embodied meanings in his or her own idiom. The knower is preoccupied with understanding the other through transparent signs which represent cognitive objects. Husserl himself adopted just such a paradigm of consciousness in *Cartesian Meditations* where he attempted to establish that existence was characterized by more than the intentionality of a monad. Even Husserl's 'community' of intentional beings started outward *from* the knower to the expressive experience of the other.[32] As a result, the knower could not conceive of the addressive partner except as explicitly or implicitly in communion with the knower's consciousness. Two separate worlds of intentional beings, each with its own language, were 'incompossible' because both worlds were sublimated in the knower's intuition of the utterer's meant object.

It is worth repeating Merleau Ponty's analysis here. He points out in *Signs* that the central problem with such an effort to reach an other, both face-to-face and analogically, is that, in our context, the knower's consciousness reaches the experience of the other if the knower's consciousness posits the other as a projection of the knower's being: 'to be conscious is to constitute, so that I cannot be conscious of another person, since that would involve constituting him as constituting, and as constituting in respect to the very act through which I constitute him.'[33] To understand the non-knower, as an analogical apperception, ignores that the non-knower's experiencing body exists as an obstacle to the knower's theoretical conception of the non-knower, however empathetic the knower aims to be with the non-knower. Merleau Ponty, so perceptive when considered in the context of the modern legal discourse, makes the basic point in his early works – such as his chapter on 'The Body as Expression, and Speech' in *Phenomenology of Perception*[34] – that the knower cannot, and does not, communicate with an other's thoughts. Applied to our issue of the *differend* between the knower and the non-knower, nothing really passes between a non-knower's expression of his or her indigenously experienced harm and a knower's act of listening if the knower – or for that matter any scholar – tries to understand through his or her consciousness or knowledge of the other. The experience of communication in such a project is illusory for the knower believes that he or she has reached the pain of the non-knower, all the while that the knower remains within the knower's own consciousness. The embodied meanings of the non-knower remain concealed. In this respect, the juridical officer's effort to understand the stories of a non-knower through conceptions or even through well intentioned analogical apperception continues Western metaphysics. As Derrida points out more generally, such a project reduces language to thought.[35] In sum, the effort of juridical officials to reach the non-knower's experience of pain through a legal consciousness, without an account of the legal sign, continues the language of Western metaphysics.

Notes

1 *Republic* (Paul Shorey trans.) in *The Collected Dialogues of Plato* (Edith Hamilton and Huntington Cairns eds.; Princeton: Princeton University Press, 1961): Book V, 479e.

2 Ibid., Book VI, 501 d-e.

3 Ibid., Book VI, 490b.

4 Ibid., Book VII, 524e.

5 Ibid., Book IX, 580 (re tyrannical persons); Ibid., Book IX, 577c (re tyrannical states).

6 The Panopticon was the type of prison introduced during the late eighteenth century which architecturally allowed a few prison guards to maintain surveillance

over the bodies of all prisoners from a centre about which the cells were located. It is discussed in general in the works of Jeremy Bentham on the criminal law and in Michel Foucault, *Discipline and Punish: The Birth of the Prison* (Alan Sheridan trans.; New York: Vintage, 1977): 195–228.

7 Jean-François Lyotard, 'A Memorial of Marxism: For Pierre Souyri' in *Peregrinations: Law, Form, Event* (New York: Columbia University Press, 1988): 46.

8 *Republic*, note 1 *supra*, 348a-c.

9 Jean-François Lyotard, *The Differend: Phrases in Dispute* (Georges van den Abbeele trans.; Minneapolis: University of Minnesota Press, 1988; *Theory and History of Literature*, vol. 46): 26.

10 Benedict Spinoza, *Ethics* in *The Collected Works of Spinoza* (Edwin Curley ed and trans.; Princeton: Princeton University Press, 1985): vol. 1, 408–617, Pt III, D2.

11 Gilles Deleuze, *Nietzsche and Philosophy* (Hugh Tomlinson trans.; New York: Columbia University Press, 1983): 97.

12 Ibid., 13.

13 Ibid., 108.

14 Gilles Deleuze and Felix Guattari, *Anti-Oedipus: Capitalism and Schizophrenia* (Robert Hurley trans.; Michel Foucault preface; Minneapolis: University of Minnesota Press, 1983): 25.

15 See Deleuze's discussion of this point more generally in *Nietzsche and Philosophy*, note 11 *supra*, 110.

16 See Emmanuel Levinas, *Totality and Infinity* (Alphonso Longis trans.; Pittsburgh: Duquesne University Press, 1969; Philosophic Series No. 24): 132, 124.

17 Ibid., 157.

18 Georg Lukacs, 'Reification and Class Consciousness' in *History and Class Consciousness* (Rodney Livingstone trans.; Cambridge Mass: MIT Press, 1971).

19 Ibid., 18–19.

20 Louis Althusser, 'Ideology and Ideological State Apparatuses (Notes Toward an Investigation)' in *Lenin and Philosophy and Other Essays* (New York/London: Monthly Review Press, 1971).

21 Ibid., 165.

22 Ibid., 180.

23 Kenneth Burke, *Permanence and Change* (Los Altos, Calif: Hermes, 1954): 74. This pietic character of the signified relations in a secondary genre lies behind Jean-François Lyotard's argument in *Just Gaming* that a paganistic political philosophy is needed in the post-modern condition: Jean-François Lyotard, *Just Gaming* (Minneapolis: University of Minnesota Press, 1985; *Theory and History of Literature*, vol. 20): esp. 62–72.

24 Husserl supports such a view in Edmund Husserl, 'The Logic of Geometry' in *The Crisis of the European Sciences and Transcendental Phenomenology* (David Carr trans.; Evanston: Northwestern University Press, 1970): 357, 364–5.

25 Edmund Husserl, Investigation I in *Logical Investigations*, vol. 2 (New York: Humanities Press, 1970): s. 7, 277.

26 Husserl, Investigation VI, ibid., s. 6, 688.

27 Maurice Merleau Ponty, 'On the Phenomenology of Language' in *Signs* (Richard C. McCleary trans.; Evanston: Northwestern University Press, 1964): 84–97, 93.

28 Ibid., 41.

29 See Husserl, Investigation I in *Logical Investigations*, note 25 *supra*, s. 7 for an analysis of this phenomenon.

30 Husserl, Investigation VI, ibid., 682–3. This phenomenon is examined generally in Maurice Natanson, *Edmund Husserl: Philosopher of Infinite Tasks* (Evanston: Northwestern University Press, 1978): 23ff.

31 This phrase is Husserl's in Investigation VI, note 25 *supra*, 683.

32 Edmund Husserl, *Cartesian Meditations* (Dorion Cairns trans.; Dordrecht: Martinus Nijhoff, 1960): s. 60, 139.

33 Merleau Ponty, 'On the Phenomenology of Language', note 27 *supra*, 93–4.

34 Maurice Merleau-Ponty, *Phenomenology of Perception* (Colin Smith trans.; London: Routledge & Kegan Paul, 1962): Pt 1, ch. 6.

35 Jacques Derrida, 'Structure, Sign and Play in the Discourse of the Human Sciences' in *Writing and Difference* (Alan Bates trans.; Chicago: University of Chicago Press, 1978): 281.

8 The Retrieval of the Dialogic Relation

As with the analysis of the constitution of meant objects by knower and non-knower, the paradigm of language offers a more fruitful opening than does the paradigm of consciousness for the professional knower to understand the non-knower's stories. What type of opening would retrieve the embodied meanings of the non-knower and, indeed, of the professional knower? Further, if the concealed embodied meanings of both professional knower and non-knower were unconcealed, could the knower still attribute "authority" to his or her configuration of signs as can the knower of a modern legal discourse? To begin with, would authority remain in the ghost-like foundation or grounding of the juridical official's trace of authoritative signs? I shall respond to these issues by examining Mikhail Bakhtin's sense of a dialogic relation as he retrieves such relations in Dostoevsky's novels. I shall then ask whether one can still talk of *auctoritas* in a dialogic relationship in the same sense as I associated it with the trace of signs to the absent foundation of legal reasoning.

By retrieving the meaning-infused dialogic relations concealed inside the modern legal discourse, one can better appreciate how the search for typifications in a chain of authoritative signs idealizes how the professional knower perceives and understands the world. When the professional knower describes his or her enterprise as "practical" as opposed to "theoretical" within a paradigm of legal consciousness, all the while that he or she transforms the embodied meanings of a non-knower as the knower resignifies them, the knower participates in "newspeak". The knower takes the externally situated "facts and circumstances of the case" and the rules, principles, policies and other authoritative standards as "givens". I shall now argue that the knower may overcome the naivety in the belief in externally posited objects by resituating him or herself into a dialogic relation with the non-knower. Such a dialogic relation opens up a non-quantifiable opening which both partners may experience as they respond to each other. What type of opening characterizes the relations of dialogic partners? How is such an opening connected to the embodiment of one's meant objects?

I described in earlier chapters how the professional knower has tended to bring oneself *towards* external "givens". The "practice" of the knower has induced the knower to deny that both he or she and the non-knower actually constitute meaning as they read a text or hear the stories of witnesses. This denial has encouraged a naivety about the interpretive act. Furthermore, the denial has had the effect of concealing the rise of an untranslatable gap between the hidden embodied meanings of the knower and those of the non-knower. Once one begins to unconceal such embodied meanings through a dialogic relation between knower and non-knower, the possibility of such a *differend* becomes apparent. The knower has hitherto failed to recognize the non-knower's indigenously experienced pain through the non-knower's own idiom. Even the effort of the knower to analogically apperceive the non-knower in the knower's consciousness has left the non-knower as a victim in Lyotard's sense. The opening to the knower's effort to reach the signified experience of the non-knower lies in the phenomenon of a responsive relation between dialogic partners. So long as the knower responds by representing a non-knower's utterance as a recognizable sign of a secondary genre, the recognition may remain foreign to the non-knower's 'environing world'. Indeed, the recognition reinforces the boundaries of the knower's legal consciousness. The modern knower's "discourse" remains monologic. Only if the professional knower and the non-knower respond to each other's utterances in a dialogic relation will the knower be able to account for his or her and the non-knower's embodied meanings.

The Infusion of Meaning

First, a responsive relation is infused with the dialogic partner's constitution of meanings. As Bakhtin points out in 'The Problem of Speech Genres', a dialogic partner embraces the speaker's speech plan or speech will.[1] Referring to my examples of Haldane and Holmes, each dialogic partner has an 'environing world' which exists *before* the juridical official ever utters sounds or makes marks. In a dialogic relation, the 'environing worlds' of each partner enter one's response to the other. Indeed, the speaker and listener might well share similar horizons of meaning even though, under the earlier analysis of legal representation, they seem to employ very different configurations of signs. What is important in a dialogic relation is that a potential multiplicity of meanings dwells in the discursive field between two responding partners. Each partner's 'environing world' humanizes his or her utterance, organizes the utterance of the other, and casts the utterances of each partner through signs which signify the environing worlds of each partner. Bakhtin describes the importance of such an 'environing world' in a dialogic response when he writes that '[t]he person who understands approaches the work with his own already formed world view, from his own viewpoint, from his own position'.[2] We lawyers may well share a similar 'environing world' because of the long years of acculturation into our profession, our learning of the nomenclature and grammar of the same professional language and our implicit acceptance of the gestural rhetoric of our peers. We may well act as dialogic partners as we communicate with each other, whether verbally or in writing. We may live through each other's professional world. We may well *present* the objects of our arguments to the other knower through familiar configurations of signs, although the presentation seems to be an intellectualizing project. The lawyer may embody a piece of evidence or a doctrine or policy as if such objects stand *before* the lawyer as items which the lawyer may actively *mean*. One's meaning enriches the other partner's configuration of signs. One discloses one's meaning as an experiential, not as a metaphysical nor solely semiotic possibility.

The challenge is to bring a disclosure to the former disparate social relations of knower and non-knower.

The Opening

To begin with, I wish to suggest that the hiatus between dialogic partners offers the key to the unconcealment of embodied meanings. This hiatus is situated amidst a possibility of multiple meanings before speech and writing A dialogic relation respects such a possibility in that neither speaker nor addressee encloses the other within absent typifications which their signs represent. In a dialogue, I *respond* to the other's utterances. I *finalize* my utterance so that other lawyers may actively respond.[3] This sense of finality contrasts with the trace of legal authority in a modern legal discourse. In the latter project, the foundation of authority, to be final, must be believed to dwell external to the signs of the secondary legal genre. In a dialogue, in contrast, one's response must be final for there to be an intertextual space in which the respondent may respond. Without such a finality in the utterer's statements, the utterer would continue without an opportunity for the listener to respond and would thus be carrying on a monologue. In response of the one to the other in a dialogue, utterer and listener join in partnership. Their meant objects work to discover the hiatus or intertext of possible *multiple* meanings which dwell between their utterances. The response of one partner is immediately presented to the response of the other without the mediation of a search for the intent of the other's original statement or, indeed, without a search for the grounding of an utterance in an absent object of a sign. In a sense, dialogic partners continually *live* their discourse as they embody their configurations of signs with their respective environing worlds. Each is an addressee to the other. Indeed, it is difficult to consider each addressee an 'author' in the sense with which I introduced the term earlier in my argument. One dialogic partner does not re-present meanings to the other partner. Rather, each *interprets* the other's speech or text. There remains an 'inter' character or hiatus between speaker and listener. The partners grope towards the hiatus. Merleau Ponty calls this hiatus 'the silence of language', a term which Michel Foucault, Jacques Derrida and others pick up as crucial to understanding language. Each interprets the other's gestural meanings. In interpretive acts, the 'inter' character of interpretation dominates. One reconstitutes one's original typification of the other as one embodies the 'inter' or betweenness between dialogic partners. Living through the 'inter' of the interpretive acts, the interpreters stretch towards the meanings of each other. A *presence* or immediacy characterizes the relation of response to response. The interpretive enterprise reflects a group experience.

Interpreters do not engage in dialogue in an unconstrained manner as if a text were irrelevant. In a dialogic relation, a text no longer dwells "out there" as if its cognitive objects were absent from the configurations of signs in the text. Rather, meaning is drawn from the 'environing world' of the reader. Thus, a reader responds to the text's signs as if the text were a dialogic partner to the reader. Should there be a further interpreter, or interpreters, who are reading the same text, each strives to reach the environing world of the other as they read it.

The concrete and lived horizons of the other interpreters now become important in contrast with the project of legal analysis which treats the utterance of another interpreter as if both "interpreters" are striving to reach the absent objects signified in the text which is itself an external posited object. In a monologue, the particular experiences which utterer and listener bring into a configuration of signs play little or no part in the search for the absent objects.[4] In a dialogic relation, though, the particulars of the utterer's and listener's experiences *do* matter. A speaker *responds* to the other's environing world in order for the constitution of meant objects to be fulfilled.

Each dialogic partner draws from the silent murmur of a multiplicity of unresponded meanings as one responds to the other's utterance or reads a text. Julia Kristeva describes this murmur as a *chora* or 'a non-expressive totality formed by the drives and their states in a motility'.[5] The embodiment of an utterance or text with experience produces uncertainty and flux. In contrast, a monologue aims to reach an absent object as if the object were certain and stable and as if one could reach the object in a linear rational direction. The *chora* of a dialogue offers the possibility of meanings before they are ever signified in verbal or gestural signs. Once meaning is signified in a genre, it can be located and quantified in time and space. Moreover, the signification is directed linearly towards what is taken as a "given" – the "facts of a case", the doctrine, the principle or the policy. But the possibility of meant objects in the *chora* of the intertext between dialogic partners rises from an opague murmur. Merleau Ponty addressed this point when he wrote in 'Indirect Language and the Voices of Silence' that,

> Words, even in the art of prose, carry the speaker and hearer into a common universe by drawing both toward a new signification through their power to designate in excess of their accepted definition, through the muffled life they have led and continue to lead in us.[6]

The common universe involves 'a fold in the immense fabric of language'.[7] The murmur or fabric resembles Derrida's *differance*. The silent web of differentiating signs, locked in the hiatus between dialogic partners, induces the one to seriously take up the embodied meanings of the other. Dialogic partners are carried from the silence of language into configurations of signs which *mean* something to each partner. In order to understand the other, a dialogic partner fulfils the ever-moving, differentiating intertext from which the dialogue draws.

Merleau-Ponty exemplifies the indirect character of the intertext in a dialogue when he examines a child's sympathy for an other in *Consciousness and the Acquisition of Language*.[8] He argues that an adult does not assimilate the child's utterances into the adult's 'environing world' but, rather, momentarily enlarges his or her own 'environing world' so as to live 'for a moment in other people in a kind of egocentric sympathy'. A Gestalt spiritualizes the child–adult dialogue. The adult does not relive a past experience for the benefit of understanding the child.

Similarly, communication between a client and a lawyer possesses a *bodily* sharing. As Husserl emphasizes, an addressee 'takes the speaker to be a person [that is, subject], who is not merely uttering sounds but *speaking to him*'.[9] The bodily experiences correlate with the mental experiences of communicating persons, and the physical side of speech affects this correlation. The client's signs indicate his or her meaning – giving inner experiences to the lawyer or listener. The client endows the utterance with his or her own act of meaning.

The lawyer does not merely perceive the client as uttering sounds, but as speaking *to him or her*. The listening lawyer takes the client, in Husserl's words, 'to be a person, who is not merely uttering sounds but *speaking to him*, who is accompanying those sounds with certain sense-giving acts'.[10] The client and the lawyer share the client's inner experiences intimated in his or her expression. The listening lawyer understands the client's expression when he or she intuitively creates a picture which accurately fulfils the meaning conferred by the client. Thus, the physical element of the client's utterance awakens the experiences in the addressee. An interpersonal bond underlies this awakening. Each dialogic partner intuitively recognizes the other's meant objects in the idiom of the other. Signs and gestures take on a social character. A discourse has displaced the legal consciousness of the monologic legal genre.

Oedipus Rex

Sophocles' *Oedipus Rex* reflects how a dialogic relation draws from the hiatus of multiple meanings in contrast with a monologic imposition of external objects as the legal discourse of a modern state. Creon reports to King Oedipus that the prophet, King Phoebus, had commanded the Corinthians

> to drive out a pollution from our land,
> pollution grown ingrained within the land,
> drive it out, said the God, not cherish it,
> till it's past cure.[11]

Each addressee of the oracle – Oedipus, Tiresius, the chorus, the leader, the messenger, and the shepherd – embodies the sign with their respective environing worlds. For example, Oedipus responds to the Delphic oracle's story of a 'pollution from the land' with 'whose murder?' and then, with assertion that his father, King Laius, must have been murdered many years earlier. Tiresius interprets the murder of Laius; Oedipus revises his interpretation of the oracle as related to his own parents; Jocasta and the shepherd interpret the oracle in the light of their own experiences; and, then, Oedipus reinterprets the oracle by remembering and then responding to another divine story which he had experienced as a young man. My point is that, in a dialogic relation, embodied meanings crystallize from a preceding response from another addressee. Such a responsive relation contrasts with the search for some certain, yet absent, Object which transcends speaker and addressee. Each dialogic partner actively responds. Each response, once actively initiated, relapses into the *chora* once the listener responds to the response. Each dialogic partner becomes an antagonist rather than a protagonist. Each antagonist *presents* his or her experiences as he or she interprets the gestures and signs of the other.

Even the voices of those coloured with authority, such as Oedipus or Tiresius, do not immerse their utterances into some single transcendent voice which we professional knowers in a modern state would recognize as "the law". Nor do those with apparent authority enclose the listeners within the boundaries of the leader's reflections. Such occurs as juridical officials read their worlds in a modern legal discourse. The legal discourse of a modern state, I have argued, presupposes that one protagonist, steeped in a web of authoritative signs, authors or creates a text as if the text's objects were posited as external to the interpreter. The meaning-constituting acts of both juridical agent and of non-knower become transformed into secondary 'ossified deposits' superimposed upon the knower and non-knower alike, to use Todorov's metaphor.[12] Instead, in dialogic relations such as transpire in *Oedipus Rex*, the antagonists coordinate their past experiences and their forestructures of meaning through lived multiple interpretations which draw from the *inter*text between them.[13] Meanings are interwoven through the 'inter' of the interpretive act.

As the dialogic relations arising throughout *Oedipus Rex* indicate, each antagonist does not author or create his or her utterances as if the utterances signify hidden objects to be grasped by the listener. Most certainly, Sophocles does not do so. Sophocles offers a possibility of a multiplicity of meant objects as antagonists in the play and as we interpreters read each other's utterances. There is no one unifying monologue. Nor do the antagonists assume that some final originating *arche* or foundation grounds the authority of Oedipus's utterances and gestures. Rather than being 'acted on', to use Spinoza's term, each antagonist actively embodies the utterances of the other with meant objects. The tragedy is that their meant objects remain continually unfulfilled. Each response is alive with the environing world of embodied meanings. Each anatgonist, as an addressee, brings his or her experiences *into* the utterance of the other. A question-and-answer relation *produces* new configurations of signs which stretch from the utterer through the intertextuality between the antagonists, and from there to the environing world of the respondent. Sophocles raises the possibility that the being of each antagonist may be exposed. The possibility arises only because Sophocles does not load the antagonists with the willed typifications of authors who represent their actions as if the actions represent absent objects to be enclosed.

In her work most influenced by Bakhtin, Julia Kristeva describes the unmeasured and unmeasurable experienced space and time between dialogic partners as an intertext.[14] Each text tries to meet, absorb and transform the other. This intertextual dimension characterizes texts, whether they appear to be authored in the past, the present or the future. Texts respond to one another. The intertext possesses a multiplicity of meanings *before* binary signifying relations take hold. As noted above, the intertext is Derrida's *differance* of a multiplicity of grams. Without the *arche* of forms, a multiplicity of differences embody the interspace. Whereas a monologue emanates from an externally situated creator or situs, such as an historical author or the Spirit of an absent Object, a dialogue shifts focus to an inexhaustible possibility of lived meanings.[15] A spirit locates in the intertext. A spirit of understanding displaces the *prejudice* concealed in the former quest to picture the Spirit of legal authority.

The Deferral of the Face-to-face Relation

One's participation in a dialogic relation possesses a gestural character which goes hand-in-hand with the embodiment of meaning in a sign. In a dialogue, the non-knower is active, not acted upon, as he or she embodies. As one responds to the other, one constitutes him or herself as he or she reads the other's utterances. What is critical here is that, in a dialogue, a dialogic partner is neither a knower nor a non-knower. Knowledge about absent objects is an aside. The addressee of the non-knower awakens the meaning-constituting acts of the knower: each stretches through the intertext as they respond to each other. This is what Bakhtin means when he suggests that:

> As a living, socio-ideological concrete thing, as heteroglot opinion, language, for the individual consciousness, lies on the borderline between oneself and the other. The word in language is half someone else's.[16]

Any monologic language, such as the legal discourse of the modern state, denies the social constitution of meaning.

Contrary to what Levinas suggests, a dialogic relation involves more than the element of an intertextuality. For Levinas, the truth of our relation with the other is in 'the opening of the opening'. Likewise, for Derrida in 'Violence and Metaphysics', the opening is without intermediary and without communion.[17] Levinas adds that consciousness can never transgress the interspace between dialogic partners. Of course, by working within the paradigm of consciousness, Husserl contemplated just such a transgression in the 'Fifth Meditation'.[18] Yet, Derrida points out in 'Violence and Metaphysics' that Husserl had already acknowledged the radical alterity of the other. In other words, Husserl had already accepted that a knower could not reach the environing world of a non-knower when he began to address the issue of intersubjectivity in the 'Fifth Meditation'. That is, according to Derrida, legal consciousness could never assimilate the consciousness of a non-knower and, at best, consciousness could only analogically apperceive the non-knower as an other. In contrast, Derrida suggests, Levinas had erroneously claimed that a dialogic relation could completely close the intertext between two dialogic partners.

In this respect, I would add that once one acknowledges the importance of the 'environing world' in the constitution of meaning, both knower and non-knower are foreclosed from ever fusing their meanings into a unity with the other. Neither dialogic partner can ever understand the other's meant objects so that both gain an immediacy or presence with the other.[19] As Derrida puts it:

> ... it is impossible to encounter the alter ego (in the very form of the encounter described by Levinas), impossible to respect it in experience and in language, if this other, in its alterity, does not *appear* for an ego (in general). One could neither speak, nor have any sense of the totally other, if there was not a phenomenon of the totally other, or evidence of the totally other as such.[20]

The embodied meanings of knower and non-knower are 'irreducibly mediate'. A juridical official could recognize the non-knower only through analogical apperception and never in an original and fused immediacy that both the early critical legal studies and legal feminist movements took for granted. For this reason, the sameness of the monologic character of the secondary legal genre, described in Chapter 2, can never assimilate the non-knower's meant objects: an intertext will always remain between dialogic partners. The non-knower will always exude an element of foreignness to the knower, notwithstanding the knower's effort to perceive the non-knower analogically or to interpret the non-knower's gestures as if he or she were a partner in a dialogue. Such a formidable experiential distance between dialogic partners lies in stark contrast with the knower who works within a paradigm of consciousness. There, the knower may only conceptualize the non-knower inside the boundaries of the knower's image or fantasy of the other. The non-knower ceases to be an other to the knower. Nor is a dialogue possible in such a consciousness. Accordingly, if one wishes to unconceal the embodied meanings of knower and non-knower alike, one must become reconciled to an intertext whose configurations will never be finalized in some face-to-face social relation as has been taken for granted by legal phenomenology.

Desire in a Dialogic Relation

I explained in Chapter 4 that the legal discourse of a modern state is characterized by a special sense of desire. The juridical agent desires an absent external object beyond the agent's intellectual grasp inside the agent's consciousness. What is pivotal is to realize that dialogic partners share a very different sense of desire. What is also crucial is that the student of law understand this difference if he or she wishes to work to unconceal the dialogic relations which the secondary legal genre has overlaid with layers and layers of configurations of signs.

In a dialogue, I disclose my environing world as I respond to the other. An externally posited object, whether it be the "facts and circumstances of a case" or a doctrine or a public policy, does not 'act on' my experiential body as if my body too is an external object to other juridical officials in the secondary genre. My desires are not cognate of some absent object represented by a secondary configuration of signs. I am earth.[21] I act as I respond to the other.

One can best gain a sense of this unfamiliar sense of desire in a dialogic relation by returning to Spinoza.[22] I have pointed out that if one's affections are believed to depend upon externally authored objects, the knower will feel constrained by the gaze of an outside object or, at least, by the surrogate who represents such an object. So, the lower court judge interprets as if he or she is constrained by the gaze of the higher court judge. The latter is presumed to possess a closer insight to the absent object, the doctrine or its application. So too, the juridical official, according to legal theorists as diverse as Hans Kelsen, H.L.A. Hart or Ronald Dworkin, must strive to read primary rules, principles and institutions coherently as if some external source or founding moment constrained the official. Hart writes that the official is "haunted" by the gaze of such a source. In such a world, both the knower and non-knower passively react to the external absent object or source. Even Hercules is so constrained to act passively as he constructs one grand cohesive narrative. Precisely because the object of a rule or principle or norm is absent from the signs of the knower, the knower desires to acquire it, to assimilate it, to colonize it and to terminate it. The object – whether it be a "fact" or legal doctrine, a rule or a principle – is believed to be the end-point of a sign. But because the sign may only approximate the object, it being forever beyond the grasp of legal consciousness, the juridical official is driven in a never-ending conquest. At best, the juridical official can only imagine or picture the object. The knower brings him or herself *to* the externally situated object. One interprets as if the object is the source of knowledge of a sign. The absent object, not the meant object which a juridical agent intuitively presents in a moment of action, is believed to be the source or grounds of the "fact" or doctrine. It is even believed to enclose the experiences of time and space, as I showed in the context of the 'reasonable time' doctrine during the Canadian repression of 1980–83.

In contrast to being acted upon, the dialogic partners, which I am presently unconcealing from inside the modern legal discourse, act through their experiential bodies as they respond to the other's utterance or text. Bodily affections, according to Spinoza, correspond to the passage from one experiential state of the body to another. As I have described of the movement of embodied meanings in the responsive relation of a dialogue, the experiential body increases or diminishes as it passes from one experience into another.[23] Movement and rest, slowness and speed characterize it. In a dialogue, a partner does not strive to reach an unreachable object – whether cognitive or physical or social – because the object is believed to rest "out there" in a world of objects. Rather, a dialogic partner *acts* so as to bring the respondent's utterance *into* the partner's 'environing world'. If a dialogue comes to a "conclusion" that a certain object is valued, this is so because the actions of the partners have reached such a conclusion, not because the object is valued in itself. Spinoza describes this point more generally with respect to his sense of desire: 'we *neither strive for, nor will, nor want, nor desire anything because we judge it to be good*; on the contrary, we judge something to be good because we strive for it, will it, want it, and desire it.'[24] Instead of representing a unifying standardized object beyond the knower and non-knower alike, justice dwells in the possibility of a multiplicity of embodied meanings in the intertext between the dialogic partners. A dialogic relation just does not continue as if a posited object possessed some invisible essence "out there" beyond the gaze of the partners.

This helps explain what I meant above when I suggested that, in a dialogic relation, I exist. My desire emanates from just such an existence, not from the absence of an object. I strive to experience the many contradictions of my existence as I engage in dialogue with another through the intertext between us. My environing world either changes or it struggles with the other's gestures. Joy infects my struggle to respond to the other.[25] Essence does not dwell "out there", beyond an interpreter, in the absent object. Turning Plato upside down, Spinoza suggests that essence involves existence, not some metaphysical conception of the good life.[26]

But what is the engine of desire in this bodily sense if some absent object no longer functions as the centre of the interpretive act? Here, one may best draw from Spinoza's commentary about ethics: if one succumbs to desiring an absent object, one's standardized typifications will enclose and deny the experiential body of both knower and non-knower. If there were no experiential body, there would be no lived meanings. The dialogic partner becomes a knower, once more, and the knower becomes a servant of the body-denying typifications. The other's body is denied as a possibility of multiple meanings. Without an other with which to dialogue, the dialogic relation collapses. As Spinoza puts it, as soon as one ceases to affirm the present existence of one's body (or the body of an other), one's consciousness evaporates[27] as also does the power of imagining the absent objects which signs represent. In contrast with the absence of an inaccessible object, what drives a dialogic relation is the experiential body which lives through its 'environing world'. Thinking involves action, rather than being acted on.

My unconcealment of the dialogic relations embedded inside the secondary legal genre of a modern state, then, requires that the knower acknowledge a radically different sense of desire than that which has plagued modern legal authority. What exists is not some absent object, but the passions of the experiential body. A dialogic partner *produces* meanings. The utterances of the other do not lie "out there" to be resignified, consumed and resituated in the search for some transcendent Object. An embodied desire draws from a social relationship.

Accordingly, only an *embodied* desire embedded in the social relation drives a dialogue. All desiring is the *production* of meaning by active subjects, not the consumption of signified commodities, as I showed in Chapters 2 and 3 in the context of the secondary legal genre. The juridical agent's quest for a foundation which can ground legal authority stifles this productive activity of an embodied desiring. This consumptive process transforms the production of meanings into the representational world of imagined objects. Myths, such as the myth of a state of nature or a state's founding fathers, become necessary in such a secondary signitive world in order to bring a transcendent coherence and unity to textual fragments. A dialogue affirms what the trace of authority denies, however – the possibility of recognizing the other's *embodied* meanings as responsive to the environing worlds of dialogic partners. One has to recognize such meant objects of the other's environing world in order to continue with a dialogue. If justice is the language of the other, then justice is possible through a dialogic relation. In such a dialogic relation, the knower would have to acknowledge the other as a radical other whose body can neither be denied nor expelled from the cognitive objects signified in a secondary genre. The body of the non-knower arouses a duty in the knower *towards* the non-knower. The knower finally addresses the non-knower's experiences through shared configurations of signs which remain alive while the dialogic partners embody the signs with meant objects.

A Multiplicity of Bodies

A dialogic relation, then, shares a radically different sense of a body than the passive body which is 'acted on' by an object which is absent and external to a sign. A typification or category encloses the experiential body of both the knower and non-knower alike in a secondary legal genre. The passivity of the body helps to reinforce the monologic character of the knower's discourse. But, in a dialogic relation, each individual experiencing body, instead of being enclosed within a cognate object, *means* an object through its gestures. Gilles Deleuze calls this movement of a body a 'rhizome'. Each rhizome ceaselessly varies and alters its distance in relation to other rhizomes.[28] Of course, Deleuze and Guattari fail to attribute lived meanings to each body because they fail to appreciate the meaning-constituting acts which an experiential body reads *into* configurations of signs: '[t]here is no such thing as either man or nature now, only a process that produces the one within the other and couples the machines together.'[29] For Deleuze, meaning is simply an issue of usefulness within the body as a signifying machine. An anonymous body is configured from that semiotic machine.

There is no author in the Roman sense of a creator or originator of a text in a dialogic relation. Indeed, the interchanges between the professional knower and the non-knower take on the character of what Deleuze calls an 'indirect discourse'[30] which emanates from the intertext between dialogic partners. The continual exchange of responses slowly transforms the meaning-constituting acts of each partner, thereby modifying their initial cognitive positions. The response to a response is the key to a dialogue. In a real sense, the responsive relations mould, colour and expose the assumptions and signifying relations of each partner. A magical chain of responses holds the knower and the non-knower together.

The intertext between each partner, as I have described, reflects an anonymous murmur with possibilities of multiple meanings. Neither the partners nor the dialogue itself associates any single response with an historically contingent beginning and a final end. Finality is absent from the dialogue in the sense of some ultimate grounding to the discursants' ideas or cognate objects. Accordingly, dialogic partners present their meant objects rather than represent them as signs which others in their genre will recognize as authoritative..

A dialogic relation lacks finality. Such a relation thereby lacks the authority associated with a modern state. The Castle of authoritative laws is really an empty unity: its rooms remain inaccessible, in a secondary legal genre, because its custodians guard absent objects all the while that they resignify the particular experiences of the non-knowers through signs which represent something authoritative for the knowers. The Castle seems real only because the professional knower idealizes his or her own and the non-knower's embodied meanings. A non-knower may clash with the custodians, briefly exchange strident words and then fade into the night as the grand narrative, believed to be authored by some Hercules, continues to represent the non-knower's stories in configurations which only the surrogates of Hercules will recognize. The search for the absent foundation works to exclude or, at best, to assimilate the non-knower's idiom into standardized representations of a legal discourse. The typification of the knower includes and excludes before the non-knower can even respond to the knower. The typification bars all of the aggrieved's questions in advance. The typification – the rule, principle, doctrine or other legal standard – stands "out there" beyond knower and non-knower alike. Yet, the legal discourse invents such a typification. Indeed, its custodians invent the author whose gaze appears to be so all-controlling.

Consumption versus the Production of Signs

Let me return to the secondary legal genre. Bakhtin points out that if there were a dialogic interrelationship between a reported speech or reported text on the one hand and the narrating text of a judge, for example, on the other, one would no longer need to describe the reported text as a commodity or 'work'. The professional knower would no longer consume the non-knower's configuration of signs as if the knower were driven to desire the non-knower's signs as absent objects. For the situs of knowledge in a dialogic relation lies in the embodied meanings, rather than in some absent object, of the partners. In a sense, neither dialogic partner is an *auctor* in the Roman sense of a creator of ideas because ideas emanate from the responses through the intertext rather than from an externally situated source. The ghostly spectre of an absent Object no longer 'acts upon' a professional knower or non-knower.[31] In a dialogic relationship, the *production* of meanings between a text (such as the Delphic oracle) and an addressee/interpreter overshadows the knowledge of the experts.

Because the betweenness is so important to dialogue, the 'environing world' of each addressee expands. What is disclosed is the meaning-constituting act of a partner, not some absent object. Such a disclosure renders a text 'historically effective', to use Gadamer's term. Lived meanings embody an 'historically effective' text. The intertext of a dialogue lacks a fixity of meaning because there is no one external author who can be said to create an idea. Dialogic partners produce meaning; they do not consume signs in the quest for an Archemedian point beyond the signs. Time and space are immeasurable in a dialogue because there is no external object which can function as a guidepost for measurement.[32]

Nor does a text represent some external object in a dialogic relation. Ambivalency colours a text in a dialogic relation because meaning is drawn from the intertext between knower and non-knower even though the one or the other may simply report an event or another text as if it had been posited independently of both the knower and non-knower. An interpreter imitates, parodies, or distorts a reported text so that the abstract evaporates through the act of interpretation. The knower and the reported speech transform each other. Indeed, not only does the reported character of testimony dissipate as the knower *responds* to the report of the testimony, so too does the need for a juridical agent to enforce the intent of a legislature simply because any contingent configuration of signs bears the imprint of all the dialogic partners. Meaning is made concrete as signs are configured, and the idealism of the legal discourse of a modern state collapses. Indeed, the professional knower need no longer search for the identity of an external author. He or she need no longer begin analysis as if a fact or doctrine or founding father has been posited beyond the control and construction of the interpreter. The "author" is situated *there*, in the space of intertextuality – but as an *inter*preter. The *auctoritas* of a presupposed *arche* collapses. And with it, so too does the monologic discourse of a modern state.

Humour helps in this enterprise. Humour displaces or resituates the typifications which the secondary legal genre takes for granted in the juridical official's search for a grounding to legal signs.[33] It returns one to a proximity with the intertext between the knower and non-knower.[34] The *auctoritas* of the Romans is dismantled. And the possibility of an ethnic cleansing of the physical bodily remainder to such an *auctoritas* evaporates.

In a dialogue the knower is a *social* being who is no longer acted on by external uncontrollable objects. For the situs of the social lies in the *chiasm* between dialogic partners. Each partner is there *with* others (*mitsein*), in a multiplicity of possible meanings which, as a surrogate of the foundation located external to the secondary signs, the knower had previously attempted to enclose within the typifications represented by his or her secondary signs. The knower now means objects as a social being, not because he or she is driven by a desire to be recognized by the other, as in Hegel's master–slave relationship, but because the knower must recognize the non-knower even *before* they begin to enter into a dialogic relationship! The knower must recognize his or her dialogic partner as an actor rather than as an object to be 'acted on'. The non-knower's experiences become a condition for the knower to carry on a dialogue with him or her.

Their relationship is linked through an intertext from which each draws his or her response to the other. The addressee no longer passively treats the world as if he or she were 'acted upon' by posited objects. No voice goes unresponded. Rather, knower and non-knower are social partners who *participate* in bringing embodied meaning into the intertextuality *between* themselves.

Understanding Through Dialogue

New spirits take hold of the unconcealed social relations embedded inside a secondary legal genre. These spirits are unlike Montesquieu's Spirit of the Laws – a divine-like Spirit which is believed to transcend all secondary signifying configurations. Nor is the new spirit the perfectly pure will in Kant's supersensible realm of fixed, dead concepts – a world which Hegel so forcefully undermines in his chapter on understanding in his *Phenomenology of Spirit*. Rather, a new spirit of understanding overtakes dialogic partners. This understanding is an inverted world of dynamic and vital bodily interchange between dialogic partners in which a certain idea may be spontaneously associated with utterances. But as the responses take over, Merleau Ponty reminds us, 'each word of a difficult text awakens in us thoughts which were ours beforehand, but these meanings sometimes combine to form new thought which recasts them all ...'[35]. Consequently, an *indeterminacy* characterizes the meaning-conferring acts of each dialogic partner. One's utterance remains unfulfilled in the utterance of the other. Because of this indeterminate fulfilment,. one partner takes up the other's thought through the other's configurations of signs. If one partner took on the former role of a professional knower, he or she would discontinue the dialogue the moment that he or she believed that his or her utterances had been fulfilled in the absent external object. In such a circumstance, the knower might even enforce external objects. But a dialogue grows from the intertext between partners, not from the knower's cognate objects. Again, Merleau-Ponty made this same point in his essay, 'Indirect Language and the Voices of Silence': 'the idea of *complete* expression is nonsensical and ... all language is indirect or allusive – that is, if you wish, silence.'[36] A dialogic partner enriches his or her own meanings by responding through the indirect silence.

Thus, one does not understand another in a dialogic relation as one does in the paradigm of consciousness. One incurs an inner experience beneath, and before, one signifies the experience as a sign.[37] A speaker does not project a sentence for the hearer to catch.[38] Rather, a dialogic partner understands when he or she takes up the other's meant object in a manner which transforms each partner's own environing world. The transformation takes place through meant objects. A dialogic partner understands the other's utterance when he or she hears what is *meant* and no longer hears only sounds. The traditional appeal to binaries (fault/strict liability, *mens rea/actus rea*, tort/contract, public/private, reasonable/unreasonable time, and the like) does not clarify the meaning intended by a dialogic partner. That is why I argued in Chapter 2 that the search for the authority of a secondary legal genre possesses a monologic character. A dialogic relation is an *inter*subjective relation. One's meant object is reciprocated with that of the other. When the utterer's 'environing world' shares a confluence of 'environing worlds', the partners understand:[39] they share meanings.

There is a risk, though, that this sense of understanding disguises the domination of one's 'environing world' over the other's. I engage in dialogue with the other through *my* experiential body and *my* signifying relations. I bring the other's intentions and gestures within *my* environing world, although the boundaries of my environing world are admittedly extended and transformed through our dialogue. Our understanding may seem to have a mono-origins. I cannot translate the full meaning of my environing world through the other's idiom. As Merleau Ponty reminds us, '[w]e may speak several languages, but one of them always remains the one in which we live'.[40] In order to share a complete understanding, he adds, 'it would be necessary to make the world which it expresses one's own, and one never does belong to two worlds at once'. Understanding between knower and non-knower always occurs at the risk of losing the language of one partner or that of the other.[41] Indeed, Merleau Ponty arguably succumbs to just such a risk in his lectures entitled *The Prose of the World*.[42] Here, he describes the social relation in terms echoing the fusion of the non-knower into the consciousness of the knower: a 'unified system' links self and other.[43] Even when, as a knower, I listen, 'I project myself into the other person, I introduce him into my own self'.[44] In a manner reminiscent of a dialogue, a knower magically crosses the silent *chiasmus* of language where cognitive objects possess a multiplicity of significations. But a dialogue collapses when the one partner assimilates the other, much as Merleau Ponty himself advocates of a phenomenology of language: 'the other whom I respect gets his life from me as I get my life from him.'[45]

Notwithstanding his acknowledgement of the surplus of silence which precedes one's speech, Merleau Ponty lectures in a crucial passage in *The Prose of the World*, 'the experience of the other is always that of a replica of myself, of a response to myself'.[46] The other is a 'strange articulation' from 'the very depths of myself'. Why? Because 'I am a totality'. What does this mean? I inhabit the world by carrying on a monologue even though I realize that I draw from the silent murmur of multiple meanings in the hiatus between speaker and listener. I would recognize the aggrieved only 'by coming, whether directly or not, within *my* range, by reckoning in *my* experience, entering *my* world'.[47] A private totality 'fraternizes with the social whole'.[48] But as between 'two rival totalities', agreement between knower and non-knower is impossible because speech *fuses* the aggrieved into the language of the more dominant. Just as Merleau-Ponty had set out to do in *Phenomenology of Perception*, I as a subject and the other as an object have collapsed into lived relations of dialogic addressees.

Notes

1 Mikhail M. Bakhtin, 'The Problem of Speech Genres' in *Speech Genres and Other Late Essays* (Vern W. McGee trans.; Austin: University of Texas Press, 1986): 77.

2 Bakhtin, 'From Notes Made in 1970–71' in ibid., 142.

3 For the constituent of finalization in a dialogic relation, see Jacques Derrida, 'The Law of Genre' in *Critical Inquiry*, vol. 7 (1980–81): 55–81, 76–8.

4 Hans-Georg Gadamer, *Truth and Method* (New York: Crossroad, 1985): 165.

5 Julia Kristeva, 'Revolution in Poetic Language' in Toril Moi ed., *The Kristeva Reader* (Oxford: Basil Blackwell, 1986): 93.

6 Maurice Merleau Ponty, 'Indirect Language and the Voices of Silence' in *Signs* (Richard C. McCleary trans.; Evanston: Northwestern University Press, 1964): 39–83 at 75.

7 Ibid., 42–3, 45.

8 Maurice Merleau Ponty, *Consciousness and the Acquisition of Language* (Hugh J. Silverman trans.; Evanston: Northwestern University Press, 1973): ch. 1, esp. 39.

9 This bodily character of communication is examined in Edmund Husserl, Investigation I, *Logical Investigations*, vol. 2 (New York: Humanities Press, 1970): 277. (Husserl's emphasis.)

10 Ibid., 277..

11 *Sophocles* (David Grene trans.; Chicago: University of Chicago Press, 1984; Phoenix Bks): vol. 1, lines 96–8.

12 Tzvetan Todorov, *Mikhail Bakhtin: The Dialogic Principle* (Minneapolis: University of Minnesota Press, 1984; Theory and History of Literature, vol. 13): 20.

13 Roland Barthes describes a similar intertextuality in connotation in *S/Z: An Essay* (Richard Miller trans.; New York: Hill & Wang, 1974): 8. However, as noted earlier, connotation is a representative meaning whereas I am trying to describe a dialogue as possessing presentative meanings.

14 Julia Kristeva, 'Word, Dialogue and Novel' in *Reader*, note 5 *supra*, 34–61 at 36–7.

15 This point is also made by Julia Kristeva in 'Revolution in Poetic Language' in *Reader*, note 5 *supra*, 89–136 at 99. One can also trace the point to Barthes and Derrida.

16 Mikhail M. Bakhtin, 'Discourse in the Novel' in *The Dialogic Imagination* (Michael Holquist ed.; Caryl Emerson and Michael Holquist trans.; Austin University of Texas Press, 1981): 259–422 at 293.

17 Jacques Derrida, 'Violence and Metaphysics: An Essay on the Thought of Emmanuel Levinas' in *Writing and Difference* (Alan Bass trans.; Chicago: University of Chicago Press, 1978): 79–153, 91.

18 See Emmanuel Levinas, *Totality and Infinity* (Alphonso Lingis trans.; Pittsburgh: Duquesne University Press, 1969; Philosophic Series No. 24): 67–8; and 'The Phenomenological Theory of Being' in *The Levinas Reader* (Sean Hand ed.; Oxford: Basil Blackwell, 1989): 11–28.

19 See Derrida, note 17 *supra*, 120–21. This point is raised in John Llewelyn, *Beyond Metaphysics? The Hermeneutic Circle in Contemporary Continental Philosophy* (New Jersey: Humanities Press, 1985): 198–200.

20 Derrida 'Violence and Metaphysics', note 17 *supra*, 123. (His emphasis.)

21 Gilles Deleuze and Felix Guattari, *Anti-Oedipus: Capitalism and Schizophrenia* (Robert Hurley trans.; Michel Foucault Preface; Minneapolis: University of Minnisota Press, 1983): 144. Nietzsche and early Greek philosophers also suggest the earth as a metaphor. Antigone described the earth as the situs of the gods.

22 Spinoza's view is discussed in Karl Kosik, *The Dialectics of the Concrete: A Study on Problems of Man and World* (Dordrecht-Holland/Boston: D. Reidel Publ. Co., 1976; Boston Studies in the Philosophy of Science): vol. 52, at 13, 17, 151, 154.

23 Benedict Spinoza, *Ethics* in *The Collected Works of Spinoza*, vol. 1 (Edwin Curley ed. and trans.; Princeton: Princeton University Press, 1985): Pt III, D 3.

24 Ibid., Pt II, P 10 Schol.

25 Ibid., Pt III, P 25.

26 Ibid., Pt I, D 1.

27 Ibid., Pt II, P 11 Schol.

28 Deleuze and Guattari, *Anti-Oedipus*, note 21 *supra*, 2; *A Thousand Plateaus: Capitalism and Schizophrenia* (Brian Massumi trans. and foreword; Minneapolis: University of Minnesota Press, 1987): 30.

29 Deleuze and Guattari, *Anti-Oedipus*, note 21 *supra*, 109. Also see ibid., 84.

30 Gilles Deleuze, *Kant's Political Philosophy* (Hugh Tomlinson and Barbara Habberjam trans.; Minneapolis: University of Minnesota Press, 1984): 55.

31 Hans Robert Jauss, *Question and Answer: Forms of Dialogic Understanding* (Michael Hays ed. and trans.; Minneapolis: University of Minnesota Press, 1989; Theory and History of Literature, vol. 68): 219–31.

32 See, for example, Julia Kristeva, 'Women's Time' in *Reader*, note 5 *supra*, 187–213 at 210.

33 Levinas, *Totality and Infinity*, note 18 *supra*, 91–2.

34 Both Bakhtin and Levinas emphasize the role of laughter and humour in their works. Also note how Duncan Kennedy offers humour as one of the tactics to break up the enclosures of legal doctrines in text *supra*, Chapter 1.

35 Maurice Merleau Ponty, *Phenomenology of Perception* (Colin Smith trans.; London: Routledge & Kegan Paul, 1962): 178.

36 Merleau-Ponty, 'Indirect Language and the Voices of Silence' in *Signs*, note 6 *supra*, 43.

37 Merleau Ponty, *Phenomenology of Perception*, note 35 *supra*, 182.

38 Ibid., 183–4.

39 When Merleau Ponty analyses the structure of language in his later works, he does not reduce language to a phenomenal body. He asks how the structure of language changes through changed meanings.

40 Merleau Ponty, *Phenomenology of Perception*, note 35 *supra*, 187.

41 Ibid., 188. (His emphasis.)

42 Maurice Merleau-Ponty, *The Prose of the World* (John O'Neill trans.; Claude Lefort ed.; Evanston: Northwestern University Press, 1973).

43 Ibid., 18.

44 Ibid., 19.
45 Ibid., 86.
46 Ibid., 135.
47 Emphasis added.
48 Merleau Ponty, *The Prose of the World*, note 42 *supra*, 145.

Conclusion: Living Laws

In aspiring to *know* the particular other's experience as an object of his or her consciousness in a secondary legal genre, the professional knower encloses the non-knower within the invisible boundaries of the knower's absent cognate objects. One can break from such a colonialist project of the modern legal discourse only if one turns from a knowledge of the other to the language of the other. In particular, a dialogic relation maintains the possibility of a multiplicity of meanings in the intertext between dialogic partners. The knower comes to recognize the non-knower's story for the meanings which the non-knower brings through his or her environing world. The non-knower is a dialogic partner. The praxis of meaning contexualizes "facts", texts and doctrines.

The interspace from which a dialogic partner represents his or her meanings dwells experientially *before* the knower ever attempts to conceptualize the non-knower. A partner *embodies* a sign with *prejudice* before the other resignifies the sign into the dialogue. A dialogic partner completes or finalizes his or her response so that the other can respond. A dialogue takes on a *spirit* of its own. The partner cannot fuse with the 'environing world' of the other because a heteroglot of voices separate the partners. The dialogic partners remain linguistically separate, yet socially joined.

What has happened to the authority of the text in a dialogic relation? Can one describe a dialogic partner as an author? Can one consider the partners as creators or originators of signs? Do the partners begin their project by bringing themselves *to* an absent Object, such as a fact or a doctrine? Is there a finality to a dialogic relation?

The critical point to a dialogic relation is that the partners *act* towards their *meant* objects: they do not react to a witness's story or to the "facts and circumstances of a case" or a rule or principle as if the latter pre-existed the interpretive act. They *participate* in the constitution of meaning. The "facts and circumstances of a case", as well as the legal doctrines, do not originate a dialogue, for the partners embody their meanings from the past experiences and the future expectations which constitute their 'environing worlds'. Dialogic partners communicate in a never-ending revision of their configurations of signs. A spirit takes hold. This spirit, as suggested in the previous chapter, is not the Spirit of a Roman sense of *auctoritas* – a Spirit, situated in an objectless transcendent realm, which gazes down upon the knower from afar. That Spirit possesses a ghostly identity. The knower envisages or pictures the identity as he or she configures signs in the secondary legal genre. Rather than being situated external to such signs, the spirit of a dialogue is embedded *inside* the discourse itself! The spirit of a dialogue takes form from the heterology of voices which condition the response of one partner to the other. Because their meanings draw from the possibility of a multiplicity of differences, the partners cannot claim to represent some one unifying, bodiless Object. At best, they can respond to the other in a signifying context which takes on living meanings as they embody its signs. Because each partner directs his or her meanings towards meant objects, the meanings may not be fulfilled in a posited, externally situated object. An indeterminacy of fulfilment of meanings characterizes the dialogic relation. The partner acts, rather than reacts. Accordingly, one can hardly describe the dialogic partner as a passive applier of external objects, such as texts and doctrines. The dialogic partner does not originate or create ideas which he or she represents in a text. The partner is not an author. He or she *continues* a discourse which pre-dates him or her. He or she *responds* to the other. And the shared objects are *meant*, not posited as external givens.

The Meant Object

The knower's desire for an absent object, whether it be a fact or a legal doctrine, colours the knower's narrative in a secondary legal genre. For the knower narrates *about* the pain of a non-knower through configurations of signs which re-present the pain as other knowers "understand" it. The external situs of the objects of the legal discourse excuses the knower for pursuing what the non-knower may take as a monologue.

Once one appreciates how the juridical agent in a secondary legal genre is situated externally to both agent and the agent's signs, what the knower has hitherto taken as an objective, formal and authoritative sign reinforces the trace of authority to some referentless object. Both the knower and non-knower *act* towards *meant* objects; they are not acted upon by some envisaged ghostly surrogate of the external foundation of authority. Both the knower and non-knower embody their objects with their past experiences and expectations drawn from past experiences. What one says or writes becomes a referent to the other's response. The one reads *into* the utterance or text of the other. Both speaker and listener embody an utterance by bringing it into their 'environing worlds'. The respondent *acts* as he or she embodies the utterance or text of the other. The utterance or text, as a referent, is not an external given. The referent does not constrain the listener. Moreover, the respondent fulfils the utterer's constituted meaning when the respondent's meant object overlaps with the utterer's. Perhaps, that may occur in the circumstance when the partners, like the knowers of a profession which trains and acculturates the knower over many years, come to share a similar environing world. The alterity of each dialogic partner remains, though, even in such a circumstance. Thus, the dialogue may not necessarily follow a linear direction from an author towards some external absent object as represented. The finality of one's utterance conditions the dialogic relation with a particular other's environing world. The intertext draws from a multiplicity of possible differences. Such a heteroglot ensures that respondents remain separate from each other, even though the one claims to be able to represent some distant inaccessible foundation. The colonialism which plagues the paradigm of the other's consciousness in a secondary legal genre evaporates. An addressee's *relation* with another addressee destabilizes all typifications which the knower had formerly used to enclose the non-knower's particular experiences.

Mutual respect reigns. When a dialogic partner recognizes the respondent – and such recognition must occur for there to be a dialogue – one does not represent nor conceive nor picture the other. The other is not another externally posited object which one can, at best, represent as a signified object. The dialogic partner's understanding of the other is a lived understanding precisely because the one embodies the signs of the other. The particular other is meant. The one responds to the other, not to some vision of an object. A peace, quite alien to the bourgeois peace of the legal discourse, imbues the dialogic relation. The partners are respondents, not authors.

Narrative versus Discourse

A dialogic partner responds to the other through a *discourse,* not through a narrative. A narrative encodes sentences so as to signify them and to situate the signification in some order with a beginning, a plot and an end. A narrative is authored. The narrator impartially recounts events as if the event existed in the past and external to the narrator. The narrator writes and speaks as if past events, out of his or her control, constrain the narration. I have argued that just such a project, which hinges upon the presupposed givenness of external objects, idealizes the events which the narrator recounts. Furthermore, the narrative project conceals the dialogically produced meant objects of the non-knower as well as of the interpreter, the narrator, the judge, the lawyer, the teacher and the student. Such a role is lived because each knower brings the event into his or her own environing world. And the knower recognizes the non-knower, whose pain is recounted, as a particular other whose utterance is the object of the knower's response. The narrator's objectivist project belies the concealed meaning-constituting acts of the narrator. Both narrator and narrated speak through environing worlds which contextualize the response of the other. They *respond* to each other and that response, expected or actual, shapes a speaker's utterance from the outset. Thus, what one may have taken as a narrator really is an addressee, but an addressee who actively participates in privileging the configuration of signs from the heterologic potential in the intertext between addressees. Unlike the narrative of legal discourse, an addressee in a dialogic relation can gain access to the significatory project by embodying its signs. One gains an addressive experience of the other.

The configuration of signs in a dialogue is not self-referential and self-binding as it was in the representative project of a secondary legal genre, as argued in Chapter 2 and demonstrated in Chapter 3, for each addressee embodies signs whose configurations represent a potential heterology of voices. Each dialogic partner is an addressee to the other – an other to the other. Although each finalizes an utterance in order for the other to respond, the dialogue itself is never finalized, nor can it possess the finality of a transcendent grounding and therefore the posited character which permeates the secondary legal genre of a modern state. Because each addressee is recognized as responding across an intertext and through each one's 'environing world', the dialogue is alive with the felt bodily experiences. One's own configuration of signs meets with resistence and struggle from the other. The struggle is impassioned with the sentiments of the body. The knowledge of external objects is tentative and in a state of flux. The possibilities of fulfilment of a meaning are inexhaustible. In addition, meaning is *personal* and *particular*. Configurations of signs are *presented* from one's 'environing world' towards meant objects, which, themselves, are fluid. One does not passively listen to a narration, nor does one just accept the enforcement of its cognate enclosures. The addressee actively participates. He or she is an *interpreter*.

The addressee produces a transient configuration of signs from the heterology of possible voices in the intertext between dialogic partners. He or she does not discover an absent Object, called Truth or Justice, from within his or her consciousness.[1] In a dialogic relation, justice dwells in the heteroglot in the intertext, but is accessible in that it resides inside the discourse rather than in some ghostly singular origins beyond it. The heteroglot is an other to the discourse – a radical other, unformed and silent.

Dialogue as the Social

Legal discourse hides the social within it. The reason why the social lies within, rather than external to, the discourse lies in the phenomenon of the displacement of meanings, examined in Chapter 2. Again, the typification is a universal and is represented by a secondary sign. Concealed meanings are concrete in the sense of being context-specific. For meaning to be concrete, it draws from an environing world which provides a context which means and fulfils the meaning of an other. An interpreter reaches out to respond to the other's 'environing world'. The 'environing world' of the one partner fulfils the meaning-constituting act of the other. Such a fulfilment makes the interpretation concrete.

When a dialogic partner configures signs, the partners embody the signs with their prior experiences and expectations. Such an embodiment draws from their environing worlds. The addressees live *through* such environing worlds. If one addressee ignores the bodily element of the constitution of meaning – that is, if one forgets the role of the environing world through which an addressee reads the response of the other – the utterer merely preaches *about* some external referent as if the essence of the referent constituted Truth and Justice. Indeed, such an utterer need not even address anyone else; he or she may as well be preaching to him or herself. The utterer's absent Object is a Oneness – a Unity which is posited as a given even though it is unrepresentable. But because a dialogue necessitates one responding to the response of the addressee, the respondent must try to recognize the *meant* objects of his or her partner and the discursive character of their relation. Thus, the discourse possesses a life of its own, independent from any absent object which the narrator may have previously taken as a given. The 'environing world' of an utterer changes as the utterer responds and understands the response of the other. Dialogue draws from the concrete context between addressees. If an addressee cannot understand and experience an other's sign – that is, if he or she cannot *mean* the sign – the sign remains dead matter in the sound waves or on a page. The addressee/other does not understand a sign when he or she passively receives a lecture, speech or sermon. But dialogic partners do not just shift from one social context to the next in a fit of rhetorical opportunism. A concrete social context awakens a particular, albeit transient, meaning from the murmur of multiple meanings.

Volosinov goes so far as to suggest that one may even engage in dialogue with oneself. One brings a meant object into a configuration of signs when one contextualizes the configuration in one's environing world. One actively responds to oneself by situating the response amongst *prejudice* in an environing world. One's thoughts, then, belong to one's past experiences. One leaves one's experiential horizons for the unknown multiplicity of the intertext between dialogic partners. As a result, then, the social dwells in the rejoinder in dialogue, not in the narrative of a presupposed external author.

The importance of the environing world in the embodiment of meaning should be emphasized. A dialogic partner embodies an other's utterance or text with meaning drawn from the first partner's environing world. Such an environing world brings a concrete context *into* the utterance or text. This concrete context contrasts with the monologue which resignifies a cognitive object. What could be more abstract than an absent object, indifferent to the felt experiences of the particular non-knower? Similarly, the configurations of signs, because they represent the absent object, are indifferent to the non-knower's biography. The environing worlds in a dialogic relation contextualize a text or utterance, thereby bringing humanity into the text. Thus, signifying configurations take on a social character. Such a social element is foreign to the secondary legal discourse of a modern state. If chains of signs are self-referring and self-binding, as they are in a modern legal discourse, one idealizes the concrete. Bakhtin goes further when he says that contact between a meant object and a concrete contingent context distinguishes a human utterance from a mere verbal sound[2] for such a contact imbues the utterance with the speaker's horizons of meaning embodied within his or her environing world. The contact brings the interpreter's passion and values into the interpretation of the utterance and embodies the utterance.

A second factor, besides the role of the environing world, works to make the concealed dialogic relations in a legal discourse constitute the social. Mindful of Spinoza's distinction between one's being 'acted on' by an absent object and the action of one's embodied interpretation, action permeates the interpretations of dialogic partners. The partners *act* as they interpret. Their action possesses a social character because they share their activity. Although they may direct their intent to some externally situated object, such as a "fact" or legal doctrine, they aim to understand each other's response rather than the absent object as in and of itself. Thus, one's utterance is no longer an instrumental good to be used and manipulated in the search for the *auctoritas* of a legal sign. Acts of interpretation in a dialogic relation are intrinsically valued in, and for, themselves as experienced. Because such meanings inhere to the environing world of each partner, a response in a dialogic relation recognizes the other partner in a manner which is context-specific or concrete in contrast to the commodified universals of a legal discourse which searches for absent objects. In contrast with the passive self-image of a knower who believes that he or she is 'acted on', the interpreter actively directs his or her meaning towards a meant object which is the concreteness of an environing world. Aristotle had such a sense of 'action' in mind when he suggested that the wise person possesses an active, as well as a passive, intellect.

This raises a third factor which works to associate the concealed dialogic relations with the social. Because one's environing world contextualizes a text in a social relation and because a possible multiplicity of meant objects may fulfil one partner's utterance to another's, a dialogue lacks the uniform unidirection of a trace for an *arche* in the secondary legal discourse. By virtue of its idealization of events, the trace of authority becomes increasingly distanced from the non-knower's meanings. In contrast, a dialogic relation connects the experiential body of one partner with that of another even though each may bring different embodied meanings into the same chain of signs. A dialogic relation, precisely because an utterance is open to the possibility of a diversity of meant objects of fulfilment in the other partner, is contradiction-ridden. Bakhtin calls such contradictions 'heteroglossia'. A word uttered in one place at one time will possess a different meaning in another context.[3] Because a response represents a meant object, a dialogue is permeated by ideological contradictions which flow from the different experiences which the partners bring into their responses to the other. Each environing world reflects a specific world-view. But, however deeply one's experiences seem like 'a second nature', a dialogue – if it is a dialogue – leaves open the possibility that interpretive acts themselves will constitute experiences. Ambiguity and indeterminacy infuse the potential fulfilment of a meaning-constituting act of each dialogic partner. Because the dialogic relation cannot be finalized in some absent constraining object, the conferring of meaning is forever indeterminate. Clashing ideologies imbue the dialogic relation against a background of communality.

A heterology of voices, then, characterizes the concealed social practices within the legal discourse of the modern state. A text or utterance awakens a plurality of experiences which the monologic narrative has left dormant. Experiences are brought into the silent intertext between dialogic partners. Each partner possesses his or her own environing world with discrete affections which move through the body. The utterance of one body affirms, contradicts, supplements and relies upon the utterance of the other. Their respective environing worlds bring concrete social circumstances to their utterances. Meaning refuses to be enclosed within the totality of an *auctor's* forms. Each body struggles to signify against the condition of the intertext. And each struggle is manifested through transient gestures which appear, have their day in court, and then die away as competing configurations take hold of addressees. Such a social struggle shatters the environing world of any one body.

The Recognition of the Particular Other

The dialogic relation takes on an ethical context.[4] Unlike the justice which is believed to transcend the signs of a secondary legal genre, the justice of a dialogic relation dwells in the murmur of multiple embodied meanings. In a sense, the possibility of multiple embodied meanings offers a very different spirit than that presupposed in an authoritative legal discourse, for this spirit lives through the embodied meanings of the dialogic partners. The Spirit of the secondary genre cannot be lived because it must remain inaccessible and external to legal signs in order to found the trace of authority in such signs. Indeed, it might be a short step for a professional knower to describe someone as "neurotic" if he or she '*destroyed* the self to make room for the other person'.[5] A spirituality of dialogue opens up the professional knower and non-knower as *inter*preters of each other's responses. Such a spirituality furthers the environing worlds of knower and non-knower alike. The knower and non-knower live *with* the other's environing world. As a dialogue takes hold, the *inter*pretive act displaces the belief in the externality of an absent object. Gadamer claims that each interpreter aspires to understand the 'said' of the other in his or her own idiom.[6] The knower does not implant his or her typifications into the non-knower's life-world; the knower completes his or her understanding of the non-knower's experience as the knower receives the non-knower's story. The knower and the non-knower, in turn, fulfil each other's meaning-constituting acts. However, contrary to Gadamer's view, the knower's reception of the non-knower dwells beyond the knower's control or the knower's conscious "knowledge" in that the hiatus between the non-knower and knower – not the knower's text itself – offers the situs for dialogic responses. Gadamer may have been hinting at this when he wrote, '[t]hrough every dialogue something different comes to be'.[7] One recognizes an other *through language* rather than through one's representation of the other in thought.[8] Language makes universality and generality possible. Because a dialogic relation takes place through the 'inter' of interpretation, Levinas suggests, 'discourse is thus the experience of something absolutely foreign, a *pure* "knowledge" or "experience", a *traumatism of astonishment*'.[9] The knower recognizes the other through shared responses rather than through some unifying monologue about the spectre of an invisible author.

The knower must *recognize* the *language* of a non-knower in order to carry on a dialogue. As the juridical agent of the absent foundation of legal authority, a professional knower compares all utterances in terms of the sameness of the knower's typifications. But in a dialogue, the knower ventures into an unknown space of intertextuality which exists prior to the knower's intentional meanings.[10] The knower and the non-knower are no longer solipsistic beings as they are when the knower plays a part in a legal narrative. Nor can the surrogate be considered an author in the sense of a creator of signs. Language is never the knower's. That is, the knower cannot treat any configuration of signs as a product to be manipulated, possessed, consumed or controlled as was possible when carrying on a monologue. The knower, like the non-knower, is an *event* which participates *through*, not in, language. What becomes important is that the non-knower and the knower are saying. Also important is what the non-knower says through his or her own idiom. Dialogue helps to recover the saying of what was said.[11]

We know now that the trace of authority in a secondary genre does not allow for an addressive rejoinder.[12] Instead, the professional knower traces authority in a unidirection towards his or her spectre of the foundation of legal authority. In such a discursive continuity, the professional knower's configurations of signs belong to nobody – that is, to no body. The author's signs stand for objects in an idealized world. The professional knower's narrative idealizes the pain of a non-knower by virtue of the absence of an addressive rejoinder from the non-knower. On the other hand, an addressive rejoinder would rupture the linear direction of the juridical agent's narrative. What the knower understands as a neutral sentence belonging to the non-knower is transformed into a living dialogue. The transformation of meaning in the secondary genre is inverted from rigid dead abstractions to lived, concrete movement.

The Authority of the Unconcealed Dialogic Relation

The big question remains: if the authority of a modern legal discourse rests in an absent foundation, can one recognize any semblance of authority in the retrieved dialogic relations which an authoritative discourse conceals? How can any one dialogic partner even parade as a professional knower of external objects to the meaning-constituting acts of the non-knower if meanings of knower and aggrieved alike are drawn from a silent formless intertext between the partners? After all, I have argued that, in a dialogic relation, each partner recognizes the other as the one responds to the other's utterances and texts. The recognition of the dialogic partner, as an opposed embodiment of meanings, contrasts with juridical recognition as a signified representation in a secondary genre. Such a signified recognition comes at the cost of the assimilation of the addressee into a linear narrative. The question which remains, indeed, is whether one can even speak of an *auctoritas* of a dialogic relation. So much of the contemporary legal process presupposes the *auctoritas* of the typifications of a transcendent *auctor* that it is difficult to understand the recovery of authority in dialogue. One thing is certain: one cannot picture such an authority in the sense of *knowing* because of the intertextual chiasmus between the texts of the *auctoritas* of a modern state on the one hand and the retrieved dialogic relations on the other. Nevertheless, one can isolate at least two conceptual possibilities.

One prospect, following Jean-François Lyotard, is to represent an authority of concealed social relations in terms of the retrieval of a multiplicity of narratives, each embedded in its own genre and each with its own chains of signifying relations. With this prospect, the *auctoritas* of a secondary genre collapses into that of many micro-narratives. Each narrative would be grounded in its own external inaccessible foundation. Each authoritative narrative would struggle to dominate other narratives in an agonistics of power.

Such a view of authority, unfortunately, plays into the very monologic character of the secondary legal genre of a modern state. Instead of one self-referential signifying machine constituting the state proper, several semiotic machines would characterize political relations. The displacement of one grand narrative in favour of several has been exemplifed in the dissolution of Yugoslavia, the former USSR and the former Czechoslavakia. Several smaller narratives are even erupting from hitherto highly commercialized and industrialized states such as Canada, the United Kingdom and Belgium. The legal genre of each smaller narrative works through secondary signifying relations. The secondary genre takes on a self-binding and self-referencing character. Each displaced, and displacing, discourse presupposes an absent transcending foundation to its authority. Each struggles to displace the signified surrogates of the dominant genre with surrogates for the seceding genre. Because the authority of a discourse, which claims to be grounded, has been associated with the state since Roman times, each displacing discourse claims to represent sovereignty. The several displacing discourses even appeal to different founding fathers and other historical authors of their respective discourses. Of course, because violence inheres in the very constitution of the identity of any one founding source, the constitutional agonistics is coloured with violence – indeed, with a barbaric violence. "Ethnic cleansing" and racial ghettoism become "second nature" to the displacement of the grand narrative with several micro-narratives. With each displacing narrative, there is always a remainder – one more other to the displacing secondary genre. The physical bodies of each remainder remind the surrogates of the displacing narratives that their project of bringing all within their consciousnesses remains incomplete. The experiential body of the other is aud must be concealed so long as the new secondary genres trace chains of signs to some presupposed absent foundation. The cleansing and ghettoism of the remainder may well be enforced authoritatively, legally. Professional knowers find little difficulty in shifting their loyalties from the discourse of the former grand narrative to that of a territorially smaller, yet just as all-exhuming, state. For all knowers in a secondary genre feel constrained by the surrogates of its foundation. The surrogates mediate between the secondary configuration of signs and the absent foundation. Each discourse pictures the foundation of authority differently. Each discourse may attribute a particular religious sect or colour of skin, or shape of the physical body, or thickness of hair to the founding fathers of the secondary genre. The picture of the physical attributes or of the cognate beliefs of the founding fathers gives an identity to the transcending, bodiless foundation of legal authority in the displacing narrative. Of course, a non-knower who does not share such physical attributes or beliefs is an outsider, an out-law, a no-body, an enemy and a threat to the centralizing and standardizing grounds of the micro-authoritative discourses. Several leviathans replace one leviathan. In the trace of its own authority, each leviathan reaches out to enclose the enemy within its self-binding narrative.

Indeed, so long as one remains within a language which takes its colour from a secondary legal genre, the production of the concealment of suffering remains problematic. Juridical officials continue to search for the identity of the founding moment of authority, and their secondary genres become distanced, once more, from the everyday languages of the non-knower who cannnot represent his or her claims except and only through the alien genre of the professional knowers of the new state. The authoritative monologues would 'endlessly hear and tell the narrative of their we', as Lyotard himself describes of the master narratives of modernity.[13] Once again, the discourse of each monologic leviathan would succeed in assimilating the embodied meanings of particular others within the consciousness of the knowers. Each legal discourse would master all other discourses: others would be excluded; some would be assimilated; still more would be interned, tortured or killed because their physical bodies would remind juridical officials that the master monologue always leaves a remainder untouched. What the multiple narratives do not enclose within their typifications, they would redefine "out of existence", as it were. That explains why savages make war, Lyotard himself argues. Although each narrative would apparently become unconcealed from the dominating 'state proper' (the final moment of Hegel's state), the multiplicities of narratives, in turn, would conceal the meaning-constituting acts of non-knowers and knowers alike. Each master narrative would remain a monologue. The only addressees would be other professional knowers.

There is a second possibility by which the concealed embodied dialogic relations could be retrieved, however. Drawing from Mikhail Bakhtin, heterologic voices – not the unilingual representations inscribed in search for the identity of a presupposed foundation – characterize the concealed embodied meanings of the *chiasmus* of a dialogue. An intertext between respondents prevents a dialogic partner from fusing the other's language into the partner's represented categories. In order to engage in dialogue, one addressee must recognize the other as unassimilable. Both the knower and non-knower bring their embodied experiences into the other's utterances and texts. An indeterminacy, which colours both the constitution of one's meanings and the fulfilment of those meanings in the meant objects of the other, characterizes the meanings of configurations of signs. A perfect coherence between utterance and interpretive act cannot be reached. The dialogue does not travel in a linear direction towards some founding author, nor is the ending of the dialogue predictable. Any consensus is transient for it crystallizes only when the partners reach similar meant objects through their dialogue.

Justice lies in the heterology of voices embedded in the silent intertext between dialogic partners. Unlike the justice associated with the modern legal discourse, one can gain access to this justice. It is accessible because it dwells concealed *inside* the legal discourse of a modern state. The embodied meanings of a non-knower have been intellectualized by professional knowers. The configurations of signs through which a non-knower represents his or her pain and suffering have dissipated in favour of the professional knower's secondary chains of signs. But the felt experiences which the non-knower had brought into her configurations remain as do his or her meant objects. Such an embodiment of the non-knower's meanings cannot be lopped off through a professional knower's cognitive act of categorization. The justice of the language of the non-knower, as an other to the language of the professional knower, is concrete and context-specific. Such a justice may be retrieved if one shirks the traditional duty of the professional knower to feel constrained by the gaze of *auctoritas*. Such a justice dwells in a formerly concealed practice of social relations and its realism contrasts with the idealism of the justice of the secondary genre. The indeterminacy of the constitution and fulfilment of meaning make it difficult to link dialogic responses to a founding source or *arche*, visible or invisible. The *arche* of the *auctoritas* of the modern state has collapsed. Texts and utterances are finally embedded in the social. But whether such texts and utterances can be described as authoritative is another question.

The sense of authority associated with the secondary legal genre has deferred to an ultimate external source or foundation or grounds of any particular text or utterance. The foundation is believed to authorize any configuration of signs. To be a foundation, the source must be final and, to be final, it must be radically other than the trace of one sign's grounds to the grounds of another sign. The ultimate foundation must be absent from the legal discourse and transcend all configurations of signs. Its situs must be external to historically contingent authors. A dialogic relation does not need such a foundation or source for it to be "authoritative". Indeed, flux and multiplicity characterize a dialogic relation. The direction of a dialogue cannot be measured in time and space, for embodied experiences constitute the responses in a dialogue. Experience is addressed. The interpretative act itself is an *addressive experience*. Addressive experiences *mean*. Although the intertext between one addressee and an other is inexhaustible, each addressee stretches to understand the environing world of the other. As one dialogic partner hears the other, the hearer stretches his or her experiences to reach the environing world of the other. The one alters his or her self-image just as the other changes his or hers. Thus, the dialogic partners reach an understanding of self and other. The most important facet of that understanding is the recognition of the other as the addressee to one's interpretive act. Because the intertext is so important and because an addressee embodies his or her response with lived meanings, one's configuration of signs neither originates in the addressee nor does it represent the will of some founding authority. One cannot associate one's chain of signs with an author or creator of an idea. For the engine of the authority of a dialogue dwells internal to the dialogue, in the silence of the intertext between dialogic partners.

The problematic which remains, however, is this: 'how does one institutionalize such a dialogic relationship without becoming entrapped in a multiple ghettoism of multiple narratives, as I raised above?' In a sense, the problem which Hegel faced in *The Philosophy of Right* remains. If the dialogic relations, concealed within the juridical language of the modern state, were retrieved into what Gadamer calls a 'free dialogue' without a referent, then some form of ordered anarchy, perhaps of the character advocated by Peter Kropotkin, might follow.[14] But I have argued that the dialogic relations, concealed within the secondary legal genre of a modern state, privilege the saying as well as the said – the silent intertext which the utterances voice as well as the utterances themselves. The silent intertext conditions the addressive experiences which speak with authority.

Husserl explains in the 'Fifth Meditation' that the sight of a particular other's physical body arouses an intention in an addressee. The experience of seeing the other's body arouses a meant object in one's own body. The meant object may well not correspond with the gestures of the other's body, but it is lived in the sense that an addressee's experiences – his or her past experiences and his or her future expectations – are directed to the object so as to give meaning to a posited text, utterance or gesture. The gestures of trying to reach the environing world of the other are contagious, Husserl suggests. All this infectious communication dwells inside the displacing and idealizing trace of a sacred ghost of the master discourse. The signified object still remains important in a dialogic relation, but meaning is not constituted merely from sign/typification relations. The signified object is *understood*. It is understood by virtue of the *embodiment* of the sign which represents the object. One's suffering will remain concealed so long as the knower analyses the language of the other in terms only of sign–object relations. One must suspend the linguistic configurations which give "form" to experience. One must orient one's analysis to the experiencing body of the non-knower instead of to the professional knower who claims to know the experiences of the non-knower through secondary configurations of signs. The professional knowers of the legal discourse of the modern state have hitherto denied such inquiries because they run counter to the presupposed claim that the knower is "acted on" by external objects. The addressive experience of a dialogic partner goes to the embodiment of a chain of signs. Such a meaning retains the possibility of an immediacy between the 'environing world' of the non-knower and that of the former claimant to knowledge. Such an identification of dialogic partners with their meanings also offers the possibility that authority draws from a concrete social context rather than from an idealizing one.

In this context, it may well be advisable to return to a point which can be retrieved in Hobbes. Hobbes described the role of the juridical office of the sovereign at the start of Chapter 30 of the *Leviathan*. There, he advises that, in addition to justifying the Representer's actions to the invisible Author, 'the author of that law [of nature], and to none but him', the Representer should procure 'the safety of the people … by a general providence, *contained in public instruction*, both of doctrine, and by example; and in the making and executing of good laws, to which individual persons may apply their own cases'.[15] We know now that the authors in a state of nature are inaccessible from the legal language of a civil society and that the

Representer to whom Hobbes appeals is the very absent founder whose identity professional knowers claim to know. I have claimed that such surrogates of the Representer owe a duty to the non-knower as an addressee, not to the founding authors themselves. The duty is to teach 'both of doctrine and by example', as Hobbes put it, and to make laws which are more than merely traceable to the gaze of some founding authors of a secondary genre. The laws must aspire to be good laws and, furthermore, to be good because the non-knower is able to live them meaningfully in his or her environing world: they are 'good laws, to which individual persons may apply their own cases'. It is ironic that one can find just such a claim concealed within Hobbes' great work of 'that immortale God, the Leviathan'. Hobbes was not alone in this regard. The dialogic relation imbues the style of Plato's dialogues. Both Plato, in his *Apology*, the *Theaetetus*, and the *Laws*, and Aristotle in his *Politics*, privilege the importance of the addressive dialogue between knower and non-knower in the law-making and law-applying actions of the knower.[16] Indeed, Plato's pedagogical theory of *elenchus* has much of the character of an authentic dialogue. Furthermore, the environing world of Socrates grows as he interprets the utterances of his peers and as the Laws speak to him. And Aristotle insisted that the authoritativeness of a text presupposes an ethics. Again, his ethics draws from the practical wisdom which derives from one's day-to-day experiences.[17]

Although such a dialogic experience seems an important part of the theory of authority which one can glean from such diverse knowers as Hobbes, Plato and Aristotle, the addressive experience is that of the knower, the 'statesman'. And the addressive experience is driven by the lack of external objects, whether they be ideas or physical objects from the material world. Once one leaves the silent intertext between dialogic partners, one enters configurations of signs which represent such externally situated objects, and the risk remains that the lack of an external object will render the dialogue asunder in favour of the savagery of multiple monologues. Institutional arrangements must be retrieved to induce a respect for an other whose environing world is the condition of understanding. At that moment, the dialogic relation will become unconcealed. So too will the trace of authority to some ghostly foundation dissipate. The addressive experiences of an interpreter, not the trace of signs to absent objects, will authorize the action in a dialogic relation. Strangely, peace will reign in such a retrieved dialogic relation. And not a juridified peace at that.

Notes

1 This point is discussed in Michel de Certeau, *Heterologies: Discourse on the Other* (Brian Massumi trans.; Minneapolis: University of Minnesota Press, 1986; Theory and History of Literature, vol. 17).

2 Mikkail M. Bakhtin, 'The Problem of Speech Genres' in *Speech Genres and Other Late Essays* (Vern W. McGee trans.; Austin: University of Texas Press, 1986): 86.

3 Ibid., 77.

4 Werner Marx develops the ethical dimension of the experiential relation between speaker and listener in *Towards a Phenomenological Ethics: Ethos and the Life-World* (Albany: State University of New York, 1992).

5 Maurice Merleau Ponty, 'Indirect Language and the Voices of Silence' in *Signs* (Richard C. McCleary trans.; Evanston: Northwestern University Press, 1964): 71. (His emphasis.)

6 Hans-Georg Gadamer, 'On the Problem of Self-Understanding' in *Philosophical Hermeneutics* (David E Linge trans.; Berkeley: University of California Press, 1976): 39–83 at 44–58, esp. 57.

7 Ibid., 58.

8 For another elaboration of this theme see Emmanuel Levinas, *Totality and Infinity* (Alphonso Lingis trans.; Pittsburgh: Duquesne University Press, 1969; Philosophic Series No. 24): 73–7.

9 Ibid., 73. (His emphasis.)

10 Michel de Certeau makes the same point in *Heterologies*, note 1 *supra*, xiii.

11 John Llewelyn understands the saying as the existential and the said as the categorical. See, generally, John Llewelyn in *Beyond Metaphysics? The Hermeneutic Circle in Contemporary Continental Philosophy* (New Jersey: Humanities Press, 1985): 205.

12 Bakhtin makes this point in 'Speech Genres', note 2 *supra*, 74.

13 Jean-François Lyotard, *The Differend: Phrases in Dispute* (Minneapolis: University of Minnesota Press, 1988; Theory and History of Literature, vol. 46): 105.

14 Peter Kropotkin in Roger N. Baldwin ed., *Kropotkin's Revolutionary Pamphlets* (New York: Dover, 1927); *Selected Writings on Anarchism and Revolution* (Cambridge Mass: MIT Press, 1970). Also see, generally, James Joll, *The Anarchists* (London: Methuen, 1964).

15 Thomas Hobbes, *Leviathan* (Michael Oakeshott ed.; New York: Collier Books, 1962): ch. 30 at 247. (Emphasis added.)

16 See, for example, Plato, *Apology*, 23a-b; *Theaetetus*, 173d-e, 174c-e, 175c-e; *Laws*, 663b and Book 7.

17 See, for example, Plato's *Gorgias*, 521; and Aristotle's *Ethics*, 1181a10–1181b10.

Bibliography

1. Author

Barthes, Roland, 'Myth Today' in *Mythologies* (Anette Lavers trans.; New York: Noonday Press, 1957): 109–59.
Barthes, Roland, 'From Work to Text' in Josu, U. Harari, ed., *Textual Strategies: Perspectives in Post Structuralist Criticism* (Ithaca: Cornell University Press, 1979): 73–81.
Barthes, Roland, 'The Theory of the Text' in Robert Young, ed., *Untying the Text: A Post Structuralist Reader* (Boston: Routledge & Kegan Paul, 1981): 31–47.
Barthes, Roland, 'Rhetoric of the Image' in Robert E. Innis, ed., *Semiotics: An Introductory Anthology* (Bloomington: Indiana University Press, 1985): 190–205.
Conklin, William, 'The Invisible Author of Legal Authority' in *Law and Critique*, vol. 7, no. 2 (1996):173–92.
Conklin, William, 'Hegel, the Author and Authority in Sophocles' *Antigone*' in Leslie Rubin, ed., *Justice v. Law in Greek Political Thought* (New York: Rowman & Littlefield, 1997): 129–51.
Derrida, Jacques, 'Sending: On Representation' (Peter and Mary Ann Caws trans.) in *Social Research*, vol. 49, no. 2 (Summer 1982): 294–326.
Edelman, Murray, 'The Political Language of the Helping Professions' in *Politics and Society*, vol. 4 (1964): 295–310.
Fish, Stanley, *Is there a Text in the Classroom?: The Authority of Interpretative Communities* (Cambridge Mass.: Harvard University Press, 1980).
Fish, Stanley, *Doing What Comes Naturally: Change, Rhetoric and the Practice of Theory in Literary and Legal Studies* (Durham NC: Duke University Press, 1989).
Foster, Hal, ed., *The Anti-Aesthetic: Essays on Postmodern Condition* (Seattle: Bay Press, 1983).
Foucault, Michel, *The Order of Things: An Archeology of the Human Sciences* (New York: Vintage Books, 1970).
Foucault, Michel, 'My Body, This Paper, This Fire' in *Oxford Literary Review*, vol. 4, no. 1 (Autumn 1979): 9–28

Foucault, Michel, 'The Subject and Power' in *Critical Theory*, vol. 8 (Summer 1982): 777–95.

Foucault, Michel, 'What is an Author?' in Paul Rabinow, ed., *The Foucault Reader* (New York: Pantheon, 1984): 101–20.

Foucault, Michel, 'The Order of Discourse' in Michael Shapiro, ed., *Language and Politics* (London: Basil Blackwell, 1984) and in Robert Young, ed., *Untying the Text: A Post Structuralist Reader* (Boston: Routledge & Kegan Paul, 1981): 48–78. Another translation of this essay is under the title, 'The Discourse on Language' in *The Archeology of Knowledge* (A.M. Sheridan Smith trans.; New York: Pantheon, 1972): 215–37.

Krieger, Murray ed., *The Aims of Representation: Subject/Text/History* (Irvine Studies in the Humanities; New York: Columbia University Press, 1987).

Nancy, Jean-Luc, *The Inoperative Community* (Peter Connor ed.; Peter Connor *et al* trans.; Minneapolis: University of Minnesota Press, 1991; Theory and History of Literature, vol. 76).

Nehamas, Alexander, 'The Postulated Author: Critical Monism as a Regulative Ideal' in *Critical Inquiry*, vol. 8 (1981–82): 133–49.

Nehamas, Alexander, 'What an Author Is' in *Journal of Philosophy* (1986): 685–91.

Nehamas, Alexander, 'Writer, Text, Work, Author' in Anthony J. Cascardi, ed. *Literature and the Quest of Philosophy* (Baltimore: Johns Hopkins Press, 1987): 265–91.

Sacks, Sheldon ed., *On Metaphor* (Chicago and London: University of Chicago Press, 1979).

Weber, Samuel, 'The Limits of Professionalism' in his *Institution and Interpretation* (Wlad Godzich afterword.; Minneapolis: University of Minnesota Press, 1987; Theory and History of Literature, vol. 31): 18–32.

2. Authority

Arendt, Hannah, 'What is Authority?' in *Between Past and Future: Six Exercises in Political Thought* (New York: Meridan, 1961): 91–141.

Conklin, William, 'The End of Judicial Review' in *Current Legal Theory* (1992) reprinted with revisions in Bert van Roermund, ed., *Constitutional Review, verfassungsgerichtsbarkeit, Constitutionele Toetsing* (Zwolle: Kluwer Law and Taxation Publishers, 1993): 33–54.

Conklin, William, 'The Invisible Author of Legal Authority' in *Law and Critique*, vol. 7, no. 2 (1996): 173–92.

Conklin, William, 'Hegel, the Author and Authority in Sophocles' *Antigone*' in Leslie Rubin, ed., *Justice v. Law in Greek Political Thought* (New York: Rowman & Littlefield, 1997): 129–51.

Conklin, William, 'The Secret Foundation of Sovereignty in Legal Positivism' in *Rechtstheorie* Beiheft 17, S. 75–84.

Derrida, Jacques, 'The Pit and the Pyramid: Introduction to Hegel's Semiology' in *Margins of Philosophy* (Alan Bass trans.; Chicago: University of Chicago Press, 1982): 69–108.

Derrida, Jacques, 'Plato's Pharmacy' in *Dissemination* (Barbara Johnson trans. with notes; Chicago: University of Chicago Press, 1982): 61–171.

Derrida, Jacques, 'Force of Law: The "Mystical Foundation of Authority"' (Mary Quaintance trans.) *Cardozo Law Review*, vol. 11 (1990): 919–1045.

Derrida, Jacques, *Specters of Marx: The State of the Debt, the Work of Mourning, and the New International* (Peggy Kamuf trans.; Bernd Magnus and Stephen Cullenberg intro.; New York/London: Routledge, 1994).

Derrida, Jacques, 'The Ends of Man' in *Margins of Philosophy*, (Peggy Kamuf, trans.; Bernd Magnus and Stephen Callenberg, intro; New York/London: Routledge, 1994): 109–36.

Derrida, Jacques, 'Form and Meaning: A Note on the Phenomenology of Language' in *Margins of Philosophy*, (Peggy Kamuf, trans.; Bernd Magnus and Stephen Callenberg, intro; New York/London: Routledge, 1994): 109–36, 155–73.

Foucault, Michel, 'Two Lectures' in *Power/Knowledge: Selected Interviews & Other Writings, 1972–1977* (Colin Gordon ed.; New York: Pantheon, 1980): 91–97.

Foucault, Michel, 'Governmentality' in Graham Burchell, Colin Gordon and Peter Miller, eds, *The Foucault Effect: Studies in Governmentality* (Chicago: University of Chicago Press, 1991): 87–104.

Krieger, Leonard, 'Authority' in Philip P. Weiner, *Dictionary of the History of Ideas: Studies of Selected Pivotal Ideas*, vol. 1 (New York: Charles Scribner's Sons, 1968, 1973): 141–62.

Layown, Mary, 'The Female Body and "Transnational" Reproduction; or Rape by any other Name?' in *Scattered Hegemonies: Postmodernity and Transnational Feminist Practices* (Minneapolis: University of Minnesota Press, 1994): 63–75.

Liu, Lydia, 'The Female Body and Nationalist Discourse: The Field of Life and Death Revisited' in Inderpal Grerval and Caren Kaplan eds., *Scattered Hegemonies: Postmodernity and Transnational Feminist Practices* (Minneapolis: University of Minnesota Press, 1994): 37–62.

Salecl, Renata, *The Spoils of Freedom: Psychoanalysis and Feminism after the Fall of Socialism* (New York/London: Routledge, 1994).

Weber, Max, 'Bureaucracy' in *From Max Weber: Four Essays in Sociology* (H.H. Genth and C. Wright Mills trans. London: Routledge & Kegan Paul, 1970): 196–244.

Weber, Max, *The Social Interpretation of Reality* (J.E.T. Eldridge ed.; New York: Charles Scribner's Sons, 1971) esp. Pt. II and III.

Young, William C., 'The Body Tamed: Tying and Tatooing among the Rashanyda Bedouin' in Nicole Sault, ed., *Many Mirrors: Body Image and Social Relations* (Peggy Reeves Sandry foreword; New Brunswick, New Jersey: Rutgers University Press, 1994): 58–75.

Zizek, Slavoj, *The Sublime Object of Ideology* (New York: Verso, 1989).

Zizek, Slavoj, *For They Know Not What They Do: Enjoyment as a Political Factor* (New York: Verso, 1991).

Zizek, Slavoj, *Tarrying with the Negative: Kant, Hegel and the Critique of Ideology* (Durham: Duke University Press, 1993).

3. Body

Atherton, Margaret, 'Cartesian reason and Gendered reason' in Louise M. Antony and Charlotte Witt, eds., *A Mind of One's Own: Feminist Essays on Reason and Objectivity* (Boulder/San Francisco/Oxford: Westview Press, 1993): 19–34.

Bakan, Mildred, 'Between Body and Thought' in David P. Shugarman ed., *Thinking about Change* (Toronto: University of Toronto Press, 1974): 25–38.

Bakan, Mildred, 'On Language, Work, and Things' in *Human Studies*, vol. 1 (1978): 221–43.

Bakan, Mildred, 'Mind as Life and Form' in R.W. Rieber ed., *Body and Mind: Past, Present and Future* (New York: Academic Press, 1980): 131–54.

Bakan, Mildred, 'Arendt and Heidegger: the Episodic Intertwining of Life and Work' in *Philosophy and Social Criticism*, vol. 12 (1987): 71–98.

Barfield, Owen, 'Poetic Diction and Legal Fiction'; 'The Rediscovery of Meaning' in *The Rediscovery of Meaning and other Essays* (Middletown, Conn: Wesleyan Press, 1977): 44–64, 11–21.

Bordo, Susan R. 'The Cartesian Masculinization of Thought and the Seventeenth Century Flight from the Feminine' in Bat-Ami Bar Or, ed., *Modern Engendering: Critical Feminist Readings of Modern Western Philosophy* (Albany: State University of New York: 1994): 3–24.

Butler, Judith, *Gender Trouble: Feminism and the Subversion of Identity* (New York/London: Routledge, 1990).

Cantrell, Carol H., 'Analogy as Destiny: Cartesian Man and the Woman Reader' in Hilde Hein and Carolyn Korsmeyer, eds., *Aesthetics in Feminist Perspectives* (Bloomington: Indiana University Press, 1993): 218–28.

Deleuze, Giles and Guattari, Felix, *Anti-Oedipus: Capitalism and Schizo-*

phrenia (Robert Hurley trans.; Michel Foucault preface; Minneapolis: University of Minnesota Press, 1983).
Deleuze, Giles and Guattari, Felix, *A Thousand Plateaus: Capitalism and Schizophrenia* (Brian Massumi trans. with foreword; Minneapolis: University of Minnesota Press, 1984).
Descartes, René, 'The Passions of the Soul' in *The Philosophical Works of Descartes*, vol. 1 (Cambridge: Cambridge University Press, 1911): 329–427.
Dreyfus, Herbert L., 'Phenomenology and Artificial Intelligence,' in James M. Edie ed., *Phenomenology in America* (Chicago: Quadrangle Books, 1967): 31–47.
Dreyfus, Herbert L., 'From Micro-Worlds to Knowledge Representation' in John Haugeland, ed., *Mind Design* (Cambridge, Mass: M.I.T. Press, 1981): 161–204.
Dreyfus, Herbert L., *Mind over Machines* (London: Basil Blackwell, 1986).
Dreyfus, Herbert L., 'Misrepresenting Human Intelligence' in Rainer Born ed., *Artificial Intelligence* (London: Croom Helm, 1987).
Emberley, Julia V., *Thresholds of Difference: Feminist Nature, Women's Writings, Postcolonial Theory* (Toronto: University of Toronto Press, 1993).
Grbich, Judith, 'The Body in Legal Theory' in M. Albertson Fineman and N. Sweet Thomadsen, eds., *At the Boundaries of Law: Feminism and Legal Theory* (New York: Routledge, 1991): 61–76.
Grene, Marjorie, 'Adolf Portmann' in *Approaches to a Philosophical Biology* (New York/London: Basic Books, 1965–68): 3–54.
Huizinga, J., 'Play and Law', chapter 4 in his *Homo Ludens: A Study of the Play-Element in Culture* (Boston: Beacon Press, 1955).
Jacob, Francois, *The Logic of Life: A History of Heredity* (Betty E. Spillmann trans.; NewYork: Pantheon, 1973, 1982).
Kosik, Karel, *Dialectics of the Concrete* (Dordrecht-Holland/Boston: D. Reidel Publ. Co., 1976; Boston Studies in the Philosophy of Science, vol. 52).
Lucas, J.R., 'Minds, Machines and Godel' in Alan Ross Anderson ed., *Minds and Machines* (Englewood Cliffs, NJ: Prentice Hall, 1964).
Miller, David, L., 'The Origin and Function of Language and the Meaning of Language Gestures' in *George Herbert Mead: Self, Language and the World* (Austin & London: University of Texas Press, 1973).
Milovanovic, Dragan, 'Inscribing the Body with a Sign: Semiotics and Punishment' in W. Richard Janikowski and Dragan Milovanovic, eds., *Legality and Illegality: Semiotics, Postmodernism and Law* (New York: Peter Lang, 1995): 47–78.
Minh-ha, Trinh, *Woman, Native, Other* (Bloomington, Indiana: Indiana University Press, 1989).

Scarry, Elaine, *The Body in Pain: The Making and Unmaking of the World* (Oxford: Oxford University Press, 1985).
Schrodinger, Erwin, *What is Life? Mind and Matter* (Cambridge: Cambridge University Press, 1967).
Scriven, Michael, 'The Mechanical Concept of the Mind' in Alan Ross Anderson (ed.), *Minds and Machines* (Englewood Cliffs, NJ: Prentice Hall, 1964): 31–42.
Shilling, Chris, *The Body and Social Theory* (London: Sage, 1993).
Shilling, Chris, 'Self-Consciousness and the Body: an Interdisciplinary Introduction' in Jose Luis Bermudez, Anthony Marcel and Naomi Eilen, *The Body and Self* (Cambridge, Mass.: MIT Press, 1995): 1–28.
Williams, Patricia, *The Alchemy of Race and Rights* (Cambridge, Mass.: Harvard University Press, 1991).
Wilson, Margaret D., 'Body and Mind from the Cartesian Point of View' in R.W. Rieber, ed., *Body and Mind: Past, Present and Future* (New York: Academic Press, 1980): 35–55.
Wolff, Janet, 'Reinstating Corporeality: Feminine and Body Politics' in *Feminine Sentences: Essays on Women and Culture* (Berkeley/Los Angeles: University of California Press, 1990): 120–41.

4. Dialogic Relation

Bakhtin, Mikhail, *The Dialogic Imagination* (Michael Holquist ed.; Caryl Emerson and Michael Holquist trans.; Austin: University of Texas Press, 1981).
Bakhtin, Mikhail, *Bakhtin School Papers* (Ann Shukman ed.; Oxford: RPT Publ, 1983; Russian Poetics in Translation 1983, no. 10).
Bakhtin, Mikhail, *Problems of Doestoevsky's Poetics* (Caryl Emerson ed. and trans.; Wayne C. Booth intro.; Minneapolis: University of Minnesota Press, 1984; Theory and History of Literature, vol. 8).
Bakhtin, Mikhail, *Speech Genres and other Late Essays* (Vern W. McGee trans.; Austin: University of Texas Press, 1986).
Bakhtin, Mikhail, *Art and Answerability: Early Philosophical Essays* (Vadim Liapunov trans.; Kenneth Boston supplementary trans.; Austin: University of Texas Press,1990).
Benveniste, Emile, *Problems in General Linguistics* (Mary Elizabeth Meek trans.; Coral Gables, Florida: University of Miami Press, 1971; Miami Linguistics Series, no. 8).
Bernasconi, Robert and Critchley, Simon, 'The Transformation of Language at Another Beginning' in *Research in Phenomenology*, vol. 13 (1983): 1–23.
Bernasconi, Robert and Critchley, Simon, 'Persons and Masks: The

Phenomenology of Spirit and Its Laws' in *Cardozo Law Review*, vol. 10 (1989): 1695–711.

Bernasconi, Robert and Critchley, Simon, *Re-Reading Levinas* (Bloomington, Indiana: Indiana University Press, 1991).

Carroll, David, 'The Alterity of Discourse: Form, History and the Quest of the Political in Bakhtin' in *Diacritics*, vol. 13, no. 1 (Summer 1983): 65–83.

de Certeau, Michael, *Heterologies: Discourse on the Other* (Brian Massumi trans.; Wlad Godzich foreword; Minneapolis: University of Minnesota Press, 1986; Theory and History of Literature, vol. 17).

Gurwitsch, Aron, *Studies in Phenomenology and Psychology* (Evanston: Northwestern University Press, 1966).

Habermas, Jurgen, 'Modernity versus Postmodernity' in *New German Critique*, no. 22, Winter (1981): 3–17.

Habermas, Jurgen, 'Law and Morality: Two Lectures' in *Tanner Lectures on Human Values*, vol. 8 (S. McMurrin, ed.; Kenneth Baynes trans. Boston: Harvard University Press, 1986): 217–79.

Habermas, Jurgen, The *Philosophical Discourse of Modernity* (Frederick Lawrence trans.; Boston: MIT Press, 1987).

Habermas, Jurgen, 'Towards a Communication–Concept of Rational Collective Will-Formation. A Thought-Experiment' in *Ratio Juris*, vol. 2 (July 1989): 144–54.

Habermas, Jurgen, *The Theory of Communicative Action*, vol. 1: *Reason and the Rationalization of Society* (Thomas McCarthy trans.; Boston: Beacon Press, 1984); vol 2: *Lifeworld and System: A Critique of Functionalist Reason* (1987).

Habermas, Jurgen, *Between Facts and Norms: Contributions to a Discourse Theory of Law and Democracy* (William Rehg trans.; Cambridge, Mass.: MIT Press, 1996).

Husserl, Edmund, *Cartesian Meditations* (Dorion Cairns trans.; Martinus Nijhoff, 1960).

Jauss, Hans Jauss, *Question and Answer: Forms of Dialogic Understanding* (Michael Hays ed. and trans.; Minneapolis: University of Minnesota Press, 1989; History and Theory of Literature, vol. 68).

Kristeva, Julia, *Revolution in Poetic Language* (Margaret Waller trans.; New York: Columbia University Press, 1984).

Kristeva, Julia, 'The Speaking Subject' in Marshall Blonsky, ed., *On Signs* (Baltimore: Johns Hopkins Press, 1985): 210–20.

Kristeva, Julia, 'Women's Time' in *The Kristeva Reader* (Toril Moi, ed.; Oxford: Basil Blackwell, 1986): 187–213.

Kristeva, Julia, 'The True-Real' in *The Kristeva Reader* (Toril Moi, ed.; Oxford: Basil Blackwell, 1986): 214–37.

Lodge, David, *After Bakhtin: Essays on Fiction and Criticism* (London and New York: Routledge, 1990).

Merleau Ponty, Maurice, *Phenomenology of Perception* (Colin Smith trans.; London: Routledge & Kegan Paul, 1962).
Morson, Gary Saul, ed., *Bakhtin: Essays and Dialogues of His Work* (Chicago & London: University of Chicago Press, 1981).
Morson, Gary Saul and Emerson, Caryl, *Rethinking Bakhtin: Extensions and Challenges* (Evanston, Illinois: Northwestern University Press, 1989).
Robbins, Jill, 'Visage, Figure: Reading Levinas's Totality and Infinity' in *Yale French Studies*, vol. 79 (1991): 135–49
Spinoza, Benedict, *A Theological-Political Treatise and A Political Treatise* (R.H.M. Elwes trans. with intro.; New York: Dover Public, 1951).
Spinoza, Benedict, *Ethics* in *The Collected Works of Spinoza* (Edwin Curley trans. and ed.; Princeton: Princeton University Press, 1985): 408–617.
Todorov, Tzvetan, 'The Origin of Genres' in *New Literary History*, vol. 8 (1976–77): 159–70.
Todorov, Tzvetan, *The Poetics of Prose* (Richard Howard trans.; Ithaca New York: Cornell University Press, 1977).
Todorov, Tzvetan, *Mikhail Bakhtin: The Dialogic Principle* (Minneapolis: University of Minnesota Press, 1984; Theory and History of Literature, vol. 13).
Todorov, Tzvetan, *Genres in Discourse* (Catherine Porter trans.; New York: Cambridge University Press, 1990).
Volosinov, V.N., *Marxism and the Philosophy of Language* (Ladislov Matejka and I.R. Titunik trans.: New York & London: Seminar Press, 1973).

5. Displacement of Discourses

Althusser, Louis, 'Ideology and Ideological State Apparatus (Notes Toward an Investigation)' in *Lenin and Philosophy and other Essays* (New York: Monthly Review Press, 1971): 127–86.
Althusser, Louis, 'Montesquieu: Politics and History' in *Montesquieu, Rousseau, Marx* (trans. Ben Brewster; Paris: Verso, 1982).
Baudrillard, Jean, *The Mirror of Production* (St. Louis: Telos Press, 1975).
Baudrillard, Jean, *For a Critique of the Political Economy of the Sign* (Charles Levin trans. with intro.; St. Louis: Telos Press, 1981).
Baudrillard, Jean, *Forget Foucault* (New York: Semiotext, 1987).
Baudrillard, Jean, *The Ecstacy of Communication* (New York: Semiotext, 1987).
Conklin, William, 'The Transformation of Meaning: Legal Discourse

and the Canadian Internment Camps' in *International Journal for the Semiotics of Law*, vol. 9, no. 27 (1996): 227–56.

Foucault, Michel, *I, Pierre Revierre, having slaughtered my mother, my sister and my brother I* (Lincoln & London: University of Nebraska Press, 1975).

Laclau, Ernesto, 'Metaphor and Social Antagonisms' in Cary Nelson and Lawrence Grossberg, eds., *Marxism and the Interpretation of Culture* (Urbana & Chicago: University of Illinois Press, 1988): 249–57.

Laclau, Ernesto, *Hegemony and Socialist Strategy: Towards a Radical Democratic Politics* (London: New Left Books, 1985): ch. 1–3.

Lakoff, Georg and Johnson, Mark, *Metaphors We Live By* (Chicago: University of Chicago Press, 1980).

Pavis, Patrice, 'Production, Reception, and the Social Context' in Anna Whiteside and Michael Issacharoff, eds., *On Referring in Literature* (Bloomington & Indianapolis: Indiana University Press, 1987): 127–37.

Sauvin, Darko, 'Can People be (Re)Presented in Fiction?' in Cary Nelson and Lawrence Grossberg, eds., *Marxism and the Interpretation of Culture* (Cary Nelson and Lawrence Grossberg trans.; Urbana & Chicago: Illinois University Press, 1988): 663–96.

White, Hayden, 'The Value of Narrativity in the Representation of Reality' in *Critical Inquiry*, vol. 7 (1980–81): 5–27.

White, Hayden, *The Content of Form: Narrative Discourse and Historical Representation* (Baltimore & London: Johns Hopkins University Press, 1987).

6. Posited Object

Brillouin, L., 'Life, Thermodynamics, and Cybernetics' in *American Scientist*, vol. 37, no. 4 (Oct., 1949): 554–69.

Burtt, Edwin A. *The Metaphysical Foundations of Physical Science: A Historical and Critical Essay* (London: Routledge & Kegan Paul, 1950): ch. 2–4.

Coplestone, Frederick, *A History of Philosophy: Late Medieval and Renaissance Philosophy* (Westminster, Md.: Newman, 1950–74) vol. 3, ch. 10 ('The Scientific Movement'): 153–67.

Gillispie, Charles Coulston, *The Edge of Objectivity: An Essay in the History of Scientific Ideas* (Princeton: Princeton University Press, 1960).

Gurwitsch, Aron, *Studies in Phenomenology and Perception* (Evanston: Northwestern University Press, 1966).

Heisenberg, Werner, *Physics and Philosophy: the Revolution in Modern Science* (London: Allen & Unwin, 1958).

Husserl, Edmund, *Phenomenology and the Crisis of Philosophy* (Quentin Lauer trans.; New York: Harper Torch Books, 1965).
Husserl, Edmund, *The Crisis of the European Sciences and Transcendental Phenomenology* (David Carr trans.; Evanston: Northwestern University Press, 1970).
Husserl, Edmund, *Reason in the Age of Science* (Frederich G. Lawrence trans.; Cambridge Mass.: MIT Press, 1981).
Koyre, Alexander, 'Galileo and the Scientific Revolution of the Seventeenth Century' in *Philosophical Review*, vol. 52, no. 4 (July, 1943): 333–48.
Koyre, Alexander, 'The Significance of the Newtonian Synthesis' in *Newtonian Studies* (London: Chapman & Hall, 1965): 3–24.
Koyre, Alexander, *Galileo Studies* (John Mepham trans.; Hassocks: Harvester Press, 1978).
Lorenz, Konrad, 'The Fashionable Fallacy of Dispensing with Description' in Richard Evans, *Konrad Lorenz: The Man and his Ideas* (New York: Harcourt, Brace Jovanovich, 1975).
Monod, Jacques, *Chance and Necessity: An Essay on the Natural Philosophy of Modern Biology* (Austyn Wainhouse trans.; New York: Alfred A. Knopf, 1971).
Simpson, George G., *The Meaning of Evolution* (New Haven: Yale University Press, 1967): 263–309.
Wilson, Margaret D., 'Body and Mind from the Cartesian Point of View' in R.W. Rieber ed., *Body and Mind: Past, Present and Future* (New York: Academic Press, 1980): 35–55.

7. Paradigm of Law as Consciousness

Benjamin, Walter, 'The Critique of Violence' in *Reflections* (Peter Demetz ed.; New York: Schocken Books, 1978): 277–300.
Conklin, William E., 'The Legal Theory of Horkheimer and Adorno' in *Windsor Yearbook Access Justice*, vol. 5 (1985): 230–57.
Goldmann, Lucien, *Lukacs and Heidegger: Towards a New Philosophy* (William Q. Boelhower trans.; London: Routledge & Kegan Paul, 1977).
Goldmann, Lucien, *The Philosophy of the Enlightenment: The Burgess and the Enlightenment* (Henry Mass trans.; Cambridge: MIT Press, 1973).
Habermas, Jurgen, 'Modernity versus Postmodernity' in *New German Critique*, no. 22 (Winter 1981): 3–17.
Habermas, Jurgen, *The Theory of Communicative Action*, vol. 1: *Reason and the Rationalization of Society* (Thomas McCarthy trans.; Boston, Beacon Press, 1984); vol. 2: *Lifeworld and System: A Critique of Functionalist Reason* (1987).

Habermas, Jurgen, 'Law and Morality: Two Lectures' in *Tanner Lectures on Human Values*, vol. 8 (S. McMurrin ed.; Kenneth Baynes trans., Boston: Harvard University Press, 1986): 217–79.

Habermas, Jurgen, *The Philosophical Discourse of Modernity* (Frederick Lawrence trans.; Boston, MIT Press, 1987).

Habermas, Jurgen, 'Towards a Communication-Concept of Rational Collective Will-Formation. A Thought-Experiment' in *Ratio Juris*, vol. 2 (July 1989): 144–54.

Habermas, Jurgen, *Between Facts and Norms: Contributions to a Discourse Theory of Law and Democracy* (William Rehg trans.; Cambridge, Mass.: MIT Press, 1996).

Hegel, Georg, *Philosophy of Right* (T.M. Knox trans.; Oxford: Oxford University Press, 1967).

Hegel, Georg, *Phenomenology of Spirit* in Chapter 6 (A.V. Miller trans.; Oxford University Press, 1977), esp. ch. 5 & 6.

Horkheimer, Max, *Critical Theory* (New York: Continuum, 1982).

Horkheimer, Max and Adorno, Theodor W., *Dialectic of Enlightenment* (New York: Continuum, 1982).

Kennedy, Duncan, 'Form and Substance in Private Law Adjudication,' in *Harvard Law Review*, vol. 89 (1976): 1685.

Kennedy, Duncan, 'The Structure of Blackstone's Commentaries' in *Buffalo Law Review*, vol. 28 (1979): 209–382.

Kennedy, Duncan, 'Toward an Historical Understanding of Legal Consciousness: the Case of Classical Legal Thought in America, 1840–1940' in S. Spitzer, ed., *Research in Law and Sociology* 3 (1980): 3–24.

Kennedy, Duncan, 'Freedom and Constraint in Adjudication: A Critical Phenomenology' in *Journal of Legal Education*, vol. 36 (1986): 518–62.

Kennedy, Duncan, 'Toward a Critical Phenomenology of Judging' in Allan C. Hutchinson and Patrick Monahan, eds., *The Rule of Law: Ideal or Ideology* (Toronto: Carswell, 1987): 141–67.

Lukacs, Georg, *History and Class Consciousness* (Rodney Livingstone trans.; Cambridge Mass.; MIT Press, 1971).

Lukacs, Georg, *Soul and Form* (Anna Bostock trans.; London: Merlin Press, 1974).

MacKinnon, Catherine, 'Difference and Dominance: On Sex Discrimination' in *Feminism Unmodified* (Cambridge, Mass.: Harvard University Press, 1987): 40–45.

Unger, Roberto, 'The Critical Legal Studies Movement' in *Harvard Law Review*, vol. 96 (1983): 561–675.

Unger, Roberto, *False Necessity: Anti-Necessitarian Social Theory in the Service of Radical Democracy* (Cambridge: Cambridge University Press, 1987).

Unger, Roberto, 'Legal Analysis as Institutional Imagination' in *Modern Law Review*, vol. 59 (1996): 1–23.

8. Paradigm of Law as a Language

Althusser, Louis, 'Ideology and Ideological State Apparatus (Notes Toward an Investigation)' in *Lenin and Philosophy and Other Essays* (New York: Monthly Review Press, 1971):127–86.

Arnaud, André-Jean, *Essai d'Analyse Structurale du Code Civil Français: La Règle du Jue Dans la Paix Bourgeois* (Michel Villey preface; Georges Mounin postface; Biblioteque de philosophie du Droit, vol 16; Paris: Librarie Generale de Droit et de Jurisprudence, 1973).

Arnaud, André-Jean, *Introduction à la logique juridique: Elements de semiotique juridique, logique des normes et logique juridique* (Paris: LGDJ, 1965).

Arnaud, André-Jean, 'Une methode d'analyse structurale en histoire du droit' in J.M. Scholteed, *Vorstudien zur Rechtshistorik* (Frankfurt-am Main: Klostermann, 1977): 263–346.

Arnaud, André-Jean, 'La Paix Bourgeois' in M. Troper, ed., *Le droit trahi par la philosophie* (Bibliotèque du Centre d'Etudes des Systèmes Politiques et Juridiques de Rouen, 1977): 51–80.

Arnaud, André-Jean, 'Du bon usage du discours juridique: analyses et méthodes' in *Langages*, vol. 53 (March 1979): 197–228.

Arnaud, André-Jean, *Critique de la Raison Juridique* 1 (Paris: LGDJ, 1981).

Arnaud, André-Jean, 'Fact as Law' in D. Carzo and Bernard Jackson, eds., *Semiotics, Law and Social Science* (Rome: Gangemi/Liverpool Law Review, 1985): 129–44.

Baudrillard, Jean, *For a Critique of the Political Economy of the Sign* (Charles Levin trans. with intro.; St. Louis: Telos Press, 1981).

Baudrillard, Jean, *The Mirror of Production* (St Louis: Telos Press, 1975).

Baudrillard, Jean, *The Ecstasy of Communication* (New York: Semiotext, 1987).

Benveniste, Emile, *Problems in General Linguistics* (Mary Elizabeth Meek trans.; Coral Gables, Florida: University of Miami Press, 1971; Miami Linguistics Series, no. 8).

Carrion-Wam, Roque, 'Semiotica Juridica' in D. Carzo and Bernard S. Jackson, *Semiotics, Law and Social Science* (Rome: Gangemi/Liverpool Law Review, 1985): 11–67.

Carzo, D. and Bernard S. Jackson, eds., *Semiotics, Law and Social Science* (Rome: Gangemi/Liverpool Law Review, 1985).

Conklin, William, *Images of a Constitution* (Toronto: University of Toronto Press, 1989).

Conklin, William, '"Access to Justice" as Access to a Lawyer's Language' in *Windsor Yearbook of Access to Justice*, vol. 10 (1991): 454–67.
Conklin, William, 'Teaching Critically within the Modern Legal Genre' in *Canadian Journal of Law and Society*, vol. 8, no. 2 (1993): 33–57.
Conklin, William, 'Human Rights, Language and Law: A Survey of Semiotics and Phenomenology' in *Ottawa Law Review*, vol. 27, no. 1 (1995): 129–73.
Conklin, William, 'The Trace of Legal Idealism in Derrida's Grammatology' in *Philosophy and Social Criticism*, vol. 22, no. 5 (1996): 17–42.
Conklin, William, 'The Transformation of Meaning: Legal Discourse and the Canadian Internment Camps' in *International Journal for the Semiotcs of Law*, vol. 9, no. 27 (1996): 227–56.
Conklin, William, 'The Invisible Author of Legal Authority' in *Law and Critique*, vol. 7, no. 2 (1996): 173–92.
Conklin, William, 'The Expressivity of the Invisible Author in the Modern Legal Genre' in Wilhem Wurzer, ed., *Invisibles* (Evanston: Northwestern University Press, forthcoming).
Cornell, Drucilla, *The Philosophy of the Limit* (New York/London: Routledge, 1993).
Cornell, Drucilla and Benhabib, Seyla, 'Introduction: Beyond the Politics of Gender' in Benhabib and Cornell eds., *Feminism as Critique* (Minneapolis: University of Minnesota Press, 1987): 1–15.
Delgado, Richard, 'Story-telling for Oppositionists and Others: A Plea for Narrative' in *Michigan Law Review*, vol. 87 (1989): 2411–41.
Delgado, Richard, 'When a Story is Just a Story: Does Voice Really Matter?' *Virginia Law Review*, vol. 76 (1990): 95–111.
Delgado, Richard, 'The Imperial Scholar Revisited: How to Marginalize Outside Writing Ten Years Later' in *University of Pennsylvania Law Review*, vol. 140 (1992): 1349–72.
Derrida, Jacques, *Speech and Phenomena: And Other Essays on Husserl's Theory of Signs* (David B. Allison trans.; Evanston: Northwestern University Press, 1973).
Derrida, Jacques, '"Genesis" and "Structure" and Phenomenology' in *Writing and Difference* (Alan Bass trans; Chicago: University of Chicago Press, 1973): 154–68.
Derrida, Jacques, 'Structure, Sign, and Play in the Discourse of the Human Sciences' in *Writing and Difference* (Alan Bass trans; Chicago: University of Chicago Press, 1973): 278–93.
Derrida, Jacques, *Of Grammatology* (Gayatri Chakravorty Spivak trans.; Baltimore & London: Johns Hopkins University Press, 1974, 1976).
Derrida, Jacques, 'The Law of Genre' in *Critical Inquiry*, vol. 7 (1980–81): 55–81.
Derrida, Jacques, 'Semiology and Grammatology' in Jacques Derrida,

Positions (Alan Bass trans.; Chicago: University of Chicago Press, 1981): 17–36.

Derrida, Jacques, 'Ousia and Gramme: Note on a Note in Being and Time' in Derrida, *Margins of Philosophy* (Chicago: University of Chicago Press, 1982): 29–67.

Derrida, Jacques, 'Differance' in *Speech and Phenomena: And Other Essays on Husserl's Theory of Signs* (David B. Allison trans.; Evanston: Northwestern University Press, 1973); reprinted in *Margins of Philosophy* (Alan Bass trans.; Chicago: University of Chicago Press, 1982): 1–27.

Derrida, Jacques, 'Sending: On Representation' in *Social Research*, vol. 49, no. 2 (Summer 1982): 294–326 (Peter and Mary Ann Caws trans.).

Derrida, Jacques, 'Force of Law: The "Mystical" Foundation of Authority' in *Cardozo Law Review*, vol. 11 (1990): 919–1045.

Derrida, Jacques, 'Before the Law' in Derek Attridge ed., *Acts of Literature* (New York/London: Routledge, 1992): 181–220.

Derrida, Jacques, *Specters of Marx* (Peggy Kamuf trans.; Bernd Magnus and Stephen Cullenberg intro.; New York & London: Routledge, 1994).

Edelman, Murray, 'The Political Language of the Helping Professions' in *Politics and Society*, vol. 4 (1964): 295–310.

Fish, Stanley, *Is there a Text in the Classroom?: The Authority of Interpretative Communities* (Cambridge Mass.: Harvard University Press, 1980).

Fish, Stanley, *Doing What Comes Naturally: Change, Rhetoric and the Practice of Theory in Literary and Legal Studies* (Durham N.C.: Duke University Press, 1989).

Foucault, Michel, 'Two Lectures' in *Power/Knowledge* (Colin Gordon trans.; New York: Pantheon, 1980): 78–108.

Foucault, Michel, *The History of Sexuality: An Introduction*, vol. 1 (Robert Hurley trans.; New York: Vintage, 1980): 78–108.

Foucault, Michel, 'The Subject and Power' in *Critical Inquiry*, vol. 8 (1982): 777–95.

Foucault, Michel, 'The Order of Discourse' in Michael Shapiro, ed., *Language and Politics* (London: Basil Blackwell, 1984): 108–38; also translated as 'The Discourse on Language' in *The Archeology of Knowledge* (A.M. Sheridan Smith trans.; New York: Pantheon, 1980):215–37.

Foucault, Michel, *The Use of Pleasure: The History of Sexuality*, vol. 2 (Robert Hurley trans.; New York: Vintage, 1986).

Foucault, Michel, 'Governmentality' in Graham Burcell, Colin Gordon and Peter Miller, eds., *The Foucault Effect: Studies in Governmentality* (Chicago: University of Chicago Press, 1991): 87–104.

Freadman, Anne, 'Structuralist Uses of Peirce, Jakobson, Metz *et al*' in *Semiotics-Ideology-Language* (Terry Threadgold *et al* ed.; Sydney: Sydney Association for Studies in Society and Culture, 1986).

Gadamer, Hans-Georg, *Truth and Method* (New York: Crossroad, 1985).

Gadamer, Hans-Georg, 'The Discrediting of Prejudice by the Enlightenment' in Kurt Mueller-Vollmer, ed., *The Hermeneutic Reader* (New York: Continuum, 1985): 257–61.

Gilligan, Carol, *In a Different Voice* (Cambridge, Mass.: Harvard University Press, 1982).

Godard, Barbara, 'The Politics of Representation: Some Native Canadian Women Writers' in *Canadian Literature*, vol. 124–25 (Summer 1990): 183–225.

Godard, Barbara, 'Translating (With) the Speculum' in *TTR*, vol. 4, no. 2 (Winter 1991): 85–121.

Goodrich, Peter, 'Rhetoric as Jurisprudence: An Introduction' in *Oxford Journal of Legal Studies*, vol. 4 (1984): 88–122.

Goodrich, Peter, *Languages of Law: From Logics of Memory to Nomadic Masks* (London: Weidenfeld & Nicolson, 1990).

Goodrich, Peter, 'Pro Lectionne Pictura Est: Images of the Legal Body in the Work of Pierre Legendre' in Kevelson, Roberta, *Semiotics and the Human Sciences*, vol. 1 (New York: Peter Lang, 1991).

Goodrich, Peter, 'Psychoanalysis in Legal Education: Notes on the Violence of the Sign' in Kevelson, Roberta, *Semiotics and the Human Sciences*, vol. 2 (New York: Peter Lang, 1991).

Goodrich, Peter, 'Fate as Seduction: The Other Scene of Legal Judgment' in Alan Norrie ed., *Closure or Critique: New Directions in Legal Theory* (Edinburgh: Edinburgh University Press, 1993): 116–41.

Greimas, Algirdas Julien, 'The Semiotic Analysis of Legal Discourse: Commercial Laws That Govern Companies and Groups of Companies' in *The Social Sciences: A Semiotic View* (Faoblo Fabbri and Paul Perron foreword; Paul Perron and Frank H. Collins trans.; Minneapolis: University of Minnesota Press, 1990): 102–38.

Harris, Roy, *Reading Saussure: a Critical Commentary on the Cours de Linguistique Generale* (La Salle Illinois: Open Court, 1987).

Hjelmslev, Louis, *Prolegomena to a Theory of Language* (Francis J. Whitfield trans.; Madison & London: University of Wisconsin Press, 1969).

Hodge, Robert and Kressin, Gunther, 'Semiotics and the Ghost of Saussure' in *Southern Review*, vol. 19 (March 1986): 38–51.

Husserl, Edmund, *Logical Investigations*, vol. 2 (New York: Humanities Press, 1970).

Indian Law Journal, 'Symposium: Semiotics, Dialectics, and the Law', vol. 61, no. 3 (1989): 315–99.

International Journal for the Semiotics of Law, 10 vols (Liverpool: Deborah Charles, 1988–).

Irigaray, Luce, *Speculum of the Other Woman* (Ithaca: Cornell University Press, 1985).
Jackson, Bernard S., *Making Sense in Law* (Liverpool: Deborah Charles, 1995).
Jackson, Bernard S., *Making Sense to Jurisprudence* (Liverpool: Deborah Charles, 1996).
Jakobson, Roman, 'Closing Statement: Linguistics and Poetics' in Robert E. Innis, *Semiotics: an Introductory Anthology* (Bloomington: Indiana University Press, 1985): 145–75.
Jakobson, Roman and Halle, Morris, in *Fundamentals of Language* (The Hague: Mouton, 1956).
Jameson, Frederick, 'The Linguistic Model' in Michael Shapiro, ed., *Language and Politics* (Oxford: Basil Blackwell, 1984): 168–94.
Johnson, Alex M., 'Racial Critiques of Legal Academia: A Reply in Favor of Context,' in *Stanford Law Review*, vol. 43 (1990): 137–65.
Kennedy, Randall, 'Racial Critiques of Legal Academia' in *Harvard Law Review*, vol. 102 (1989): 1745–819.
Kevelson, Roberta, *Semiotics and Law*, vol. 1, 2, 3 (New York/London: Plenum Press, 1987–89).
Kevelson, Roberta, *The Law as a System of Signs* (New York/London: Plenum Press, 1988).
Kevelson, Roberta, *Peirce, Paradox, Praxis: The Image, the Conflict, and the Law* (Berlin/New York: Mouton de Gruyter, 1990).
Kevelson, Roberta, *Semiotics and the Human Sciences*, vol. 1–6 (New York: Peter Lang, 1991–present).
Kline, Marlee, 'Race, Racism and Feminist Legal Theory' in *Harvard Women's Law Journal*, vol. 12 (1989): 115–50.
Lacan, Jacques, 'The Mirror Stage as Formative of the Function of I', in *Ecrits* (Alan Sheridan trans.; New York: Norton, 1977): 1–7.
Lacan, Jacques, 'The Function and Field of Speech and Language in Psychoanalysis'; in *Ecrits* (Alan Sheridan trans.; New York: Norton, 1977): 30–113.
Lacan, Jacques, 'The Signification of the Phallus', in *Ecrits* (Alan Sheridan trans.; New York: Norton, 1977).
Lacan, Jacques, 'Sign, Symbol, Imaginary' in Blonsky, *Signs* (Baltimore: Johns Hopkins University Press, 1985): 203–9.
Milovanovic, Dragan, *Postmodern Law and Disorder: Psychoanalytic Semiotics, Chaos and Juridic Exegesis* (Liverpool: Deborah Charles, 1992).
Morrison, Toni, ed., *Race-ing, En-gendering Power: Essays on Anita Hill, Clarence Thomas, and the Construction of Social Reality* (New York: Pantheon, 1992).
Peirce, Charles, S., *Collected Works* (Charles Hartshorne and Paul Weiss eds.; Boston: Harvard University Press, 1965).
Peirce, Charles, S., *Semiotic and Significs: The Correspondence Between*

Charles S. Peirce and Lady Victoria Welby (Charles S. Hardwick ed.; Bloomington: Indiana University Press, 1977): 10–119.
Pollock, Griselda, *Vision and Difference: Feminity, Feminism and the Histories of Art* (London: Routledge, 1988).
Saussure, Ferdinand, *Course in General Linguistics* (C. Bally *et al* ed.; W. Baskin trans.; NewYork: McGraw Hill, 1959).
Selecl, Renata, *The Spoils of Freedom: Psychoanalysis and Feminism after the Fall of Socialism* (London/New York: Routledge, 1994).
Strange, Carol, 'Wounded Womenhood and Dead Men: Chivalry and the Trials of Clara Ford and Carrie Davies' in Francia Iacovelter and Marianna Valveilde, eds., *Gender Conflicts* (Toronto: University of Toronto Press, 1992): 149–88.
Syracuse Law Review, 'Symposium: Law and Economics and the Semiotic Process' in *Syracuse Law Review*, vol. 42, no. 1 (1992): 1–239.
Taylor, Mark, ed., *Deconstruction in Context: Literature and Philosophy* (Chicago & London: University of Chicago Press, 1986): 396–420.
Thibault, Paul, *Re-reading Saussure* (London: Routledge, 1996).
Turpel, Mary Ellen, 'Aboriginal Peoples and the Canadian Charter: Interpretive Monopolies, Cultural Difference' in Patrick Devlin, ed., *Canadian Perspectives on Legal Theory* (Toronto: Edmond Montgomery, 1991): 503–31.
Turpel, Mary Ellen, 'Patriarchy and Paternalism: The Legacy of the Canadian State for First Nations Women' in *Canadian Journal of Women and Law*, vol. 6, no. 1 (1993): 174–92.
von Uexkull, Jacob, *Theoretical Biology* (D.L. Mackinnon trans.; London: Kegan Paul, 1926).
von Uexkull, Jacob, 'The Theory of Meaning' in *Semiotica*, vol. 92, no. 1 (1982): 25–82.
von Uexkull, Jacob, 'Neglected Figures in the History of Semiotic Inquiry: Jacob von Uexkull' in Thomas Sebeok, *The Sign and its Masters* (Austin & London: University of Texas Press, 1979): 187–207.
Yesell, Stephen C., 'Convention, Fiction and Law' in *New Literary History*, vol. 13 (1981–82): 89–102.
Williams, Patricia, *The Alchemy of Race and Rights* (Cambridge, Mass.: Harvard University Press, 1991).

9. Narratology

Bal, Mieke, *Narratology: Introduction to the Theory of Narrative* (Christine van Boheeman trans.; Toronto: University of Toronto Press, 1985).
Dworkin, Ronald, *Law's Empire* (Cambridge: Harvard University Press, 1986).

Genette, Gerard, 'Boundaries of Narrative' in *New Literary History*, vol. 8, no. 1 (1976): 1–13.
Jackson, Bernard, *Law, Fact and Narrative Coherence* (Merseyside, U.K.: Deborah Charles, 1988).
Jackson, Bernard, *Making Sense in Law: Linguistic, Psychological and Semiotic Perspectives* (Liverpool: Deborah Charles Publications, 1995).
Lind, E. Allan and O'Barr, William M., 'The Social Significance of Speech in the Citizen' in Howard Giles and Robert N. St. Clair, *Language and Social Psychology* (Oxford: Oxford University Press, 1979): 66–87.
Rimmon-Kenan, Shlomith, *Narrative Fiction: Contemporary Poetics* (London & New York: Methuen, 1983).
van Roermund, Bert, 'Narrative Coherence and the Guises of Legalism' in Patrick Nerhot, ed., *Law, Interpretation and Reality: Essays in Epistemology, Hermeneutics and Jurisprudence* (Dordrecht, Boston, London: Kluwer Academic Publishers, 1990): 310–45.
Twining, William, 'Introduction' and 'Evidence and Legal Theory' in his *Legal Theory and Common Law* (Oxford: Basil Blackwell, 1986): 1–7, 62–80.
White, Hayden, *The Content of Form: Narrative Discourse and Historical Representation* (Baltimore & London: Johns Hopkins University Press, 1987).
White, Hayden, 'The Value of Narrativity in the Representation of Reality' in *Critical Inquiry*, vol. 7 (1980–81): 5–27.

10. Phenomenology of Language

Bakhtin, Mikhail, *The Dialogic Imagination* (Austin, Texas: University of Texas Press, 1981).
Bakhtin, Mikhail, 'The Problem of Speech Genres' in *The Problem of Speech Genres and other Early Essays* (Austin, Texas: University of Texas Press, 1986): 60–102.
Barnes, Julien, *A History of the World in 10½ Chapters* (London: J. Cape, 1989).
Bernasconi, Robert and Wood, David, *The Provocation of Levinas: Rethinking the Other* (London & New York: Routledge, 1988).
Conklin, William, 'The Transformation of Meaning: Legal Discourse and the Canadian Internment Camps' in *International Journal for the Semiotics of Law*, vol. 9, no. 27 (1996): 227–56.
Gadamer, Georg, 'On the Problem of Self-Understanding' (1962), 'Man and Language' (1966), and 'The Philosophical Foundations of the Twentieth Century' (1962) in *Philosophical Hermeneutics* (David E. Linge trans.; Berkeley: University of California Press, 1976).
Gadamer, Georg, *Truth and Method* (New York: Crossroads, 1975).

Gadamer, Georg, 'The Phenomenological Movement' (1963) in *Philosophical Hermeneutics* (David E. Linge trans.; Berkeley: University of California Press, 1976).

Gadamer, Georg, 'The Rehabilitation of Authority and Tradition' in Kurt Mueller-Vollmer, ed., *The Hermeneutic Reader* (New York: Continuum, 1985): 261–7.

Gadamer, Georg, 'The Discrediting of Prejudice by the Enlightenment' in Kurt Mueller-Vollmer, ed., *The Hermeneutic Reader* (New York: Continuum, 1985): 257–61.

Grene, Marjorie, 'Adolf Portmann' in her *Approaches to a Philosophical Biology* (New York/London: Basic Books, 1968).

Hamrick, William S., *An Existential Phenomenology of Law: Maurice Merleau Ponty* (Boston: Martinus Nijhoff, 1987).

Heidegger, Martin, *Being and Time* (John Macquarie and Edward Robinson trans.; Oxford: Basil Blackwell, 1962): sect. 1–11, 21, 43, 44, 83.

Heidegger, Martin, *Poetry, Language and Thought* (Albert Hofstadter trans.; New York: Harper & Row, 1971).

Heidegger, Martin, *On the Way to Language* (Peter O. Hertz trans.; New York: Harper & Row, 1971).

Heidegger, Martin, 'The Origin of the Work of Art' in *Basic Writings* (David Farrell Krell ed. and intro.; New York: Harper & Row, 1977): 143–87.

Heidegger, Martin, 'The End of Philosophy and the Task of Thinking' in *Basic Writings* (David Farrell Krell ed.; New York: Harper & Row, 1977): 369–92.

Heidegger, Martin, 'On the Essence of Truth' in *Basic Writings* (David Farrell Krell ed.; New York: Harper & Row, 1977): 113–41.

Heidegger, Martin, 'Modern Science, Metaphysics, and Mathematics' in *Basic Writings* (David Farrell Krell ed.; New York: Harper & Row, 1977): 243–82.

Heidegger, Martin, *Early Greek Philosophy: The Dawn of Western Philosophy* (David Farrell Krell and Frank A. Capuzzi trans.; San Francisco: Harper & Row, 1875, 1984).

Hicks, Stephen C., 'An Existential Phenomenology of Law' in *Suffolk University Law Review*, vol. 24 (1991): 288–312.

Husserl, Edmund, *Logical Investigations*, vol. 2; esp. Investigations I, V, VI (New York: Humanities Press, 1970).

Kozulin, Alex, *Vygotsky's Psychology: A Biography of Ideas* (Cambridge, Mass.: Harvard University Press, 1991).

Kozulin, Alex, 'Vygotsky and Education' in *American Journal of Psychology*, vol. 105 (1992): 510–16;

Lehman, Warren, 'Existentialism and the Law: Hamrick on Merleau Ponty' in *Law and Social Inquiry*, vol. 13, no. 4 (1988): 835–43.

Levinas, Emmanuel, *Totality and Infinity: An Essay on Exteriority*

(Alphonso Lingis trans., Pittsburgh: Duquesne University Press, 1969).
Levinas, Emmanuel, 'Dialogue with Emmanuel Levinas' (with Richard Kearney) in Richard A. Cohen, ed., *Face to Face with Levinas* (Albany: State University of New York, 1968): 13–33.
Levinas, Emmanuel, 'The Trace of the Other' in Mark C. Taylor, ed., *Deconstruction in Context: Literature and Philosophy* (Chicago & London: University of Chicago Press, 1986): 345–59.
Lyotard, Jean-François, *Phenomenology* (Brian Beakley trans.; Gayle L. Ormiston foreword; Albany: University of New York Press, 1991).
Marx, Werner, *Towards a Phenomenological Ethics: Ethos and the Life-World* (Thomas Nenon foreword; Albany: State University of New York Press, 1992).
Miller, David, L., 'The Origin and Function of Language and the Meaning of Language Gestures' in *George Herbert Mead: Self, Language and the World* (Austin & London: University of Texas Press, 1973): 66–87.
Merleau Ponty, Maurice, 'The Body as Expression, and Speech' in *Phenomenology of Perception* (Colin Smith trans.; London: Routledge & Kegan Paul, 1962): 174–99.
Merleau Ponty, Maurice, *The Visible and the Invisible* (Alphonso Lingis trans.; Evanston: Northwestern University Press, 1968).
Michelfelder, Diane P. and Palmer, Richard E., eds., *Dialogue and Deconstruction: The Gadamer-Derrida Encounter* (New York: State University of New York Press, 1989).
Ratner, Carl, *Vygotsky's Sociohistorical Psychology and its Contemporary Applications* (New York: Plenum Press, 1991).
Sartre, Jean Paul, *Being and Nothingness: an Essay on Phenomenological Ontology* (New York: Philosophy Library, 1956; London: Methuen, 1957).
von Uexkull, Jacob, *Theoretical Biology* (D.L. Mackinnon trans.; London: Kegan Paul, 1926).
von Uexkull, Jacob, 'The Theory of Meaning' in *Semiotica*, vol. 92, no. 1 (1982): 25–82.
von Uexkull, Thure, 'Glossary' in *Semiotica*, vol. 92, no. 1 (1982): 83–7.
van der Veer, Rene, 'Vygotsky's Developmental Psychology' in *Psychological Reports*, vol. 59 (October 1985): 527–36.
Vygotsky, Lev, *Thought and Language* (Eugenia Haufmann and Gertrude Vaker trans.; Boston: MIT Press, 1962).
Vygotsky, Lev, *The Psychology of Art* (1965 in Russian) (Cambridge, MA: MIT Press, 1971).
Vygotsky, Lev, *The Historical Meaning of the Crisis in Psychology* (1982 in Russian) Sobranie Sochinenii [Collected Papers], vol. 1, Moscow: Pedagogika, 1982.
Vygotsky, Lev, *Thought and Language* (1934 in Russian), reprinted in

1956 and 1982, and published in English (Alex Kozulin, trans.; Cambridge MA: MIT Press, 1965, 1986).
Wertsch, James V., *Vygotsky and the Social Formation of Mind* (Cambridge Mass: Harvard University Press, 1985).
Wertsch, James V., *Culture, Communication and Cognition: Vygotskian Perspectives* (Cambridge; New York: Cambridge University Press, 1985).

11. Phenomenology of Law

Amselek, Paul, 'The Phenomenological Description of Law' in Maurice Natanson, *Phenomenology and the Social Sciences*, vol. 2 (Evanston: Northwestern University Press, 1973): 367–450.
Broekman, Jan, 'Law, Anthropology and Epistemology' in E. Bulygin, J.-L. Gardies and I. Niiniluoto eds., *Man, Law and Modern Forms of Life* (Dordrecht, Holland: D. Reidel, 1985): 15–42.
Chang, Briankle C., 'World and/or Sign: Toward a Semiotic Phenomenology of the Modern Life-World' in *Human Studies*, vol. 10 (1987): 311–31.
Franklin, Mitchell, 'The Mandarism of Phenomenological Philosophy of Law' in Maurice Natanson, *Phenomenology and the Social Sciences*, vol. 2 (Evanston: Northwestern University Press, 1973): 451–57.
Friedmann, Wolfgang, 'Phenomenology and Legal Science' in Maurice Natanson, *Phenomenology and the Social Sciences*, vol. 2 (Evanston: Northwestern University Press, 1973): 343–66.
Friedmann, Wolfgang, 'The Phenomenon of Law' in *Law, Morality and Society: Essays in Honour of H.L.A. Hart* (Oxford: Clarenden Press, 1977): 85–98.
Gabel, Peter, 'Intention and Structure in Contractual Conditions: Outline of a Method for Critical Legal Theory' in *Minnesota Law Review*, vol. 61 (1977): 601–93.
Gabel, Peter, 'Reification in Legal Reasoning' in *Research in Law and Sociology*, vol. 3 (1980): 25–51.
Gabel, Peter, 'The Phenomenology of Rights-Consciousness and the Pact of the Withdrawn Selves' in *Texas Law Review*, vol. 62 (1984): 1563–99.
Goldmann, Lucien, *The Philosophy of the Englightenment: The Burgess and the Enlightenment* (Henry Mass trans.; Cambridge: MIT Press, 1973).
Goldmann, Lucien, *Lukacs and Heidegger: Towards a New Philosophy* (William Q. Boelhower trans.; London: Routledge & Kegan Paul, 1977).

Heidegger, Martin, *Being and Time* (John Macquarie and Edward Robinson trans.; Oxford: Basil Blackwell, 1962).
Heidegger, Martin, *Basic Writings* (David Farrell Krell ed. and intro.; New York: Harper & Row, 1977).
Jacob, François, *The Logic of Life: A History of Heredity* (Betty E. Spillmann trans.; New York: Pantheon, 1973, 1982).
Jonas, Hans, *The Phenomenon of Life: Towards a Philosophical Biology* (New York: Delta Books, 1966).
Kosik, Karel, *Dialectics of the Concrete* (Dordrecht-Holland/Boston: D. Reidel, 1976; Boston Studies in the Philosophy of Science, vol. 52).
Luijpen, W., *Existential Phenomenology* (Pittsburgh: Duquesne University Press, 1960): ch. 3 & 6.
Luijpen, W., *Phenomenology of Natural Law* (Pittsburgh: Duquesne University Press, 1967).
McBride, William Leon, 'Towards a Phenomenology of International Justice' in Graham Hughes, ed., *Law, Reason and Justice* (New York: New York University Press, 1969): 137–67.
Natanson, Maurice, 'Phenomenology and Typification: A Study in the Philosophy of Alfred Schutz' in *Social Research*, vol. 37 (1970): 1–22.
Natanson, Maurice, 'The Problem of Anonymity in the Thought of Alfred Schutz' in Joseph Biened, *Phenomenology and the Social Sciences: A Dialogue* (The Hague: Martinus Nijhoff, 1978): 60–73.
Salter, Michael, 'Towards a Phenomenology of Legal Thinking' in *Journal of the British Society for Phenomenology*, vol. 23, no. 2 (1992): 167–82.
Salter, Michael, 'Common Sense and Resistance to Legal Theory', *Ratio Juris*, vol. 5, no. 2 (1992): 212–29.
Salter, Michael, 'A Dialectic Despite Itself: Overcoming the Phenomenology of Legal Culture' in *Social and Legal Studies*, vol. 4 (1995): 453–76.
Schiff, David, 'Phenomenology and Jurisprudence' in *Liverpool Law Review*, vol. 4, no. 1 (1982): 5–18.
Schrodinger, Erwin, *What is Life? Mind and Matter* (Cambridge: Cambridge University Press, 1967).
Schultz, Alfred, 'Equality and the Social Meaning Structure' in Schutz, *Collected Papers*, vol. 2: *Studies in Social Theory* (Arvid Brodersen ed. and intro.; The Hague: Martinus Nijhoff, 1964): 226–73, at 229–62.
Schultz, Alfred, 'Symbol, Reality and Society' in *Collected Papers*, vol. 1 esp. 340–56.
Schultz, Alfred, 'On Multiple Realities' in *Collected Papers*, vol. 1: 207–59.
Schultz, Alfred, 'The Social World and the Theory of Social Action' in in *Collected Papers*, vol. 2: 3–19.

Schultz, Alfred, 'The Dimensions of the Social World' in *Collected Papers*, vol. 2: 20–63.
Schultz, Alfred, 'The Problem of Rationality in the Social World' in *Collected Papers*, vol. 2: 65–88.
Schultz, Alfred, 'Type and Eidos in Husserl's Late Philosophy' in *Collected Papers*, vol. 3: 92–115.
Schultz, Alfred, 'Some Structures of the Life-World' in *Collected Papers*, vol. 3: 116–32.
Schultz, Alfred, 'Language, Language Disturbances, and the Texture of Consciousness' in *Social Research*, vol. 17 (1950): 365–94.
Schultz, Alfred, 'Concept and Theory Formation in the Social Sciences' in Maurice Natanson ed., *Philosophy of the Social Sciences: A Reader* (New York: Random House, 1963): 231–49.
Schultz, Alfred, 'Common-Sense and Scientific Interpretation of Human Action' in Maurice Natanson ed., *Philosophy of the Social Sciences* (New York: Random House, 1963): 302–46.
Schutz, Alfred and Luckmann, Thomas, *The Structures of the Life-World* (Richard M. Zaner and H. Tristram Engelhardt trans.; Evanston: Northwestern University Press, 1973): 233–41.
Simpson, G.C., *The Meaning of Life: A Study of the History of Life and its Significance for Man* (New Haven: Yale University Press, 1967).
Taylor, H. Buckner, 'Transformations of Reality in the Legal Process' in *Social Research*, vol. 37 (1970): 88– 101.
van Eikerna Hommes, H.J., *Major Trends in the History of Legal Philosophy* (Amsterdam: North-Holland, 1979): sect 26–30.

12. Suffering

Adorno, Theodor, 'After Auschwitz' in *Negative Dialectics* (New York: Continuum, 1983): 361–64.
Aeschylus, *The Orestia* (Robert Fagles trans.; London: Penguin, 1977).
Benjamin, Walter, 'Critique of Violence' in *Reflections* (Peter Demetz ed.; New York: Schocken Books, 1978).
Bradley, A.C., 'Hegel's Theory of Tragedy' in Anne and Henry Paolucci, eds., *Hegel on Tragedy* (Garden City, New York: Doubleday, 1962): 367–88.
Conklin, William, 'Husserl, the Differend, and Kafka's *The Trial*', (M. Kronegger and A.-T. Tymieniecka eds., *Analecta Husserliana*, vol. 49 (Kluwer Academic Publishers, 1996): 115–25.
Foucault, Michel, *Madness and Civilization* (Richard Howard trans.; New York: Vintage, 1973).
Foucault, Michel, *Discipline and Punish: The Birth of the Prison* (Alan Sheridan trans.; New York: Vintage 1977).
Foucault, Michel, 'The Dangerous Individual' in *Politics, Philosophy,*

Culture: Interviews and other Writings 1977–84 (Alan Sheridan and others trans.; Lawrence D. Kritzman ed.; New York: Routledge, 1988).

Harris, H.S., *Hegel: Phenomenology and System* (Indianapolis: Hackett, 1995).

Hegel, Georg F., *Phenomenology of Spirit* in Chapter 6 (A.V. Miller trans.; Oxford University Press, 1977).

Irigaray, Luce, 'The Eternal Irony of the Community' in *Speculum of the Other Woman* (Gillian C. Gill trans.; Ithaca, New York: Cornell University Press, 1985): 214–26.

Kaufmann, Walter, 'Hegel's Ideas about Tragedy' in Warren E. Steinkraus, *New Studies in Hegel's Philosophy* (New York: Holt, Rinehart & Winston, 1971): 201–22.

Lyotard, Jean-François, *The Differend: Phrases in Dispute* (Georges van den Abbeele trans.; Minneapolis: University of Minnesota Press, 1988; Theory and History of Literature, vol. 46).

Lyotard, Jean-François, *The Inhuman Condition: Reflections on Time* (Stanford, Calif: Stanford University Press, 1991).

Scarry, Elaine, *The Body in Pain: The Making and Unmaking of the World* (Oxford: Oxford University Press, 1985).

Scheler, Max, *The Nature of Sympathy* (Peter Heath trans.; Hamden, Conn: Archon Books, 1970).

Sophocles, *Sophocles: The Plays and Fragments*, Pt 3: Antigone (Richard C. Jebb trans.; Amsterdam: Servio Publishers, 1962).

Sophocles, *The Three Theban Plays: Antigone, Oedipus the King, and Oedipus at Colonus* (Robert Fagles trans.; New York & Harmondsworth: Penguin, 1982, 1984).

Sophocles, *Sophocles 1* (David Green trans.; Chicago: University of Chicago Press, 1984; Phoenix Books).

Index

www.ingramcontent.com/pod-product-compliance
Lightning Source LLC
LaVergne TN
LVHW010630300926
849162LV00001B/105

9781138360792